EYEWITNESS TRAVEL

SLOVENIA

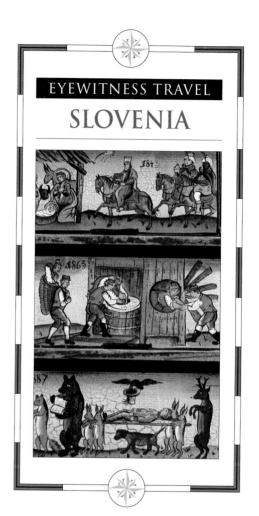

EYEWITNESS TRAVEL

SLOVENIA

LONDON, NEW YORK,
MELBOURNE, MUNICH AND DELHI
www.dk.com

MANAGING EDITOR Aruna Ghose

SENIOR EDITORIAL MANAGER Savitha Kumar

SENIOR DESIGN MANAGER Priyanka Thakur

PROJECT EDITOR Shikha Kulkarni

PROJECT DESIGNER Shruti Singhi

EDITOR Parvati M. Krishnan

DESIGNER Rupanki Arora Kaushik

SENIOR CARTOGRAPHIC MANAGER Uma Bhattacharya

CARTOGRAPHER Subhashree Bharati

SENIOR DTP DESIGNER Azeem Siddiqui

DTP DESIGNER Rakesh Pal

SENIOR PICTURE RESEARCH CO-ORDINATOR Taiyaba Khatoon

CONTRIBUTORS
Jonathan Bousfield, James Stewart

PHOTOGRAPHERS
Demetrio Carrasco, Linda Whitwam

ILLUSTRATORS
Chinglemba Chingtham, Sanjeev Kumar,
Arun Pottirayil, Shruti Soharia Singh

Reproduced in Singapore by Colourscan
Printed and bound by Vivar Printing Sdn Bhd, Malaysia

First published in Great Britain in 2012
by Dorling Kindersley Limited
80 Strand, London WC2R 0RL

12 13 14 15 10 9 8 7 6 5 4 3 2

Copyright © 2012 Dorling Kindersley Limited, London
A Penguin Company

ISBN 978-1-40535-894-1

Front cover main image: Lake Bled

MIX
Paper from
responsible sources
FSC FSC™ C018179
www.fsc.org

Beautifully painted exterior of
the Cooperative Bank, Ljubljana

CONTENTS

Stunning view of the Triglav
mountain peaks

◁ Picturesque valley with the Alps in the background

Statue of Giuseppe Tartini in the Tartinjev trg, Piran

LJUBLJANA AREA BY AREA

Painted Attic cup,
Tolmin Museum

SLOVENIA REGION BY REGION

TRAVELLERS' NEEDS

View of the boats moored at the
marina in Izola

Bogenšperk Castle

6

HOW TO USE THIS GUIDE

HOW TO USE THIS GUIDE

This guide helps you get the most from your visit to Slovenia. It provides detailed practical information and expert recommendations. *Introducing Slovenia* maps the country and its regions, sets them in a historical and cultural context and describes events through the entire year. *Slovenia Region by Region* is the main sightseeing section. It covers all the important sights, with photographs, maps and illustrations. Information on hotels, restaurants, shops and markets, entertainment and sports is found in *Travellers' Needs*. The *Survival Guide* has advice on everything from travel to medical services, telephones and post offices.

1 Area Map
Sights are numbered on a map. Within a chapter, information on each sight follows the numerical order on the map. Sights in this area are also located on the Ljubljana Street Finder maps on pages 96–9.

A locator map shows where you are in relation to other parts of the city.

LJUBLJANA AREA BY AREA

Slovenia's capital, dealt with in a separate section, is divided into four sightseeing areas. Each area has its own chapter, which opens with an introduction and a list of sights described. All sights are plotted on an *Area Map*. The key to the map symbols is on the back flap.

The visitors' checklist provides all the practical information needed to plan your visit.

2 Detailed information
Major towns have maps with sights picked out and described individually.

A town map has all the town's major sights numbered and plotted on it.

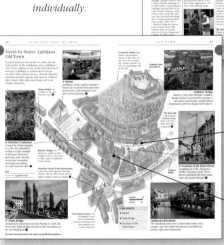

A suggested route for a walk is shown in red.

3 Street-by-Street map
This gives a bird's-eye view of the key area in the chapter.

SLOVENIA REGION BY REGION

Apart from Ljubljana, Slovenia is divided into three regions, each with a separate chapter.

Sights at a glance lists the chapter's sights by category: Historic Streets and Buildings, Museums and Galleries, Parks and Gardens, and so on.

1 Introduction

The landscape, history and character of each region is outlined here, revealing how the area has developed over the centuries and what it offers visitors today.

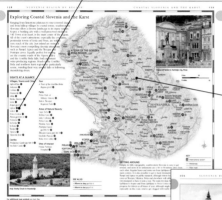

2 Regional Map

This map shows the road network and gives an illustrated overview of the region. All the sights are numbered and there are useful tips for getting around.

3 Detailed information

Important places to visit are described individually. Addresses, telephone numbers, opening hours and other practical information are provided for each entry.

Each region can be identified by its colour codes, which are listed on the front inside cover.

Driving tours explore areas of special interest.

4 Major sights

Top sights and historic buildings are dissected to reveal their interiors, while museums have colour-coded floor plans to help find the most important exhibits. Stars indicate the main features visitors should not miss.

INTRODUCING
SLOVENIA

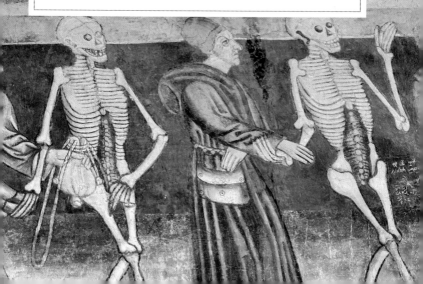

DISCOVERING SLOVENIA

Located at the junction of the Alps, the Mediterranean and the Pannonian plain, Slovenia offers a patchwork of varied terrain. Much of the country is easily accessible from Ljubljana, its compact and lively capital. To the north of Ljubljana, the peaks of the Karavanke range and the Julian Alps

Hand-painted salt box

tower above lake-filled valleys. To the west is the cave-studded limestone plateau of the karst region and the country's short strip of coast, with its Venetian-style architecture and lush Mediterranean vegetation. Eastern Slovenia is different again, with gently rolling hills and rich agricultural flatlands.

LJUBLJANA

- **Captivating Old Town**
- **Galleries and museums**
- **Vibrant nightlife**

A quaint Baroque town with an alpine backdrop, **Ljubljana** *(see pp40–99)* is one of Europe's smaller capitals, and is perfect for relaxed strolling. The main focus of tourist interest is the **Old Town** *(see pp44–55)*, with historic churches and townhouses crowding the banks of the Ljubljanica river. Perched on a hilltop above the city, the medieval **Ljubljana Castle** *(see pp52–3)* offers panoramic views. East of the river, Ljubljana's **New Town** *(see pp56–69)* has a variety of 20th-century architectural styles, with its many Art Nouveau and Art Deco buildings. Outside the centre, the 19th-century **Tobacco Factory** *(see p73)*, now a museum and cultural centre, and the former barracks at

Ferry on the Ljubljanica river in the Old Town, Ljubljana

Metelkova Mesto *(see p77)*, a buzzing area of clubs and galleries, mix historical heritage with contemporary cool. The meadows of **Tivoli Park** *(see p74)* and the wooded **Rožnik Hill** *(see p75)* provide opportunities for great walks. With good transport connections Ljubljana makes an ideal base for trips to the market town of Škofja Loka *(see pp86–7)* and the Bogenšperk Castle *(see pp90–91)*.

THE ALPS

- **Triglav National Park**
- **Lakes Bled and Bohinj**
- **Soča Valley activities**

Slovenia's most attractive mountain wonderlands are the alpine chains that run along its northern border. **Bled** *(see pp108–9)*, just northwest of Ljubljana, serves as an ideal introduction to the area, with its tranquil lake set against a backdrop of snow-capped summits. Southwest of Bled and fringed by plunging mountains, **Lake Bohinj** *(see pp114–5)* is the ideal base from which to explore the **Triglav National Park** *(see pp112–3)*, an expanse of verdant pastures, dense spruce forest and granite peaks. Bohinj is the starting point for the popular hike to Mount Triglav, the three-pronged peak that serves as Slovenia's national symbol. On the northern edge of the national park, the

Snow-capped peaks and verdant meadows in the Triglav National Park

◁ *Dance of Death* fresco at the Holy Trinity Church, Hrastovlje village of **Kranjska Gora** *(see p116)* stands at the centre of Slovenia's most varied skiing region. West of Triglav, the **Soča Valley** *(see pp118–9)* is an increasingly well-known venue for adventure sports, with rafting, canoeing and bungee-jumping among the most popular activities. Further east, the **Kamniško-Savinjske Alps** *(see pp122–3)* contain some of Slovenia's most bewitching highland valleys, with **Logarska dolina** *(see p122)*, in particular, drawing a stream of hikers and cyclists.

Spectacular limestone formations, Škocjan Caves

COASTAL SLOVENIA AND THE KARST

- **Venetian architecture**
- **White Lipizzaner horses**
- **Spectacular caves**

Slovenia's Adriatic coastline is a mere 46 km (29 miles) long, but offers much for visitors to take in. The busiest of the coastal resorts is **Portorož** *(see p132)*, fashionable since the 19th century and still pulling in the summer crowds with its strip of hotels, bars and restaurants. The historic port towns of **Piran** *(see pp130–31)*, **Izola** *(see p133)* and **Koper** *(see pp134–5)* couldn't be more different, with squares, fountains and palaces offering a distinctly Venetian flavour. Popular excursions from the coast include visits to see the medieval church frescoes at **Hrastovlje** *(see p136)*, the ancient hilltop village of **Štanjel** *(see p141)* and the stud farm at **Lipica** *(see p137)*, where Lipizzaner horses are bred and trained.

Further inland is the karst region, an arid limestone plateau famous for its spec-tacular rock formations. The fabulous **Postojna Caves** *(see pp150–51)* and **Škocjan Caves** *(see pp138–9)*, with underground lakes and stalagmite-filled caverns, are among the most popular destinations in the country. **Predjama Castle** *(see pp148–9)*, pressed into the mouth of a cavern, is no less

memorable. On the north side of the karst, the former mercury-mining settlement of **Idrija** *(see p146)* offers an insight into the area's industrial heritage. Tucked into an isolated valley nearby, the **Franja Partisan Hospital** *(see p147)* is now one of Slovenia's most popular museums.

Lipizzaner horse

SOUTHERN AND EASTERN SLOVENIA

- **Monasteries and castles**
- **Relaxing spa resorts**
- **Charming Ptuj**

Southern Slovenia offers a diverse wealth of unspoilt nature, beginning with the dense forest of **Kočevski Rog** *(see p161)* and the rolling hills of Bela Krajina. The main centre of the south is **Novo Mesto** *(see p162)*, attractively

located in a loop of the Krka river. The town makes a good base to explore the **Krka Valley** *(see p165)*, taking in the castle of Otočec, before arriving at the castle at Brežice, now a museum.

The lumpy hills along Slovenia's southern border are famous for their mineral springs. Spa resorts such as **Rogaška Slatina** *(see p167)* offer ample opportunities for indulging in rest cures, beauty treatments, or simply splashing around in swim-ming pools. The region's rich collection of ecclesiastical architecture includes the fine monasteries at **Pleterje** *(see p164)* and **Olimje** *(see p167)*, while the ruined Carthusian **Žiče Monastery** *(see pp174–5)* provides an insight into Slovenia's medieval monastic orders.

Dominating the northeast is bustl-ing **Maribor** *(see pp176–7)*, which boasts the kind of cultural scene and nightlife that one would expect from Slovenia's second-largest city. Just outside town is Mariborsko Pohorje, site of Slovenia's biggest ski area.

The historic jewel of eastern Slovenia is **Ptuj** *(see pp178–9)*, a town that combines Roman, medieval and Baroque elements with a charming riverside setting. Near the Hungarian border are the towns of **Murska Sobota** *(see p182)* and **Lendava** *(see p183)* and villages such as **Velika Polana** *(see p183)*, home to a seasonal population of storks.

Colourful buildings around the main square in Maribor

Putting Slovenia on the Map

Slovenia is one of Europe's smaller states, with an area of 20,273 sq km (7,825 sq miles). It has borders with Austria to the north, Hungary to the east, Croatia to the south and Italy to the west. There is a short stretch of Adriatic coastline and the main mountain chains are the Karavanke and the Julian Alps. The principal river is the Sava, which rises in the Julian Alps before flowing southeast towards Croatia then Serbia, where it joins the Danube. The capital, Ljubljana, stands at the centre of the road and rail network. From here, even the furthest regional attractions can be reached in a couple of hours.

Satellite image of the capital, Ljubljana

HUNGARY
Zalalövő
Gornji
Petrovci
Murska
Sobota
Lenti
Strass
Šentilj
Maribor
Radizel
Ljutomer
ograd
Poborje Massif
Velenje
Slovenska
Bistrica
Ptuj
Ormož
Varaždin
Slovenske
Konjice
Celje
Rogaška
Slatina
CROATIA
Laško
Kozje
adeče
Sevnica
Krško
Brežice
Šmarješke
Toplice
Zagreb
Novo
Mesto
ske
Metlika
Crnomelj
Karlovac

Drava
Mura
Krka
Kolpa

CROATIA

KEY

✈ International airport
━━ Motorway
━━ Major road
━━ Minor road
━━ Railway
━·━ International border

EASTERN EUROPE

POLAND
CZECH
REPUBLIC
GERMANY
SLOVAKIA
UKRAINE
AUSTRIA
HUNGARY
SLOVENIA
Ljubljana
CROATIA
ROMANIA
BOSNIA AND
HERZEGOVINA
SERBIA
Adriatic Sea
ITALY
MONTENEGRO
BULGARIA

0 km   20
0 miles   20

A PORTRAIT OF SLOVENIA

Few countries pack so much variety into such a small geographical area as Slovenia. The landscape changes swiftly from the high Alps to arable plains, and from dense deciduous forests to the palm-fringed Mediterranean coastline. At the centre of the country is the capital Ljubljana, a vibrant city combining graceful architecture with a certain joie de vivre.

Outside the capital, characteristic alpine farmhouses and whitewashed hilltop churches are scattered across the landscape of central and eastern Slovenia. To the west, however, Mediterranean styles are more evident and coastal towns such as Koper and Piran have an instantly recognizable Venetian character. This diversity reflects Slovenia's geographical position at the junction of Central Europe, the Balkans and the Mediterranean.

The country has a population of just over 2 million, of which 83 per cent are Slovenians. Small but significant others include Albanians, Bosnians, Croats and Serbs, who came to Slovenia during the Yugoslav period. Slovenians themselves are descendants of the Slav tribes who settled here from the 6th century AD onwards. The Slovenian language is closely related to other Slav tongues such as Croatian, Serbian, Czech and Slovak, although it retains many unique characteristics.

Despite being ruled by foreign dynasties for much of their history, the Slovenians have proved to be remarkably resilient. Slovenia's status as a federal republic in Communist Yugoslavia after 1945 gave the nation stable borders for the first time in its history, although the country did not achieve full independence until 1991.

Intricately patterned Idrija lace

Lake Bohinj, against the backdrop of the fog-covered Alps

◁ Slovenians dressed in historical costumes parading the streets of Škofja Loka

Visitors enjoying a ride on a horse-drawn wagon, Logarska dolina

SOCIETY

Slovenia's culture is vibrant and maintains its bold, forward-looking approach. During the 1970s and 80s, it emerged as a major centre of contemporary art, music and design, and even today, boasts the kind of film, newspaper and publishing industries that are the envy of its neighbouring countries. Until the early 20th century, however, Slovenia was predominantly a peasant country, and traditional costume, folk music and village festivals remain an important part of life.

Given Slovenia's spectacular mountainous terrain, the great outdoors features prominently in the national psyche. Hiking and skiing are popular, and facilities for winter sports

Sculpture outside Gruber Palace, Ljubljana

are of a very high standard. The primeval forests of Kočevski Rog and the vine-cloaked hill villages of the southwest are no less compelling in terms of unspoilt nature. Slovenia is also famous for its breathtaking limestone formations in the karst region.

PEOPLE

Slovenia's status as a cultural crossroad has also had an impact on its national character. Typical Central European traits such as honesty, hard work and cheerfulness are valued, although Mediterranean qualities such as style, sociability and a taste for good food also fit the nation's psychological profile. Slovenian attitudes to the Balkan regions to the southeast are more complex. Indeed, "Balkan" was considered an unpleasant word in the aftermath of independence in 1991, when Slovenians were eager to emphasize their complete break with former Yugoslav nations. Today, however, supposedly Balkan characteristics such as warmth, spontaneity and vivacity are viewed more positively by most Slovenians.

Slovenia is a predominantly Catholic country, although the tone of everyday life is secular. A third of all marriages end in divorce, which is somewhere near the European average.

POLITICS

Despite the dissolution of Yugoslavia in 1991, attitudes towards the Yugoslav heritage still remain complex. Pride in Slovenia's economic achievements often exists side-by-side with a feeling of nostalgia for

Exhibition on Communism, at a gallery in Idrija

a Communist system that offered more in the way of social justice and job security. Even though the Yugoslavia of President Tito was a one-party state with limited political freedoms, the nation was still culturally open to the outside world.

The Communist-led partisan struggles of World War II are still seen by most as a genuinely heroic period in the nation's history; many streets and squares bear the names of partisan divisions and heroes. This is especially true in western Slovenia and Slovenian Istria, which would not have been part of the country today were it not for the partisans. Yet, at the same time, there is little nostalgia for Communism as a political system, and Slovenians are enormously proud of the "Slovene Spring" of the late 1980s, when citizens successfully challenged Communist authority.

Since 1990, Slovenia has been a parliamentary democracy with power passing fairly painlessly between right- and left-wing parties. The main planks of post-independence policy – membership of NATO and the EU, and acceptance of the euro as the national currency – were greeted positively by the majority of Slovenians and are widely recognized today.

SLOVENIA TODAY

Of all the former Communist countries of Europe, Slovenia has enjoyed the easiest transition to a Capitalist democracy. Even during the Communist period, Slovenia was a highly educated society with competitive manufacturing industries, a modicum of private enterprise and a vibrant consumer culture. Post-independence, Slovenia has become a technocratic society in which young educated people are frequently employed in high positions. Most Slovenian professionals want to stay and work in their home country, and Slovenia has thus experienced little of the economic emigration suffered by other former Communist states.

Tourism is a major industry, with Slovenia's alpine terrain offering a wealth of hiking and skiing opportunities. Recent developments have seen the rise of adrenaline sports such as rafting and canyoning, and the emergence of Ljubljana as one of Central Europe's prime holiday destinations. Slovenia's reputation as a "green" destination of unspoilt countryside, ecological consciousness and organic food has only served to increase the country's appeal.

Grape harvest at a vineyard near Ljutomer

Landscape and Wildlife

Slovenia packs an extraordinary variety of flora and fauna into what is, by European standards, a relatively small country. The landscape changes swiftly from the snow-covered peaks and glacier-carved valleys of the alpine north to the rolling farmlands of the southeast, to the palm-fringed Adriatic resorts of the southwest. The most distinctive part of the Slovenian landscape is the karst, an arid plateau of porous limestone that stretches across the west of the country. Rich in caves and potholes carved by centuries of rainfall, the karst makes for some of the most dramatic underground scenery in Europe.

Wild flowers in the Alps

Traditional salt pans in Sečovlje, coastal Slovenia

ALPINE SLOVENIA
Northern Slovenia is dominated by mountains. The Julian Alps in the northwest boast the highest peaks, including Mount Triglav. Much of alpine Slovenia is covered in evergreen forest and its lush highland meadows are perfect for dairy farming.

COASTAL SLOVENIA
Slovenia's short strip of coastline enjoys a warm Mediterranean climate – vines and olive trees cover the hills above the shore and palm trees line the seafront promenades. The waters of the Adriatic are rich in shellfish and crustaceans.

Alpine ibex *roam the high-altitude pastures in the spectacular Triglav National Park.*

Olive trees *are grown on the slopes overlooking the coast for their highly prized oil.*

Brown bears *can be quite easily spotted in Slovenia's alpine region.*

Bottlenose dolphins *can be seen frolicking off the Slovenian coast.*

The primula *blooms in spring and can be found all over alpine Slovenia.*

Vipava valley *is an important vine-growing region famous for its dry white wines.*

FORESTS OF SLOVENIA

Over 50 per cent of Slovenia is covered with woodland, making it one of the most densely forested countries in Europe. The Julian Alps are carpeted with a mixture of spruce, beech and larch. Beech trees predominate the deep, primeval forests of southern Slovenia, notably the Kočevski Rog area, which serves as an important habitat for wolves, lynx and bears. Common in all areas of Slovenia is the linden, a deciduous tree whose heart-shaped leaves are a national symbol.

Forest-dwelling dormouse on the branch of a tree

Linden tree at the Lipica stud farm, where a tree is planted every time a foal is born

THE KARST

The limestone uplands of western Slovenia are famous for their subterranean cave systems, carved out over the millennia by underground rivers. The caves at Postojna and Škocjan are among the most visited speleological attractions in Europe.

Bats, *including the lesser horseshoe and the greater mouse-eared species, inhabit the caves in the karst.*

Human fish (Proteus anguinus) *grow up to a length of 30 cm (1 foot) and can live for as long as 100 years.*

The persimmon, *with its succulent golden flesh, is the most common garden fruit in the western karst.*

THE PANNONIAN PLAIN

The rolling lowlands of the Pannonian plain stretch from eastern Slovenia across much of Hungary, eastern Croatia and northern Serbia. It is a rich agricultural area with sunflower, rape, pumpkin and grape among the most important crops.

White storks *spend late spring and early summer in the villages of eastern Slovenia, migrating southwards in August.*

Pumpkins *are harvested for their seeds, which yield delicious oil.*

Sunflowers, *which fill the fields during summer, are an important agricultural crop.*

Architecture

Slovenia's location between Central Europe and the Mediterranean has placed it at the crossroads of architectural styles throughout history. During the Middle Ages, a wealthy and ambitious church built monasteries throughout the country, frequently employing Gothic styles imported from Northern Europe. During the Counter-Reformation, Slovenia welcomed a wave of architects influenced by Italian Baroque. In the 20th century, Slovenia became a breeding ground for Modernist trends: Art Nouveau was eagerly adopted in the years before World War I, while more functionalist styles became popular in the years that followed.

Sculpture, Ljubljana

Baroque fountain by Francesco Robba on Mestni trg, Ljubljana

GOTHIC

The medieval church was the organization most responsible for the spread of Gothic style in Slovenia, with its construction of churches and monasteries. Apart from major 12th-century projects such as the Carthusian Monastery at Žiče or the Cathedral of St John the Baptist at Maribor, there are a number of exquisite parish churches scattered throughout the country.

The Baroque belfry, added in the 18th century

The Church of St John (see p115) *on the eastern shores of Lake Bohinj, is a typical example of a Gothic-era village church, with a rib-vaulted ceiling and well-preserved frescoes.*

St James's Church (see p86) *is a late-Gothic church in Škofja Loka that contains superb examples of complex rib-vaulting, with exuberant floral motifs filling the spaces in between.*

BAROQUE

Through the 16th and 17th centuries, an influx of architects from Italy brought the best of Baroque to Slovenia's main towns. Prominent among them was Andrea Pozzo, architect of the capital's famous St Nicholas's Cathedral.

Maribor Castle's façade (see p176) *showcases the Baroque taste for swirly decorative details with its crests and mouldings. The castle is also home to a spectacular Baroque staircase.*

St Nicholas's Cathedral (see p50) *boasts a typically ornate Baroque interior, with frescoes by Giulio Quaglio and statues by Francesco Robba.*

ART NOUVEAU

The dominant architectural style in Ljubljana at the beginning of the 20th century was Art Nouveau. Many city-centre apartment blocks still bear decorative details associated with the movement.

Centromerkur Building (see p48) *now the Galerija Emporium, a fashion store, was built in 1903. Among its original features are a cast-iron canopy and a beautiful Y-shaped staircase.*

Coloured tiles

Hauptman House (see p59) *was decorated in a lively geometric style by local architect Ciril Metod Koch, using a mixture of paint and glazed tiles.*

Ljubljana's Co-operative Bank (see p58) *was the work of architect Ivan Vurnik. He took Art Nouveau one step further, drawing on Slovenian folk motifs to produce this highly original decorative scheme.*

CONTEMPORARY (20TH CENTURY)

The main currents of modern architecture all left their mark on Slovenia. The country's greatest 20th-century architect was Jože Plečnik, who combined modern styles with elements from the ancient world to create a unique personal style.

Ljubljana City Museum

Arched top-floor windows add decorative charm

Nebotičnik (see p58) *is a stately Art Deco building, best appreciated by taking a trip to the top-floor café.*

National and University Library (see pp68–9) *is Plečnik's masterpiece, combining locally quarried marble with red brick to create a dappled façade.*

MEDIEVAL CASTLES

Slovenia was, for centuries, a feudal society run by landowning warlords, and their castles are still scattered across the landscape. Although much altered in the intervening period, dramatically located hilltop castles at Ljubljana, Bled and Celje retain plenty of their original medieval features. Many castles were converted during the Renaissance and Baroque eras to serve as aristocratic dwellings – those at Ptuj, Predjama, Bogenšperk, Škofja Loka and Kromberk are popular museum destinations today, packed with fine furnishings and objects d'art.

Predjama Castle, pressed against the mouth of a cave in the karst region

Folk Art and Music

Despite entering the 21st century as a modern and technologically advanced society, Slovenia has retained a good deal of its folk traditions. Each region has a distinct musical style, with age-old songs and dances kept alive by local societies and schools. Regional folk costumes no longer form part of everyday dress, but are still very much in evidence during Slovenia's busy calendar of festivals and fairs. The products of traditional craftspeople can be seen in ethnographic museums all over the country – one of the most characteristic folk arts being painted wooden beehive panels, featuring fanciful scenes with human and animal figures.

Folk dancers in the regional costume of the Dolenjska area.

TRADITIONAL DRESS

Each region has its traditional costume that is still worn on festive occasions. Intricate geometric or floral patterns on skirts, blouses and tassled shawls were specific to an area and helped identify a person's village. Black ankle-length skirts are the most common attire for women. Typical for men are waistcoats, breeches and a hat.

Slovenian bonnet called the *avba*, frequently decorated with lace, ribbons and embroidery, is an important national symbol.

The umbrella is a characteristic accessory, usually bright orange-red with coloured concentric stripes.

FOLK MUSIC

Slovenian folk music is still widely performed in rural areas, especially at weddings, feast days and local celebrations. The most widely distributed form of traditional music is the polka- and waltz-dominated style of the alpine region. Featuring an accordion backed by strings, it is joyful, melodic and ideal for dancing in couples. Its commercial music form, perfected by the Avsenik brothers from the Bled region, has enjoyed international success, selling millions of records in alpine Europe. Two current groups inspired by folk music are Terrafolk and Katalena, whose experiments in folk-rock fusion are contemporary in flavour.

Pan pipes or *trstenka*

The accordion is a key component in almost every folk group.

Zither, a common musical instrument

Live music *is an important part of social life, especially during summer, when most towns and villages organize festivals and celebrations that often involve groups playing on an open-air stage.*

PAINTING AND OTHER CRAFTS

Painting, embroidery and lace-making added style, colour and spiritual symbolism to the traditional Slovenian home. Furniture was frequently painted to add brightness to living and sleeping rooms, while intricately patterned textiles created an aura of wealth and comfort. One widespread form of popular art involved the painting of religious images on glass panes.

Detail of Idrija lace

Traditional lace-making in progress

Beehive panels *were highly decorative and were used to identify the hive and its owner. Seasonal agricultural activities usually formed the subject matter.*

Intricate lace, *from the town of Idrija (see p146), is traditionally made by intertwining threads from a series of small bobbins, a complicated procedure that requires nimble fingers.*

Painted Easter eggs *are traditionally decorated with colourful blobs of melted wax, a custom that has been preserved in the villages of southern Slovenia.*

Furniture, *such as wardrobes, bedsteads and cradles, were frequently painted in bright colours. Flowers, geometric shapes and figures of angels were the most common decorations. Painted wooden chests played a ritual role in weddings and were part of a bride's dowry.*

Gingerbread *made in various shapes and iced in bright colours, is a gift often given on festive occasions. The gingerbread heart (lectovo srce) is the traditional love token – although it is likely to be hung on a wall as a memento rather than eaten.*

FOLK ARCHITECTURE

Folk architecture, with farmhouses and barns constructed from traditional materials, still survives in rural areas. In alpine Slovenia, timber houses with flower-decked verandahs is the dominant style, followed by modern house builders too. In the karst and on the Adriatic coast, most houses were made from stone blocks, grouped around narrow alleys – this can be seen in karst villages such as Štanjel. One of the characteristics of traditional houses was the black kitchen, consisting of an open hearth and no chimney. Smoke rose up through the beams of the house, curing grain and meats in the process.

Traditional timber-built house, common in Slovenia's highland region

Slovenian Art

Slovenia has long been a melting pot of European
artistic styles, and has frequently been at the
epicentre of major cultural movements. The history
of Slovenian art closely follows that of the country's
architecture, with Gothic art flourishing throughout
the Middle Ages and a major explosion of Baroque art
occurring during and after the Counter-Reformation
of the 16th century. From the late 19th-century
onwards, art was often closely related to national
politics, with the Slovenian Impressionists aiming
to modernize national culture while remaining
true to its traditional ideals. Slovenia's post-World
War I generation eagerly embraced Cubism,
Constructivism and other modern art movements.

Woman Drinking Coffee by
Ivana Kobilca

THE MEDIEVAL PERIOD

Medieval Christianity provided a fertile ground for the growth
of a rich artistic culture, with frescoes, stained glass and
sculpture filling the country's churches and monasteries.

Dance of Death, *Hrastovlje, was painted in 1490 by John of
Kastav. This animated frieze is the best known of a series
of frescoes that fill Hrastovlje's village church.*

St George, *Gabrska Gora, an
anonymous mid-15th century
wood sculpture, is a compelling
example of late-Gothic art.*

BAROQUE ART

The Counter-Reformation encouraged new styles in the
arts, with an enhanced sense of spiritual drama visible in
both painting and sculpture. Artists from Italy flooded
Ljubljana, bringing with them the best in Baroque style.

**Frescoes in the
Seminary Library**,
Ljubljana (see p51),
*were painted by
Giulio Quaglio
together with his
son Raffaello in
1721. They depict a
mixture of Christian
figures and Classical
deities. Clever use
of perspective
creates the illusion
of added height.*

Fountain of the Three Rivers by
Francesco Robba (see p49) *shows
Slovenia's three main rivers symbolized
by a trio of Titans pouring water from
jugs, with fish providing a playful touch.*

THE 19TH CENTURY

The early 19th century saw a growing middle-class, in Ljubljana and other towns, who were wealthy enough to buy pictures for their homes, and frequently commissioned family portraits from local artists. Painters Matevž Langus, Jožef Tominc and Mihael Stroj mixed pictorial realism with domestic warmth and sentiment.

Julija Primic With Her Brother Janez by Matevž Langus *was one of his many portraits of Primic, subsequently a celebrated beauty and object of unfulfilled desire for poet France Prešeren.*

IMPRESSIONISM

Taking their lead from the French Impressionists, Slovenian artists such as Ivan Grohar, Rihard Jakopič, Matija Jama and Andrej Sternen brought a new sense of colour and atmosphere to Slovenian painting. Choosing to depict local landscapes and rural subjects, the Slovenian Impressionists saw their art as a patriotic duty, creating truly Slovenian paintings for a Slovenian audience.

The Sower by Ivan Grohar *was painted in 1907. This enigmatic depiction of a toiling peasant, face turned away from the viewer, has become something of a national icon.*

MODERNISM

Slovenian artists enthusiastically took up new ideas after World War I, with Avgust Černigoj experimenting with Constructivism and Ferdo Delak publishing avant-garde magazine *Tank!* Expressionism and New Objectivity influenced the work of painters Veno Pilon and Tone Kralj.

In the Café by Veno Pilon *is a 1926 work dating from Pilon's period in Paris. It illustrates the enduring fascination of Slovenian artists with Western Europe.*

POST-WAR AND CONTEMPORARY ART

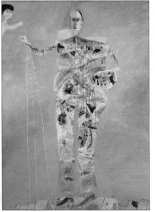

Unlike some more strictly controlled Communist countries, Slovenia remained open to international art trends after World War II, and frequently stood at the forefront of the global avant-garde. The 1960s art group OHO (Marko Pogačnik, David Nez, Milenko Matanović, Andraž and Tomaž Šalamun) was one of the leading conceptualists of the era, performing "actions" and publishing theoretical texts rather than producing artworks as such. In the 1980s, the art collective, IRWIN, produced a provocative mixture of painting, political symbolism and performance art that still exerts a strong influence on artists elsewhere.

Big Bright Self-Portrait by Gabriel Stupica, *painted in 1959, is an example of the versatile and prolific artist's use of mixed elements of Expressionism, Surrealism and Abstraction over a long and influential career.*

Skiing in the Slovenian Alps

Slovenians have been skiing since the 18th century, so it is of little surprise that skiing is the most popular activity in the country and that Slovenia has produced several Olympic and World Cup champions. Most of the country's resorts lie in the alpine northwest or are strung along the Pohorje massif near Maribor. Although each has its own character and pistes for most levels, Slovenian resorts are small and relaxed compared to the more famous ones elsewhere in Western Europe. The resorts here are also far cheaper, even though they provide the same facilities as the more celebrated resorts in Austria and Italy.

Vogel *is one of the most scenic skiing destinations in Slovenia. This mountain lies in the Triglav National Park (see pp112–14). There are pistes for beginners and mid-level skiers, while experts have the opportunity to go off-piste as well as to ski on one of Slovenia's best "black" runs, Žagarjev graben. There is a snowboarding park too.*
Star attractions: Spectacular views; off-piste skiing

Kranjska Gora, *Slovenia's oldest and best-known ski resort (see p116), is famous for its World Cup links and awesome ski jumps in Planica. It has everything from child-friendly runs to steep competition pistes in nearby Podkoren. Off-piste skiing is possible when conditions allow. There is also a wide variety of hotels, family activities and a range of après-ski activities.*
Star attractions: Alpine scenery; excellent holiday facilities

Kobla is a modern intermediate-level resort above Bohinjska Bistrica, which has the distinction of being the only Slovenian ski destination that can be accessed by train.

Cerkno, a small resort in Primorska, is not as busy as those further north. It has 18 km (11 miles) of pistes that suit all levels of skiers, from children and novices to thrill-seekers.

Mount Kanin, *at 2,300 m (7,546 ft), has Slovenia's highest pistes and its greatest vertical descent. The scenic mountain offers skiing late into spring as well as views of the Adriatic on clear days. It also allows the unique opportunity of skiing to the Italian resort, Sella Nevea.*
Star attractions: All ski slopes above 2,000 m (6,562 ft); long skiing season; skiing into Italy

STATISTICS

KRANJSKA GORA
Resort at: 810 m (2,648 ft)
Skiing altitude: 1,210–800 m
(3,937–2,625 ft)
Pistes: 20 km (12 miles)
Maximum descent: 813 m
(2,667 ft)
Ski lifts: 19
Cross-country trails: 40 km
(25 miles)
Season: Dec–Mar

MARIBORSKO POHORJE
Resort at: 325 m (1,066 ft)
Skiing altitude: 1,150–325 m
(3,773–1,066 ft)
Pistes: 42 km (26 miles)
Maximum descent: 1,010 m
(3,314 ft)
Ski lifts: 20
Cross-country trails: 25 km
(16 miles)
Season: Dec–Mar

MOUNT KANIN
Resort at: 460 m (1,509 ft)
Skiing altitude: 2,300–1,600 m
(7,546–5,249 ft)
Pistes: 30 km (19 miles)
Maximum descent: 1,840 m
(6,036 ft)
Ski lifts: 5
Cross-country trails: 16 km
(10 miles)
Season: late Nov–early May

MOUNT VOGEL
Resort at: 570 m (1,870 ft)
Skiing altitude: 1,800–570 m
(5,905–1,870 ft)
Pistes: 18 km (11 miles)
Maximum descent: 1,231 m
(4,039 ft)
Ski lifts: 8
Cross-country trails: 35 km
(22 miles)
Season: Dec–mid-Apr

Mariborsko Pohorje, *located next to Maribor (see pp176–7), the second-largest city in Slovenia, is the country's largest ski resort and one of its most popular. With pistes spread over a 220-ha (544-acre) area, the resort caters best to intermediate and novice skiers, although there are challenging runs for experts too.*
Star attractions: Only 30 minutes from Maribor centre; 10-km (6-mile) long night-time piste; cross-country forest trail

Velika Planina is popular with day trippers. The slopes are gentle for beginners and cross-country skiing is spectacular.

Kope is the highest part of the Pohorje range and enjoys one of the longest seasons.

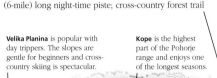

Rogla, popular with advanced skiers and snowboarders, is the training base for the Slovenian Olympic team. Most of its 12 km (8 miles) of pistes are ranked in the intermediate level.

Krvavec is very popular with the residents of Kranj *(see p120)* – the cable car to the ski base is just 17 km (11 miles) from Kranj's city centre. Krvavec's smooth alpine meadows permit skiing even under a thin blanket of snow and its pistes are well equipped for all activities, including snowboarding.

KEY

✈ International airport

▲ Peak

▬ Motorway

▬ Major road

▬ Minor road

— Railway

▬▪ International border

FAMILY FUN

Winter sports are family activities in Slovenia. Many children start to ski or toboggan as toddlers and most resorts have nursery slopes for youngsters. There are myriad activities to tempt younger skiers on to the slopes in places such as Kranjska Gora, Vogel or around Lake Bled. Here, pistes are set aside for those who want to toboggan on sledges or rubber rings, go snowshoe trekking, sleigh-riding, snowboarding or dog-sledding. Daring youngsters can sled at night on floodlit slopes.

Children playing at Krvavec

SLOVENIA THROUGH THE YEAR

Anation with distinct seasons, Slovenia has warm springs, long and hot summers, golden autumns and crisp cold winters. Spring and early summer tend to be dry and warm but rarely stifling, making them ideal times to visit the country. July and August are the peak periods for holidaying on Slovenia's stretch of the Adriatic

Dancing in traditional dress

coast, while the winter sports season can last from mid-December right through to Easter. Whatever the time picked to travel, there are always plenty of events to plan a trip around, from seasonal celebrations of local folklore to major arts and music festivals, which attract a large number of big-name international participants.

Skiiers at the Golden Fox tournament, Maribor

SPRING

Spring comes early to lowland Slovenia, with café tables spilling out on to the pavements. In the alpine parts of the country, however, snow can linger until Easter or beyond. By May, the weather is warmer and drier all over the country, heralding the first of the year's open-air cultural festivals.

MARCH

World Cup Ski Flying *(mid-Mar)*, Planica, near Kranjska Gora. The winter sports calendar reaches a climax with international competitions at Planica *(see p116)*, the highest ski-jumping hill in the world.

APRIL

Ljubljana Tango Festival *(mid-Apr)*, Ljubljana. This festival brings together dancers from Latin America

and Europe. There are plenty of opportunities for audience participation.
Spring Festival *(2nd half of Apr)*, Ljubljana. This is a 2-week season of electronic music concerts and avant-garde art exhibitions.
Salt Festival *(weekend closest to 23rd Apr)*, Piran. The local salt-making industry is celebrated with a weekend of

handicraft fairs, outdoor concerts and church processions, all in honour of Piran's patron saint, St George.

MAY

May Day *(1st May)*, nationwide. This is traditionally celebrated with the erection of the *mlaj*, a tall spruce trunk that is stripped of most of its branches except a few twigs at the top. Coloured ribbons and the Slovenian flag are hung from its tip.
Druga godba *(mid-May)*, Ljubljana. With concerts taking place in the open-air Križanke complex *(see p69)*, this is one of Europe's foremost world music festivals, featuring top-name participants from across the globe.
Cerkno Jazz *(mid-May)*, Cerkno. An eclectic selection of top-class jazz, jazz rock, jazz noise and ethno jazz, with internationally known

Dancers at the Ljubljana Tango Festival

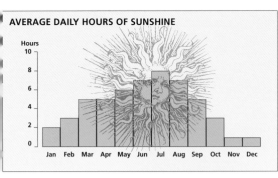

AVERAGE DAILY HOURS OF SUNSHINE

Hours

Jan Feb Mar Apr May Jun Jul Aug Sep Oct Nov Dec

Climate chart
The greatest number of sunny days occur between May and September. The least occur from November to January, when the hours of daylight are shorter. Hours of sunlight pick up again in February and March when the winter scenery is at its best.

names performing on Cerkno's main square, followed by after-party events around town.
Magdalena *(May)*, Maribor. A prestigious festival for young designers and graphic artists, with exhibitions in the daytime and gigs along with DJ events in the evenings.

SUMMER

There is a rich and varied menu of festivals in the summer, with many towns organizing a season of open-air concerts.

JUNE

Kino Otok Film Festival *(early–mid-Jun)*, Izola. A festival of international feature films and short films, often featuring a strong Third-World angle, with screenings taking place on Izola beach.
SEVIQC Brežice *(Jun–Aug)*, various venues. A season of early music concerts, takes place in historic buildings throughout Slovenia.
Ljubljana Jazz Festival *(late Jun–early Jul)*, Ljubljana. A week of outstanding jazz performances from international stars, with concerts in Križanke and other venues around the capital city.
Summer in the Old Town *(Jun–Sep)*, Ljubljana. A summer-long series of classical and jazz concerts held in historical buildings and courtyards.
Medieval Festival *(last weekend of Jun)*, Škofja Loka. Pageants, jousts

Conductor at the Ljubljana Festival

and feasting in one of the nation's best-preserved historic towns.
Rock Otočec *(last weekend of Jun)*, Otočec. This 3-day festival is Slovenia's biggest outdoor rock event. Local and international bands perform in a field near the Otočec Castle.
Lent Festival *(late Jun–early Jul)*, Maribor. One of

Slovenia's prime summer events, offering a fortnight of rock, jazz, theatre and folklore on outdoor stages on the riverbank and outside the town hall.

JULY

Ana Desetnica *(early Jul)*, Ljubljana. An international festival of street theatre with drama, circus acts and dance.
Bled Festival *(Jul)*, Lake Bled. A month-long programme of music and theatre in a range of venues around Lake Bled, featuring new contemporary work as well as the classics.
Ljubljana Festival *(Jul and Aug)*, Ljubljana. A season of major operas, symphonic concerts and chamber music using the Križanke outdoor stage.
Trnfest *(late Jul–late Aug)*, Ljubljana. A month-long series of open-air rock gigs and DJ events organized in the Trnovo district by the KUD France Prešeren Cultural Centre.

SEVIQC Brežice concert in progress at a historic building

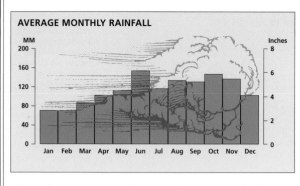

AVERAGE MONTHLY RAINFALL

MM
200
160
120
80
40
0

Inches
8
6
4
2
0

Jan Feb Mar Apr May Jun Jul Aug Sep Oct Nov Dec

Rainfall chart
The heaviest rainfall occurs in the summer months, although it is concentrated in the mountains. The lowland regions remain significantly drier. In winter, precipitation takes the form of snowfall, which can be dramatic, especially in the Alps.

AUGUST

Tartini Festival *(Aug and Sep)*, Piran. Outstanding classical soloists and chamber musicians perform in Piran's Minorite Monastery *(see p130)* and other historical buildings.
Radovljica Festival *(early Aug–mid-Aug)*, Radovljica. A 3-week festival of early music, with concerts in Radovljica manor house (free bus for concert-goers from Ljubljana).
Kamfest *(mid-Aug)*, Kamnik. The centre of Kamnik is taken over by a 2-week programme of concerts featuring rock, pop and world music.

AUTUMN

Autumn sees several major cultural festivals, with film and theatre featuring prominently. One massively popular seasonal activity is mushroom-picking, an all-the-family affair that gets into full swing by mid-September and can last until mid-November. The best harvests occur after a good period of rain.

SEPTEMBER

Nagib Contemporary Dance Festival *(mid-Sep)*, Maribor. A week of challenging dance performances by international and local artistes. Performances take place in a variety of venues throughout the city.
The Cows' Ball *(2nd or 3rd weekend of Sep)*, Bohinj. A long weekend of feasting, drinking and folk dancing, celebrating the transhumance of the dairy herds from the alpine meadows to pastures on the valley floor.

Biennial of Graphic Arts *(Sep and Oct, odd years)*, Ljubljana. A major event attracting the world's best printmakers, designers and illustrators. Exhibitions are spread across several major galleries.

OCTOBER

Slovene Film Festival *(early Oct)*, Portorož. A review of the year's best Slovenian feature films, short films and documentaries. Prizes are awarded to the best directors.
BIO (Biennial of Industrial Design) *(Oct, even years)*, Ljubljana. A prestigious international design festival, embracing product design, graphic arts and fashion, with exhibitions at Ljubljana's Fužine Castle *(see p81)*.
Borštnikovo srečanje *(mid-Oct)*, Maribor. Slovenia's premier contemporary

Onlookers and participants at the Cows' Ball festival, Bohinj

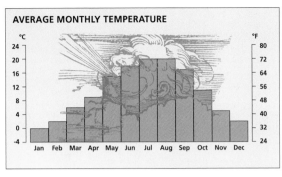

AVERAGE MONTHLY TEMPERATURE

Temperature chart
Summer is generally mild, with average temperatures peaking at 20° C (68° F) in July, although summers in the mountains can be significantly cooler. Winters tend to be harsh, with the temperature often dropping below zero from December.

theatre event, repeating the outstanding performances of the previous year.

NOVEMBER

St Martin's Day *(11th Nov)*, nationwide. Traditionally the day on which the year's new wine is ready to be drunk, St Martin's Day is marked with drinking and feasting – roast goose is the traditional dish.
LIFFE International Film Festival *(mid-Nov)*, Ljubljana & Maribor. A 10-day showcase of recent art movies from around the world, with lectures by visiting directors.

WINTER

The opening of the ski season in mid-December is marked with DJ parties at the main resorts. The main folkloric event of late winter is Shrovetide, when archaic Lenten rituals take place in Ptuj, Cerkno and the villages of the southwest.

DECEMBER

Advent *(Dec)*, Ljubljana. This market brings craft and delicatessen stalls on to the streets of the Old Town.
Living nativity scenes *(Dec)*, Postojna Caves. Local high-school students re-create scenes from the New Testament in Slovenia's most-visited cave.
Outdoor Film Festival *(last week of Dec)*, Bovec. This

Revellers dressed as *kurenti* during Kurentovanje, Ptuj

innovative festival of films focuses on documentaries dealing with sports, nature and the environment.

JANUARY

Golden Fox (Zlata lisica) *(mid-Jan)*, Maribor. Women's world-cup skiing on the pistes of the Mariborsko Pohorje *(see p177)*.

Hand-painted clock sold at Advent

FEBRUARY

MED (Maribor Electronic Destination) *(late Feb)*, Maribor. The Kibla Multimedia Centre in Maribor celebrates experimental electronic music with a week-end of concerts.
Kurentovanje *(Shrove Sunday)*, Ptuj. The most famous of Slovenia's pre-Lenten carnivals is held in Ptuj, where the *kurenti*

(traditional carnival figures) dance and leap through the town clad in animal skins and masks to drive away the evil spirits of winter as they go.

PUBLIC HOLIDAYS

New Year's Day (1 Jan)
Prešeren Day (Day of Slovene Culture, 8 Feb)
Easter Sunday (variable)
Easter Monday (variable)
Day of the Anti-Fascist Uprising (27 Apr)
May Day (1 and 2 May)
Pentecost (7th Sunday after Easter)
Day of Slovene Statehood (25 Jun)
Assumption Day (15 Aug)
Reformation Day (31 Oct)
All Saints' Day (1 Nov)
Christmas (25 Dec)
Independence and Unity Day (26 Dec)

THE HISTORY OF SLOVENIA

*L*ocated at the junction of the Central European, Mediterranean and Balkan worlds, Slovenia was, for a large part of its history, a marginal space squeezed between more powerful nations and cultures. That the Slovenians emerged as a coherent national group with a state of their own is a remarkable story of its people's resilience as well as survival.

Archaeological finds have suggested that Slovenia was already settled during the Paleolithic Age; however, evidence of the first well-established human culture in the area dates back to 4000 BC, when pile-dwellings were built in the Ljubljana Marshes, south of what is now the capital.

Bronze Age situla vessel, Novo Mesto

Constant migrations brought in new ethnic groups such as the Illyrian-speaking tribes that settled in the alpine region. By the 2nd millennium BC, a Bronze Age society based on hilltop fortresses was emerging in western Slovenia. The more sophisticated cultures of the 1st millennium BC were famous for their jewellery and situlae (ritual bronze vessels decorated with reliefs). The Vače Situla in the National Museum in Ljubljana is the finest example.

Migrating Celts arrived somewhere around 300 BC, bringing with them technical innovations such as the horse-drawn chariot and the potter's wheel. Celts assumed leadership of the pre-existing population and carved out several states, of which the most powerful was Noricum, a tribal federation covering northern Slovenia and much of Austria.

THE ROMANS

In the 2nd century BC, the Romans began to expand towards present-day Slovenia. This was a gradual and largely peaceful process in which the Romans extended their power through trade agreements and favourable alliances. It was under Emperor Augustus (63 BC–AD 14) that the region was fully absorbed into the Roman state and divided between the provinces of Italia in the west, Noricum in the northeast and Pannonia in the southeast. Roman legionaries were encouraged to settle in Emona (present-day Ljubljana), which soon became a thriving centre of trade and commerce. Celeia (Celje) and Poetovio (Ptuj) were the other main urban centres that developed during this period. Some of the best-preserved Roman ruins can be found around these towns.

By the middle of the 5th century AD, these Roman towns had been abandoned, with the populace seeking sanctuary in the hills from incursions by a succession of invaders. The Ostrogoths overran large parts of Slovenia in the 5th century only to be displaced by the Lombards several generations later.

TIMELINE

Bronze Age helmet

500 BC Artisans in central Slovenia produce the bronze Vače Situla, a high point of Iron Age art

Romans expand into Slovenia, 200 BC

00 BC	1000 BC	AD1	AD 500

300 BC Much of Slovenia is occupied by Celts

AD 15 The Romans establish Emona (Ljubljana) and Poetovio (Ptuj)

◁ Fresco from the Besenghi degli Ughi Palace, Izola

Painting depicting the Magyars invading Central Europe, AD 896

ARRIVAL OF THE SLOVENIANS

The Slovenian nation has its origins in the great migrations of the 6th century AD, when Slav tribes from the east settled in what is now Slovenia and southern Austria. They became the dominant ethnic group and were briefly drawn into a tribal federation led by Frankish merchant Samo in the mid-7th century. After Samo's death in 658, the Slavs formed their own state, which came to be known as the Duchy of Carantania. The 8th and 9th centuries saw the gradual absorption of these territories into the Frankish Empire. Frankish control helped ease the progress of Christianization, a process largely carried out by missionary priests from Salzburg and Aquileia. Frankish rule was profoundly shaken in the 10th century due to raids by the Magyars, and the Holy Roman Empire (the name adopted by a confederation of German rulers) expanded into Slovenia to fill the vacuum. Priests and warlords from the German province of Bavaria were awarded lands, creating a German-speaking aristocracy that held sway in Slovenia until the end of the 19th century.

HABSBURGS AND OTTOMANS

Medieval Slovenian society was dominated by a small number of super-powerful landowning dynasties – notably the Spannheims and the Counts of Celje – who controlled central Slovenia in the 14th and 15th centuries. Apart from building castles, the Counts of Celje made donations to Pleterje Monastery and the pilgrimage church at Ptujska Gora. Another feudal family increasing its holdings in the region were the Habsburgs, and, by the late 15th century, Slovenia had effectively become a province of the Habsburg Empire. Throughout the period of the Habsburg reign, the language for politics and culture was German, and Slovenian was spoken only among the peasantry.

Italian culture exerted an influence over the western Slovenian lands, where Slovene-inhabited villages

TIMELINE

630 Present-day Slovenia becomes part of a Slav federation under Samo

700 Slovenians begin to convert to Christianity

Conversion to Christianity depicted on a wall in the Church of the Holy Cross, Kojs

600	800	1000

658 Slavs form the Duchy of Carantania

740 Slovenians come under Bavarian rule

A page from the Freising Manuscripts

972 Carinthian monks compile the *Freising Manuscripts*, the earliest-known text in Slovenian

were in close proximity to the largely Italian-speaking area along the Adriatic coast. Slovenians and Italians mingled in the multi-ethnic port city of Trieste, which became a Habsburg possession in 1382. The nearby towns of Capodistria (Koper) and Pirano (Piran), meanwhile, came under the rule of Venice.

The Ottoman conquest of Bosnia in 1463 suddenly made Central Europe vulnerable to a new and powerful enemy. The Ottomans immediately started raiding Slovenian territory, leading to the fortification of towns, villages and churches throughout the country. Slovenians fought in the Habsburg armies that defeated the Ottomans at the Battle of Sisak in 1593, removing the threat of invasion for several generations.

Artist's view of the addition of Trieste to the Habsburg Empire (1382)

REFORMATION AND COUNTER-REFORMATION

Slovenian society was shaken by the emergence of Protestantism in the early 16th century. The preacher Primož Trubar became leader of the local Protestants, but was forced to leave for Germany in 1548 when the authorities clamped down on the new creed. Prayer books, published by Trubar in Tübingen, were the first books to be printed in the Slovenian language. Most of Slovenia's gentry and townsfolk accepted Protestantism by the 1560s, but the high aristocracy remained loyal to the Catholic

Bronze relief depicting the spread of Christianity, Ljubljana Cathedral

faith. The Jesuits arrived in Ljubljana in 1597 to spearhead the Counter-Reformation and, in 1628, the Habsburg emperor, Ferdinand II, enforced Catholic obedience on all high state officials. The Counter-Reformation won over the peasantry by encouraging new popular forms of worship, in which the cult of the Virgin Mary and mass participation in pilgrimages played increasingly important roles. The 17th century witnessed a renewed interest in Slovenian history and culture, led by geographer Janez Vajkard Valvasor. In 1689 he published his most important work, *Honour of the Duchy of Carniola,* on the natural history of his homeland.

Detail of Dance of Death *fresco*

1282 The Habsburgs gain a foothold in the region

1490 Janez of Kastav decorates Hrastovlje Church with his *Dance of Death* fresco

1515 A peasant revolt ruthlessly put down by pro-Habsburg aristocrats

00 | 1400 | 1600

1365 The Habsburg ruler, Rudolf IV, founds Novo Mesto

Duke Rudolf IV

1456 Death of Ulrich II, last Count of Celje; lands acquired by Habsburgs

1597 Jesuits arrive in Ljubljana to spearhead the Counter-Reformation

1593 Habsburgs defeat the Ottomans at the Battle of Sisak

SLOVENIA'S NATIONAL AWAKENING

Intellectual life in Ljubljana began to take off at the turn of the 18th century, with learned societies such as the Academia Operosorum as well as the Academia Filharmonicorum encouraging literature, music and the arts. Renewed interest in the Slovenian language was promoted by the intellectuals grouped around Žiga Zois, an enlightened baron whose collection of minerals became the basis for the Slovene National Museum. Among Zois's circle were Valentin Vodnik, editor of the first Slovenian newspaper, and Jernej Kopitar, linguist and philologist.

Further impetus to Slovenian culture came from a brief period of French rule (1809–1813), when Ljubljana became the capital of the "Illyrian Provinces", which included

Habsburg's coat of arms

Slovenia and western Croatia. The Slovenian language was introduced in schools, increasing the demand for Slovenian books. Even though Austria returned to power after the end of the Napoleonic Wars (1799–1815), interest in Slovenian culture continued. The epic verses of Romantic poet France Prešeren demonstrated that Slovenian language was fit for fine literature as well as the marketplace.

Social upheavals in 1848 raised hopes that the Habsburg Empire would be decentralized, leading to some autonomy for the Slovenians. However, the authorities in Vienna retained their grip on power, and the 1850s saw a return to absolutist rule. In 1867, the Habsburg Empire was divided into Austrian- and Hungarian-administered halves, creating the Dual Monarchy of Austria-Hungary. Most of Slovenia fell within the Austrian part, although the Slovenians of the eastern province of Prekmurje found themselves under Hungarian rule. Between 1868 and 1871 Slovenian intellectuals launched what became known as the Tabor Movement, a series of mass meetings calling for the reunification of Slovenians, nurturing a new sense of patriotism. Most Slovenians believed their country was too small to be a viable political entity on its own and campaigned for a self-governing Slav unit within Austria-Hungary. However, gaining ground by the close of the 19th century was the concept of Yugoslavism – the idea that those south-Slav peoples who shared similar languages (Slovenians, Croats and Serbs) should form a common state.

Poet France Prešeren's statue, Prešernov trg, Ljubljana

TIMELINE

1751 Baroque sculptor, Francesco Robba, completes the *Fountain of the Three Rivers* in Ljubljana

1778 Four climbers reach the summit of Mount Triglav

1799 Napoleonic Wars begin

1809 Ljubljana capital of French-run "Illyrian Provinces"

1700

1750

1800

Fountain of the Three Rivers *by Robba*

1768 Monk Marko Pohlin publishes Carniolan grammar

Congress of Vienna that led to the end of the Napoleonic Wars, 1815

An 1845 engraving showing an aerial view of Ljubljana

WORLD WAR I AND THE BIRTH OF YUGOSLAVIA

During World War I, Slovenians were drafted into Habsburg armies and served on all fronts. Italy declared war on Austria-Hungary in 1915, hoping to conquer ethnic Slovenian territory in the Adriatic hinterland. Three years of bitter warfare along the Soča (Isonzo) river followed, with huge casualties on both sides. After the October 1917 breakthrough at Kobarid, the Austro-Hungarian forces won at the Soča Front but faced collapse elsewhere, leading to a disintegration of authority.

With the defeat of the Austro-Hungarian Empire in October 1918, Slovenia's leaders rushed to declare a union with their south-Slav neighbours, creating the Kingdom of Serbs, Croats and Slovenians. Trieste and its hinterland were awarded to Italy, disappointing Slovenians who considered it to be part of their national heritage. The Slovenians of Trieste soon became the target of Italian nationalist attacks and the Slovene Cultural Centre (Narodni dom) was burnt down by a Fascist mob in 1920. The German-Slovenian areas around Klagenfurt in Carinthia were subjected to a plebiscite in October 1920, with the majority voting for incorporation into Austria. Slovenians initially thought that the new south-Slav state would be a loose federation in which they would enjoy a measure of autonomy. However, the Constitution of 1921 created a centralized country with a single parliament in Belgrade. Slovenian politicians tried to reform the system, but the new state remained politically unstable. After the fatal shooting of Croat leader Stjepan Radić in parliament (1928), Serbia's King Alexander established a royal dictatorship. The state was renamed "Yugoslavia" in the hope that officially-enforced Yugoslav patriotism would end ethnic quarrels.

Political frustrations aside, Slovenian culture flourished in the inter-war period, with the extension of local-language education, the founding of Ljubljana University and a boom in publishing. Winter tourism and skiing became a national obsession, with ski-jumping emerging as the most popular spectator sport.

Austro-Hungarian soldiers at the Soča Front, 1915

France Prešeren's Toast (Zdravljica)

	1849 Ljubljana connected to Graz and Vienna by rail	**1867** Habsburg Empire divided; Slovenia falls under Austria		**1914** World War I begins
1850			**1900**	
1844 France Prešeren's *Toast (Zdravljica)* published; serves as the national anthem today	**1868** Tabor Movement launched	**1918** Habsburg Empire collapses		*Impressionist painter Ivan Grohar's iconic* The Sower, *1907*

Socialist Realist painting in the Museum of
Contemporary History, Ljubljana

WORLD WAR II, TITO AND THE
YUGOSLAV FEDERATION

The Kingdom of Yugoslavia came to
an end with the German invasion in
April 1941 and Slovenia was divided
between Germany and Italy. An anti-
Fascist partisan movement under the
Communists became increasingly influential. Some conservatives collaborated
with the occupiers, swelling the ranks
of the Quisling-controlled *domobranci*
or home guard. Ably led by the half-
Slovenian, half-Croatian Josip Broz
Tito, the partisan movement
became a liberation army,
sweeping the occupiers out of
Slovenia by May 1945. Over the
next few months about 12,000
domobranci were massacred by
avenging partisans, their bodies
dumped in mass graves.

With the war over, Slovenia
became a federal republic in
Communist Yugoslavia. The fate
of Trieste and its hinterland remained
undecided until 1954, when it was
returned to Italy. Koper, Piran and
Portorož were ceded to Slovenia.
Federal Yugoslavia was initially allied
to the USSR, but Soviet leader Stalin
harboured a profound distrust of Tito,
and engineered Yugoslavia's expulsion
from the Eastern-bloc Cominform

organization in 1948. Tito stayed in
power, borrowed money from the
West, and built a popular form of
Communism. The 1950s saw a rise in
living standards and a boom in con-
sumerism. Slovenian goods, such as
Gorenje domestic appliances, Cockta
soft drinks and Lisca lingerie, became
household names and are exported
even today. Although Yugoslavia was
relatively open to Western culture,
freedom had its limits. The Intellectual
magazine, *Revija 57*, was closed down
in 1958 after publishing articles critical
of Socialism (their author Jože Pučnik
was jailed) and the journal, *Perspektive*,
faced a similar fate in 1964.

As the most economically advanced
republic in the federation, Slovenia
frequently felt short-changed by a system where funds were channelled to
subsidize projects in the poorer south.
In 1969, money for Slovenian road-
building was diverted to other republics owing to pressure from Belgrade.

Slovenian Communist leader Stane
Kavčič was forced out of power
in 1972 for defending Slovene
interests. Paradoxically, a new
constitution in 1974 gave more
autonomy to the republics,
leaving Slovenia's Communists
relatively free to run their own
affairs. Yugoslavia's decentralized system worked as
long as living standards
improved, and the popular
Tito remained at the helm. With
his death in 1980, and the economic
crisis, the federation disintegrated.

Bust of Josip
Broz Tito

THE "SLOVENE SPRING"

In Slovenia, the emergence of punk
rock in the late 1970s unleashed
subcultures that the Communist
authorities failed to control. National

TIMELINE

1938 Vladimir Bartol publishes historical novel
Alamut, an international bestseller decades later

1980 Yugoslavia enters a period of
crisis following Tito's death

1948 Tito's Yugoslavia expelled
from Cominform

1940   **1955**   **1970**

1941
Germany
invades
Yugoslavia

1945 Slovenia becomes one
of six republics forming
Communist Yugoslavia

*Packaging from
the Tito era*

1972 Liberal Stane Kavči
forced out by conservati

1966 Tito sacks secret police
chief Aleksandar Ranković

youth organizations enthusiastically adopted alternative culture, and the magazine, *Mladina,* became increasingly daring in its criticisms of Communist bureaucracy. The Slovene League of Communists, led by reformist Milan Kučan, relaxed its grip on censorship, allowing these new social phenomena to flourish. In January 1987, the journal, *Nova revija,* discussed the possibility of independence from Yugoslavia.

Monument to Communist leader, Boris Kidrič, Maribor

Slovenia's reformist path was regarded as dangerous by conservative institutions, notably the JLA (Yugoslav People's Army). When a plot to destabilize Slovenia was unearthed by journalists from *Mladina,* the JLA put them on trial in a Ljubljana military court. Beginning in July 1988, the trial provoked huge demonstrations, leading to the creation of a mass civil rights organization. The Slovene League of Communists appeared to sympathize with the demonstrators. The final Congress of the Yugoslav League of Communists was held in 1990. The Slovenian delegation walked out when it realized that their reformist ideas would be rejected by Communists from other republics.

Slovenia's first multi-party elections took place in April 1990, with DEMOS (coalition of non-Communist parties) becoming the leading force in parliament. After the December 1990 referendum, independence was declared on 25 June 1991. The JLA occupied strategic points in the republic, but were outmanoeuvred by Slovenian forces, bringing an end to the so-called Ten-Day War. Slovenian independence was recognized by the European Union nations on 15 January 1992.

SLOVENIA TODAY

Slovenia soon established itself as one of the economic and political successes of post-Communist Europe. Parliamentary elections at four-year intervals produced relatively smooth exchanges of power from right-of-centre to left-of-centre coalition governments. For whoever was in power, the main plank of policy throughout the 1990s remained Slovenia's integration into European and global institutions – an ambition achieved in 2004 with the country's admission to both NATO and the EU. Slovenia's adoption of the euro in January 2007 served to confirm the country's extraordinary voyage from a Yugoslav republic to equal partner in a new Europe.

Yugoslav army convoy during the Ten-Day War in Slovenia

1991 Slovenia becomes independent on 25 June

2008 Hammer-thrower, Primož Kozmus wins gold at the Beijing Olympics.

Primož Kozmus celebrates his Olympics gold

45

2000

2015

European Union flag

2004 Slovenia becomes a member of the European Union and NATO

2010 Slovenia's footballers qualify for the FIFA World Cup for the second time since independence

LJUBLJANA
AREA BY AREA

Ljubljana at a Glance

Most of Ljubljana's historic sights are located in
the Old Town, squeezed between Castle Hill
and the Ljubljanica river. However, many of the city's
architectural highlights and keynote museums are in
the New Town, on the west bank of the river. Both
parts of the city are very compact and can easily be
explored on foot. Attractions outside the centre, such
as Tivoli Park and Metelkova Mesto, are also within
walking distance. Suburban sights such as the Žale
Cemetery and the Museum of Architecture are
accessible by bus.

**Winged Retable, National
Museum of Slovenia**

**Orthodox Church of Sts Cyril and
Methodius** (see p58), *built in
the Byzantine style in the 1930s,
is decorated with colourful
modern frescoes executed
in the style of medieval Serbian
church murals.*

NEW TOW
(see pp56–

Tivoli Mansion
(see p74),
*contains a
gallery devoted
to contemporary
graphic art
from around
the world.*

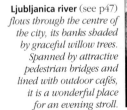

Ljubljanica river (see p47)
*flows through the centre of
the city, its banks shaded
by graceful willow trees.
Spanned by attractive
pedestrian bridges and
lined with outdoor cafés,
it is a wonderful place
for an evening stroll.*

◁ **Magnificent view of the Old Town, Ljubljana**

Dragon Bridge (see p51) *is a much-loved urban landmark, celebrating the beast that, according to local legend, once ruled over the Ljubljana Marshes.*

| 0 meters | 500 |
| 0 yards | 500 |

Metelkova Mesto (see p77), *an alternative arts and nightlife centre, is located in a former barracks, and is famous for its offbeat bars and clubs.*

AROUND THE CENTRE
(see pp70–81)

D TOWN
pp44–55

Slovene Ethnographic Museum (see pp78–9) *is everything that a contemporary museum should be, with varied and colourful exhibits arranged in eye-catching displays.*

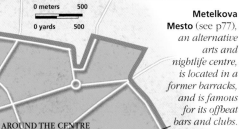

Fountain of the Three Rivers (see p49) *is one of the finest examples of Ljubljana's Baroque heritage. The work of sculptor Francesco Robba, its replica now stands in the Old Town.*

OLD TOWN

Ljubljana is often described as one of the most Mediterranean of Central European cities and it is in the Old Town that this is most apparent. There is a distinct Italian flavour to the Baroque mansions and churches rising above its cobbled streets. The focal point is the Triple Bridge that links Prešernov trg on the west bank of the Ljubljanica river with the colonnaded Market on the east. South of the Market are the pedestrianized Mestni trg and Stari trg, home to quirky shops and lively restaurants. Looming above the town is Ljubljana Castle, offering unrivalled views of the city.

One of the dragons on the Dragon Bridge

SIGHTS AT A GLANCE

Historic Buildings, Sites and Streets
Bishop's Palace **8**
Fountain of the Three Rivers **4**
Gruber Palace **16**
Ljubljana Castle pp52–3 **11**
Seminary **9**
Stari trg **12**
Town Hall **5**

Bridges
Dragon Bridge **10**
Triple Bridge **3**

Churches and Cathedrals
Franciscan Church of the Annunciation **2**
St Florian's Church **14**
St James's Church **15**
St Nicholas's Cathedral **7**

Square
Prešernov trg **1**

Gallery
ŠKUC Gallery **13**

Places of Interest
Market **6**

KEY

	Street-by-Street area *pp46–7*
	Funicular
P	Parking
i	Visitor information

GETTING AROUND

The Old Town is a 5-minute walk from central Ljubljana and is a joy to explore on foot. A fast modern funicular saves visitors the steep climb to the castle.

SEE ALSO

- **Where to Stay** pp188–90
- **Where to Eat** pp202–4

◁ **Exquisite interior of St Nicholas's Cathedral**

Street-by-Street: Ljubljana Old Town

Located between the medieval castle and the leafy banks of the Ljubljanica river, Ljubljana's Old Town contains some of the best-preserved Baroque buildings in southeastern Europe. Arcaded 18th-century houses, domed churches, fountain-studded piazzas and narrow cobbled alleys lined with cafés and shops add to its elegant character.

★ **Market**
Ljubljana's lively outdoor market is known for its fresh herbs and dried mushrooms, sold alongside every kind of local produce ⑥

Dragon Bridge, an example of the Art Nouveau style ⑩

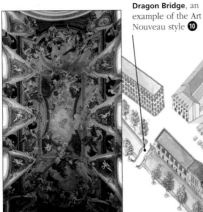

St Nicholas's Cathedral
Created by Giulio Quaglio in 1706, the cathedral's ceiling is a fine example of Baroque illusionist painting, with cherubs, saints and evangelists seemingly ascending through heavenly skies ⑦

Butchers' Bridge was opened to public in 2010. Couples in love come here to affix engraved padlocks to the parapet.

KEY

– – – Suggested route

Franciscan Church of the Annunciation is the city's most attractive Baroque church, with an 18th-century altar by Italian sculptor, Francesco Robba ②

★ **Triple Bridge**
Designed for pedestrians by Jože Plečnik in 1929, the three-lane Triple Bridge was part of the renovation of the riverbank area ③

The Prešeren Statue, one of Ljubljana's best-known landmarks, honours Romantic poet and national icon, France Prešeren.

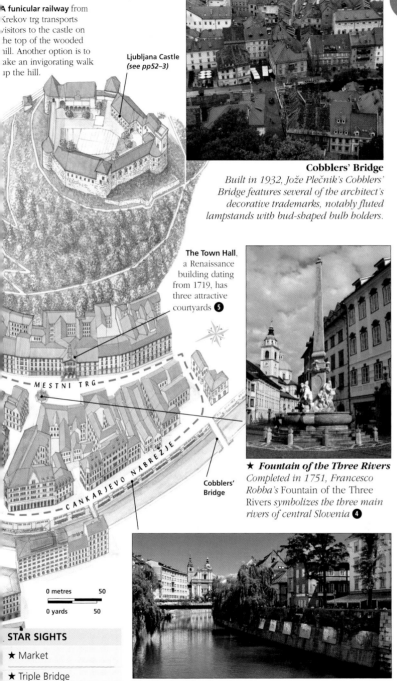

A funicular railway from Krekov trg transports visitors to the castle on the top of the wooded hill. Another option is to take an invigorating walk up the hill.

Ljubljana Castle (see pp52–3)

Cobblers' Bridge
Built in 1932, Jože Plečnik's Cobblers' Bridge features several of the architect's decorative trademarks, notably fluted lampstands with bud-shaped bulb holders.

The Town Hall, a Renaissance building dating from 1719, has three attractive courtyards ❺

MESTNI TRG

CANKARJEVO NABREŽJE

Cobblers' Bridge

★ **Fountain of the Three Rivers**
Completed in 1751, Francesco Robba's Fountain of the Three Rivers *symbolizes the three main rivers of central Slovenia* ❹

0 metres   50
0 yards   50

STAR SIGHTS

★ Market

★ Triple Bridge

★ Fountain of the Three Rivers

Ljubljanica Riverbank
The east bank of the river is lined with willow trees, orange- and red-roofed townhouses and fabulous terrace cafés and restaurants.

Prešernov trg ❶

City Map D2 & D3.

Located between Ljubljana's Old Town and the 19th-century districts on the west bank of the Ljubljanica river, Prešernov trg is, in many ways, the symbolic heart of the city. It is named after France Prešeren, the Romantic poet whose patriotic verses were central to the development of a Slovenian national consciousness. The poet is immortalized by a monument in the centre of the square, with a poetry book in hand, accompanied by a scantily clad muse wielding a sprig of laurel. The unveiling of the statue in 1905 was a major political event, bringing thousands of patriotic Slovenians out on to the street at a time when the city was still ruled by the Habsburg Empire.

Around the square are some of the finest Art Nouveau structures in Ljubljana. The **Centromerkur Building**, on the northeastern corner, was built in 1903 by Austrian architect Friedrich Sigismundt to serve as a department store. Crowning the building is a statue of Mercury, the Roman god of trade. Now occupied by the fashion store Galerija Emporium, the interior retains some stunning Art Nouveau

Centromerkur Building, now occupied by the Galerija Emporium

details, with carved female heads at the bottom of the Y-shaped staircase and some ornate light fittings above.

On the opposite side of the square is the mid-19th-century Hauptman House, renovated in 1904 by the city's leading Art Nouveau architect, Ciril Metod Koch. Edged with green and turquoise tiles, it is an outstanding example of the Viennese-inspired decorative style of the age.

Just behind it, the building at Wolfova No. 4 features a relief of the 19th-century beauty Julija Primic peering from a mock first-floor window. Primic was the object of Prešeren's unrequited love, an obsession that inspired the air of romantic melancholy which characterized much of his writing.

Franciscan Church of the Annunciation ❷
Frančiškanska Cerkev Marijinega oznanjenja

Prešernov trg. **City Map** D2.
⏰ 9am–noon & 3–7pm daily.

Dominating the northeast corner of Prešernov trg is the 17th-century Franciscan Church, containing a wealth of Baroque interior detail.

The main attraction is the high altar by Francesco Robba, the Venetian sculptor who spent most of his adult life in Ljubljana and made a huge artistic contribution to the city. Expressive statuettes of St Mary and other saints on either side of the altar showcase Robba's work at its graceful best. The ceiling frescoes were painted by Slovenian artist Matevž Langus in the mid-19th century, and re-worked by Slovenian Impressionist Matej Sternen following damage during the 1895 earthquake.

Triple Bridge ❸
Tromostovje

City Map D3.

If the capital city has one immediately recognizable landmark, it is probably the

Pedestrians crossing the Triple Bridge towards the Franciscan Church of the Annunciation

Triple Bridge, the three-lane crossing designed in 1929 by the city's most prolific architect, Jože Plečnik *(see p73)*. Faced with the problem of how to widen the city's main crossing point to accommodate increasing traffic levels, Plečnik decided to retain the 19th-century bridge in the middle, adding two angled side bridges for pedestrians. It was an inspired piece of town planning, turning Prešernov trg into the focal point of the city and bringing life to both banks of the river.

The bridge is embellished with the kind of decorations typical of Plečnik, with stone baubles sprouting from the parapets alongside curvy lampstands tipped with buds of milk-coloured glass. The elegant balustrades bring a Venetian sense of style to the whole ensemble.

Fountain of the Three Rivers ❹
Vodnjak treh kranjskih rek

Mestni trg. **City Map** D3.

Surrounded by water and rising above the cobblestoned Mestni trg, this tall triangular obelisk, is the most celebrated work of Ljubljana-based Venetian sculptor, Francesco Robba. The fountain gets its name from the three pitcher-wielding giants at its base, thought to symbolize the Ljubljanica, Sava and Krka, the three main rivers of the historical duchy,

The 18th-century *Fountain of the Three Rivers*

Carniola. The fountain was commissioned in 1743, although it was another eight years before the project reached completion – Robba was in any case constantly busy with church-commissioned jobs throughout the city. Probable inspiration for the work was Bernini's Fountain of the Four Rivers

Arcaded inner courtyard with a well in the Town Hall

in Rome's Piazza Navona. What visitors see today is actually a replica – the original fountain was moved to the National Gallery *(see pp60–61)* in 2008, where a modern glass-covered atrium protects it from the elements.

Town Hall ❺
Mestna hiša

Mestni trg 1. **City Map** D3.

Adding an air of distinction to Mestni trg's western side is Ljubljana's 18th-century Town Hall, a Renaissance-influenced structure with an arcaded ground floor and a hexagonal clock tower rising from its pediment. Just inside the entrance is a 17th-century statue of Hercules wielding a club and preparing to batter a wild beast. According to local myth, Hercules visited Ljubljana in the company of Jason and the Argonauts who, having sailed up the Danube and Sava rivers, had to pull their boat overland in order to secure passage to the Adriatic Sea.

Beyond the statue lies a trio of arcaded inner courtyards, which frequently host exhibitions of art or photography. The central courtyard is decorated with a sgraffito frieze featuring horn-blowing cherubs and frolicking unicorns. Slightly hidden in the corner of the courtyard is a fountain overlooked by a statue of Narcissus, attributed to Francesco Robba's workshop.

FRANCE PREŠEREN (1800–1849)

The Romantic poet France Prešeren was the first to demonstrate that Slovenian – hitherto considered a peasant language – could serve as the vehicle for great literature. His verse contained a strong patriotic undercurrent, spurring the development of a modern national consciousness. His collection, *Crown Of Sonnets* (1834), used the author's own sense of unfulfillment as a metaphor for Slovenia's position in the Habsburg Empire. More optimistic is *Zdravljica* (1844), the wine drinking song, the 7th strophe of which later became the text for Slovenia's national anthem. A lifelong drinker himself, Prešeren did not live long enough to enjoy the fame his works ultimately generated.

Prešeren's statue, Prešernov trg

Seafood on sale in Ljubljana's Market Colonnade

Market ❻

Glavna tržnica

Vodnikov trg. **City Map** D3, E2 & E3.
Market Colonnade ◯ 7am–4pm
Mon–Thu, 7am–2pm Sat.

The northern end of Ljubljana's Old Town is largely taken up by the city's sprawling market. Apart from being the local fruit and vegetable market, the place also has numerous stalls selling souvenirs, herbs and speciality foods.

Dominating the market's northern side is the **Market Colonnade**, a gently curving riverside structure that looks like an elongated Graeco-Roman temple. It was designed by Jože Plečnik (see p73) in 1942 to provide shelter for a row of food stalls. Spiral staircases descend to the colonnade's lower storey, home to a fish market filled with piles of Adriatic octopus, squid and lobster. The lower storey also contains a seafood snack bar and an arcaded terrace looking out on to the river.

Plečnik initially planned to build a covered bridge linking the eastern end of the colonnade to the opposite bank of Ljubljanica river – a project that did not take off due to lack of funds. The original plan was partly carried out with the construction of the Butchers' Bridge (Mesarski most) in 2010. Guarding the approaches to the bridge are the statues of Adam, Eve and Prometheus by local sculptor Jakov Brdar (b.1949). To the east of the colonnade is the main fruit-and-vegetable market, where trestle tables

fill the broad expanse of Vodnikov trg. Presiding over the southern end of the square is a statue of Valentin Vodnik, the priest and poet whose works helped to shape the modern Slovenian language.

Immediately east of Vodnikov trg, at the corner of Poljanska cesta and Kapiteljska ulica, is the so-called Flat Iron (Peglezen), a four-storey apartment built by Jože Plečnik in 1932. Named after its narrow wedge shape and flat roof, the building is a typical example of Plečnik's architectural style – a mix of Modernist, Rennaissance and Classical – with an arcaded ground floor and geometrical window frames on the first floor.

St Nicholas's Cathedral ❼

Stolna Cerkev sv Nikolaja

Dolničarjeva 1. **City Map** D3.
Tel (01) 234 2690. ◯ 6am–noon & 3–7pm.

Towering above the market are the twin towers of the Baroque St Nicholas's Cathedral. Built on the site of an earlier church by leading

Jesuit architect Andrea Pozzo in 1707, this cathedral is dedicated to St Nicholas, patron saint of fishermen and sailors. The relatively plain exterior is enlivened by the two bronze doors made to commemorate Pope John Paul II's visit to Slovenia in 1996. Each door is decorated with expressive reliefs. The west door depicts scenes from the history of Slovenian Christianity – the top of the door portrays Pope John Paul II peering from a window, while towards the bottom is an illustration of the baptism of the Slovenian nation. The south door shows the tall mitred profiles of six of Slovenia's 20th-century bishops praying at Christ's tomb.

Angel sculpture in the cathedral

Inside, the cathedral has a richly decorated sequence of side chapels as well as a nave dominated by an Illusionist ceiling painting of the Crucifixion by Giulio Quaglio the Elder (1610–58). The cathedral is particularly rich in Baroque sculpture. It has a Corpus Christi altar (1752) by the Italian sculptor Francesco Robba, which is flanked by statuettes of angels. Niches in the transept hold four statues of the bishops of Roman-era Emona carved by the 17th-century sculptor, Angelo Putti.

Richly decorated interior of St Nicholas's Cathedral

Frescoes on the ceiling of the Seminary's library

Bishop's Palace ❽
Škofijski dvorec

Ciril Metodov trg 4. **City Map** D3.
Tel (01) 234 2600. ☐ Mon–Fri.

Connected to the cathedral by a covered pedestrian bridge is the Bishop's Palace, a distinguished ochre building facing the Ljubljanica river. It was originally built for Bishop Ravbar in 1512. However, its arcaded courtyard, added in the 18th century, gives the building its charm.

The French Emperor Napoleon Bonaparte stayed here after routing Austrian armies in 1797. The palace subsequently served as the official residence of the Governor-General of the French-ruled Illyrian Provinces between 1808 and 1813.

Seminary ❾
Semenišče

Dolničarjeva ulica 4. **City Map** D3.
Tel (01) 433 6109.

Immediately northeast of the cathedral is the Seminary, a grand Baroque structure built by the architect Carlo Martinuzzi between 1708 and 1714. The most impressive feature on the exterior is the south portal, an arched doorway flanked by a pair of stone Titans carved by Angelo Putti. The seminary's first-floor library was the first public library in Ljubljana

and preserves its Baroque interior. The ceiling vaults are filled with frescoes by Giulio Quaglio. Books are stored in ornate wooden cases made by local cabinet maker Josip Wergant. Visits to the library can be arranged in advance through the Ljubljana Tourist Information Centre (see p95).

Dragon Bridge ❿
Zmajski most

City Map E2.

Located just beyond the market's eastern boundary, the Dragon Bridge was the first major Art Nouveau project to be built in the city. Designed by the architect Jurij Zaninovič, it was built in 1901 to mark the 60th birthday of Austro-Hungarian Emperor Franz-Josef I. The bridge gets its name from the bronze dragons that stand guard over its ends. It is said that the legendary voyagers, Jason and the Argonauts, fought with and killed a dragon in the marshes south of Ljubljana before continuing on their journey towards the Adriatic.

Rising from the bridge's parapet is a line of Art Nouveau lampposts, decorated with gryphon motifs and crowned with fruit-like clusters of glass globes. A plaque halfway along the bridge honours Ivan Hribar (1851–1941), the mayor of Ljubljana who oversaw the bridge's construction. The western end of the bridge provides a fine view of Ljubljana's market halls, with the twin towers and dome of the cathedral rising in the distance.

A bronze dragon on the Dragon Bridge

VALENTIN VODNIK (1758–1819)

One of the founding fathers of Slovenian literary culture, Valentin Vodnik wrote some of the first poems ever to be published in Slovenian. He also edited the first Slovenian newspaper, *Lublanske novice*. Vodnik was particularly inspired by the Illyrian Provinces, which introduced the local language in schools. His poem *Illyria Revived* (1816) argued that Illyria deserved to be treated as a nation in its own right. The poem became a rallying cry for late 19th-century Slovenian patriots, for whom the notion of Illyria provided a welcome alternative to the harsh realities of Habsburg power.

Statue of Vodnik, Vodnikov trg

Ljubljana Castle ⑪
Ljubljanski Grad

Tourist sign

Perched atop a cone-shaped hill, Ljubljana Castle looms above the Old Town. The city's most instantly recognizable landmark originally dates from the 11th century, when the Spannheims adopted Ljubljana as their feudal power base. Following the city's absorption by Austria in 1355, the castle became the property of the Habsburg family, before going on to serve as a barracks, then a refuge for the poor and a prison. The castle is now a popular tourist destination, with many attractions around its irregular courtyard.

Sculpture in the grounds behind the castle

Restaurant

Wedding hall

Pentagonal Tower
The 15th-century Pentagonal Tower once guarded the main entrance to the courtyard. Its restored interior now serves as an atmospheric exhibition space for contemporary art.

★ Virtual Museum
A 25-minute 3D animation film on Ljubljana's history, with commentary in various languages, is shown here.

Entrance

Funicular
This state-of-the-art metal and glass box zooms up in under a minute to the castle from Krekov trg in the Old Town. It runs during the castle's opening hours.

STAR SIGHTS

★ Virtual Museum

★ Clocktower

★ Courtyard

★ Clocktower

The clocktower, built in 1848 to serve as a viewing platform and tourist attraction, provides a wonderful panorama of the city, with the Karavanke range clearly visible to the north.

Virtual Museum

Chapel of St George

This 15th-century Gothic chapel's ceiling is decorated with the coats of arms of the noble families of Carniola, accompanied by those of Habsburg emperors Rudolf I and Charles IV. They were painted in 1747 as a romantic expression of nostalgia for the medieval feudal order.

★ Courtyard

During summer evenings, the courtyard is used for music and drama performances. It is also a popular venue for weddings, which are held on Saturdays throughout the year.

Estate Hall

Casemates

Views

The castle parapet offers a bird's-eye view of central Ljubljana's terracotta roofs with the Alps in the background.

Visitors at a charming open-air café on Stari trg

Stari trg ⑫

City Map D4.

The main thoroughfare of the Old Town is Stari trg, a narrow cobbled street overlooked by well-preserved Baroque and Neo-Renaissance houses. Once inhabited by Ljubljana's wealthier merchant families, the street now hosts smart designer clothes boutiques, craft shops and funky restaurants. A lattice of alleyways connects Stari trg to Cankarjevo nabrežje, the café-lined promenade that runs along the riverbank to the west.

The 18th-century Schweiger House (Schweigerjeva hiša), at No. 11, has a portal overlooked by a stone figure of a man holding his finger up to his lips – a witty allusion to the building's original owner, Franz Karl Schweiger von Lerchenfeld; Schweiger in German means "Silent One". A bust mounted on the wall beside the doorway honours one of the house's most famous residents, the poet Lili Novy (1885–1958).

ŠKUC Gallery ⑬
Galerija ŠKUC

Stari trg 21. **City Map** D4. *Tel (01) 251 6540.* ☐ *11am–7pm Tue–Sun.* **www**.skuc.org

Occupying the front half of a corner house at the junction of Stari trg and Gornji trg, ŠKUC Gallery has been Ljubljana's primary venue for contemporary art ever since it first opened its doors in 1978.

Founded as a student cultural centre (Študentski kulturni center, hence the acronym), ŠKUC soon became the focus of radical activity. It has promoted artists from all over Yugoslavia, released punk-rock records under its own label, supported minority rights groups and organized intellectual discussions. Most of the civil rights activists who shaped the Slovene Spring *(see pp38–9)* of the 1980s were part of ŠKUC at some stage in their lives. The centre organizes the literature festival, Live Literature (Živa književnost), in June, when international authors give book readings on the street outside the gallery. Let's Meet at ŠKUC (Dobimo se pred Škucem) is a series of outdoor concerts organized in July.

The ŠKUC Gallery still looks like an alternative cultural space, with black doorways and darkened windows eloquently conveying the message that this not a mainstream art gallery. A full programme of exhibitions presents a great opportunity to see artists from Slovenia as well as from other countries.

St Florian's Church ⑭
Cerkev sv Florjana

Gornji trg. **City Map** E4.

Presiding over the mansard-roofed Baroque houses on the picturesque Gornji trg is the onion-domed St Florian's Church, dedicated to the patron saint of firefighters. A 17th-century structure,

Restored interior of the 17th-century St Florian's Church

Gruber Palace, formerly a school of hydrology and navigation

damaged by fire in 1774, it was restored by Jože Plečnik (see p73) in 1933.

The church is rarely open to the public, but there are plenty of interesting details on the exterior, such as the faded 18th-century fresco of Our Lady of Mercy, high above the main door. Occupying a niche on the street-facing side of the church is Francesco Robba's (1698–1757) lively sculpture of the Czech martyr St John of Nepomuk. Here, the saint is portrayed being thrown into the Vltava river, as cherubs cling to his robes.

St James's Church ⓯
Cerkev sv Jakoba

Gornji trg 18. **City Map** D4.
Tel (01) 252 1727. 🔼 8am, 9:30am & 5pm Sun, 6:30pm Mon–Sat.

Rising to the south of Stari trg is St James's Church, a church of Gothic origins that received a Baroque makeover when the Jesuits adopted it as their base in 1598. The basilica was damaged in the 1895 earth-quake. A second wave of rebuilding resulted in the addition of the Neo-Gothic spire that is the church's focal point today.

The interior remains one of Ljubljana's most outstanding displays of Baroque religious art. There are parallel rows of altars, full of extravagant statuary, including Francesco Robba's high altar (1732),

which is flanked by a graceful pair of angels depicted with their hands clasped in prayer.

The octagonal St Francis Xavier Chapel (1709) on the northern side of the church features more angels sculpted by Paolo Groppelli (1677–1751) and female figures by Jacopo Contieri personifying the continents of Europe and Africa – the latter exotically clad in grasses and feathers.

Gruber Palace ⓰
Gruberjeva palača

Zvezdarska 1. **City Map** D4.
Tel (01) 241 4200. 🔲 by appt.

Marking the southern extent of the Old Town is Gruber Palace, a stately yellow building that now houses the State Archives. It originally served as a school of hydrology and navigation, built in 1770s on the initiative

of Jesuit priest and engineer Gabriel Gruber (1740–1805). One of the best-equipped schools of the era, it housed manufacturing workshops, a chemistry laboratory and an astronomical observatory.

A relief just left of the main door shows the school's founder holding a varied collection of scientific instruments. The interior, visits to which can be arranged through Ljubljana's Tourist Information Centre (see p95), contains a chapel decorated with paintings by the late-Baroque Austrian artist Kremser Schmidt (1718–1801). There is also a richly stuccoed oval stair-case that is overlooked by frescoes of figures symbol-izing scientific endeavour.

Gruber's other great contribution to Ljubljana was the construction of the canal that runs south of Castle Hill, diverting seasonal floodwaters away from the city centre.

Sculpture by Francesco Robba in St James's Church

NEW TOWN

Stretching west of the Ljubljanica river is the bustling downtown area of department stores, government ministries and cultural institutions. It was mostly laid out on a grid plan in the 19th century, although the area retains some wonderfully atmospheric Baroque alleyways huddled beside the river. Apart from the

Hunting target in the City Museum

best of the city's Art Nouveau architecture, the New Town contains notable examples of 20th-century Modernism. There are set-piece open spaces – the leafy expanse of Kongresni trg and the courtyards of the Križanke complex – and the pick of museums, including the National Gallery, National Museum of Slovenia and the City Museum.

SIGHTS AT A GLANCE

Buildings and Sights
Cooperative Bank **1**
Križanke **16**
National and University
   Library **14**
Nebotičnik **2**
Opera House **8**
Philharmonic Hall **12**
Slovene Parliament **9**
University of Ljubljana **13**

Churches and Cathedrals
Orthodox Church of Sts Cyril
   and Methodius **4**

Museums and Galleries
Ljubljana City
   Museum **15**

Modern Gallery **5**
National Gallery pp60–61 **3**
National Museum of
   Slovenia **6**
Natural History Museum **7**

Squares
Kongresni trg **11**
Trg Republike **10**

KEY

▦	Street-by-Street area *pp66–7*
🅿	Parking
✚	Church
	Pedestrian street

0 meters   250
0 yards   250

GETTING AROUND
The New Town is just a hop across the river from the Old Town, and most of its attractions are within a 10-minute walking distance of each other. The central artery, Slovenska cesta, is the place to catch buses to various sights in the suburbs.

SEE ALSO
• *Where to Stay* pp188–90
• *Where to Eat* pp202–4

◁ Striking façade of the Art Nouveau Cooperative Bank

Colourful façade of the
Cooperative Bank

Cooperative Bank ❶
Zadružna gospodarska banka

Miklošičeva 8. **City Map** D2.

The most vibrantly decorated building in downtown Ljubljana, the Cooperative Bank was designed by Ivan Vurnik (1884–1971), a Radovljica-born architect who studied under Otto Wagner, the doyen of Viennese Art Nouveau. Vurnik was keen to develop a Slovenian national style of architecture by blending traditional folk motifs with the best in modern design; this building is his ideological statement.

Begun in 1921, it represents a unique mixture of ethnographic detail and Art Nouveau, with jazzy chevrons and zig-zags weaving around the oriel windows on the façade. Rich in blues, yellows and brick-reds, the decorative scheme is inspired by the embroidery of rural Slovenia. Vurnik, clearly, was also influenced by folk-art patterns found throughout Slavic Europe.

The Cooperative Bank now houses the Ljubljana Land Registry Office; visitors can peek into the extravagantly decorated lobby during working hours. Geometrical patterns frame frescoes painted by Vurnik's Viennese wife, Helena Kottler, extolling the beauty of the Slovenian landscape and the virtues of its hard-working peasants.

Nebotičnik ❷

Corner of Štefanova and Slovenska ulica. **City Map** C2. **Kavarna Nebotičnik** ☐ 8–3am daily.

Adding a dash of Art Deco elegance to Ljubljana's main shopping street is Nebotičnik (Skyscraper), an upmarket residential block designed by Vladimir Šubic in 1933. Although it looks rather modest in comparison to the multistorey towers of today, this 13-storey structure was the tallest in Yugoslavia when it was constructed.

In contrast to the building's stern façade are the round porthole-style windows on the ground floor and the arched window frames just below the roof. An angelic female figure sculpted by Lojze Dolinar (1893–1970) occupies a plinth on the sixth floor, watching over the pedestrians on the pavement below.

Visitors can enter the lobby from Štefanova ulica to admire the faux marble walls overlooked by busts of Greek gods. The spiral staircase is accessible only to residents. However, tourists can take the lift up to **Kavarna Nebotičnik** that occupies the top three floors of the building with its café, bar and restaurant. The café's open terrace offers great views of the city.

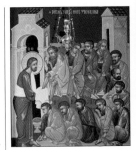

Fresco in the Orthodox Church of
Sts Cyril and Methodius

National Gallery ❸

See pp60–61.

Orthodox Church of Sts Cyril and Methodius ❹
Pravoslavna cerkev sv Cirila in Metoda

Prešernova cesta. **City Map** B2.
Tel (01) 252 4002.

Built in 1932 for Ljubljana's Serbian community, this church is inspired by the medieval monastery churches of southern Serbia, with a cluster of bulbous cupolas mounted on a high cross-shaped nave. Covering every inch of the spacious interior are frescoes by contemporary artist Dragomir Jašović (b.1937). The frescoes follow centuries-old Serbian models, with scenes from the New Testament juxtaposed with friezes of Serbian saints.

Presiding over the park in front of the church is a bust of the Reformation preacher Primož Trubar, who published the first books in Slovenian.

Visitors enjoying the view from the terrace café at the Nebotičnik

Art Nouveau Architecture in Ljubljana

Ljubljana experienced a building boom in the early 20th century, when numerous apartment houses and office blocks were being built to the north of Prešernov trg. The architecture of these buildings designed by the Slovenian Art Nouveau architects Ciril Metod Koch, Max Fabiani and Josip Vancaš was influenced by the Austrian Secessionist style as well as by Slovenian design motifs.

Sculpture of Mercury

KEY
Area illustrated

Čuden House ④
Built in 1901, this is one of Koch's most ostentatious buildings.

Krisper House ⑥
Designed by Max Fabiani, this elegant apartment block looks out on to the leafy Miklošičev park.

0 metres 100
0 yards 100

City Saving Bank ⑪
This bank bears statues symbolizing Slovenian industry and commerce.

Union Hotel ⑧
Designed by Josip Vancaš, this statue-encrusted structure was the largest building in Ljubljana when it was built in 1905.

MIKLOŠIČEV PARK

AJDOVŠČINA

Hauptman House ⑩
This wedge-shaped building is decorated with geometric shapes and floral swirls.

Centromerkur Building ⑨
Now a fashion store, this building is famous for its petal-shaped Art Nouveau canopy.

PREŠERNOV TRG

LIST OF KEY SITES

National Gallery ❸
Narodna galerija

Slovenia's national art collection occupies an elegant 19th-century building full of stucco ceilings and ornate chandeliers. Erected in 1896 to serve as the Slovene Cultural Centre, the building became home to the National Gallery in 1925. A modern annexe was opened in 2001, with a glass-fronted atrium at the junction of the old and new buildings, holding the collection's pride and joy – Francesco Robba's *Fountain of the Three Rivers*. The collection is particularly rich in Gothic statuary and Baroque religious paintings. Space is also devoted to the Slovenian Impressionists: Rihard Jakopič, Matija Jama, Ivan Grohar and Matej Sternen.

Visitors in one of the brightly lit exhibition areas

Fountain of the Three Rivers
Robba's 18th-century sculptural masterpiece is surrounded by balconied walkways, providing some wonderful viewpoints. At the base of the fountain are three Tritons pouring water from jugs, symbolizing the three main rivers of Slovenia.

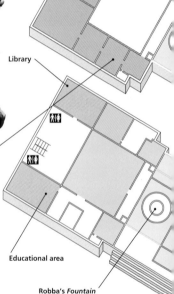

Library

★ The Krakovo Madonna
Correctly entitled The Madonna on Solomon's Throne, *this delicate 13th-century relief from Ljubljana's suburb of Krakovo was the work of an anonymous mason known as the Master of Solčava.*

Educational area

Robba's *Fountain of the Three Rivers*

GALLERY GUIDE
The original 19th-century wing contains the national collection of Slovenian art, from Gothic to the early 20th century. A modern annexe is devoted to European painters. Joining these wings is an atrium where temporary exhibitions are held.

STAR EXHIBITS

★ The Krakovo Madonna

★ Red Parasol

★ Solomon's Verdict

THE SLOVENIAN IMPRESSIONISTS

In the years before World War I, Rihard Jakopič (1869–1943), Ivan Grohar (1867–1911), Matija Jama (1872–1947) and Matej Sternen (1870–1949) energized the local art scene by painting Slovenian subjects with the kind of style and verve previously associated with French artists such as Renoir and Monet. Initially snubbed by conservative critics, today they are regarded as the high point of the nation's art. All of them were committed landscape painters.

Bridge Over the Dobra by Matija Jama

NEW TOWN

61

Katarina Lukančič
Full of exquisitely rendered detail, this portrait owes a great deal to Flemish painting of the 17th century. It is usually attributed to the Slovenian artist Janez Frančišek Gladič, although some experts believe its quality is far too high to be one of his works.

VISITORS' CHECKLIST

Prešernova 24. **City Map** C2. *Tel* (01) 241 5418. 10am–6pm Tue–Sun. www.ng-slo.si

KEY

European paintings
Art in Slovenia
Visual collections
Exhibition area
Atrium
Non exhibition area

First floor

Ground floor

★ ***Red Parasol*, Matej Sternen**
Painted in 1904, this is arguably the best-loved canvas by Sternen (1870–1949), an artist who was particularly known for his female portraits.

★ ***Solomon's Verdict*, Franc Kavčič**
The Vienna-educated Kavčič (1755–1828) was Slovenia's greatest exponent of Neo-Classicism, painting a series of large-scale mythological or biblical subjects.

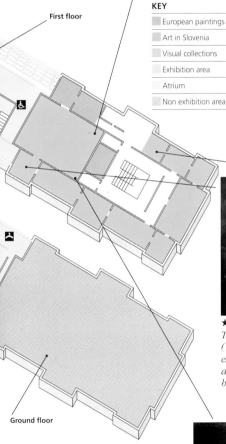

***The Card Players*, Almanach**
Almanach was a 17th-century Flemish painter who stopped off in Ljubljana during the later stages of his career. The Card Players was painted for Mark Anton, owner of Polhov Gradec castle.

The entrance to the Modern
Gallery, Ljubljana

Modern Gallery ⑤
Moderna galerija

Tomšičeva 14. **City Map** B2. *Tel (01)*
241 6800. ☐ *10am–6pm Tue–Sun.*
🖼 ♿ 🛈 www.mg-lj.si

Housed in a low grey building
designed in 1947 by Edvard
Ravnikar, a disciple of the
Swiss architect Le Corbusier,
the Modern Gallery comprises
the national collection of
post-World War II art.

Despite the imposition of
Communist ideology in the late
1940s, Slovene art was remarkably free and varied from the
mid-1950s onwards. Ample
evidence of this is provided by
the surreal figurative paintings
of Gabriel Stupica (1913–90)
and the more abstract work of

Janez Bernik (b.1933). More
perplexing is the work of the
60s art collective OHO, whose
ambiguous conceptual
performances (most famously,
dressing up in a huge dark
gown to resemble Slovenia's
highest mountain, Triglav) are
documented in a series of
black-and-white photo-
graphs. Representing the
turbulent changes of 1980s
are works by IRWIN, a
group of artists who
mixed avant-garde art
and extreme political
symbolism to produce
some ironic statements
on national identity.

Standing on the lawn
of the gallery are several
notable sculptures,
including Drago Tršar's
abstract *Manifestants*
(1959) and France
Rotar's *Dissected Sphere* (1975).

Statue of an
aristocrat

National Museum
of Slovenia ⑥
Narodni muzej Slovenije

Prešernova cesta 20. **City Map** B2.
Tel (01) 241 4400. ☐ *10am–6pm*
Fri–Wed, 10am–8pm Thu. 🖼 🛈
www.nms.si

Occupying one wing of an
imposing Neo-Renaissance
pile dating from the 1880s,
the main branch of the
National Museum of Slovenia
concentrates on the country's
archeological heritage. The

collection of applied art is
on display in a separate
branch of the museum on
Metelkova ulica *(see p77)*.

The ground floor of the
museum contains an exten-
sive collection of expressively
carved funerary monuments
from the Roman settlement
of Emona, together with a
gilded bronze statue of a
young male aristocrat.

Ancient Egypt is repre-
sented by a 6th-century
BC coffin of the priest
Isahta, decorated
with brightly painted
hieroglyphics.

First-floor galleries
contain locally excavated
pottery, decorated with
geometric designs, from
the 3rd millennium BC.
The most valued item
on display is the
6th-century BC Vače situla, a
30-cm (12-inch) high bronze
bucket that once served as
a ritual drinking vessel. On
the outer surface of the
situla are reliefs depicting
a parade of horsemen, a
drinking party and a row
of antelope-like animals
being stalked by a big cat.

Dominating the park in
front of the museum is a
monument dedicated to
Janez Vajkard Valvasor
(see pp90–91), the 17th-
century antiquarian and
publisher who pioneered
the documenting of history
in Slovenia.

School children on an educational visit to the National Museum of Slovenia

For hotels and restaurants in this region see pp188–90 and pp202–4

Natural History Museum ❼
Prirodoslovni muzej

Prešernova cesta 20. **City Map** B2. **Tel** (01) 241 0940. ◯ 10am–6pm Fri–Wed, 10am–8pm Thu. 📷 🚫 **www**.pms-lj.si

Located in the same building as the National Museum of Slovenia, the Natural History Museum offers informative insight into the flora, fauna and geology of Slovenia.

The most memorable of the museum's exhibits is an almost complete skeleton of a mammoth found near Kamnik. The museum also has an audio-visual display devoted to *Proteus anguinus* or the human fish (*see p149*), a salamander-like denizen of Slovenia's karst caves.

Opera House ❽
Operna

Cankarjeva cesta 11. **City Map** C2. **Tel** (01) 241 1700. **www**.opera.si

The home of Slovenia's national opera and ballet companies was built in 1892 by Czech architects Jan Vladimir Hrasky and Anton Hruby. Ljubljana's cultural centre has elements of Neo-Classical, Neo-Renaissance and Neo-Baroque styles, all apparent on the building's semi-circular façade.

Sculptor Alojz Gangl (1859–1935) was responsible for much of the exterior decoration, which features statues of griffins, cherubs and scantily clad nymphs on the pediment and in niches on either side of the main entrance. Above the pediment is the sculpture of an androgynous figure wielding a torch – a symbol of artistic inspiration.

The building's opulently decorated auditorium was reopened in 2011 after extensive renovation. Completed at the same time was the annexe at the back of the building, constructed to provide extra rehearsal rooms and office space.

Sculptures adorning the Slovene Parliament's façade

Slovene Parliament ❾
Parlament Slovenije

Šubičeva 4. **City Map** C3. **Tel** (01) 478 9400.

A Modernist block of concrete and glass designed by the architect Vinko Glanz in 1960, the political heart of Slovenia resembles a typical office building. However, the Slovene and European Union flags near the entrance hint at its importance.

The sculpted figures on the building's façade comprise one of former Communist Europe's more artistic statements. The work of 20th-century sculptors Zdenko Kalin and Karel Putrih, the ensemble offers a utopian vision of Socialism – workers, peasants, scientists and engineers striving together to create a new and beautiful society.

Cankar Hall, with the monument to Ivan Cankar in front

Trg Republike ❿

City Map C3.

Stretching south of the Parliament building, Trg Republike (formerly Trg Revolucije) was developed in the 1960s to provide a modern focal point to the capital's New Town. With the Maximarket department store on the eastern side, and two large office blocks, originally owned by Ljubljanska banka and the Iskra telecommunications company, to the south, the whole unit was intended as a powerful expression of socialist progress. Today, a major part of the square serves as a car park.

Located behind the two office blocks is **Cankar Hall** (Cankarjev dom), a prestigious cultural centre. Opened in 1982, it was designed by Slovenia's leading postwar architect Edvard Ravnikar and named after Slovenia's greatest novelist and playwright, Ivan Cankar (*see p85*). Covered with slabs of Carrara marble, the building contains a concert hall with seating for 1,500 people, three smaller multi-purpose halls and an exhibition gallery.

Outside the main entrance is the cube-shaped monument to Ivan Cankar by the Slovenian sculptor Slavko Tihec (1928–93). At first glance it looks rather like a rusty box, although an image of Cankar's face, formed by the dark fissures covering the monument's surface, is visible.

Ljubljanica river flowing through the Old Town ▷

Street-by-Street: Ljubljana University District

The University District contains many examples of Ljubljana's finest 19th-century architecture, much of it laid out around the leafy Kongresni trg. The area resonates with history, its buildings occupied by many of Slovenia's most important cultural and educational institutions. This part of the city is closely associated with 20th-century architect Jože Plečnik, who designed the National and University Library and renovated the courtyards of the Križanke monastery.

Sculpture near the Philharmonic Hall

Drama Theatre

★ National and University Library
The most famous of Jože Plečnik's many buildings in Ljubljana, this library features a rough-and-smooth façade of stone and brick. Its bay windows are in the shape of open books ⓮

★ Križanke
Renaissance arcades and post-Modern lamp fittings mark the former monastery of Križanke as one of Jože Plečnik's foremost restoration projects. The courtyards now host major outdoor concerts ⓰

The Illyrian Monument

KEY

 Suggested route

Academy of Arts and Sciences
The Academy is located in the Lontovž or "Landhaus", home to the provincial assembly during the Habsburg era. Presiding over a courtyard on the eastern side of the building is a Baroque statue of Neptune.

Ljubljana City Museum

Zois House, home of Baron Žiga Zois (1747–1819), was a meeting point for Slovenian intellectuals.

Café Zvezda

Occupying the eastern corner of Kongresni trg (see p68) is Kavarna Zvezda, long famous for its delicious cakes, pastries and ice cream.

Café Zvezda

KONGRESNI TRG

OVI TRG

LJUBLJANICA

University of Ljubljana

This building has witnessed many historical events, with Tito speaking from the balcony in May 1945 and political reformers addressing large crowds in June 1988 ⓭

Philharmonic Hall

The Philharmonic Hall is home to the nation's leading orchestra, which descended from the Academia Filharmonicorum, a cultural society founded in 1701 ⓬

0 metres	50
0 yards	50

STAR SIGHTS

★ National and University Library

★ Križanke

★ Illyrian Monument

★ Illyrian Monument
This stately obelisk recalls Ljubljana's role as the capital of the French-run Illyrian Provinces from 1809 to 1813. Reliefs of Napoleon Bonaparte and female heads adorn it.

Kongresni trg ⓫

City Map C3.

The gently sloping rectangle of grass and trees known as Kongresni trg, or Congress Square, takes its name from the Congress of the Holy Alliance – Russia, Austria and Prussia – held in Ljubljana in 1821. Hosted by Emperor Francis I of Austria and attended by dignitaries from all over Europe, most notably Tsar Alexander I of Russia, the Congress aimed to bring stability to the pan-European political system agreed upon at the Congress of Vienna in 1815. With four months of negotiations accompanied by an endless round of dinners, firework displays and masked balls, it was the biggest party in Ljubljana's history.

The event involved a major overhaul of the city's infrastructure; the square was levelled and expanded to host the daily military parades, roads were re-paved and street lighting was installed. The square also played an important role in the Slovene Spring (*see p39*) – mass demonstrations in support of the Ljubljana Four were held here in June 1988.

The most appealing of the buildings surrounding the square is the Baroque Ursuline Church at the western end. Most of the other buildings on the square, including the pink-hued Neo-Classical palace (Kazina) on the northern side, are from the 19th century. Originally a club for Ljubljana's

Sculpture of well-known Ljubljana mayor, Ivan Hribar in Breg

wealthier citizens, the Kazina was briefly the seat of the Slovenian parliament in the years following World War II.

Philharmonic Hall ⓬
Filharmonija

Kongresni trg 10. **City Map** D3. *Tel (01) 241 0800.* **www**. filharmonija.si

Sitting on the southeastern corner of Kongresni trg is the Philharmonic Hall, Ljubljana's main venue for classical music, built in 1891 on the site of a former German-language theatre. The inscription "1701" on the façade refers to the date of the foundation of Academia Filharmonicorum, Ljubljana's first musical society. The academy's members performed only at state occasions and society funerals, and it was not until the formation of the Philharmonic Society in 1794 that Ljubljana gained a

regularly performing orchestra. During his brief tenure as conductor at Ljubljana's Provincial Theatre, Gustav Mahler, then 21 years old, was invited by the society to play piano at their concerts in 1882.

Ljubljana did not have a full symphony orchestra in the years following World War I, until 1947, when the Slovene Philharmonic was re-founded and this building was adopted as its permanent home.

University of Ljubljana ⓭
Univerza v Ljubljani

Kongresni trg 12. **City Map** C3. *Tel (01) 241 8500.* **www**.uni-lj.si

The most prominent building on the southern side of Kongresni trg is the Neo-Renaissance palace that serves as the main headquarters of the University of Ljubljana. Built in 1902 to provide the Duchy of Carniola with a prestigious venue for meetings and receptions, the palace is adorned with ornate corner towers and spires.

Arranged in a semicircle in front of the entrance are sculptures and busts of noteworthy academic figures, including that of Ivan Hribar (1851–1941), the long-serving mayor of Ljubljana who was instrumental in getting the university off the ground. Mooted by leading Slovenian politicians in the 1890s, the university did not come into being until 1919. It is now one of the biggest universities in Central Europe, with over 65,000 students.

National and University Library ⓮
Narodna in univerzitetna knjižnica

Turjaška 1. **City Map** C4. *Tel (01) 200 1188.* ⬜ *8am–8pm Mon–Fri, 9am–2pm Sat.* 🎫 *book in advance.*

Located off the west bank of the Ljubljanica river, the National and University Library is considered the masterpiece of architect Jože

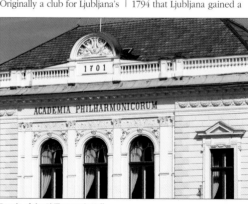

Façade of the Philharmonic Hall

Aerial view of the National and University Library building

Plečnik *(see p73)*. Completed in 1940, the building is characteristic of Plečnik's work, combining the straight lines of modern architecture with organic surfaces and inspired decorative details. The exterior features a patchwork of different hues, mixing grey hunks of Slovenian granite with terracotta-coloured brickwork. Inside, a dark stairway of polished black limestone leads to the brightly lit, first-floor reading rooms, symbolizing the transition from ignorance to knowledge. The doorknobs, window fittings and wooden beamed ceilings were all designed by Plečnik himself, fusing Art Deco with folk-influenced motifs to create a highly personalized style. For a glimpse of the reading rooms, furnished with ornate desk lamps and chandeliers, visitors are free to enter the lobby during opening hours.

Ljubljana City Museum **⑮**

Mestni muzej Ljubljana

Gosposka ulica 15. **City Map** C4. **Tel** (01) 241 2500. ◯ 10am–6pm Tue–Sun, 10am–9pm Thu. 🖼 ♿ 🖥 🛈 www.mestnimuzej.si

Occupying the 17th-century Auersperg Palace, at the eastern end of Trg francoske revolucije, this museum is one of the principal venues for large-scale themed exhibitions in Ljubljana. The museum was given a bold contemporary facelift

between 2000 and 2004. A curved glass atrium was added along with a spiral walkway that links the building's basement to the upper floors. Archaeological finds, such as bits of Roman road and medieval brickwork, unearthed during renovation, are on display in the basement.

The museum's permanent collection features a variety of artifacts illustrating the daily life of the city dwellers in the past. Exhibits include painted targets used by archers in the 19th century as well as a Fičko (Fiat 750), the car that became a symbol of Slovenia's burgeoning consumer society in the 1960s. Art on display includes an 18th-century bust of Emperor Charles VI by Francesco Robba as well as 15th-century statues of Adam and Eve that once stood in niches on the façade of the Town Hall *(see p49)*.

Križanke **⑯**

Trg francoske revolucije. **City Map** C4. 🎭 *Ljubljana Festival (Jul & Aug)*.

South of the National and University Library lies Križanke, a former monastery complex that now serves as a concert venue. It is also where orchestral events are held during the Ljubljana Festival as well as major rock, jazz and world music concerts from spring through to autumn. Classical music concerts are held in the indoor Knight's Hall throughout the year. Križanke dates from the 13th century, when Duke Ulrich III of Spannheim invited the Teutonic Knights to Ljubljana to develop schools and hospitals for the poor. The complex of ceremonial halls and interlocking courtyards dates from the 16th and 18th centuries. The monastery fell into disrepair after the Communists moved the monks out in 1945; Plečnik was given the task of restoring it as a cultural centre.

Painted archery target

The main courtyard is usually open only to concertgoers, although visitors are free to explore the entrance courtyard (Malo dvorišče), where a bust of Plečnik adorns a balustrade. The courtyard is lined by arcades on three sides, with bold sgraffito decorations conveying an air of Renaissance gaiety. The occasional outdoor chamber concerts held in the Peklensko dvorišče, an intimate quadrangular courtyard, are worth buying tickets for.

Exhibition room in the Ljubljana City Museum

General view of the sprawling Tivoli Park

SIGHTS AT A GLANCE

Historic Buildings, Streets and Neighbourhoods
Kodeljevo Castle ⓴
Krakovo ❷
Metelkova Mesto ⓯
Plečnik House ❹
Sokol Hall ⓲
Tivoli Mansion ❼
Tobacco Factory ❺

Churches and Cathedrals
Church of St Francis
   of Assisi ⓮
St Bartholomew's
   Church ⓬
St John's Church ❸

Museums and Galleries
Brewery Museum ⓫
*Slovene Ethnographic
   Museum pp78–9* ⓱
Museum of Architecture
   and Design ㉑
Railway Museum ⓭
Slovene Museum of
   Contemporary History ❽
Slovene National
   Museum (Metelkova) ⓰

Parks and Sanctuaries
Botanical Garden ⓳
Tivoli Park ❻
Zoological Gardens ❿

Sites of Interest
Roman Wall ❶
Rožnik Hill ❾
Žale Cemetery ㉒

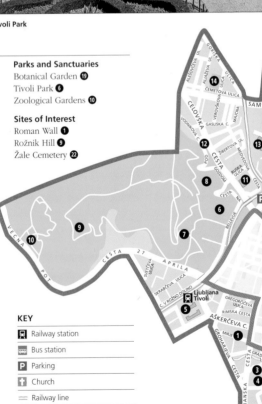

KEY
🚉	Railway station
🚌	Bus station
P	Parking
✝	Church
═	Railway line

AROUND THE CENTRE

Arranged in an arc around the centre, Ljubljana's suburbs are surprisingly rich in attractions. Many of the sights of interest lie within easy strolling distance of the Old and New Towns – in particular the neighbourhoods of Krakovo and Trnovo, which are characterized by vegetable gardens and willow-lined waterways. Equally refreshing are the open spaces of Tivoli Park, where a tangle of footpaths and cycle tracks leads past flowerbeds and open meadows. Within the park are the Tivoli Mansion, home to superb seasonal art exhibitions, and the Slovene Museum of Contemporary History, with displays devoted to

Statue in St John's Church, Trnovo

Slovenian independence. West of Tivoli Park is Rožnik Hill, where woodland paths and a polyphony of bird-song provide a taste of the Slovenian countryside. The main destination north of the centre is the former military barracks, Metelkova Mesto – home to both an alternative arts centre and an emerging museum quarter with an outstanding ethnographic collection. The work of prolific architect Jože Plečnik looms large in suburban Ljubljana. The Church of St Francis of Assisi in Šiška, Žale Cemetery and the Museum of Architecture and Design in Fužine Castle are all important places to visit while on a tour of Plečnik's works.

GETTING AROUND

Krakovo, Tivoli Park and Metelkova Mesto can be reached on foot from the city centre in only a few minutes. Other sights can be reached quickly and easily on Ljubljana's well-organized bus network. Most bus routes pass along the central Slovenska cesta, which serves as the city's main public transport interchange.

SEE ALSO

- *Where to Stay* pp188–90
- *Where to Eat* pp202–4

Roman Wall ❶
Rimski zid

Mirje.

The long straight street of Mirje marks the southern end of the original Roman settlement of Emona (modern-day Ljubljana), founded between AD 14 and 25 as a legionary base and subsequently a major mercantile city. Parallel to the street, a 300-m (985-ft) long stretch of the Roman Wall that bordered the settlement has been partially rebuilt, providing an evocative indication of what Emona's boundaries once looked like. The architect Jože Plečnik (see p73) was responsible for the reconstruction. He added various decorative details of his own – notably the brick pyramid rising above an arched gateway halfway along the wall.

Behind the house at No. 4 Mirje, is the **Jakopič Garden**, where the remains of a 1st-century Roman house can be seen. Consisting of four separate apartments grouped around an entrance hall, the dwelling was warmed by a heating system under the floor. The building was abandoned some time in the 5th century.

The garden gets its name from the Impressionist painter Rihard Jakopič (1869–1943), who had a studio in the adjacent house. The garden can be visited by appointment through the Ljubljana City Museum (see p69).

The 19th-century St John's Church, Trnovo

Krakovo ❷

Despite its location on the fringes of central Ljubljana, the suburb of Krakovo is famous for having preserved its medieval street plan and rustic appearance. Narrow streets such as Krakovska, Kladezna and Rečna feature rows of houses standing with their backs to the road in typical village style, many featuring three windows on the street-facing gable – a surviving relic of medieval edicts that specified how many and what kind of windows each house could have.

Detail on the altar, St John's Church

Krakovo originally served as the quarter for boatmen and fishermen, although, from the mid-19th century, locals increasingly turned towards vegetable growing and market trading. Krakovo's vegetable plots are still a major feature of the suburb, providing a refreshingly bucolic contrast to the relatively dense urbanization on show elsewhere in the city.

St John's Church ❸
Cerkev sv Janeza Krstnika

Kolezijska 1. **Tel** (01) 283 5060.
🕐 7:30am & 6:30pm Mon–Sat, 8am, 9:15am, 11am & 6:30pm Sun.

With its Neo-Romanesque twin towers soaring above the willow-lined Gradaščica stream, St John's Church is one of the most inspiring sights in southern Ljubljana. According to local legend, it was here that the Romantic poet France Prešeren (see p49) first set eyes on Julija Primic, the woman who was the unattainable object of his desire and provided the inspiration for many of his love poems. Renovation of the church's interior was entrusted to Jože Plečnik, who added several characteristic design details such as the small brass lamps that hang from the ceiling and the pillars.

Gateway in the Roman Wall leading to a park

For hotels and restaurants in this region see pp188–90 and pp202–4

Desk in the workshop at Plečnik House

In front of the church is the Trnovo Bridge (Trnovski most), a Plečnik-designed single-arch bridge, with pyramid-shaped obelisks protruding from the parapet. Standing between the obelisks is the sculptor Nikolaj Pirnat's (1903–48) statue of St John the Baptist, with his face turned towards the church.

Plečnik House ❹
Plečnikova hiša

Karunova 4. **Tel** (01) 280 1600.
🕒 10am–6pm Tue–Thu, 10am–3pm Fri, 9am–3pm Sat. 📷 📹
www.aml.si

The architecture of Jože Plečnik is visible at every step in Ljubljana, and a visit to his former home provides an ideal introduction to his life and work.

After studying in Vienna and enjoying early success in Prague, Plečnik returned to Ljubljana in 1922 and set about transforming this property into a home and studio. The two traditional-style houses that came with the plot accommodated Plečnik's housemaid and gardener. Behind these, he built a modern two-storey house for himself and his brother.

Hourly guided tours of the house begin with the light-filled entrance lobby, decorated with some of the

stubby classical columns left over from Plečnik's building projects. Also on the ground floor is Plečnik's study, a circular room whose curving windows admit light whatever the time of day. Roosting on a corner of Plečnik's desk, a sleek black trophy in the shape of an eagle made for the Orel or Eagle gymnastics society, demonstrates Plečnik's artistry as a designer. Elsewhere are plans, models and photographs of his major works. Most famous among his unfinished projects is the Slovene Acropolis, a monumental parliament building in the form of a huge cone, originally intended for Ljubljana's Castle Hill. A more down-to-earth aspect of his taste is revealed by the rustic wood-panelled meeting room, filled with folksy ornaments brought from Czechoslovakia.

Looking out on to the rectangular vegetable garden is the sunny conservatory, accommodating a handful of palm and fig trees.

Tobacco Factory ❺
Tobačna tovarna

Tobačna. **Tel** (01) 241 2500.
🕒 11am–7pm Tue–Sat, 11am–3pm Sun.

Founded in 1871, Ljubljana's Tobacco Factory was a major regional cigarette manufacturer until 2004, when production at this site ceased. Although Imperial Tobacco still has an administrative office here, plans are afoot to turn the rest of the complex into a residential and business quarter.

One restored building houses the Tobačna 001 Cultural Centre, home to a gallery of contemporary art as well as the **Tobacco Museum**. The museum covers the history of smoking, as well as that of cigarette production in the capital. Sepia pictures show life on the factory floor, with its mainly female workforce, known as the cigar ladies.

Exhibit at the Tobacco Museum, Tobacco Factory

JOŽE PLEČNIK (1872–1957)

Few men have left such a lasting imprint on their home city as Jože Plečnik, the Vienna-educated architect whose work can be seen throughout Ljubljana. Initially an exponent of the Art Nouveau movement, Plečnik developed a uniquely eclectic style, blending Graeco-Roman models with Egyptian motifs and Slovenian folk art. His development of a Slovenian national style won him prestigious commissions, notably Ljubljana's Market, the National and University Library and the Žale Cemetery. A master of innovative forms and inspired decoration, he is considered to be one of the greatest architects of the 20th century.

Bust of Plečnik, Trnovo

Tree-lined pedestrian path leading up to Tivoli Mansion

Tivoli Park ❻

Park Tivoli

Indoor Swimming Pool *Tel* (01) 431 5155. ☐ 6–11am & 6–10pm Tue–Fri, 10am–8pm Sat–Sun.

Stretching to the west of the city centre is Tivoli Park, a leafy expanse much loved by strollers, joggers and dog-walkers. Named after the Jardins de Tivoli in Paris, it was first laid out during the period of Napoleonic rule in the early 19th century.

Today, it offers an appealing mix of order and wilderness, with well-tended lawns and trimmed shrubs alternating with wildflower meadows and thickets of trees. The park's main avenue, Jakopičevo sprehajališče, is lined with display stands where outdoor exhibitions of art and photo-graphy are held.

The northern end of the park is dominated by the Tivoli Hall (Hala Tivoli), Ljubljana's main venue for basketball, ice hockey and big rock and pop concerts. Designed by architect Marjan Božič (b.1932), this grey-brown rectangular building was a much admired example of architectural Modernism when it first opened in 1965.

The northern end of the park also contains a popular **Indoor Swimming Pool** (Kopalisce Tivoli), tennis courts and a playground for children.

Tivoli Mansion ❼

Tivolski grad

Pod turnom 3. *Tel* (01) 241 3800. ☐ 11am–6pm Wed–Sun. 📷 ☐ 🎨 *Biennial of Graphic Arts (Jun–Sep: every odd-numbered year).* www.mglc-lj.si

Built in the 18th century as a villa for the local Jesuit hier-archy, Tivoli Mansion stands at the top of a stone staircase guarded by sculptures of fierce-looking dogs. The mansion subsequently served as the summer residence of the Ljubljana archbishops before it was presented in 1852 to the 86-year-old hero of Habsburg military cam-paigns, Field Marshal Josef Radetzky. Radetzky was a much-loved symbol of

Fountain surrounded by flowers, Tivoli Park

Austrian patriotism, a status immortalized by Johann Strauss the Elder's famous tune *Radetzkymarsch*.

The mansion now houses the International Graphic Arts Centre (Mednarodni grafični likovni center), which organizes the prestigious Ljubljana Biennial of Graphic Arts, the world's longest-running graphic-arts expo-sition. The centre also holds high-quality exhibitions of posters, prints and drawings.

Slovene Museum of Contemporary History ❽

Muzej novejše zgodovine Slovenije

Celovška cesta 23. *Tel* (01) 300 9610. ☐ 10am–6pm Tue–Sun. 📷 ♿ www.muzej-nz.si

Located behind Tivoli Hall is a stately pink-coloured mansion that was built in 1752 for Count Leopold Karl Lamberg. The building was adapted to house the Museum of the Revolution in 1952 and became the Slovene Museum of Contemporary History following the end of the Communist regime in 1991.

Parked in front of the building is an ex-Yugoslav army (JLA) tank comman-deered by the Slovenian terri-torial defence forces during the Ten Day War of July 1991.

Inside, the museum tells the story of 20th-century Slovenia using film footage and sound recordings to bring each period to life. The 30-minute film with English subtitles, documenting the impact of World War I on Slovenia is well worth a watch; visitors can ask the curator if they wish to see it. There is also a re-creation of World War I trenches and a display of World War II uniforms and weaponry.

Other exhibits reveal the good and bad sides of Tito's Yugoslavia – a collection of posters and consumer products pays tribute to social progress under Communism, while a side room commemorates the anti-communist activists who were imprisoned during the same period.

Rožnik Hill ⑨

Rising above the western end of Tivoli Park are a series of small wooded hills grouped around the 390-m (1,285-ft) high Rožnik Hill, a popular destination for weekend walkers. The main route to the hill begins just south of the Slovene Museum of Contemporary History, looping around the 430-m (1,410-ft) high peak of Šišenski hrib before following an undulating trail to Rožnik.

Occupying the ridge just below the summit is the Gostilna Rožnik inn, where novelist and playwright Ivan

Church of the Visitation, Rožnik Hill

Sea lion display at the Zoological Gardens

Cankar (see p85) lived from 1910 to 1917. The innkeeper's wife, Štefanija Franzotova, was a childhood friend of Cankar's, and offered the writer free use of an attic room in the hope that his presence at the inn would bring in added custom. The impoverished Cankar's appetite for free food and drink soon took its toll on his friendship with the innkeeper's family, and the writer was eventually persuaded to move out. Occupying the former barn opposite the inn, the **Ivan Cankar Memorial Room** (Spominska soba Ivana Cankarja) preserves his writing desk and other possessions.

Just uphill from the inn is the 18th-century **Church of the Visitation** (Cerkev Marijinega obiskanja), a rose-coloured structure that contains a painting of the *Visitation* by Jurij Šubic (1855–90). The church is rarely open outside Sunday mass times. The meadow below the church is the scene of an all-night bonfire party on 30th April, an annual celebration of spring that involves much drinking and feasting.

Ivan Cankar Memorial Room
Rožnik. *Tel (01) 241 2506.*
☐ Apr–Oct: 11am–6pm Sat & Sun. www.mm-lj.si

🏛 **Church of the Visitation**
Rožnik. 🕆 May–Sep: 10:30am Sun.

Bust of Ivan Cankar

Zoological Gardens ⑩
Živalski vrt

Večna pot 70. *Tel (01) 244 2188.*
🚌 May–Sep: 23. ☐ May–Oct: 9am–7pm; Nov–Apr: 9am–4pm.
🎫 ♿ 🅿 📷 www.zoo.si

Spread across the densely wooded southern slopes of Rožnik Hill is Ljubljana's zoo, which houses a wide variety of creatures from around the world. Near the entrance is a selection of animals such as horses, goats and geese that one might find on the average Slovenian farm. A re-created thatch-roofed farm cottage displays the kind of insects and rodents that traditionally live in proximity to humans. Further on is a varied collection of more exotic animals such as giraffes, Siberian tigers, Persian leopards and an energetic family of gibbons that can be seen leaping from branch to branch in their enclosure. The zoo extends quite a long way up the hillside, with wooded paths leading to large enclosures housing wild cats, wolves and bears.

The Zoological Gardens made international news in May 1969, when the bears Piki and Miki broke out of their enclosure and had to be tracked by hunters through Ljubljana's western suburbs.

Locomotives on display in the Railway Museum

Brewery Museum ⑪
Pivovarski muzej

Pivovarniška 2. **Tel** *(01) 471 7330.*
⬤ *8am–1pm 1st Tue of the month.*
📷 📹 www.pivo-union.si

Dominating the horizon just north of Tivoli Park is the tall grey façade of the Union Brewery (Pivovarna Union), Slovenia's second-largest beer producer. A small museum in an old malting house depicts the history of the brewery along with a display of brewing equipment through the ages. Of particular

Old poster, Brewery Museum

interest are the horse- and hand-drawn carts once used to deliver the brew around the city. Visitors can also visit the factory floor and sample a selection of the company's products.

The brewery was founded by Kočevje-born Germans Ivan and Peter Kosler in 1864; the latter used the wealth he amassed from beer brewing to purchase the Lamberg Mansion in Tivoli Park, which is today the Slovene Museum of Contemporary History *(see pp74–5)*. Popular legend maintains that Kosler had beer delivered from the brewery to his palatial home via an underground pipe, enabling him to test the quality of the brew whenever he wanted to.

St Bartholomew's Church ⑫
Cerkev sv Jerneja

Celovška cesta.

A grey-brown edifice that looks more like a village church, St Bartholomew's dates from around the 1370s and is thought to be the oldest surviving place of worship in the city. The church was extensively refurbished in the 1930s by Jože Plečnik *(see p73)*, who added colonnaded porches to the front and back of the building. Standing at the bottom of the staircase beside the church is another example of Plečnik's architectural style – a lampstand made up of bubble-like forms mounted one on top of the other.

Display of brewing equipment at the Brewery Museum

Railway Museum ⑬
Železniški muzej

Parmova 35. **Tel** *(01) 291 2641.*
⬤ *9am–6pm Tue–Sun.* 📷 📹
www.slo-zeleznice.si

The history of railways in Slovenia began with the Südbahn, the line southwest from Vienna that reached Maribor in 1844 and Ljubljana in 1849. Many of the locomotives that plied this route are on display in the Railway Museum's main exhibition space – a crescent-shaped engine shed packed with vintage rolling stock. The oldest locomotive on show is the sleek SB 718, built in Vienna by Scottish engineer John Haswell in 1861 and in use in Yugoslavia until 70 years later. More elegant still is the SB 17c, an express locomotive built in 1896, which rattled along at a speed of 80 kmph (50 mph). Particularly delightful are the squat locomotives with funnel chimneys; once used on Slovenia's numerous narrow-gauge railways.

A hall across the road from the shed displays antiquated signalling equipment. There is also a re-created station-master's office from the 1920s. A room full of railway uniforms reveals the different styles adopted by the various states to have ruled over the region, from the Ruritanian finery of the Habsburg era to the black overalls and red-star insignia adopted during the early years of Communist rule.

Church of St Francis of Assisi ⑭
Cerkev sv Frančiška Asiškega

Černetova ulica 20. **Tel** *(01) 583 7270.* 🚌 *1, 3, 5 (to Šiška).*
✝ *7am, 8am & 7pm daily.*

Located in the suburb of Šiška and begun in 1924, the Church of St Francis of Assisi was one of the first major projects by Jože Plečnik in Ljubljana and contains many of the distinctive elements associated with his style.

Pyramid-shaped high altar, Church of St Francis of Assisi

On approaching it from the east, the church looks like a Classical temple, with a façade supported by four columns. Adorning the pediment is a statue of St Francis, with his head tilted to one side as if sermonizing. The most bizarre part of the structure is the hollow belfry, with two tiers of colonnades topped by the greenish cone of a spire.

The main entrance to the church is on the southern side, where a small courtyard is illuminated by lamps that resemble large eggs. The interior features a host of equally inventive touches; the central chandelier is made up of small dangling lanterns and the tall main altar is shaped like a pyramid.

Metelkova Mesto ⓯

Corner of Masarykova cesta and Metelkova ulica.
www.metelkovamesto.org

Visitors looking for a glimpse into contemporary Ljubljana will enjoy spending time in Metelkova Mesto, the city's alternative social centre that occupies one half of a large area of old army barracks to the east of Ljubljana Railway Station. Built by the Habsburgs and subsequently used by the Yugoslav People's Army (JLA), the abandoned barracks were encroached upon by a varied group of musicians and artists in the early 1990s. The city authorities initially wanted them evicted, but ultimately let them stay, allowing Metelkova to develop into one of the most vibrant alternative communities in Central Europe. Metelkova's buildings, covered in colourful murals and splashes of mosaic, house a number of bars, clubs, artists' workshops and NGOs, driving home the non-conformist message.

In many ways Metelkova is the natural successor to the post-punk alternative culture of the 1980s, from which Slovenia's civil rights movement was born. Providing a link to the past is **Hostel Celica**, which occupies a former military prison at No. 8. It was here that the Ljubljana Four were incarcerated in 1988 (see p37) sparking demonstrations that ultimately led to Slovenia's independence. The rooms in the former cells have been redesigned by contemporary artists.

Otherwise, Metelkova Mesto is a night-time attraction – its large central courtyard is usually filled with revellers attracted by its bars and live-music venues (see pp94–5).

Hostel Celica
Metelkova 2. **Tel** (01) 230 9700.
2pm daily. www.souhostel.com

Slovene National Museum (Metelkova) ⓰

Narodni muzej Slovenije (Metelkova)

Maistrova 1. **Tel** (01) 230 7030. 10am–6pm Tue–Sun. www.nms.si

The grand-looking trio of Habsburg-era barrack buildings at the southern end of Metelkova ulica is being converted into a museum complex that will include a contemporary art museum in the future.

Occupying the eastern side of the complex's central plaza is the Metelkova branch of the National Museum of Slovenia (see p62). It has displays of costumes, toys and applied art through the ages. There is also a furniture collection, which includes ornate medieval storage chests and opulent Baroque wardrobes as well as the mass-produced plywood furniture eagerly purchased by Slovenian households in the 1960s. Temporary historical exhibitions take place on the ground floor of the building.

Colourful façade of a building in Metelkova Mesto

Slovene Ethnographic Museum ⑰
Slovenski etnografski muzej

Opened in stages between 2007 and 2009, the Slovene Ethnographic Museum is one of the most imaginative of its kind in Europe, exhibiting artifacts from Slovenia and around the globe in a series of visually captivating displays. The collection is brought to life with the help of documentary films, sound recordings and a computer lounge allowing visitors to access audio-visual content. The setting is itself impressive, occupying a 19th-century barracks to which a futuristic glass-and-steel façade has been added. The museum is particularly suited to younger visitors, with interactive toys on the top floor, an ethnoalphabet display and a merry-go-round and see-saw on the lawn outside the café.

Shrovetide costume

View of the permanent exhibition on the second floor

Folk costumes

Objects of Life, Objects of Desire
This room on the third floor sheds light on the industrious and creative side of human society, with traditional trades such as shoe-making and clock-making displayed alongside wonderful examples of folk costume, painting and wood sculpture.

First floor

International Ethnography

★ Čupa
This dug out canoe, carved out of a log, dominates the Water and Earth section, which is devoted to local agriculture and trade. It was used for fishing by Slovenians living on the Adriatic coast north of Trieste (now in Italy).

Temporary exhibition space is used for changing exhibitions.

Workshops
Artisans in the museum's ground-floor workshops are on hand to demonstrate traditional pottery and weaving techniques. Visitors can buy textiles, including contemporary accessories such as ponchos, bags and scarves with folk motifs.

STAR EXHIBITS

★ Čupa

★ Painted Beehive Panels

★ Folk Costumes

Painted Furniture
Children's cradles and chests are among the most popular pieces of painted furniture on display on the third floor.

VISITORS' CHECKLIST

Metelkova 2. **City Map** F2.
Tel *(01) 300 8745.*
◯ *10am–6pm Tue–Sun.*
📷 *free every last Sun of the month.* 🖩 ♿ 🖥 📷
www.etno-muzej.si

Third floor

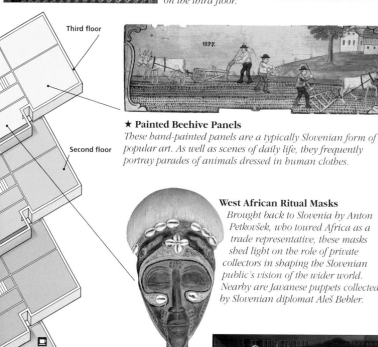

Second floor

★ Painted Beehive Panels
These hand-painted panels are a typically Slovenian form of popular art. As well as scenes of daily life, they frequently portray parades of animals dressed in human clothes.

West African Ritual Masks
Brought back to Slovenia by Anton Petkovšek, who toured Africa as a trade representative, these masks shed light on the role of private collectors in shaping the Slovenian public's vision of the wider world. Nearby are Javanese puppets collected by Slovenian diplomat Aleš Bebler.

Ticket desk

Ground floor

Workshop space

KEY

- Slovene life and culture
- I, We and Others
- Temporary exhibition space
- Non-exhibition space

★ Folk Costumes
The colourful display includes costumes from all regions of Slovenia and the fine clothes worn by 19th-century town-dwellers. There is also a fascinating collection of bonnets, important symbols of regional and national identity.

GALLERY GUIDE
The ground floor is devoted to craft workshops, café and a shop. The permanent collection begins on the second floor with a display, "I, We and Others," which looks at ethnography globally. The third floor showcases Slovene life and culture through the ages.

Visitors taking a stroll through the lush Botanical Garden

Sokol Hall ⑱
Sokolski dom

Tabor 13. **Tel** *(01) 232 2528.*
www.sportnodrustvo-tabor.si

This sports hall was one of the most unconventional buildings to emerge from the Slovenian Modernist Movement of the 1920s. It was designed for the Sokol (Falcon) Sports Club by Ivan Vurnik, architect of the Cooperative Bank *(see p58)*. The building features rows of Graeco-Egyptian columns, each decorated with zig-zags, chevrons and other geometric shapes inspired by Slavic folk art.

Originally founded in Prague in 1862, the Sokol Movement sought to encourage solidarity among the Slavs of the Habsburg Empire by promoting physical exercise, especially gymnastics. Like its Czech counterpart, the Slovenian branch of the Sokol used sport as a means to nurture national values among the youth by organizing gymnastic displays that were rousingly patriotic as well as spectacular to watch. Now the property of the Tabor Sports Association (Športno društvo Tabor), the hall retains its social importance for the locals, offering sporting and fitness programmes for all ages.

Botanical Garden ⑲
Botanični vrt

Ižanska cesta 15. **Tel** *(01) 427 1280.* ☐ *Apr–Jun, Sep & Oct: 7am–7pm daily; Jul–Aug: 7am–8pm daily; Nov–Mar: 7am–5pm daily.*
www.botanicni-vrt.si

Located to the southeast of the Old Town, Ljubljana's small Botanical Garden was founded in 1810 during French rule. The linden tree planted by French governor Marshal Marmont still presides over a compact park featuring an array of beech, pine and chestnut trees, while paths weave their way through shrubs and flowers indigenous to central Europe. A palm house at the southern end of the garden has displays of more exotic flora.

Kodeljevo Castle ⑳
Grad Kodeljevo

Koblarjeva ulica 34. **Lunapark Pizzeria Tel** *(01) 544 3067.* ☐ *11am–10pm daily.*

Built by the Thurn family in the early 17th century, Kodeljevo Castle is one of Ljubljana's best-preserved Renaissance residences. It gets its name from the Codelli family, who bought it in 1700 and added the Baroque chapel to the building's western wing. Lavishly decorated with frescoes by France Jelovšek (1700–1764), the chapel is rarely open to the public. A plaque on the castle wall honours its most famous resident, Baron Anton Codelli von Fahrnenfeld (1875–1954), the first man to drive an automobile – a Benz Comfortable acquired in 1898 – on the streets of Ljubljana.

Several of the castle's atmospheric rooms are occupied by the **Lunapark Pizzeria**.

Façade of the early 20th-century Sokol Hall

Museum of Architecture and Design ㉑

Muzej za arhitekturo in oblikovanje

Pot na Fužine 2. **Tel** *(01) 540 9798.* ☒ *20.* ◯ *10am–6pm Tue–Sun.* 🎫 📷 🚻 ♿ *Biennial of Industrial Design (Oct–Nov: every even-numbered year).* **www**.aml.si

Occupying an attractive riverside site on the city's eastern outskirts, this museum makes for a rewarding excursion, not least because of its setting in **Fužine Castle** (Grad Fužine). The castle was originally built in the mid-16th century by the Kisls, a family of merchants attracted by the iron foundries around the Ljubljanica river. Restored in the 1990s, it is a fine example of a Renaissance chateau, with cylindrical corner towers and an arcaded central courtyard.

Apart from hosting the Biennial of Industrial Design, the museum is also the permanent home of the Plečnik Exhibition, a collection of materials including plans, models, furniture first shown at Paris's Centre Pompidou in 1986. Visitors can enjoy scale models of Plečnik's most famous buildings as well as maquettes of projects that were never built. The most famous of these designs is the Slovenian Acropolis, a magnificent parliament house topped by a huge conical spire that sadly never left the drawing board *(see p73).*

Candle offerings at a grave in the Žale Cemetery

Žale Cemetery ㉒

Med hmeljniki 2. **Tel** *(01) 420 1700.* ☒ *2.* ◯ *Apr–Sep: 7am–9pm daily; Oct–Mar: 7am–7pm daily.* **www**.zale.si

On the city's northeastern outskirts, Žale Cemetery is another of the iconic sights associated with architect Jože Plečnik. The cemetery itself has been Ljubljana's main burial ground since 1906, but it was in 1937 that Plečnik – then at the height of his career – was given carte blanche to redesign the entrance and provide facilities for mourners. The graveyard is entered via an archway flanked by two-tiered

Sculpture at Žale Cemetery

colonnades, intended by Plečnik to mark the transition from the world of the living to that of the dead.

Immediately beyond the gateway lies the All Saints' Gardens (Vrt vseh svetih) with a cluster of Plečnik-designed chapels, executed in radically differing styles to express humanity's religious and cultural diversity. Both the central prayer room *(molilnica)* and the nearby Chapel of St John (kapela sv Janeza) follow Classical models with triangular pediments held up by Doric and Ionic columns, flanked by amphora-like urns.

In total contrast are the Chapel of St Agathius (kapela sv Ahaca), an ivy-covered cone inspired by Etruscan grave mounds, and the octagonal Chapel of St Peter (kapela sv Petra), which recalls the Moorish styles of southern Spain.

To the north of the chapel lies the graveyard proper, a grid of plots edged by trimmed hedges and shrubs. To the east is the Ossuary of Victims of World War I, an impressive rotunda designed by Plečnik's student, Edvard Ravnikar, in 1939. It commemorates the Slovenians who served in the ranks of the Austro-Hungarian army; the remains of Russian and Serbian POWs are also housed within. The entrance to the ossuary is via a stepped bridge watched over by Lojze Dolinar's (1893–1970) statue of a soldier.

Running between the central part of the cemetery and the newer plots to the north is the Path of Remembrance and Comradeship (Pot spominov in tovarištva), a 33-km (21-mile) long walking and cycling route. This path follows the barbed wire fence that was built around Ljubljana by Fascist Italian occupiers in 1942. Visitors who want to explore the route can pick up maps from the Ljubljana Tourist Information Centre *(see p95).*

Fužine Castle, home to the Museum of Architecture and Design

FURTHER AFIELD

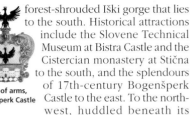

Coat of arms, Bogenšperk Castle

The area of low hills and farmland that lies beyond Ljubljana's suburbs holds a lot of potential for day trips. Immediately south of the city lie the flatlands of the Ljubljana Marshes (Ljubljansko barje), crisscrossed with tracks that provide the perfect terrain for cyclists. Enthusiastic hikers can tackle the Šmarna Gora hill, located just north of the capital, or venture into the forest-shrouded Iški gorge that lies to the south. Historical attractions include the Slovene Technical Museum at Bistra Castle and the Cistercian monastery at Stična to the south, and the splendours of 17th-century Bogenšperk Castle to the east. To the north-west, huddled beneath its Baroque castle, well-preserved Škofja Loka offers the perfect taste of small-town Slovenia.

SIGHTS AT A GLANCE

Historic Buildings
Bistra Castle **5**
Bogensperk Castle pp90–91 **12**
Polhov Gradec Castle **3**
Stična Monastery **10**
Turjak Castle **9**

Towns and Villages
Škofja Loka pp86–7 **6**
Vrhnika **4**

Sites of Interest
Arboretum Volčji Potok **11**
Iški gorge **8**
Lake Zbilje **2**
Ljubljana Marshes **7**
Šmarna Gora **1**

GETTING AROUND
Many of the destinations in this area lie at the end of Ljubljana's municipal bus routes. Distant sites such as Škofja Loka and Vrhnika are connected by inter-city buses operating from the main bus station on Trg Osvobodilne fronte. However, for some destinations, such as Stična or Bogenšperk, private transport is required.

KEY
Urban area
✈ International airport
Motorway
Major road
Minor road
Railway

SEE ALSO
• *Where to Stay* pp188–90
• *Where to Eat* pp202–4

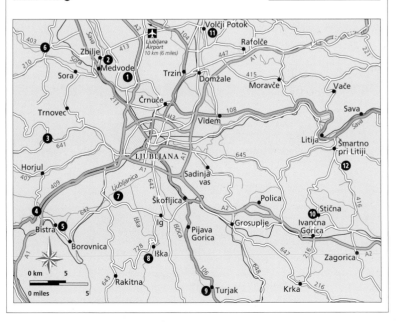

◁ **Statue in the grounds behind Bogenšperk Castle**

Šmarna Gora ❶

Road Map B3. 6 km (4 miles)
N of Ljubljana. 🚌 *from Ljubljana.*
www.smarnagora.com

Rising above Ljubljana's northern suburbs, the smooth-topped Šmarna Gora is a popular destination for Ljubljana dwellers seeking to stretch their legs. The hill has two peaks: the 676-m (2,218-ft) high Grmada lies to the west and the 669-m (2,195-ft) high Šmarna Gora lies to the east. Most people head straight for the latter, where the fortified Church of the Holy Mother crowns the summit, and expansive views of the city open up to the south. Also at the summit is the miraculous Bell of St Anthony. According to legend, Ottoman raiders were ordered to capture Šmarna Gora before noon. The bell tolled half an hour early, confusing the attackers and sending them into retreat. It is said that the wishes of those who ring the bell come true.

The hill is particularly busy on fine Sundays, when it seems as if the entire city is swarming up and down its slopes. Numerous paths lead up the hill, although the most popular is the ascent that begins in the suburb of Tacen. A steeper approach heads up the eastern side of the hill from the village of Šmartno. Both suburbs are accessible by bus from central Ljubljana.

Hiker walking up one of the several trails on Šmarna Gora

Lake Zbilje ❷
Zbiljsko jezero

Road Map B3. 20 km (13 miles) NW of Ljubljana.

A reservoir fed by the Sava river, Lake Zbilje came into being with the construction of a dam at Medvode in 1953. It soon became a popular location for summertime swimming and boating, with the village of Zbilje at the lake's northern end offering a number of recreational facilities.

Stretching south of the village is a grassy lakeside area featuring cafés, a children's play park and boat-renting facilities. Although busiest in summer, it is a popular place for walks throughout the year, with abundant swans, ducks and other waterfowl adding to the charm.

Polhov Gradec Castle ❸
Polhograjska grascina

Road Map B3. 22 km (14 miles) W of Ljubljana; Polhov Gradec 61. **Tel** (01) 364 5694. 🚌 *from Ljubljana.* ⏰ 10am–5pm Tue–Fri & Sun. 📷 **www.**tms.si

Nestling among wooded hills, the village of Polhov Gradec grew around its castle, a medieval stronghold that was rebuilt as an aristocratic residence during the Baroque period. During the late 16th century, the castle was owned by Jurij Kisl, grandson of Vid Kisl, founder of Fužine Castle – now the Museum of Architecture and Design *(see p81)* – in Ljubljana. Jurij Kisl was a statesman, intellectual and soldier who distinguished himself in campaigns against the Ottoman Turks.

The castle now houses the Slovene Museum of Post and Telecommunications, which has colourful and entertaining displays. There are also specimens of Morse code machines, telephones through the ages and postal uniforms. Visitors can also admire the castle's richly stuccoed chapel before taking a stroll in the 19th-century ornamental park.

Picturesque Lake Zbilje against the backdrop of Zbilje and the Alps

For hotels and restaurants in this region see pp188–90 and pp202–4

View of the octagonal St Leonard's Church, Vrhnika

Vrhnika ❹

Road Map B3. 32 km (20 miles) SW of Ljubljana. 🏘 *18,000.* 🚌 *from Ljubljana.* 🛈 *Jelovškova 1; (01) 755 1054.* **www**.*zavod-cankar.si*

Spread between low hills, Vrhnika is a pleasant market town that was originally the Roman town, Nauportum, in the 1st century AD. Nothing from that period has survived. However, there is a pleasant ensemble of historic buildings near the central Cankarjev trg, starting with the octagonal St Leonard's Church facing the broad mansard roof of the former Court House.

The most visited spot in town is the **Ivan Cankar Memorial House**, just west of the centre in the Na klancu district. It was here that the famous Slovenian writer Ivan Cankar was born in 1876. The house itself is not original, having been built on the site of the earlier Cankar family cottage, which burnt down in a fire in 1880. The interior contains photographs and manuscripts, alongside the kind of furniture that a 19th-century artisan's family would have owned.

🏛 **Ivan Cankar Memorial House**
Na klancu 1. **Tel** *(01) 755 1054.* ☐ *Apr–Oct: 9am–1pm Tue–Fri, 2–6pm Sat & Sun.* 🖼

Bistra Castle ❺
Grad Bistra

Road Map B3. 36 km (22 miles) SW of Ljubljana.

Set against a hillside some 3 km (1 mile) east of Vrhnika, Bistra Castle began life as a Carthusian monastery founded by Ulrich III of Spannheim in 1260. Later an aristocratic residence, Bistra was an important centre for saw-milling throughout its history, and several reconstructed water-powered workshops lie alongside the stream that runs through the heart of the estate. The castle now provides a rather grand home to the **Slovene Technical Museum** (Tehniški muzej Slovenije), one of the country's most varied collections.

A pavilion near the entrance to the castle houses vintage trams and automobiles, including several official cars that were once used by Yugoslav president Josip Broz Tito. Elsewhere, there are exhaustive displays of agricultural, forestry and fishing equipment, alongside early examples of steam power and electricity generation. Carrying on with the technological theme is a room devoted to Nikola Tesla (1856–1943), the prolific Yugoslav-born inventor who spent most of his career in the USA, developing alternating current, electric light systems and radio waves in the process.

🏛 **Slovene Technical Museum**
Bistra 6. **Tel** *(01) 750 6670.* ☐ *Mar–Jun & Sep–Nov: 8am–4pm Tue–Fri, 9am–5pm Sat; Jul & Aug: 10am–6pm Tue–Fri, 9am–5pm Sat.* 🖼 🏛 **www**.*tms.si*

Model of an old petrol station in the Slovene Technical Museum

IVAN CANKAR (1876–1918)

Few writers have shaped the modern Slovenian psyche in the way that Ivan Cankar has. The writer's vast output of poetry, novels and plays occupies a dominant position in Slovenian culture. His works rarely offered a flattering portrayal of Slovenian society, frequently focusing on ineffectual dreamers, corrupt managers and cruel officials. Cankar always supported the downtrodden, conveying a new sense of sympathy for the aspirations of the rural and urban poor. His most famous short story is "Hlapec Jernej" (Jernej the Bailiff), in which an ageing servant is deprived of his rights – a metaphor for the Slovenia under Austrian domination. Cankar was a supporter of the Yugoslav ideal but insisted on the uniqueness of Slovenian language and culture.

Ivan Cankar

Škofja Loka ⑥

Coat of Arms, Mihelič Gallery

Located at the confluence of two branches of the Sora river and backed by wooded ridges, Škofja Loka (Bishop's Meadow) is one of the most attractively situated towns in Slovenia. It gets its name from the bishops of Freising, who were granted ownership of the town by King Otto II of Germany in AD 973. A major trade and craft centre throughout the Middle Ages, the town was hit by an earthquake in 1511 and rebuilt in a uniform, early-Baroque style. More recently, Škofja Loka became famous for its Passion Play, written by a Capuchin friar in 1721 and revived in 1999. Involving hundreds of costumed locals, the play is enacted at Easter every six years.

Detail on the ceiling of St James's Church

🏛 Mestni trg

Central Škofja Loka consists of a warren of streets woven tightly around the oblong Mestni trg, the medieval market square. Dominating the square's northern end is the 16th-century Homan House (Homanova hiša), whose lively façade features jutting oriel windows, squiggly sgraffito patterns and a larger-than-life painting of St Christopher. Occupying the building's ground floor is the Café Homan, long the centre of the town's social life and once the favoured sketching spot of Impressionist painter Ivan Grohar (1867–1911).

Midway along the square is the former Town Hall (Mestna hiša), its façade enlivened by the fragmented remains of 17th-century frescoes. They are unexpectedly exotic in content, showing friendly looking sphinxes squatting on ivory-choked pillars. Diagonally opposite the Town Hall is the Plague Column, topped by a serene statue of the Virgin and Child. The column was erected in 1751 to ensure divine protection from disease and other natural disasters.

🏛 St James's Church

Cankarjev trg 13.
Built in 1471, St James's Church (Cerkev sv Jakoba) has preserved much of its late-Gothic appearance. Of note is the delicate stone

Dancers at the medieval festival in the Old Town centre

relief above the main entrance showing Judas grasping a bag of money, watched expectantly by Herod's soldiers. After the earthquake in the early 16th century, the church's belfry was remodelled, when it acquired a characteristically bulbous Baroque spire.

Inside, the ceiling is a masterpiece of Gothic vaulting, with brightly coloured floral designs filling the spaces between the stone ribs. Hovering above the pews is a forest of brass chandeliers and lanterns, added by 20th-century architect Jože Plečnik (see p73). Behind the church stands a sturdy 16th-century schoolhouse, with a plaque honouring its founder Michael Papler, lord of Škofja Loka Castle (Grad Škofja Loka).

🏛 Mihelič Gallery

Spodnji trg 1. **Tel** (04) 517 0400.
⏰ by appt only. 🎫 for a fee.
www.loski-muzej.si
Dominating Spodnji trg is a 15th-century granary, a severe-looking stone building with tiny rectangular windows. This was once one of the most important buildings in town, housing the food supply as well as the citizens' tax records. Today, the granary's timber-beamed upper storeys accommodate the Mihelič Gallery (Galerija Mihelič), devoted to artist France Mihelič (1907–98), who was born in Škofja Loka.

Mihelič is primarily known for his distinctively surreal graphic works, in which human forms were made to resemble twig-like creatures and distorted insects. Among his most striking works are the series of lithographs depicting the Kurenti, masked men who lead the Kurentovanje revels in Ptuj.

🏛 Castle Museum

Grajska pot 13. **Tel** (04) 517 0400.
⏰ Apr–Sep: 10am–6pm Tue–Sun, Nov–Mar: 10am–5pm Tue–Sun. 🎫
www.loski-muzej.si
Squatting on a hillock directly above the town centre, Škofja Loka's Baroque castle served as the seasonal residence

The so-called "black kitchen" in the 16th-century Nace's House

VISITORS' CHECKLIST

Road Map B3. *23 km (15 miles)
NW of Ljubljana.* 🚉 *22,100.*
🚏 🚌 *from Ljubljana.* 🛈 *Mestni
trg 7; (04) 512 0268.*
🏛 *Mon–Sat.* 🎭 *Medieval
festival (late Jun).* **www**.
skofjaloka.info

for the bishops of Freising and was the seat of their administration when the prelates were away. Easily reached via a winding pathway from Mestni trg, the building now houses the extensive and varied collections of the Town Museum (Mestni muzej).

Highlights of the museum include the brightly decorated pottery used in Loka households through the ages, as well as painted wooden furniture and original wares from the lace- and hat-making workshops that once figured prominently in the local economy. The corridors are filled with canvases by local painters, including several works by Ivan Grohar.

Displayed in the castle's octagonal chapel are four 17th-century altars from the Church of St Lucy in Dražgoše. Each altar is encrusted with gilded statuettes of saints and gambolling cherubs.

🏛 **Nace's House**
Puštal 74. **Tel** *(04) 176 9425.*
◻ *by appt.* 📷 🎫 *for a fee.*
www.nacetovahisa.com
Southeast of the centre, on the opposite bank of the Poljanska Sora, spreads the suburb of Puštal, a pleasant neighbourhood of one- or two-storey houses surrounded by gardens and orchards. The oldest of the surviving dwellings in this part of town is the

16th-century Nace's House (Nacetova hiša), a beautifully preserved, largely timber building whose spindly wooden balconies are sheltered under a steep overhanging roof.

Named after its early 19th-century owner Ignac "Nace" Homan, the house served as an inn until 1907 – it was here that farm workers would return to from the fields, have a drink and change into their town clothes before venturing homewards. The interior is packed with traditional furnishings and original features. One of them is the archaic "black kitchen" so-called because it did not have a standard chimney – smoke from the fire escaped upwards through the rafters, drying the household's grain and curing sausages as it went. A traditional timber granary and a hay barn can be seen in the garden.

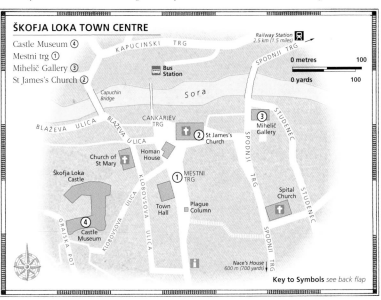

ŠKOFJA LOKA TOWN CENTRE

Castle Museum ④
Mestni trg ①
Mihelič Gallery ③
St James's Church ②

*Railway Station
2.5 km (1.5 miles)*

0 metres   100
0 yards   100

KAPUCINSKI TRG
SPODNJI TRG
Bus Station
Capuchin Bridge
Sora
BLAŽEVA ULICA
BLAŽEVA ULICA
CANKARJEV TRG
③ Mihelič Gallery
STUDENEC
② St James's Church
Homan House
Church of St Mary
Škofja Loka Castle
① MESTNI TRG
SPODNJI TRG
KLOBOVSOVA ULICA
Town Hall
Plague Column
Spital Church
STUDENEC
④ Castle Museum
GRAJSKA POT
KLOBOVSOVA ULICA
SPODNJI TRG
🛈
*Nace's House
600 m (700 yards)*

Key to Symbols *see back flap*

Ljubljana Marshes **7**

Ljubljansko barje

Road Map B3. 10 km (6 miles) S of Ljubljana. **www**.ljubljanskobarje.si

Stretching beyond Ljubljana's southern suburbs, the grassy plain known as the Ljubljana Marshes began life as a shallow lake formed at the end of the last Ice Age. It was an important centre of Neolithic culture in the 4th millennium BC, when locals lived in wood-pile dwellings above the lake's surface and used log-carved canoes to commute. With time the lake dried out, leaving a soggy area of peat bog. From the 18th century onwards, the digging of drainage ditches rendered the area suitable for agriculture, and in 1830, the marsh was sold off as plots, largely to soldiers for whom the land purchase offered exemption from further military service. The bogs were over-harvested for peat and only survive in isolated pockets nowadays. However, they remain an important breeding ground for birds, with herons, curlews and corncrakes among the regular nesters. The best way to explore the marshes is by bike, thanks to a network of trails that run alongside the drainage channels.

The area's one prominent architectural attraction is the **Church of St Michael** (Cerkev sv Mihaela) in the village of Črna vas. Built between 1925 and 1939 by architect Jože Plečnik (see p73), the structure utilizes local wood as well as a mixture of grey limestone and red brick – a technique also employed in the National and University Library (see pp68–9) in Ljubljana. The ivy-covered bell tower, perforated with arches of various sizes, is one of Plečnik's most arresting creations. The church features a nave raised above ground level to guard it against seasonal flooding, and is entered via an unusual arched stairway. Inside, wooden pews and timber ceiling beams contrast with the warm sheen of a high altar constructed with burnished copper sheets.

Bell tower of the Church of St Michael, Ljubljana Marshes

Iški gorge **8**

Iški Vintgar

Road Map C3. 25 km (16 miles) S of Ljubljana.

Flowing into the Ljubljana Marshes from the south, the Iška river cuts through the dolomite rock of the Bloke plateau to form the Iški gorge, a V-shaped valley with steep, densely wooded sides.

The most interesting stretches of the gorge lie just beyond the Gostišče Iški Vintgar, a guesthouse accessible via the paved road from the marshes. From the guesthouse, a footpath leads along the bank of the river, passing a sequence of cataracts and pools. The going gets more difficult as the gorge narrows,

and visitors should be prepared to get their feet wet to be able to enjoy the waterfalls and rock formations of the gorge's upper stretches.

For those who want to explore the hilly terrain above the gorge, a path ascends west from the Gostišče Iški Vintgar towards the Orlek ridge, before descending into an isolated dell, site of the Krvavice Partisan Hospital during World War II – a few wooden huts remain. More ambitious hikers can carry on uphill to the 1,107-m (3,632-ft) high summit of Krim hill, which offers wonderful views back across the marshes towards Ljubljana.

Turjak Castle **9**

Grad Turjak

Road Map C4. 25 km (16 miles) SE of Ljubljana. **Tel** (01) 788 1006. ◯ May–Oct: noon–7pm Sat & Sun.

An important stronghold in the Middle Ages, Turjak Castle got its present form in the 16th century, when the castle's characteristic barrel-shaped bastions and arcaded inner courtyard were built. The masters of the castle were the Auerspergs, who turned it into a key stronghold in Austria's defences against Ottoman incursions. The famous Andreas Auersperg led the Carniolan forces during the 1593 battle of

Wooden water mill at the Iški gorge

Permanent exhibition at Turjak Castle

Sisak, when a combined Croatian-Slovenian force crushed an advancing Ottoman army. Andreas is credited with the capture of a bridge crucial to the struggle, causing the enemy to flee.

Several rooms in the castle can be visited. These include the Renaissance Knights Hall and the castle chapel, decorated with 15th-century frescoes. Temporary exhibitions of arts and crafts are held in one of the towers. Below the castle are the ruins of alms-houses built by the owners for their ageing servants.

Stična Monastery ⑩
Samostan Stična

Road Map C3. 35 km (22 miles) SE of Ljubljana. *Tel* (01) 787 7100. ☐ 8am–noon & 2–5pm Tue–Sat, 2–5pm Sun. 🖾 🗹

Set among meadow-carpeted hills just north of the main road from Ljubljana to Novo Mesto is Stična Monastery. It was founded in 1136 by Patriarch Peregrine I of Aquileia, who was keen to provide the Cistercian order with a base from which to spread their teachings. The monastery was one of the richest in Slovenia and became an important centre of education and manuscript production. Heavily fortified in the 15th and 16th centuries in order to withstand Ottoman raids, Stična has retained its sturdy outer appearance to

this day. Emperor Joseph II's decision to dissolve the big monasteries in 1781 led to the abandonment of Stična and the sale of its treasures. It was re-founded in 1898 by Cistercian monks from Bavaria.

The 12th-century monastery church retains several original Romanesque features, although repeated re-buildings during the Baroque era bequeathed a bulbous belfry and an altar-filled interior. The monastery's administrative buildings now house the Slovene Religious Museum, crammed with reliquaries, candelabras and religious paintings. Highlights include 15th-century fresco fragments painted by Master Janez of Ljubljana for one of the monastery chapels.

Sculpture, Stična

Arboretum Volčji Potok ⑪

Road Map C3. 22 km (14 miles) NE of Ljubljana; Volčji potok 3. *Tel* (01) 831 2345. ☐ Mar & Oct: 8am–5pm; Apr–Aug: 8am–7pm; Sep: 8am–6pm; Nov: 8am–3:30pm daily. 🖾 🗹 🖾 🗋 **www.** arboretum-vp.si

Just north of the Domžale exit on the Ljubljana-Maribor motorway lies the Arboretum Volčji Potok, once Ljubljana University's botanical study centre and now the most popular horticultural attraction in the country.

Formerly a landscaped park belonging to the Souvan estate, the arboretum features 3,000 species of trees and shrubs, neat ornamental gardens and numerous floral displays. Seasonal attractions include tulips in April, a wide range of blossoms in May, roses from June onwards and an explosion of autumn colours in October. An autumn pumpkin festival celebrates one of Slovenia's best-loved vegetables. Facilities for children include an attraction-packed play park, a maze and a tractor-pulled train dressed up to look like a vintage steam locomotive.

The arboretum's shop is a great place to buy seeds. There is an 18-hole golf course situated right next to the arboretum.

Flowers blooming in the Arboretum Volčji Potok

Bogenšperk Castle ⑫
Grad Bogenšperk

The Renaissance castle of Bogenšperk was built for the Wagen family in the early 16th century. Its place in Slovene history is due to Janez Valvasor, the antiquarian and author who bought the castle in 1672 and turned it into his printing workshop. Here, he produced the copper-plate engravings subsequently published as part of his magnum opus, *The Glory of the Duchy of Carniola*. Printing debts forced Valvasor to sell his books and artifacts, but his castle survives as a popular tourist attraction.

Performer at the castle courtyard

Flowering plants adorning the stark courtyard walls

★ **Folk Costumes**
Clothes worn by Slovenians in the 17th century are re-created in this display of costumes from all over the country.

Entrance

STAR FEATURES

★ Folk Costumes

★ Re-created Study

★ Copper-engraving Workshop

Ticket office

JANEZ VAJKARD VALVASOR'S WORK

A traveller, historian and collector, Valvasor is primarily remembered for the four-volume work, *The Glory of the Duchy of Carniola* (Die Ehre des Herzogtums Crain), published in Nuremberg in 1689. It was the first fully researched description of central and western Slovenia, containing comments on history and human geography.

The Glory of the Duchy of Carniola, *a 3,500-page illustrated work, remains valuable for researchers. Valvasor spent 15 years preparing the book and was ruined by the cost of its publication, forcing him to sell the castle in 1692.*

Valvasor *sold his library to the Bishop of Zagreb, and died in poverty in Krško in 1693.*

Former Library
The largest room in the castle, Valvasor's former library is nowadays mainly used as an atmospheric venue for wedding ceremonies.

VISITORS' CHECKLIST

Road Map C3. 41 km (26 miles) E of Ljubljana. **Tel** *(01) 898 7664.* 🚗 🅿 🚻 *Apr–Oct: 10am–5pm Tue–Sat, 10am–6pm Sun; Mar & Nov: 10am–5pm Sat & Sun.* **www. bogensperk.si**

Hunting room

★ **Re-created Study**
Period furnishings shed light on Valvasor's day-to-day working life. Also on display is an original copy of The Glory of the Duchy of Carniola.

★ **Copper-engraving Workshop**
This display of 17th-century paper-making and printing machines reveals just how labour-intensive book production was.

Death *was a popular subject for Baroque illustrators, focusing minds on the transience of earthly life.*

Printing *was complex and expensive in the 17th century. Valvasor was a leader in the production of beautiful books and many people came especially to Bogenšperk Castle to study his technique.*

Accurately drawn townscapes *were an important element of Valvasor's book on Carniola, which aimed to be a visually appealing complete guide to the nation's riches as well as a scholarly text.*

SHOPPING IN LJUBLJANA

Souvenir on sale, Ljubljana

Central Ljubljana is a treasure trove of characterful shops, with the boutiques of the Old Town offering everything from kooky arts and crafts to haute couture. There are also plenty of souvenir outlets, with lace, embroidery, handmade chocolates and Slovene wines featuring among the most popular wares. Visitors to the capital city also have the option of browsing the market stalls – the fresh fruit, vegetable and fish stalls in Ljubljana's Market are an attraction in their own right; while the weekly bric-a-brac market on the riverbank is also a social event. In December, the Advent market in the Old Town generates plenty in the way of Christmas gift ideas alongside a festive atmosphere.

Daily morning fruit and vegetable market, Vodnikov trg

OPENING HOURS

Shops in Ljubljana are usually open from 9 or 10am until 7 or 8pm from Monday to Friday and from 9 or 10am until 1 or 2pm on Saturday. Be aware that almost all shops in the city centre – supermarkets and newspaper kiosks included – are closed on Sunday. The best places to shop for basic provisions on Sundays are the shopping centres on the eastern outskirts of Ljubljana or petrol stations throughout the city.

DEPARTMENT STORES AND SHOPPING CENTRES

Central Ljubljana's main department store is **Nama**, offering five storeys of clothes, accessories, household goods and toys. A range of up-market international fashion brands is sold at **Galerija Emporium**, which occupies the Centromerkur building (see p59) on Prešernov trg. Otherwise, the best places for general shopping, ranging from clothes to homeware, are the large mall-style complexes on the outskirts of the city. The biggest of these are **BTC City**, 4 km (3 miles) east of the centre, and **Citypark** right next to it. The BTC complex also boasts a multiplex cinema, an aquapark and other leisure facilities.

MARKETS

Ljubljana's colourful Market (see p50), at the northern end of the Old Town, offers a wide variety of fresh fruit and vegetables, featuring local seasonal produce. Indigenous vegetables include asparagus in spring and mushrooms in autumn. The Market's riverside colonnade is the place for fresh seafood from the Adriatic. There are also specialist stalls selling honey, olive oil and dried herbs.

The antiques and bric-a-brac market on the riverside on Breg every Sunday morning is full of potential discoveries. It is also an occasion for the locals to enjoy coffee and conversation in the nearby cafés after browsing the stalls.

FOOD AND DRINK

Many Slovenian specialities such as honey, olive oil and pumpkin oil can be picked up in the Market, although you will find a better choice of delicacies in specialist stores spread throughout the centre. **Kraševka** is the place to seek out goods from the karst region including home-cured *pršut* (ham), teran red wine, and olive oil. Handmade chocolates are on offer at **Čokoladnica Cukrček** – who count *Prešernove kroglice* (chestnut paste and chocolate balls) among their specialities – and **Čokoladni atelje**, known for their chocolate-coated figs, plums and pralines. Souvenir bags of Piran sea salt crystals (see p133) can be bought from **Piranske soline**. The **Maximarket**, located in the subterranean

Antiques on display at the riverfront market

Contemporary gifts on display at the Ika shop

shopping mall on Trg republike *(see p63)*, has an extensive delicatessen selection and a good choice of Slovenian wines. A selection of Slovenian wines can be found in any large supermarket, although if you need specialist advice on what to buy, head for **Vino Boutique** or **Vinoteka Dvor**, both in the city centre on the western side of the river. **Vinoteka Movia**, in the Old Town, sells quality wines from the Movia estates in Goriška Brda *(see p145)*.

CRAFTS AND SOUVENIRS

A wide range of folksy textiles, ceramics and crafts can be found in the boutiques of Ljubljana's Old Town. **Galerija Rogaška** sells a range of cut glass and crystalware from the famous glassworks in Rogaška, while traditional hand-woven lace from Idrija *(see p146)* can be bought at **Galerija Idrijske čipke** store nearby. **Etnogalerija Skrina** has a broad selection of authentic crafts, including embroidered blouses, glass paintings and painted beehive panels *(see p111)*. For more contemporary gifts and souvenirs, head for **Ika**, which sells affordable fashion accessories and goods made by young Slovene designers.

MUSIC

The best place to buy CDs by contemporary Slovenian artists is **Big Bang** in the BTC shopping centre. The centrally located **Dallas Mute Shop** is particularly good for rock, pop, jazz and world music. Ljubljana is also a good place to browse for second-hand recordings. Former Yugoslavia was home to a huge music industry, releasing albums by local and international artists and collectors will find a lot of them in specialist stores such as **Vom Second Hand** near Prešernov trg and **Spin Vinyl** in the Old Town.

BOOKS

Ljubljana's biggest bookshop, **Mladinska knjiga Konzorcij** offers a wide choice of books about Slovenia in various languages, alongside a selection of English-language fiction. The small and welcoming **Knjigarna Behemot**, tucked away on a stepped alleyway, is a gold mine of English-language books, with plenty of literary fiction and a wealth of titles on the culture and history of Slovenia and its surroundings.

Racks of albums for sale at the Spin Vinyl record shop

DIRECTORY

DEPARTMENT STORES AND SHOPPING CENTRES

BTC City
Šmartinska 152.
Tel *(01) 585 1310.*

Citypark
Šmartinska 152g.
Tel *(01) 587 3050.*

Galerija Emporium
Prešernov trg 5A.
City Map D2.
Tel *(01) 308 4210.*

Nama
Tomšičeva 1. **City Map**
C2. **Tel** *(01) 425 8300.*

FOOD AND DRINK

Čokoladni atelje
Trg republike 1. **City Map**
C3. **Tel** *(01) 425 3141.*

Čokoladnica Cukrček
Mestni trg 11. **City Map**
D3. **Tel** *(01) 421 0453.*

Kraševka
Ciril-Metodov trg 10.
City Map D3.
Tel *(01) 232 1445.*

Maximarket
Trg republike 1. **City Map**
C3. **Tel** *(01) 476 6800.*

Piranske soline
Mestni trg 19. **City Map**
D3. **Tel** *(01) 425 0190.*

Vino Boutique
Slovenska cesta 38.
City Map C2.
Tel *(01) 425 2680.*

Vinoteka Dvor
Dvorni trg 1. **City Map**
D3. **Tel** *(01) 251 3644.*

Vinoteka Movia
Mestni trg 4. **City Map**
D3. **Tel** *(01) 425 5448.*

CRAFTS AND SOUVENIRS

Etnogalerija Skrina
Breg 8. **City Map** D4.
Tel *(01) 425 5161.*

Galerija Idrijske čipke
Mestni trg 17.
City Map D3.
Tel *(01) 425 0051.*

Galerija Rogaška
Mestni trg 22.
City Map D3.
Tel *(01) 241 2701.*

Ika
Ciril-Metodov trg 13.
City Map D3.
Tel *(01) 232 1743.*

MUSIC

Big Bang
BTC. **Tel** *(01) 309 3768.*

Dallas Mute Shop
Rimska 14.
City Map C4.
Tel *(01) 252 4591.*

Spin Vinyl
Gallusovo nabrežje 13.
City Map D4.
Tel *(01) 251 1018.*

Vom Second Hand
Čopova ulica 14.
City Map C2.
Tel *(01) 252 7921.*

BOOKS

Knjigarna Behemot
Židovska steza 3.
Tel *(01) 251 1392.*

Mladinska knjiga Konzorcij
Slovenska cesta 29.
City Map C2.
Tel *(01) 241 4761.*

ENTERTAINMENT IN LJUBLJANA

Ljubljana may not be one of the biggest European capitals but it is extraordinarily vibrant for its size. Local classical music, dance and theatre companies are of the highest quality, and the city's year-round repertoire of cultural festivals attracts a steady stream of international names. The city's vibrant bar culture provides

Drummer at a historical event

a wealth of nightlife opportunities, especially in the summer, when the café-lined banks of the Ljubljanica river take on a Mediterranean joie de vivre. The city also has a history of pop, rock and alternative music, a heritage that manifests itself in an impressive range of concert venues and clubs.

Visitors watching artists perform on Prešernov trg

PRACTICAL INFORMATION AND TICKETS

The Ljubljana Tourist Office website features a list of the major cultural events. The best way to find out about the events being organized in the city is to consult the websites of the venues that host them.

Tickets for many events can be bought through **Eventim**, which has outlets in the **Ljubljana Tourist Information Centre** and in the international travel company, **Kompas'** offices. The Eventim website also offers tickets on sale and is a handy, if limited, guide to upcoming attractions.

CULTURAL CENTRES

Playing a crucial role in Ljubljana's cultural life are the multi-purpose cultural centres that host a wide range of events from classical music to theatre, cinema, jazz and rock. The main venue for cultural events is Cankar Hall *(see*

p63) in the city centre, a large, partly underground complex comprising concert halls, congress facilities and an art gallery. Less formal venues include **KUD France Prešeren**, just south of the centre in Trnovo; **Stara Elektrarna**, an atmospheric former power plant near the train station; and **Španski borci** in the western suburb of Moste – all of which host a mix of jazz, theatre and children's events.

OPERA AND CLASSICAL MUSIC

Ljubljana's most prestigious venues for classical art forms are the 19th-century **National Theatre Opera and Ballet**, where opera and ballet performances are staged; and the Philharmonic Hall *(see p68)*, home to the national symphony orchestra. Križanke *(see p69)*, with outdoor and indoor stages, is a great venue for classical music. Local and international recitals also take place in Cankar Hall.

ROCK AND JAZZ

The capital regularly plays host to major international rock acts, with performances in the **Arena Stožice** or the slightly smaller Tivoli Hall *(see p74)*. The best venue for medium-sized acts is **Kino Šiška**, a restored cinema with great sound. The other major location for live music is the Metelkova Mesto Alternative Cultural Centre, with clubs such as **Menza pri koritu**, **Gala Hala** and **Channel Zero** all grouped around a central courtyard. Outdoor jazz, rock and world music gigs also take place in Križanke through the summer. **Jazz Club Gajo**, founded by drummer Drago Gajo, hosts regular concerts and jam sessions.

THEATRE

Theatre is of a very high standard in Ljubljana, with several European directors of renown working in the city's theatres. Performances are in

Bass player of the Marc Duret Trio band during a gig, Ljubljana

Kinodvor theatre, a venue for art films

Slovenian, unless visiting companies are in the city. However, most productions feature a level of movement and stagecraft that will hold the audience's interest. The Slovene National Theatre Drama (Slovensko narodno gledališče), also known as Drama; and the **Ljubljana City Theatre** (Mestno gledališče ljubljansko) concentrate on the classics and on contemporary local and international drama. Slightly more edgy is the **Youth Theatre** (Mladinsko gledališče), founded in 1955 specifically

for young people. Nowadays, it stages experimental drama for all ages. Established in 1970, **Gledališče Glej**, the oldest independent performing arts venue in Ljubljana, has a line-up of experimental, but accessible, productions.

CINEMA

Films are screened in their original language with Slovenian subtitles. Hollywood movies are shown in multi-plexes, the biggest of which is **Kolosej**, 4 km (3 miles) east

of the centre. The best places for watching new international movies are the two-screen **Kinoklub Vič**, which also has a popular bar, and **Kinodvor**, which shows art films and has a daytime café and bookshop. **Kinoteka** is the place to watch cinema classics.

NIGHTLIFE

Ljubljana's vibrant nightlife focuses on the cafés and bars along the Ljubljanica river, a majority of which remain open until the early hours. The areas around Prešerenov trg and Cankarjevo nabrežje are very lively in spring and summer. The **Kavarna Nebotičnik** bar, on the top floors of the Art-Deco skyscraper (see p58), offers superb views of the city.

The club life, with venues such as **Klub Top**, **Cvetličarna**, **K4** and **Orto Bar**, offers a mix of live music and DJ-driven sounds. K4 hosts a gay night usually on Sundays.

DIRECTORY

PRACTICAL INFORMATION AND TICKETS

Eventim
www.eventim.si

Kompas
Pražakova 4.
Tel (01) 200 6300.
www.kompas-online.net

Ljubljana Tourist Information Centre
Adamič-Lundovo nabrežje 2. **City Map** D3.
Tel (01) 306 1215.
www.visitljubljana.si

CULTURAL CENTRES

KUD France Prešeren
Karunova 14. *Tel (01) 283 2288.* www.kud.si

Španski borci
Zaloška 61.
Tel (01) 620 8784.
www.spanskiborci.si

Stara Elektrarna
Slomškova 18. **City Map** E1. *Tel (01) 231 4492.*
www.bunker.si

OPERA AND CLASSICAL MUSIC

National Theatre Opera and Ballet
Cankarjeva 11/1. **City Map** C2. *Tel (01) 241 1700.* www.opera.si
www.balet.si

ROCK AND JAZZ

Arena Stožice
Vojkova 90.
Tel (01) 430 6660.

Channel Zero
Metelkova 4. **City Map** F1. www.ch0.org

Gala Hala
Masarykova 24. **City Map** F1. www.galahala.com

Jazz Club Gajo
Beethovnova 8.
City Map C2.
www.jazzclubgajo.com

Kino Šiška
www.kinosiska.si

Menza pri koritu
Metelkova. **City Map** F1.
www.menzaprikoritu.org

THEATRE

Drama
Erjavčeva 1. **City Map** B3.
Tel (01) 252 1462.
www.drama.si

Gledališče Glej
Gregorčičeva 3.
City Map B3. *Tel (01) 251 6679.* www.glej.si

Ljubljana City Theatre
Čopova 14. **City Map** C2.
Tel (01) 251 0852.
www.mgl.si

Youth Theatre
Vilharjeva 11.
Tel (01) 425 3312.
www.mladinsko.com

CINEMA

Kinodvor
Kolodvorska 13. **City Map** E1. www.kinodvor.org

Kinoteka
Miklošičeva 38. **City Map** D2. www.kinoteka.si

Kinoklub Vič
Trg mladinskih delovnih brigad. *Tel (01) 241 8410.*

Kolosej
Šmartinska 152.
www.kolosej.si

NIGHTLIFE

Cvetličarna
Kranjčeva 20.
www.cvetlicarna.eu

K4
Kersnikova 4. **City Map** C1. *Tel (01) 438 0261.*
www.klubk4.org

Kavarna Nebotičnik
Štefanova 1. **City Map** C2. *Tel (040) 60 1787.*
www.neboticnik.si

Klub Top
Tomšičeva 2. **City Map** B2. *Tel (040) 66 8844.*
www.klubtop.si

Orto Bar
Grabloviceva 1.
Tel (01) 232 1674.
www.orto-bar.com

STREET FINDER

The map on the right shows the areas of the capital city, Ljubljana, which are covered by the Street Finder maps on the following pages. All map references given for sights, entertainment venues and shops described in this section of the guide refer to the Street Finder maps. Map references are also provided for Ljubljana hotels *(see pp188–90)* and restaurants *(see pp202–4)* as well as for useful addresses in the *Travellers' Needs* and

Deer crossing signage

the *Survival Guide* sections at the back of the book. The main sights in the city's Old Town, the New Town and some in the Around the Centre areas can be found on pages 98–9. The letter and the number that follows in the map reference indicate the map's grid for the entry. There is also an index of street names opposite for quick reference. The symbols used to represent sights and useful information on the Street Finder maps are listed in the key given below.

Visitors enjoying an open-air music performance at Prešernov trg

KEY TO STREET FINDER

■	Major sight	P	Parking
■	Other sight	✚	Hospital
■	Other building	▣	Police station
▣	Railway station	✝	Church
▣	Bus station	⊠	Post office
▣	Funicular	═	Railway line
ℹ	Visitor information		Pedestrian street

SCALE OF MAPS 1–2

0 metres	200
0 yards	200

Street Finder Index

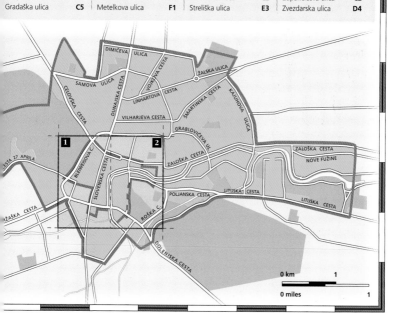

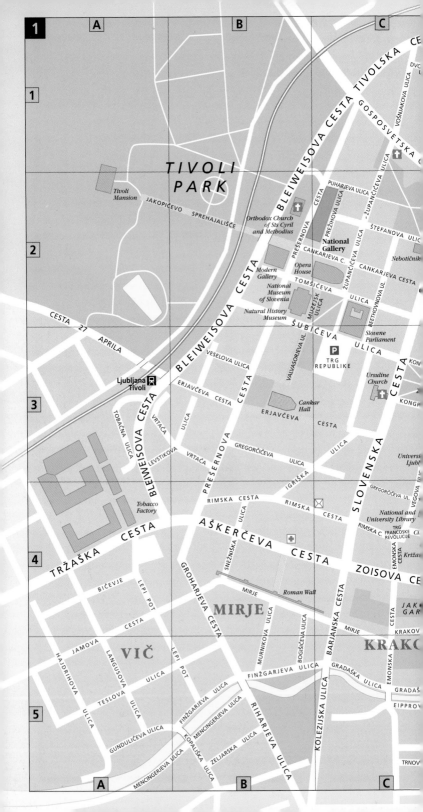

1

A   **B**   **C**

1

TIVOLI PARK

Tivoli Mansion

JAKOPIČEVO SPREHAJALIŠČE

BLEIWEISOVA CESTA

TIVOLSKA CE

GOSPOSVETSKA

VOŠNJAKOVA ULICA

DVO

PUHARJEVA ULICA

PREŠERNOVA CESTA

PREŠIHOVA ULICA

ŽUPANČIČEVA ULICA

ŠTEFANOVA ULIC

Orthodox Church of Sts Cyril and Methodius

National Gallery

CANKARJEVA C.

ŽUPANČIČEVA ULICA

CANKARJEVA CESTA

Nebotičnik

2

Modern Gallery

Opera House

National Museum of Slovenia

Natural History Museum

TOMŠIČEVA

ULICA

MUZEJSK ULICA

ŠUBIČEVA

BEETHOVNOVA ULICA

Slovene Parliament

CESTA

CESTA 27 APRILA

BLEIWEISOVA CESTA

VALVASORJEVA UL.

VESELOVA ULICA

KON

ULICA

TRG REPUBLIKE

Ursuline Church

KONGR

Ljubljana Tivoli

ERJAVČEVA CESTA

CESTA

Cankar Hall

CESTA

SLOVENSKA

CESTA

3

TOBAČNA ULICA

BLEIWEISOVA CESTA

VRTAČA

LEVSTIKOVA ULICA

ERJAVČEVA

VRTAČA

GREGORČIČEVA

ULICA

ULICA

Univers Ljub

GREGORČIČEVA UL.

VEGOVA

PREŠERNOVA

IGRIŠKA

Tobacco Factory

CESTA

RIMSKA CESTA

ULICA

RIMSKA

CESTA

National and University Library

RIMSKA C.

TRG FRANCOSKE REVOLUCIJE

Cı

4

TRŽAŠKA CESTA

AŠKERČEVA

CESTA

ZOISOVA CE

BIČEVJE

LEPI POT

CESTA

GROHARJEVA CESTA

SNEŽNIŠKA ULICA

Roman Wall

MIRJE

BARJANSKA CESTA

EMONSKA CESTA

Križan

JAK GAR

KRAKOV

HAJDRIHOVA ULICA

JAMOVA

LANGUSOVA ULICA

TESLOVA ULICA

VIČ

LEPI POT

CESTA

MIRJE

MURNIKOVA ULICA

BOGIŠIČEVA ULICA

MIRJE

EMONSKA

CESTA

KRAKO

GRADAŠ

EIPPRO

5

GUNDULIČEVA ULICA

FINŽGARJEVA ULICA

KOVALIŠKA ULICA

MENCINGERJEVA ULICA

ZELJARSKA ULICA

RIHARJEVA ULICA

FINŽGARJEVA ULICA

KOLEZIJSKA ULICA

GRADAŠKA ULICA

TRNOV

MENCINGERJEVA ULICA

A   **B**   **C**

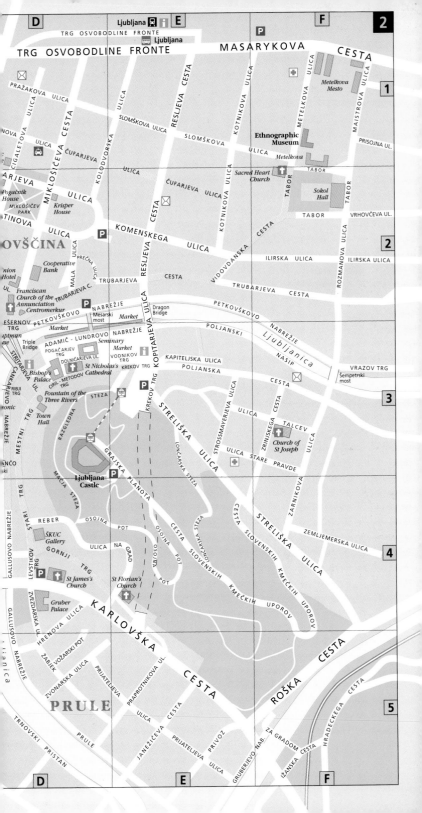

SLOVENIA REGION BY REGION

Slovenia at a Glance

Koper Museum

The landscape in Slovenia frequently changes within the space of a short car ride. Much of the country comprises mountains, cloaked in dark green forest, especially in the north with its dramatic alpine terrain. From the grey peaks of the Triglav National Park to the turquoise waters of the Soča river, the scenery is exhilarating. The topography of central and eastern Slovenia is more gentle, with green hills merging with the Pannonian plain. In the west, the limestone caves give way to a narrow strip of coast.

Bled (see pp108–9) *offers lakeside scenery with an island church and a breath-taking mountain backdrop.*

Kranjska Gora (see p116), *a leading ski resort, is the perfect base for exploring the Triglav National Park.*

THE ALPS
(see pp104–125)

LJUBL
(see pp4

COASTAL SLOVENIA AND THE KARST
(see pp126–155)

Goriška Brda (see p145), *a region of rolling hills close to the Italian border, is famous for its vineyards.*

0 km	25
0 miles	25

Piran (see pp130–31) *is a former salt-trading town and fishing port with numerous fine examples of Venetian architecture.*

◁ Idyllic view of Lake Bled and the island with a church

Maribor *is Slovenia's second main city (see pp176–7). It is famous for its lively riverfront, where modern café-bars share space with medieval walls and towers.*

Ptuj *(see pp178–9), one of Slovenia's most attractive towns, features medieval castles and Roman-era remains.*

SOUTHERN AND
EASTERN SLOVENIA
(see pp156–183)

Novo Mesto *(see p162) is the ideal base from which to explore the castles of the Krka river and the Kočevski rog forests.*

Kolpa Valley *(see p161), marking the border between Slovenia and Croatia, offers unspoilt countryside, historic castles and churches as well as opportunities for cycling, fishing and white-water rafting.*

THE ALPS

*S*pectacular alpine scenery coupled with a rich history make northwest Slovenia the most acclaimed and visited region in the country. The focus for walkers, skiers and adrenaline sports enthusiasts alike is the picturesque Triglav National Park, whose mountains form the heart of the area. Soaring above all is Mount Triglav, so iconic that it features on the national flag.

Excavations around Most na Soči reveal that a rich Bronze and Iron Age culture, which traded with ancient Greece and Italy, flourished in the upper Soča Valley. The Romans settled in the valley in the 1st century AD and established a military base at what is now Kranj. That site was developed in the 7th century by early Slavic tribes, who also established an island settlement at Lake Bled.

The 12th century brought a period of cultural vitality to this protectorate of Frankish aristocracies. Churches were built throughout the region and towns such as Radovljica, Kamnik and Kranj developed. The latter two emerged as important trade and religious centres in the Middle Ages and both served as capitals of Carniola until the Habsburgs won control of the area in the late 13th century. Until the 20th century, farming was the region's mainstay, with dairy herds being taken to high alpine meadows in summer and returned to the lowlands in September. Apiculture reached its zenith through Carnolian honeybee breeding in the 17th century. Logging was another minor industry.

Tourism began in the late 19th century. Lake Bled morphed from a health retreat to a fashionable resort frequented by Viennese high society. Austro-Hungarian and Slovenian hikers began to explore the area.

The greatest upheaval in the region's history came during World War I, when the Soča Valley saw horrific fighting between Italian and Austro-Hungarian forces. Farming returned to the area and was joined by tourism in the 1990s. Today, Soča Valley, Kranjska Gora and Lake Bled are trademark destinations.

Visitors hiking in the Julian Alps, Triglav National Park

◁ Soča river, making its way through Triglav National Park

Exploring the Alps

The Triglav National Park, with its crown of limestone mountains rising above picturesque glaciated lakes at Bled and Bohinj, is the poster-destination of the Alps. Bohinj, due to its good resort facilities and fairy tale setting, makes an excellent base for day trips to the medieval cores of Radovljica and Kranj. To the north, the country's leading ski resort, Kranjska Gora, doubles as a gateway to the beautiful Soča Valley, which is littered with reminders of the three-year conflict between Austro-Hungary and Italy during World War I, a bloody and futile story best explained by a museum in Kobarid. The spectacular Kamniško-Savinjske Alps, the meadows of Velika Planina and the stupendous Logarska dolina valley lie to the east.

Boats waiting to take visitors to Lake Bled Island

SEE ALSO

• *Where to Stay* pp190–91

• *Where to Eat* pp205–6

Museum of Triglav National Park, Trenta

GETTING AROUND

The easiest way to visit the Alps is by car. Traffic is only heavy around Lake Bled in high season. The roads are open year round except the one over Vršič Pass, which may close due to snow from November to April. Buses connect most destinations, although services to villages are infrequent. Rail links go from Ljubljana to some of the destinations; a car train also runs from Bohinjska Bistrica, 6 km (4 miles) east of Lake Bohinj.

Brilliant blue waters at Most na Soči

SIGHTS AT A GLANCE

Villages, Towns and Cities
Bled ❶
Bovec ⓫
Kamnik ⓲
Kamniška Bistrica ⓴
Kanal ⓯
Kobarid ⓬
Kranj ⓰
Kranjska Gora ❼
Radovljica ❹
Tolmin ⓭
Trenta ❾
Tržič ❺
Velika Planina ⓳

Tour
A Tour of the Kamniško-
   Savinjske Alps pp122–3 ㉑

National Park
Triglav National Park
pp112–15 ❻

Areas of Natural Beauty
Pokljuka gorge ❸
Vintgar gorge ❷
Vršič Pass ❽

Resort
Krvavec ⓱

Historical Sites
Kluže Fortress ❿
Most na Soči ⓮

KEY

✈	International airport
═══	Motorway
───	Main road
═ ═	Minor road
⊶⊶	Railway
::::	Road tunnel
::::	Railway tunnel
▬▬	International border
△	Peak

Hikers on a wooden walkway over the river at Vintgar gorge

Vintgar gorge ❷
Soteska Vintgar

Road Map B2. 4 km (2 miles) NW of Bled. **Tel** (04) 572 5266. 🚌 May–Sep: tourist shuttle from Bled. ⏰ late Apr–Oct: 8am–7pm daily. 🅿️ 🚻

Located just north of Bled, Vintgar gorge is a 2-km (1-mile) long ravine carved by the rushing waters of the Radovna river. It was discovered by chance in February 1891 during a period of unusually low water level in the river. The local mayor and a cartographer friend were amazed at the beauty of this usually impass-able ravine and established a committee to construct wooden walkways to cater to the increasing number of visitors to Bled. The gorge became a major tourist attraction as soon as it opened in August 1893.

Visiting the gorge remains an exhilarating experience as the trail winds along sheer cliffs, passing gurgling rapids and whirlpools, criss-crossing the river on bridges. The walkway culminates at the 16-m (52-ft) high Šum waterfall, which marks the northern end of the gorge. The cascade is at its most impressive during spring, when its thundering torrent throws up clouds of spray and even steam on very cold days. From here, Bled is within easy walking distance

via a pretty footpath up Hom hill that leads to the village of Zasip and the 15th-century Church of St Catherine (Cerkev sv Katarine) with good views over the area.

Pokljuka gorge ❸
Pokljuška soteska

Road Map B2. 7 km (4 miles) W of Bled. 🚌 from Bled.

Not as popular as the Vintgar gorge, the 2-km (1-mile) long Pokljuka gorge, which spears into the national park west of Bled, is a destination for more isolated walking in pristine scenery. Although the gorge has some walk-ways, most of the route is along a permanently dry, rough river bed, so walking boots are advisable.

Façade of Šivec House, Radovljica

Other sights in the gorge include the Pokljuka cave (Pokljuška luknja), with a fallen roof that permits light into the cave; and tiny circular fields formed in the limestone depressions, known locally as *vrtci*, meaning little gardens. The prettiest formation is just beyond the ravine's narrowest part.

Access to the gorge is easiest from Krnica village, situated below the pictur-esque centre of the ravine, where the walls rise 40 m (130 ft) high. By bus, the ravine can be accessed along a short woodland path from Krnica. A car park is sign-posted above the village at the entrance of the ravine. Maps of the area are sold at the Bled information centre.

Radovljica ❹

Road Map B2. 5 km (3 miles) SE of Bled. 🏠 18,000. 🚆 from Ljubljana & Kranj. 🚌 from Bled or Kranj. 🛈 Gorenjska cesta 1, (04) 531 5300. 🎷 Classical music (mid Aug). **www**.radovljica.si

The pretty core of Radovljica is one of the Gorenjska region's best-preserved old towns, defensively perched 75 m (246 ft) above the Sava river valley. Cocooned from traffic, Linhartov trg is boxed in by painted Gothic and Renaissance burgher mansions that testify to medieval prosperity. The mansion at No. 23 has a fresco of St Florian dousing a fire in the 18th-century town, while No. 24, the late-Gothic Malijeva House (Malijeva hiša), retains a penalty bench used to chain criminals. The museum and gallery **Šivec House** (Šivečeva hiša) is late-Gothic with Renaissance living quarters.

The square's architectural highlight is the large Thurn Mansion. Built as a ducal castle, then renovated into a palace and given a decorative Baroque façade, it houses the fascinating **Museum of Apiculture** (Čebelarski muzej). Displays of quirky carved bee-hives show, for example, a Turk in bloomers with a treasure casket. A marvellous collection of painted beehive panels helps bring to life this Slovenian folk tradition. A municipal museum on the first floor documents the life of Slovenian dramatist Anton Tomaž Linhart (1756–1795).

Off the square is the late-Gothic Church of St Peter (Cerkev sv Petra). It has a Baroque high altar with a statuary by the architect of St Nicholas's Cathedral, Ljubljana, Angelo Pozzo. The choir stalls have a carved boss depicting Pozzo in a hat and blue tunic.

Environs
Located about 10 km (6 miles) south of Radovljica, Kropa is a blacksmiths' village which, in its 18th-century heyday, had 50 forge waterwheels. The **Iron Forging Museum** (Kovaški muzej) displays wares, and a smithy opposite sells decorative ironwork. The village of Brezje, 8 km (5 miles) south-east of Radovljica, annually hosts about 300,000 pilgrims at the nation's most revered shrine – a miracle-working Madonna and Child painting in the Basilica of the Virgin (Marija Pomagaj).

🏛 Šivec House
Linhartov trg 22. *Tel* (04) 532 0523. ☐ Jun & Sep: 10am–noon & 5–7pm Tue–Sun; Jul–Aug: 10am–noon & 6–8pm Tue–Sun; Oct–May: 10am–noon and 4–6pm Tue–Sun. 🖼 www.muzeji-radovljica.si

🏛 Museum of Apiculture
Linhartov trg 1. *Tel* (04) 532 0520. ☐ Jan–Feb: 8am–3pm Tue–Fri; Mar–Apr & Nov–Dec: 8am–3pm Tue, Thu & Fri, 10am–noon & 3–5pm Wed, Sat & Sun; May–Oct: 10am–6pm Tue–Fri. 🖼 www.muzeji-radovljica.si

🏛 Iron Forging Museum
Kropa 10. *Tel* (04) 533 7200. ☐ Jan–Feb: 8am–3pm Tue–Fri; Mar–Apr & Nov–Dec: 10am–noon & 3–5pm Wed, Sat & Sun, 8am–3pm Tue, Thu & Fri; May–Oct: 10am–6pm Tue–Fri. 🖼 www.muzeji-radovljica.si

Model at the Tržič Museum, dedicated to shoe-making

Tržič ❺

Road Map B2. 23 km (14 miles) E of Bled. 🏔 15,000. 🚌 from Kranj & Radovljica. 🚊 Trg svobode 18, (04) 597 1536. www.trzic.si

Lying just below the foothills on the Austrian border, the riverside town of Tržič was synonymous with the artisan handicrafts of wheel- and shoe-making. Both withered in the face of industrial mass production leaving the town a sleepy one-street place – only carriage-sized portals on the high street, Trg svobode, hint at the booming 18th and 19th centuries.

The modest **Tržič Museum** (Tržiški muzej), located in a former tannery at the upper end of the town, illustrates shoe-making as well as the leatherwork trade that fed it.

Around 3 km (2 miles) north lies the Dovžan gorge (Dovžanova soteska). This narrow ravine is a protected natural monument due to the abundance of Palaeozoic fossils found here, which were laid down when the area was covered by a warm shallow sea. Carved out by the rushing Tržiska Bistrica river, the gorge begins just beyond a road tunnel.

🏛 Tržič Museum
Muzejska ulica 11. ☐ 9am–3pm Mon, Tue, Thu & Fri, 9am–5pm Wed. 🖼

Painted beehive panels in the Museum of Apiculture, Radovljica

PAINTED BEEHIVE PANELS
No folk tradition is more Slovenian than that of painting beehive panels. During the mid 1600s, hives were created as shelf-like units allowing bee-keepers to harvest individual honeycombs without damaging the entire hive. Panels were – and still are – coloured to guide bees home but the practice of painting on to their front panels emerged in the mid 1700s and reached its zenith during the 19th century. Religious motifs and battle scenes are popular, but the jokes and satirical images appeal the most: a hunter carried on a stretcher by his quarry, for example, or the gossip whose tongue is sharpened by the devil.

Triglav National Park ❻
Triglavski narodni park

Established in 1961, Slovenia's only national park is centred on the country's highest mountain, the 2,864-m (9,396-ft) high Triglav. Starkly beautiful outcrops of bare limestone characterize the higher altitudes of the park, while its lower reaches encompass forests of spruce and beech, which are home to a fantastic range of flora and fauna. An outstanding network of picturesque trails, valleys, deep blue lakes and peaks makes Triglav National Park one of the most visited places in the country.

Vršič Pass, a spectacular mountain road cutting through the heart of the park, features an exhilarating sequence of hairpin bends.

Alpinum Juliana
Located on the southern approaches of the Vršič Pass, this lush botanical garden showcases the diverse flora of the Slovenian Alps. About 600 botanical species can be found here.

ITALY

PLANICA VALLEY

TAMAR VALLEY

Kra

Vršič

Strmec

Log pod Mangartom

MLINARICA GORGE

Trenta

Kršovec

Zgornja Bavšica

Soča

206

TRENTA VALLEY

Gre La

Soča

Pristava Lepena

Bla

Kc
1,520 m (4,98

LOWER BOHINJ MO

Krn
2,182 m
(7,159 ft)

Tolm
Rav

Soča Trail
This 20-km (12-mile) long trail runs along the Soča river as it carves its way through the pine-fringed Trenta valley to the tiny hamlet of Kršovec.

0 km   5

0 miles   5

Valley of the Triglav Lakes
One of the park's most captivating sights, this sequence of seven glacial lakes is surrounded by boulders and spruce trees.

Vrata Valley
A classic glacial valley on the northern side of Triglav, Vrata valley is overlooked by towering limestone rock formations.

VISITORS' CHECKLIST

Road Map A2. 26 km (16 miles) W of Bled. ☒ from Bled.
🛈 **Bled** Ljubljanska cesta 27, (04) 578 0200; **Trenta** Na Logu, (05) 3889 330; **Zgornja Radovna** Pocar Farm, Zgornja Radovna 25, (04) 5780 200. 🛈
⛴ at Lake Bohinj, Bled and Kranjska Gora, just outside the park. www.tnp.si

The Radovna cycle route leads visitors through verdant farmland dotted with traditional villages.

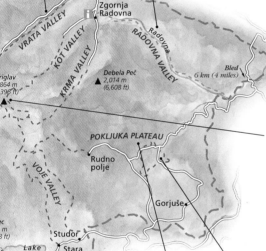

Gozd Martuljek

Zgornja Radovna

VRATA VALLEY

KOT VALLEY

KRMA VALLEY

Radovna

RADOVNA VALLEY

Bled
6 km (4 miles)

Triglav
2,864 m
9,396 ft)

Debela Peč
2,014 m
(6,608 ft)

POKLJUKA PLATEAU

VOJE VALLEY

Rudno polje

Gorjuše

vec
51 m
78 ft)

Studor

Lake Bohinj

Stara Fužina

nc   904

Ribčev Laz

el
2 m (6,306 ft)

Lake Bohinj *(see pp114–115)* is the largest water body in Slovenia.

Triglav
Slovenia's highest peak, Triglav is a national symbol; its three-peaked silhouette appears on the national flag.

The Goreljek Peat-Bog Nature Trail passes through unspoilt wetlands, rich in cranberries, bilberries and the insect-devouring sundew plant.

KEY

🛈	Visitor information
▲	Peak
═	Minor road
- -	Walking trail
- -	Cycle route
▪ ▪	Park boundary
▪–▪	International border

Pokljuka Plateau
This unspoiled area of pine forests and pastures is crisscrossed by nature trails. The highlight is the Pokljuka gorge, which burrows through the plateau's northern flanks.

Triglav National Park: Lake Bohinj

Tucked into the southeastern corner of Triglav National
Park, Lake Bohinj (Bohinjsko jezero) is a beautiful
expanse of water with high mountains on almost all
sides and surrounded by some of Slovenia's best-
preserved rustic villages. Fed by clear mountain streams,
it is ideal for swimming and kayaking and an excellent
base from which to explore the region's hiking trails.
In winter, Vogel, to the south of the lake, is a popular
spot for skiing and snowboarding, while the frozen
lake provides a great opportunity for ice skating.

**Visitors canoeing near Ribčev Laz,
at the eastern end of Lake Bohinj**

Slap Savica
*A popular walking trail west from
Ukanc leads to Slap Savica, a pair of
waterfalls surrounded by high cliffs.
Their waters feed the Sava river,
which flows southeast to meet the
Danube at Belgrade in Serbia.*

Slap Savica
1.5 km (1 mile)

A World War I Cemetery
holds the graves of
about 300 Astro-
Hungarian soldiers
buried between
1915 and 1917.

Savica

UKANC

**The cable car to
Vogel** begins from
the southern
shores of Bohinj.

Vogel
1.5 km (1 mile)

Ukanc
*The small village of Ukanc, at the
lake's western end, has pebbly
beaches and is surrounded by
Komna plateau and Pršivec peak.*

Vogel
*At an altitude of 1,922 m (6,306 ft), the
Vogel resort is a paradise for skiers in winter
and hikers in summer. The cable car from
the shores of Lake Bohinj ascends to a
plateau that offers breathtaking views of the
snow-clad Triglav massif to the north.*

Stara Fužina
*With charming alpine farmhouses, Stara Fužina is one
of the best-preserved traditional villages in western
Slovenia. The 13th-century St Paul's Church on the
outskirts of the village is also worth a visit.*

0 metres   500

0 yards   500

Lake Bohinj

STARA FUŽINA

Church of
St John

RIBČEV
LAZ

Kozolec
*The meadows around
Stara Fužina are
dotted with canopied
hay-drying racks
or* kozolec, *a
common feature of
Slovenian farms.*

The Church of the Holy Spirit
*(Cerkev sv Duha) has a fine
bell tower and contains a
number of notable 15th-
and 16th-century frescoes.*

KEY

	Visitor information
	Parking
	Church
	Cemetery
	Cable car
	Camp site
═	Minor road
–	Trail

Ribčev Laz
*The main settlement at the eastern end of Lake Bohinj,
Ribčev Laz is famous for its dainty parish Church of St John
(Cerkev sv Janeza), which has some late-Gothic frescoes.*

Façade of the traditional Liznjek House, Kranjska Gora

Kranjska Gora ❼

Road Map A2. 39 km (24 miles) NW
of Bled. 👥 5,500. 🚌 from Bled &
Ljubljana. 🛈 Tičarjeva ulica 2; (04)
580 9440. **www**.kranjska-gora.si

Beautifully located in the
Sava Dolinka valley beneath
jagged alpine peaks, Kranjska
Gora is the northern gateway
to the Soča Valley. This former
dairy village was a key supply
base for the Soča Front (see
p119) during World War I.

Since the 1930s it has been
Slovenia's premier winter
sports playground. In early
March, the village hosts the
Vitranc Cup in slalom and
giant slalom for the ski World
Cup. The World Ski-Flying
Championship is held at
Planica, the world's highest
ski-jumping hill, 3 km (2 miles)
to the west. In summer,
Kranjska Gora is a popular
base for hiking in Triglav
National Park (see pp112–115).

Starting at Mojstrana, 13 km
(8 miles) east of Kranjska Gora,
the Triglavska Bistrica walking
trail runs up the ruggedly
beautiful Vrata valley before
reaching the forbidding north
face of Mount Triglav.

The Church of the
Assumption (Cerkev Device
Marije Vnebovzete) on the
town's main square dates
from Kranjska Gora's earliest
days in the 14th century. A
Romanesque bell tower survives from the original building but the church has been
rebuilt in Gothic style and
features fine roof vaulting.

Beyond the church is **Liznjek
House** (Liznjekova domačija),
which provides a glimpse into
the past of this traditional
alpine village. This shingle-
roofed residence of a wealthy
landowner was built in 1781. It
has a brick ground floor and a
smoke-stained "black kitchen".
Traditional furnishings such as
painted trousseau chests and a

grandfather clock in the living
quarters date back to the
1800s, as does the religious
iconography in a tiny bed-
room. The former stables have
displays on local author Josip
Vandot (1884–1944), a popular
children's writer who penned
tales about an inquisitive
shepherd boy called Kekec.

🏠 **Liznjek House**
Borovška cesta 63. **Tel** (04) 588
1999. 🕐 May–Oct: 10am–6pm Tue–
Sat, 10am–5pm Sun; Dec–Apr:
10am–4pm Tue–Fri, 10am–5pm Sat &
Sun. **www**.gornjesavskimuzej.si

Vršič Pass ❽

Road Map A2. 51 km (32 miles)
NW of Bled. 🚌 late Jun–Aug:
from Kranjska Gora & Bovec.
🛈 Tičarjeva ulica 2, Kranjska
Gora; (04) 5889 440. 🖥 ✉

The drive over this 1,611-m
(5,285-ft) high mountain
saddle, with its crisp clear air
and close-up views of cork-
screw peaks, is arguably the
most spectacular in Slovenia.
The route's 50 hairpin bends
are negotiable in most vehicles between May and
October – snowfall can close
the pass at other times, so it
is best to check conditions
in Kranjska Gora or Bovec
(see p118) before attempting
a crossing. The road is
unsuitable at all times if
towing a trailer or caravan.

Originally a shepherds'
track, the road south of
Kranjska Gora was created

Breathtaking view of snow-covered Alps from Vršič Pass

o supply ammunition and
ood to Austro-Hungarian
roops on the Soča Front
luring World War I. Russian
risoners of war who were
ut to the task of building the
oad, suffered hard labour,
tarvation, frostbite and
unstroke. The 13,000 POWs
lso faced avalanches – one
ipped through a work camp
n March 1916 and claimed
round 300 lives. A tiny
Russian chapel (Ruska kapela)
t bend 8, serves as a memo-
ial to the victims. An Austro-
Hungarian military graveyard
ies beneath a hikers' hostel-
estaurant before bend 22.
his remote spot affords good
iews of Prisank mountain.

Sheltered from chilly north
winds, the route downhill is
ess spectacular but provides
occasional sweeping views
down the broad valley. At
end 48 is a monument to
Or Julius Kugy (1858–1944), a
botanist who promoted the
beauty of these mountains
while hunting for new alpine
species. Off the hairpin bend
below, a dirt-track leads to a
ar park from where begins
he 2-km (1-mile) walk to the
ource of the Soča river, a karst
spring that gushes out from a
left and down a rockface to
begin its 136-km (85-mile) long
ourney to the Adriatic Sea.

Trenta ❾

Road Map A2. 64 km (40 miles)
V of Bled. 🚶 115. 🚌 late Jun–
ep: from Kranjska Gora & Bovec.
🛈 Trenta 31; (05) 388 9330.
www.trenta-soca.si

On the banks of the Soča
iver is Trenta – home to
hepherds and lumberjacks.
ts villagers led the first hikers
nto the Julian Alps in the
ate 1800s. A votive plaque
t the northern entrance to
he village commemorates
n injured woodcutter's
ucky rescue by a walker in
891. Just uphill from this,
lovenia's only alpine
otanical garden, the **Alpinum**
uliana (Alpski botanični vrt
uliana), spills down the
illside. The 600-plus alpine
nd karst species found here
epresent the diversity of the

Monument to botanist Julius
Kugy, Vršič Pass

nation's alpine flora. There
are plants from the Julian and
Friuli Alps, the karst region
and pre-alpine meadows as
well as from the Kamnik-
Savinja Alps. The best time to
visit the garden is in May and
early June, when the flowers
are in bloom.

Downhill, in the heart of
the village, **Trenta Lodge**
(Dom Trenta) contains an
excellent information centre
for the Triglav National Park.
It also houses a local museum
on geology and fauna, with
displays on shepherd and
mountaineering traditions,
including a re-creation of a
shepherd's dwelling.

❧ Alpinum Juliana
Trenta. **Tel** (05) 388 9306. ⬚ May–
Sep: 8:30am–6:30pm daily. 📷

🏛 Trenta Lodge
Na Logu vi Trenti. **Tel** (05) 388 9330.
⬚ Apr–Oct: 10am–6pm daily; Dec–
26 Apr: 10am–2pm daily. 📷 ♿
www.trenta-soca.si

Kluže Fortress ❿
Trdnjava Kluže

Road Map A2. Trg golobarskih žrtev
8, Bovec; 84 km (52 miles) W of Bled.
Tel (05) 388 6758. ⬚ May–Jun &
Sep–Oct: 9am–5pm Sun–Fri, 9am–
6pm Sat; Jul–Aug: 9am–8pm daily.
📷 🎭 Music and Theatre Festival
Kluže (late Jul). www.kluze.net

Impressively located
between the Koritnica
gorge and Mount Rombon,
Kluže Fortress is the last
of a number of strongholds
that once guarded the
valley. It is believed that
the Romans originally had
a fort here, which was
supplanted by a wooden
fortress. Today's massively
fortified bastion was built
to serve as a command
post during the Soča Front
campaign (see p119). The
fortress withstood repeated Italian
shelling, protected by its
sheltered location and 2-m
(7-ft) high reinforced walls.

Inside the fortress are
displays on its history and
on the Soča Front. The
courtyard serves as the venue
for mock battles organized
by the Slovene Cultural and
Historical Foundation in July
and August. The gorge of
the Koritnica river forms a
70-m (230-ft) deep natural
moat around the fortress;
the bridge across it affords
breathtaking views of the
Alps and the gorge.

A path off the main road
leads to Fort Hermann, the
twin fortress that was nearly
obliterated during the Soča
Front campaign.

Kluže Fortress against the backdrop of Mount Rombon

Bovec ⓫

Road Map A2. 84 km (52 miles) W
of Bled. 👥 *1,700.* 🚌 *from Tolmin &
Ljubljana; from Kranjska Gora (late
Jun–Aug).* 🚕 *Jul–Aug: 7am–5pm
daily, Sep–Jun: 8am–4pm daily.*
ℹ️ *Trg golobarskih žtrev 22–23, (05)
389 6444.* **www**.bovec.si

Once a dairy centre, Bovec has
transformed into a premier
adrenaline sports destination in
Slovenia mainly because of its
spectacular setting between
high alpine peaks and the
china-blue Soča river.

   Between April and October,
several agencies organize
whitewater rafting, kayaking
and canyoning trips. There are
signposted trails for mountain
biking and a dedicated bike
park; a brochure available in
the tourist office outlines the
routes. In winter the focus is
on Kanin which at 2,300 m
(7,546 ft) is the highest skiing
destination in Slovenia. It can
be reached by a cable car that
also provides access to high-
altitude walking paths in
summer as well as a stunning
view that stretches to the
Adriatic Sea.

   More astounding scenery
lies 6 km (4 miles) south at
the Boka waterfall (Slap Boka)
near Žaga, which plummets
106 m (348 ft) from a cliff.

Kobarid ⓬

Road Map A2. 91 km (57 miles) SW
of Bled. 👥 *1,500.* 🚌 *from Bovec,
Nova Gorica & Ljubljana.* ℹ️ *Trg
svobode 16, (05) 380 0490;
Gregorčičeva 8, (05) 389 0167.*
www.dolina-soce.com

Italian influence can be seen
in Kobarid's shuttered houses,
dusty pastel paintwork and
fine restaurants. Italy occupied
this town between the world
wars and during the battle for
the Soča Front, until the first
blitzkrieg in Europe broke the
stalemate between Italy and
Austro-Hungary.

   The excellent **Kobarid
Museum** (Kobariški muzej), a
block north of the central
square, provides detailed information on the war. Other war
reminders can be seen along
the **Kobarid Historical Walk**

**Boka waterfall plummeting
down a cliff**

(Kobariška zgodovinska pot),
whose 5-km (3-mile) circuit
starts from Trg svobode.

🏛 **Kobarid Museum**
Gregorčičeva 10. ℹ️ *(05) 389 0000.*
⏰ *Apr–Sep: 9am–6pm Mon–Fri,
9am–7pm Sat & Sun; Oct–Mar:
10am–5pm Mon–Fri, 10am–6pm Sat
& Sun.* 🖼 **www**.kobariski-muzej.si

🎣 **Kobarid Historical Walk**
Gregorčičeva 8. ℹ️ *(05) 389 0167.*
⏰ *by appt only.* 🖼 📷
www.potmiru.si

Tolmin ⓭

Road Map A3. 75 km (47 miles) SW
of Bled. 👥 *3,800.* 🚌 *from Bovec,
Nova Gorica & Ljubljana.* ℹ️ *Petra
Skalarja 4, (05) 380 0480.* 🎪 *Metalcamp (mid-Jul), Reggae Riversplash
(mid-Jul).* **www**.dolina-soce.com

This area's administrative
centre, Tolmin warrants a
visit for its absorbing archaeological collection in the
Tolmin Museum.
Displayed on
the first floor are
grave finds, jew-
ellery and pottery that
attest to the presence of
sophisticated prehis-
toric cultures. Some   **Painted Attic cup,**
items were imported,   **Tolmin Museum**
such as an exquisite
Attic cup that has become the
trademark of the museum.

Environs
Located nearby are the Tolmin
gorge (Tolminska korita) and
Dante's Cave (Zadlaška jama).

🏛 **Tolmin Museum**
Mestni trg 4. **Tel** *(05) 381 1360.* 🖼
www.tol-muzej.si

Most na Soči ⓮

Road Map A3. 70 km (44 miles)
SW of Bled. 👥 *240.* 🚉 *from
Bohinjska Bistrica & Nova Gorica.*
🚌 *from Tolmin & Idrija.*

One of the most advanced
prehistoric settlements in
Slovenia developed on this
peninsula created by the confluence of the Soča and Idrija
rivers. Over 7,000 grave sites
from the Bronze and Iron Age
have been excavated, ranking
it among Europe's most important settlements. The Romans
were here too, and an archaeological trail visits the remains
of a Roman villa among its 21
sites. Other sites on this
cultural treasure hunt include a
re-created Bronze Age Hallstatt
dwelling in the local school
(accessed through the Tolmin
Museum) and the Church of
St Lucy (Cerkev sv Lucije).

Kanal ⓯

Road Map A3. 95 km (59 miles) SW
of Bled. 👥 *1,500.* 🚉 *from Nova
Gorica.* 🚌 *from Most na Soči.*
ℹ️ *Pionirska 2, (05) 398 1213.*
🏊 *High Diving World Cup (early Jul).*
www.tic-kanal.si

There is an iconic single-span
bridge that crosses into this
small town, from which
competitors in the High Diving
World Cup plunge 23 m (56 ft)
into the Soča river below. On
the opposite side of the bridge
an archway beside the church
is a post-World War I
rebuild of the
16th-century
original.
   Through this is
the Kontrada court-
yard, the oldest part
of the town, which
began as a castle in
1140 and developed
into a square village
protected by walls and two
gatehouse towers. The tower
on the north side survives and
houses the **Galerija Rika
Debenjaka**, showcasing the
work of Kanal-born 20th-
century artist Riko Debenjak.

🏛 **Galerija Rika Debenjaka**
Pionirska ulica bb. **Tel** *(05) 163 6930.*
⏰ *10am–noon Tue, 5–7pm Fri.*

The Soča Front

In January 1915, in a bid to weaken Austro-Hungary with a war on two fronts, the Allies lured Italy into World War I with the promise of territorial gains. Italy poured 50 per cent of its forces over the border into the Soča Valley in Austro-Hungarian Slovenia. So, the Soča Front (Isonzo in Italian), a 90-km (56-mile) frontline

Medal, Kobarid Museum

extending from Mount Rombon near Bovec to the Adriatic, came into being and witnessed some very brutal fighting. The casualties in the 12 offensives during the 30-month war are estimated to have been around 1.2 million.

After rapid Italian gains, the front stagnated into a war of attrition between two entrenched armies.

THE 12TH OFFENSIVE

On 24 October 1917 the 12th Offensive began. A lightning-fast action routed the Italians near Bovec. The next day the 14th Austro-German army (formed when Austro-Hungarian Emperor Karl I sought help from Germany's Wilhelm II) seized Kobarid and by 28 October, the Italians had been chased back to the Friulian plain, a chaotic retreat described by author Ernest Hemingway, who served on the front, in *A Farewell to Arms*. The "miracle of Kobarid" was one of the most decisive actions in World War I.

Kobarid Museum *displays maps and relief models showing the positions of the troops as well as weapons and other memorabilia.*

Machine gun posts *have been restored to their former positions and can be visited near Bovec and Kobarid.*

KEY

■ Austro-German army

■ Italian army

---- Battlefront

--- International border

Italian troops, *unable to advance, endured two crippling winters on mountains that were barely passable even in summer. The Austro-Hungarian and German forces fared little better due to poor supplies and Italian shelling.*

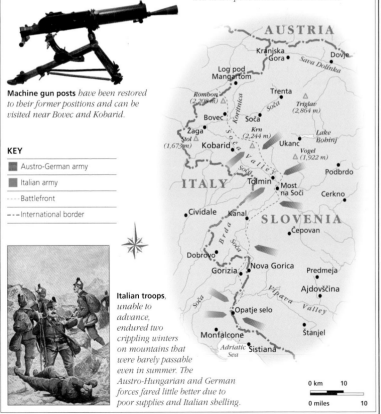

AUSTRIA

Kranjska Gora • Dovje • *Sava Dolinka*
Log pod Mangartom
Rombon (2,208 m) △ Trenta
Soča Triglav (2,864 m)
Bovec • Soča
Žaga Krn (2,244 m) *Lake Bohinj*
Stol △ (1,673 m) Kobarid Ukanc
Vogel △ (1,922 m)
Valley Podbrdo
ITALY Tolmin Most na Soči Cerkno
• Cividale Kanal SLOVENIA
Brda • Čepovan
Dobrovo
Gorizia Nova Gorica Predmeja
Ajdovščina
Vipava Valley
• Opatje selo Štanjel
Monfalcone *Adriatic Sea* Sistiana

0 km   10

0 miles   10

Kranj ⑯

Road Map B3. 27 km (17 miles) SE of Bled. 🏠 *53,000*. 🚉 *from Ljubljana*. 🚌 *from Ljubljana, Bled, Kamnik & Škofja Loka*. 🛈 *Glavni trg 2; (04) 238 0450*. **www**. tourism-kranj.si

The country's fourth largest settlement and an industrial centre, Kranj has an appealing Old Town spread along a promontory, the site of early Celtic and Roman settlements.

Kranj is known for its links with France Prešeren (*see p49*), the most celebrated of Slovenia's poets. The modest residence in which he spent the last three years of his life, **Prešeren House** (Prešernova hiša), contains his personal effects as well as a display dedicated to his muse Julija Primic, the unrequited love of his life.

The heart of the Old Town is Glavni trg. Located on this square is the former city hall, which houses the **Gorenjska Museum** (Gorenjski muzej), with displays on regional archaeology and charming exhibits of folk culture. The museum has a ceremonial Renaissance hall as well as sculptures by the Modernist sculptor Lojze Dolinar (1893–1970), a student of the Croatian sculptor Ivan Meštrovič (1883–1962). Also on the square is the grandest hall church in Slovenia, the Church of St Cantianus and Disciples (Cerkev sv Kancijana in tovarišev). The *Star of Beautiful Angels*, a fresco depicting angels, dating from

Interior of a room in Prešeren House, Kranj

Exterior of the chapel at Little Castle, Kamnik

the 15th century, adorns the ceiling of the nave. The church was built over the country's largest Slavic grave-yard. Visits to the ossuary can be arranged through the Gorenjska Museum.

Off the square is the Church of the Holy Rosary (Roženvenska cerkev) and next to it, a ceremonial stair-case by Jože Plečnik (*see p73*).

🏛 **Gorenjska Museum**
Glavni trg 4. **Tel** (04) 201 3980. ⏰ *10am–6pm Tue–Sun*. 📷 **www**.gorenjski-muzej.si

🏛 **Prešeren House**
Prešernova ulica 7. **Tel** (04) 201 3983. ⏰ *10am–6pm Tue–Sun*. 📷

Krvavec ⑰

Road Map C2. 59 km (37 miles) SE of Bled. 🚠 *winter: 8am–5pm daily; summer: 7am–5pm Mon–Fri, 8am–6pm Sat & Sun*. 🛈 *Grad 76; (04) 252 5911*. 🍴 💻 ☕ **www**.rtc-krvavec.si

Its proximity to Ljubljana and Kranj ensures that this ski destination, located on the 1,853-m (6,079-ft) high Krvavec mountain, is one of the busiest in Slovenia. Access to the mountain summit, marked by a tall radio antenna, is by cable car from a small ski resort at

Gospinca at an altitude of 1,480 m (4,856 ft). It can be reached on a narrow twisting road, or, during snowfall, by a cable car north of Cerklje. From Gospinca, marked trails ascend to the summit; the blue, 3-km (2-mile) long Path of History (Poti zgodovine) takes visitors past a modern chapel and the excavated site of a 10th-century settlement. The mountain is also popular in summer due to the good walking and mountain-biking opportunities it affords.

Kamnik ⑱

Road Map C3. 52 km (32 miles) SE of Bled. 🏠 *26,600*. 🚉 *from Ljubljana*. 🚌 *from Ljubljana & Kranj*. 🛈 *Glavni trg 2; (01) 831 8250*. 📅 *Tue & Sat*. 🎭 *Medieval Days (2nd weekend of Jun), Kamfest (mid-Aug), National Costumes Festival (2nd weekend of Sep)*. **www**.kamnik-tourism.si

This pleasing old-fashioned town was a regional capital in the Middle Ages. The Franciscan Monastery (Frančiškanski samostan) off Glavni trg, the town's main square, has a library that houses a rare copy of the Bible (1584) by the Slovenian translator Jurij Dalmatin (1547–1589); visits can be arranged through the tourist office. The attached Baroque Church of St James (Cerkev sv Jakoba) houses the **Chapel of the Holy Sepulchre** (Kapela Božjega groba), which was created in 1952 by Jože Plečnik and is full of motifs of Resurrection.

Perched atop the rocky hillock at the end of Glavni trg is the so-called **Little Castle** (Mali grad). All that remains of this fortification, first documented in 1202, is a two-storeyed chapel. Its portal bears a Romanesque carving of angels and a crucifix, but the architecture within is Gothic and adorned with restored Baroque frescoes. Another reason to visit the chapel is the panorama it affords over Kamnik, up to the Kamniško-Savinjske Alps.

Šutna, the town's main street and Kamnik's former medieval thoroughfare, ends beneath the **Intermunicipal Kamnik Museum** (Medobčinski muzej Kamnik). The museum has displays of archaeological finds, memorabilia of the 19th-century bourgeoisie and bentwood furniture from a local factory. Outside the museum is a lapidarium with specimens of traditional granaries from the Tuhinj valley.

Environs
Volčji Potok Arboretum, 4 km (2 miles) south of Kamnik and en route to Radomlje, is Slovenia's finest botanical park. Its 88 ha (218 acres) are beautifully and creatively landscaped in a number of gardening styles.

🏠 **Little Castle**
Glavni trg. ⏰ mid-Jun–mid-Sep: 9am–noon & 2–7pm daily. 📷

🏛 **Intermunicipal Kamnik Museum**
Muzejska pot 3. **Tel** (01) 831 7662. 🔴 Mon. 📷 www.muzej-kamnik-on.net

🌺 **Volčji Potok Arboretum**
Volčji Potok 3. **Tel** (01) 831 2345. 🔴 during snowfall. ⏰ summer only. 📷 🖥 www.arboretum-vp.si

View of the forest and the Kamniška Bistrica river

Velika Planina ⑲

Road Map C2. 76 km (47 miles) E of Bled. 🚌 from Kamnik. 🚠 open daily. 🛈 Kamniška Bistrica 2; (01) 832 7258. 🍴 🖥 📷 🔺 www.velikaplanina.si

The world's fourth longest unsupported cable car, which starts midway up the Kamniška Bistrica valley, provides access to the 1,666-m (5,466-ft) high Velika Planina. This mountain plateau is the best destination from which to get a sense of the Kamniško-Savinjske Alps.

Velika Planina is a popular destination for skiing in winter and walking in summer. During summer the local herdsmen migrate to their picturesque settlements to graze cattle on the plateau's lush alpine meadows. Most of the unique, shingle-roofed

Altar at the Chapel of the Holy Sepulchre

wooden huts were rebuilt after they were destroyed during World War II – the Germans suspected that this area was a base for resistance fighters. **Preskar's Hut** (Preskarjev stan), which survived the onslaught, has been preserved as a museum. It is located about an hour's walk south of the upper cable car terminal, near the Church of Our Lady of the Snows (Kapela Marije Snežne).

🏛 **Preskar's Hut**
Kamniška Bistrica 2. ⏰ Jul–Aug: 10am–4pm Sat & Sun. 📷

Kamniška Bistrica ⑳

Road Map C2. 65 km (40 miles) E of Bled. 🚌 from Kamnik. 🛈 Tomšičeva 23, 1240 Kamnik; (01) 831 8250. 🍴 📷

Around 4 km (2 miles) north of the lower cable car station to Velika Planina, the Kamniška Bistrica river valley terminates in a stupendous amphitheatre of Alps that are over 2,000 m (6,561 ft) high. Serious hikers can ascend from the car park at the terminal through pine woods and climb up to the saddles that lie between the jagged summits. A short walk takes visitors to the Orglice waterfall (slap Orglice), which falls 30 m (98 ft) from a cleft. A similar walk leads to a woodland hunting lodge, known as Plečnik's Mansion (Plečnikov dvorec), built in 1932 for the Yugoslav King Aleksander I by Jože Plečnik.

Shingle-roofed herdsmen's huts, Velika Planina

A Tour of the Kamniško-Savinjske Alps ㉒

Sculpture, Gornji Grad

As the road twists uphill east of Kamnik, the farming villages and agricultural landscapes of the Dreta valley give way to alpine settlements in the valley on the northern side of the Kamniško-Savinjske Alps. Off its upper reaches are two of the most beautiful alpine valleys in Slovenia – Robanov kot and Logarska dolina – each enclosed by a jagged wall of peaks. Logarska dolina literally means Loggers' Valley, referring to the timber industry, which, along with farming, was the main livelihood of the people of the valley. Today, tourism is the area's largest industry.

Rinka waterfall ⑧
A footpath from the car park at the head of the valley leads to this 80-m (262-ft) high waterfall.

AUSTRIA

Solčava

428

KAMNIŠKO-SAVINJSKE A

⑦ P i

⑥

Logarska dolina ⑦
Lush meadows, speckled by wildflowers and clear rivers, backdropped by a wall of the Alps at its head, make this U-shaped valley one of the most picturesque.

⑧ P   ▲ Ojstrica
2,350 m

KEY

▬▬	Tour route
═══	Other road
i	Visitor information
P	Parking
✲	Viewpoint
▲	Peak
–·–	International border

Robanov kot ⑥
Accessed only via footpaths, this alpine valley, with steep wooded slopes framing the 2,350-m (7,710-ft) high Ojstrica mountain, is popular with walkers who seek unspoilt nature.

Snow Cave ⑤
Visitors carry carbide lamps to view the ancient limestone features and ice formations, preserved year long because of very low temperatures, inside this cave in Raduha mountain. Access to the cave is via a forest road.

Gornji Grad ①
The main attractions in this small town are the Cathedral of Sts Hermagor and Fortunat, and the summer residence of the Ljubljana bishops. The latter houses an ethnographic museum displaying old religious books.

Radmirje ②
This is a pretty agricultural village known for its traditional *kozolci* haystacks and the Church of St Francis Xavier. Its treasury contains a golden chalice donated by the 18th-century Habsburg Empress Maria-Teresa and mantles gifted by Polish and French royalty.

TIPS FOR DRIVERS

Starting point: Gornji Grad
Length: 40 km (25 miles).
Duration: 2 hours; allow half a day each to walk around Robanov kot and Logarska dolina.
Driving conditions: the roads are narrow and winding but well signposted.
Stopping-off points: there are restaurants and cafés in the towns, and a tourist office in Luče ob Savinji.
Visitor Information: Logarska dolina 9, (03) 838 9004, **www.** logarska-dolina.si

Ljubno ob Savinji ③
Until as late as the 1950s, Ljubno ob Savinji, located at the confluence of the Ljubnica and Savinja rivers, maintained a tradition of *flosarji* (rafters) who navigated felled logs to markets as far afield as Hungary. A small museum documents the tradition's history, with displays on how the rafters lived while afloat.

Luče ob Savinji ④
A small town in the upper Savinja valley, Luče ob Savinji is where most of the local administrative infrastructure, including a bank, supermarkets, cafés and an outstanding inn, is located.

Snow covered peaks of Mount Triglav ▷

COASTAL SLOVENIA AND THE KARST

S *lovenia is often described as a transitional zone between Mediterranean and alpine Europe. This is most apparent in southwestern Slovenia, where the craggy ridges and highland meadows of the limestone plateau, known as the karst, descend suddenly to meet a lush coastal strip rich in olive groves, palms as well as a number of important historic towns.*

Western Slovenia has long been the meeting point of Slav and Italian cultures. The region's inclusion in Slovenia was largely the result of the partisan struggles of World War II and memories of the Communist-led liberation movement are still cherished. War memorials are an important feature of regional towns and many streets and squares still named after partisan heroes. Many Italian speakers left the coastal towns when they were awarded to Slovenia after World War II, but Italian is the official language and street signs are bilingual.

The region's arid sunny climate produces some of Slovenia's best-known wines, including the famous crisp white wines from the Goriška Brda and Vipava regions, and the sharp red teran from the coast. The spectacular mix of cultural influences is evident in the food as well, with menus fusing seafood from the Adriatic with truffles, mushrooms and home-cured ham, *pršut* from the inland towns and villages.

Slovenia's short Adriatic coastline is packed with variety. Historic ports such as Koper and Piran, which were ruled by Venice for five centuries, still bear that city's architectural imprint. Nearby, Portorož is Slovenia's prime beach resort, offering boisterous nightlife in summer and soothing spa tourism the whole year round. Inland, the karst region is riddled with gorges and caverns, of which the renowned show-caves at Postojna and Škocjan are the most visited. A dramatically situated castle at Predjama, mercury mines at Idrija and the white horses of Lipica add to the broad palette of attractions.

Terraced vineyards in the Goriška Brda wine-making region

◁ Boats moored in the harbour at the Adriatic seaport of Izola

Exploring Coastal Slovenia and the Karst

Ranging from limestone plateaux to vine-covered slopes and from hilltop villages to coastal towns, southwestern Slovenia offers a diverse landscape to its many visitors. Koper, a bustling city with a well-preserved medieval Old Town at its heart, is the main centre of the region. All of the coast's attractions, especially the evocative, peninsular towns of Izola and Piran, are within easy reach of the city. Just inland are some of Slovenia's most compelling day-trip attractions such as Štanjel, Lipica and the Škocjan and Postojna caves. Equally perfect for touring are the country roads of the Vipava valley and the Goriška Brda hills, both important wine-producing regions. Roads in the Goriška Brda and northern karst regions are particularly scenic, winding their way around hills or following meandering rivers.

SIGHTS AT A GLANCE

Villages, Towns and Cities
Ajdovščina **14**
Ankaran **6**
Cerkno **20**
Hrastovlje **8**
Idrija **19**
Ilirska Bistrica **32**
Izola **5**
Koper pp134–5 **7**
Lipica **10**
Lokev **9**
Nova Gorica **17**
Piran pp130–31 **1**
Portorož **2**
Sečovlje **4**
Sežana **11**
Štanjel **16**
Vipava **13**
Vipavski križ **15**

Castles
Predjama Castle pp148–9 **22**
Snežnik Castle **30**

Tour
A Tour of the Goriška Brda Region p145 **18**

Parks
Pivka Park of Military History **25**
Rakov Škocjan Regional Park **27**

Areas of Natural Beauty
Cape Seča **3**
Križna Cave **29**
Lake Cerknica **28**
Pivka Cave **24**
Planina Cave **26**
Postojna Caves pp150–51 **23**
Reka river valley **33**
Škocjan Caves pp138–9 **12**
Snežnik Plateau **31**

Sites of Interest
Franja Partisan Hospital **21**

Holy Trinity Chuch in Hrastovlje

SEE ALSO
• *Where to Stay pp192–4*
• *Where to Eat pp207–9*

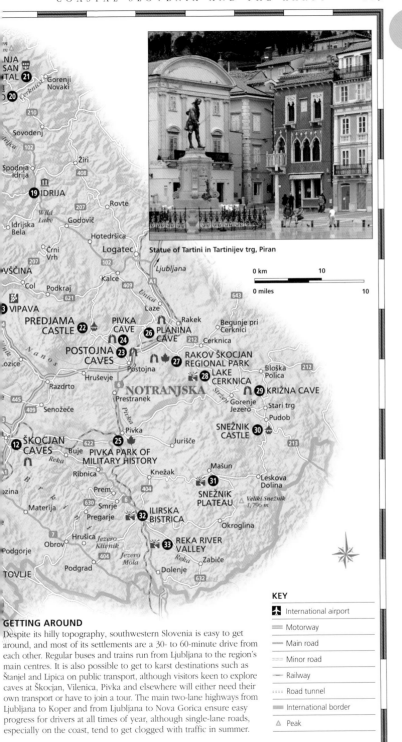

NJA
SAN
TAL **21**
20

Gorenji
Novaki

`210`

Sovodenj

`102`

Žiri
`408`

Spodnja
Idrija

🏛 **19** IDRIJA
`207`
Rovte

Wild
Lake
Idrijska
Bela
Godovič
Hotedršica

Črni
Vrh
Logatec

Statue of Tartini in Tartinijev trg, Piran

VŠČINA
`207`
Col
Podkraj
`621`

Kalce
`409`

Ljubljana
A1

Unica

`643`

0 km   10

0 miles   10

3 VIPAVA

PREDJAMA
CASTLE **22**

N a n o s

ozice

PIVKA
CAVE
24

26 PLANINA
CAVE

Laze

Rakek

Begunje pri
Čerknici

`212` Cerknica

POSTOJNA **23**
CAVES

Postojna

RAKOV ŠKOCJAN
27 REGIONAL PARK

Bloška
Polica
`212`

HrušEvje

Razdrto
`445`

`6`

28 LAKE
CERKNICA

29 KRIŽNA CAVE

`409` Senožeče

NOTRANJSKA

Prestranek

Pivka

Gorenje
Jezero

Stari trg

Strzen

Pudob

12 ŠKOCJAN
CAVES

`622`

Buje
Reka

25
PIVKA PARK OF
MILITARY HISTORY

Jurišče

SNEŽNIK **30**
CASTLE

`213`

Pivka

Ribnica

ozina
B

Knežak

Mašun

31

Leskova
Dolina

Materija

Prem

`630` Smrje

`404`

`6`

SNEŽNIK
PLATEAU

Veliki Snežnik
△ 1,796 m

Pregarje

32
ILIRSKA
BISTRICA

Okroglina

`7`

Hrušica Jezero
Klivnik

33 REKA RIVER
VALLEY

Obrov
`404`

Jezero
Mola

Reka Zabiče

Podgorje

Podgrad

Dolenje
`632`

TOVLJE

KEY

✈	International airport
═══	Motorway
───	Main road
═ ═ ═	Minor road
┅┅	Railway
┄┄┄	Road tunnel
▬▬▬	International border
△	Peak

GETTING AROUND

Despite its hilly topography, southwestern Slovenia is easy to get around, and most of its settlements are a 30- to 60-minute drive from each other. Regular buses and trains run from Ljubljana to the region's main centres. It is also possible to get to karst destinations such as Štanjel and Lipica on public transport, although visitors keen to explore caves at Škocjan, Vilenica, Pivka and elsewhere will either need their own transport or have to join a tour. The main two-lane highways from Ljubljana to Koper and from Ljubljana to Nova Gorica ensure easy progress for drivers at all times of year, although single-lane roads, especially on the coast, tend to get clogged with traffic in summer.

Piran ●

Cherub on the fountain

A delightful warren of pastel-coloured houses squeezed on to a small peninsula, Piran represents coastal Slovenia at its most charming. It has largely preserved its medieval street plan, with narrow alleys emerging into unexpected squares. A walled town with a grand cathedral, Piran's wealth was built on the salt produced at Sečovlje *(see pp132–3)* and shipped to Venice. Piran became part of Slovenia in 1954 and a majority of the Italian-speaking population left town, to be replaced by Slovenians from the interior. Long an important port, the town retains a few fishing boats and some excellent seafood restaurants.

Tartinijev trg with St George's Cathedral in the background

🎠 Tartinijev trg

Piran is centred around the oval-shaped Tartinijev trg, which occupies the former inner harbour *(mandrač)*. The harbour was filled in at the end of the 19th century to free the town of the stench of stagnant water, and the resulting space was named after local-born violinist and composer, Giuseppe Tartini (1692–1770). The square's focal point is the 19th-century statue by Venetian artist Antonio dal Zotto portraying the composer with a violin bow, as if addressing an audience of students.

On the western side of the square is the Neo-Renaissance Town Hall (Občinska palača), built in 1879. The building's four Corinthian columns are decorated with cherubs holding garlands. Jutting out on to the square's northern side is the wine-red 14th-century Venetian House

(Benečanka hiša), boasting delicate Gothic windows and a balustraded, L-shaped balcony with stone-carved human and animal heads.

Nearby, the Neo-Classical St Peter's Church (Cerkev sv Petra) contains a 14th-century crucifix that shows Jesus nailed to an unusual fork-shaped cross thought to symbolize the Tree of Life.

🏛 Tartini House

Kajuhova 12. **Tel** (05) 663 3570.
◯ *Jun–Aug: daily; Sep–May: Tue–Sun.* 🖾

Tucked away in a small plaza north of Tartinijev trg, Tartini House (Tartinijeva hiša) has a modest collection of the composer's heirlooms, including one of his violins. Also on display are Tartini's death mask, old musical scores, letters as well as artworks that were inspired by Tartini's music.

🏛 Piran Art Gallery

Tartinijev trg 3. **Tel** (05) 671 2080. **Herman Pečarič Gallery** Cankarjevo nabrežje. ◯ *Jun–Aug: 5–10pm Tue–Sat, 8–10pm Sun; Sep–May: 11am–5pm Tue–Sat, 11am–1pm Sun.* **www**.obalne-galerije.si Located just off the square, the Piran Art Gallery (Obalne galerije Piran), with a regular programme of exhibitions by local and international artists, is one of the best places to see contemporary art in south-western Slovenia.

A branch of the gallery is located a short distance south of Tartinijev trg in the **Herman Pečarič Gallery**, housed in a beautifully restored late 19th-century house. The gallery's schedule of contemporary exhibitions is augmented by a display of paintings and graphics bequeathed to the town by local artist Herman Pečarič (1908–81), best known for his Istrian landscapes and seascapes.

🔓 St George's Cathedral

Adamičeva ulica. **Tel** (05) 673 3440.
◯ *10am–5pm Wed–Mon.* 🖾 🖾
Narrow streets climb uphill from Tartinijev trg towards St George's Cathedral (Stolna cerkev sv Jurija), a single-nave structure begun in 1641. It has splendid side altars that feature several depictions of St George by Venetian Baroque painters. The church can be accessed via a passageway from the small Parish Museum (Župnijski muzej) in the baptistery. The museum displays the church silverware,

Interior of the 17th-century St George's Cathedral

including an 18th-century statuette of St George studded with semi-precious stones.

Topped by a statue of the Archangel Michael, the church's free-standing campanile is a faithful copy of that in St Mark's Cathedral in Venice.

🏰 Town Wall
Adamičeva ulica. ◻ daily. 🎫
A steep walk uphill from the cathedral is a 200-m (660-ft) long stretch of the Town Wall, built in 1470. Visitors can scale the gate tower and walk along a stretch of the parapet, which offers a sumptuous panorama of the town and surrounding coast.

🏛 Prvomajski trg
Northwest of Tartinijev trg is a maze of alleys and a trio of minor squares, of which the largest, Prvomajski trg, has an elaborate Baroque fountain. Built in 1776 on top of the town's balustraded cistern, the fountain is fronted by an imposing pair of statues symbolizing Law and Justice. A stone cherub holding an amphora stands on one corner of the balustrade. The guttering of a nearby house is fed into pipes that point down towards the cherub, so that rainwater from the gutter gushes out of the amphora.

Display of diving suits at the Museum of Underwater Activities

🐟 Piran Aquarium
Kidričevo nabrežje 4. **Tel** (05) 673 2572. ◻ daily. 🎫
Located beside the harbour is the Piran Aquarium (Akvarij Piran), with a large selection of fish and crustaceans indigenous to the Adriatic. A large tank has shark, grey mullet and sea bass swimming freely. Colourful, well labelled and educational, it is ideal for children to visit.

🏛 Sergej Mašera Maritime Museum
Cankarjevo nabrežje 3. **Tel** (05) 671 0040. ◻ Tue–Sun. 🎫 www.pommuz-pi.si
On the southeastern side of the harbour, this museum (Pomorski muzej Sergej

VISITORS' CHECKLIST
Road Map A5. 120 km (75 miles) SW of Ljubljana. 👥 16,000. 🚌 from Koper & Portorož. ℹ️ Tartinijev trg 2; (05) 673 4440. 🎉 Piran Salt Festival (early May). 📧 Mon–Fri. www.portoroz.si

Mašera) recounts the town's history as a trading centre and fishing port. Many exhibits are displayed in glass-covered compartments on the floor.

The museum is dedicated to Yugoslav Navy Lieutenant Sergej Mašera, who drowned in April 1941 when he destroyed his ship off the Croatian coast to prevent it from falling into enemy hands.

🏛 Museum of Underwater Activities
Župančičeva 24. **Tel** (04) 168 5379. ◻ Jun–Sep: daily; Oct–May: Fri–Sun. 🎫 www.muzejpodvodnihdejavnosti.si
The small but absorbing collection in this museum (Muzej podvodnih dejavnosti) is dedicated to the history of diving in the Adriatic Sea, exhibiting deep-sea diving suits and helmets. A section is devoted to underwater warfare, with models of submarines and the uniforms of their crews on display.

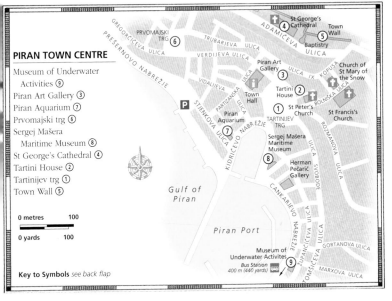

PIRAN TOWN CENTRE

Museum of Underwater Activities ⑨
Piran Art Gallery ③
Piran Aquarium ⑦
Prvomajski trg ⑥
Sergej Mašera Maritime Museum ⑧
St George's Cathedral ④
Tartini House ②
Tartinijev trg ①
Town Wall ⑤

0 metres 100
0 yards 100

Key to Symbols see back flap

Portorož ➋

Road Map A5. 2 km (1 mile) SE of Piran. 🏙 *3,000.* ✈ 🚌 *from Koper, Ljubljana & Piran.* 🛈 *Obala 16; (05) 674 0231.* **www**.portoroz.si

Draped along a curve of Piran Bay, Portorož is Slovenia's biggest and most stylish beach resort. Despite the presence of a grand Habsburg-era hotel – the Kempinski Palace, built in 1911 (*see p194*) – most of Portorož dates from the post-World War II period; a number of modern hotels, cafés and casinos border the palm-lined main boulevard. There is a large crescent of beach made up of imported sand – there are no naturally sandy beaches on this part of the Adriatic. Boutiques selling major fashion labels and jewellery cater to an increasingly upmarket clientele.

As well as being very busy in summer, Portorož is a popular spa resort throughout the year, thanks to a warm microclimate and the therapeutic qualities of the local seawater. The **Portorož Auditorium** (Avditorij) has a year-round programme of music, drama and film, and in summer, stages concerts in its outdoor amphitheatre.

🎭 **Portorož Auditorium**
Senčna pot 10. **Tel** (05) 676 6777.
www.avditorij.si

Black-winged stilt at the beautiful Sečovlje Salt-pan Nature Park

Cape Seča ➌
Rt Seča

Road Map A5. 5 km (2 miles) SE of Piran. 🚌 *from Portorož.*

Dominating the horizon south of Portorož is Cape Seča, a hilly peninsula with holiday cottages, vineyards and olive groves. The olive-covered western flanks of the cape provide stunning views of the Sečovlje salt pans, which fill the bay that forms the border between Slovenia and Croatia.

A path leads around the cape from the southern side of Portorož's yachting marina on to an open stretch of seafront beneath grey-brown cliffs. Just beyond the cape's western-pointing tip is the Cactus Garden (Vrt kaktusov),

a privately owned collection of prickly plants that is open to the public during the summer months. Another route from Portorož goes over the ridge of the cape, passing **Forma Viva**, an open-air sculpture park. The park features over 130 works, many of which are strikingly abstract.

🏛 **Forma Viva**
Seča. **Tel** (05) 671 2080.
www.obalne-galerije.si

Sečovlje ➍

Road Map A5. 9 km (6 miles) SE of Piran. 🏙 *590.* 🚌 *from Portorož.*
www.kpss.soline.si

A small village just short of the Croatian border, Sečovlje is famous for the salt pans that stretch across the neighbouring Gulf of Piran. This arrestingly beautiful manmade grid of shallow pools is important both as a wildlife sanctuary and an industrial heritage site. Although salt extraction still takes place in a section of the pans, since 2001 they have been protected under the the Sečovlje Salt-pan Nature Park (Krajinski park Sečoveljske soline).

The main entrance to the park is at the northern end of the pans and is easy to reach on foot or by bike from

Visitors enjoying themselves at Portorož's popular promenade

For hotels and restaurants in this region see pp192–4 and pp207–9

Portorož. From the entrance, a dyke-top path leads towards the visitors' centre, which has a display on conservation issues. A second entrance at the southern end of the salt pans is by the Croatian border – the access road is in a no-man's land between the Slovene and Croatian frontier posts. This leads to the **Sečovlje Salt Museum** (Sečoveljske muzej), located in one of the blocks where seasonal workers used to live.

A unique area of man-made wetland, the pans are home to flora typical of salty marshland environments, and also serve as an important stop-off for migrating birds in spring and autumn. Nesting species include the yellow-legged gull, the common tern and the Kentish plover; white egrets often visit the area to hunt.

🏛 **Sečovlje Salt Museum**
Sečovlje. *Tel* (05) 671 0040. ⏰ Jun–Aug: 9am–8pm daily; May, Sep & Oct: 9am–6pm daily. ⏰ Nov–Apr. 📷 💻 www.pommuz-pi.si

Izola ❺

Road Map A5. 11 km (7 miles) NE of Piran. 🏠 14,600. 🚌 from Koper. ℹ Sončno nabrežje 4; (05) 640 1050. 🎬 Kino Otok Film Festival (Jun). www.izola.eu

A lively fishing port squeezed on to a thumb-shaped peninsula, Izola is a typical Mediterranean town of narrow alleys, shuttered windows and potted palms. It is one of the most pleasant spots in Slovenia for a sea-side stroll, with its horseshoe-shaped harbour bordered by seafront gardens fragrant with lavender, sage and rosemary. Stretched around the peninsula's northern end are a sequence of concrete bathing platforms, each boasting views across the bay towards Koper and Trieste.

Dominating the high ground at the heart of the peninsula is the Church of St Maurus (Cerkev sv Mavra), with a striped orange-and-cream façade and a free-standing belfry. Below the church is the former palace of the Besenghi degli Ughi family, sporting

Sail boats docked in the scenic harbour of Izola

fancy wrought-iron window grilles and a stone balustrade adorned with carvings of human faces. It is now a music school.

Hidden in the alleys of the Old Town is the **Parenzana Railway Museum** (Muzej Ozkotirne Železnice Parenzana), celebrating the narrow-gauge railway line that once ran through Izola from Trieste in Italy to Poreč in Croatia. Closed in 1937, the Parenzana is remembered through old photographs and a model of a short stretch of the line displayed in the museum. The museum's collection of model locomotives recalls the days when the Izola-based toy manufacturer Mehanotehnika, active from

1954 to 2008, produced train sets that were very popular with children across the former Yugoslavia. Today the railway line serves as a foot- and cycle-path.

🏛 **Parenzana Railway Museum**
Alme Vivoda 3. ⏰ 9am–3pm Mon–Fri. 📷

Ankaran ❻

Road Map A4. 28 km (17 miles) NE of Piran. 🏠 3,000. 🚌 from Koper. ℹ Jadranska cesta 25;. (05) 652 0444. www.koper.si

Hugging the slopes of the Mirje peninsula just across the bay from Koper, the quiet settlement of Ankaran grew around a former Benedictine monastery, which was abandoned in 1641 after a plague. It became a hotel and campsite in the 1920s.

A huddle of holiday villas were subsequently built among the coastal pines and cypresses. Ankaran is a good base for undemanding coastal walks, with paths leading west towards Debeli Rt, a rugged cape made up of stone plates and boulders. Alternatively, the well-signposted Bebler Mountain Path (Beblerjeva planinska pot) climbs inland from the town's centre to the ridgetop village of Hrvatini, passing through olive groves, vineyards and pine forest.

SALT PANS OF SEČOVLJE

Sečovlje has been known for salt production since the Middle Ages, although it was only in the 19th century that it became the region's main industry. Dykes were constructed across the bay, creating shallow pans in which seawater would evaporate, leaving pure salt crystals. The salt was then raked into piles and loaded on to barrows, before being exported all over the Mediterranean. Traditionally, the salt-harvesting season lasted from St George's Day on 23 April to St Bartholomew's Day on 24 August, when many families from the Piran region would converge on the salt pans to work until the harvest was over. The pans were neglected during the Communist period and the quality of the salt declined. Today, Sečovlje salt under the brand-name Piranske soline *(see p93)* make popular gastronomic souvenirs.

View of the salt pans

Koper ❼

Now Slovenia's main port, Koper began as a small Roman settlement known as Insula Caprea (Goat Island). It became a major trading centre under the Venetian Empire, and boasts an attractive Old Town rich in Venetian-influenced architecture. The city was home to a largely Italian-speaking population until it became part of Slovenia in 1954. The Italian heritage remains ever-present, street signs are bilingual and many of the locals speak Italian. Modern Koper is girdled with industrial zones and modern shopping centres, although the city centre remains a real historical gem, with an enjoyable network of medieval, pedestrianized streets at its heart.

🏛 Titov trg
Galerija Loža ⬜ 11am–5pm Tue–Sat, 11am–1pm Sun.

Many of central Koper's narrow alleyways meet at Tito Square, home to some spectacular historical buildings. The most eye-catching is the Praetorian Palace (Pretorska palača), a striking example of Venetian-Gothic style. Embedded in the façade are the coats of arms of leading Koper families and busts of prominent city administrators. Opposite the palace is the 15th-century Loggia, boasting Venetian-Gothic windows and a 16th-century statue of the Virgin and Child. Its ground-floor arcade is now a café. A side door leads to the first-floor **Galerija Loža**, a gallery for contemporary artists.

Detail on Loggia

🏛 Cathedral of the Assumption
Titov trg. **City Bell Tower** ⬜ 10am–1pm Sat & Sun.

On the eastern side of Titov trg is the Cathedral of the Assumption (stolnica Marijinega vnebovzetja), a pleasing amalgam of Romanesque and Baroque elements. On the right side of the transept is an animated painting of the *Virgin and Child Accompanied by Saints*, attributed to the Venetian painter Carpaccio, who is thought to have lived in Koper for some time. Hidden behind the main altar is the medieval sarcophagus of local protector St Nazarius, with an effigy of the saint on the lid. One side of the slab has a delicately carved relief of Nazarius holding a model of Koper, complete with city walls and cathedral spire. Slightly away from the cathedral is the Venetian-style **City Bell Tower**, a medieval defensive tower that was turned into a belfry in the 15th century. Steep steps lead up to a bird's-eye view of the city centre. Behind the cathedral is a 12th-century rotunda that was originally a baptistry.

🏛 Fontico
Trg Brolo.

One of the Old Town's most characterful buildings is the Fontico. A 15th-century grain warehouse, it is now occupied by municipal offices. The Fontico's busy exterior is studded with the crests of local merchant families, many bearing intriguing decorative details such as birds of prey and bare-breasted nymphs. Next door is the plain ochre Church of St Jacob (Cerkev sv Jakoba), a simple 14th-century Gothic structure.

De Ponte Fountain
Prešernov trg.

The delightfully elaborate Fontana da Ponte is located at one of the prettiest small squares in the Old Town's southern end. Dating from 1666, the fountain's octagonal base is spanned by an arch in the form of a balustraded bridge. On the southern end of the square is the Muda

View of the red-tiled roofs in Koper's main square, with the harbour in the background

For hotels and restaurants in this region see pp192–4 and pp207–9

Prešernov trg with the De Ponte Fountain

Gate, a 16th-century archway with reliefs of the city's official symbol – a fiery-tongued sun with a smiling face.

🏛 Regional Museum

Kidričeva 19. **Tel** (05) 663 3570.
◯ *9am–5pm Tue–Fri, 9am–1pm Sat & Sun.*

Occupying the Belgramoni-Tacco Palace, the Regional Museum (Pokrajinski muzej) hosts a rich collection of fossils, archaeological finds and medieval stonework including several carved beasts salvaged from crumbling medieval churches. Overlooking the staircase are 17th-century portraits of the local Tarsi family. Paintings on display upstairs include a panorama of Koper in the 1600s, showing the salt pans that once surrounded the town, and a copy of the *Dance of Death* fresco from the Holy Trinity Church, Hrastovlje *(see p136).* Exhibitions of historical interest are held in the Muzejska galerija, two doors further down the street.

🚇 Taverna

Carpacciov trg.
The western entrance to the Old Town is marked by the Taverna, a buttressed stone structure with open arches on each side. Originally a salt-storage warehouse, the building gets its name from the number of inns that were once clustered around it. It is now a venue for summer concerts. Diagonally opposite the Taverna is the market area.

🏛 Ethnographic Collection

Gramšijev trg 4. **Tel** (05) 663 3570.
◯ *May–Sep: 10am–6pm Tue–Fri, 9am–1pm Sat.*

Surrounded by an atmospheric maze of alleys, the Ethnographic Collection (Etnološka zbirka) fills a beautifully restored Venetian-Gothic house. The displays include utensils, costumes, dry-stone construction techniques of the karst and a re-creation of a typical 19th-century kitchen.

Exhibit on the ground floor of Koper's Regional Museum

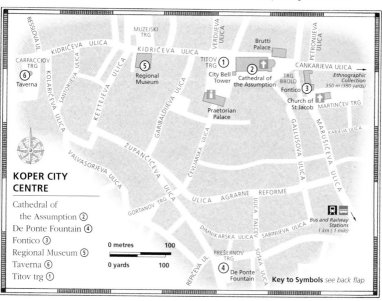

KOPER CITY CENTRE

0 metres   100
0 yards   100

Key to Symbols *see back flap*

Fifteenth-century frescoes in the Holy Trinity Church, Hrastovlje

Hrastovlje ❽

Road Map A5. 20 km (13 miles) SE
of Koper. 🚶 *140*. 🚌 *from Koper.*
ℹ️ *Hrastovlje 4; (041) 398 368.*

Located in the arid hills above
the coast, the rustic village of
Hrastovlje is home to one of
Slovenia's most outstanding
medieval treasures. Crowning
a hillock a short distance from
the rest of the village is the
12th-century **Holy Trinity
Church** (Cerkev sv Trojice), a
simple Romanesque structure
sheltered behind a high
defensive wall.

The church's interior is
covered from floor to ceiling
with dazzling frescoes painted
by local artist John of Kastav
in 1490. Painted over several
times in the subsequent years,
the frescoes were only discovered in 1949. Most famous
of the friezes is the *Dance of
Death* on the south wall, in
which a jolly-looking company of skeletons lead the old
and young, rich and poor
alike towards the grave.

Many of the other scenes
feature familiar stories from
the Bible, but with the main
characters clad in attire from
the 15th century, providing

a fascinating insight into the
lifestyles of people in the late-
medieval period. Particularly
imaginative are the scenes
depicting the Book of Genesis,
filled with exotic birds, beasts
and plants; and the Journey
of the Magi showing the three
kings journeying with a retinue
of richly clad followers on
horseback. Ceiling panels carry
delightful illustrations of local
country life at different stages
of the annual agricultural cycle
and through the seasons.

🔒 **Holy Trinity Church**
🕗 *8am–noon & 1–5pm daily.* 📷

Lokev ❾

Road Map A4. 38 km (24 miles) NE
of Koper. 🚶 *740*. 🚌 *from Sežana.*

Surrounded by green pastures
and limestone outcrops, Lokev
is a typical karst village of
modest stone houses. It is
famous for the local home-
cured ham (*pršut*) that is sold
in the shop at the huge
drying shed (*pršutarna*). At
the centre of Lokev is a
castellated round tower built
by the Venetians in 1485. The
tower now houses the **Tabor**

Military Museum (Vojaški
muzej Tabor), a private collection containing mementos
from both world wars.
Exhibits include the uniform
of General Svetozar Borojevič,
commander of the Austro-
Hungarian forces on the Soča
Front (*see p119*), and weapons
used by the partisan brigades
that liberated western Slovenia
from fascist occupiers in 1945.

Environs
Located amidst forest and
scrub 2 km (1 mile) north of
the village, **Vilenica Cave**
(Jama Vilenica) was one of
the first of the karst caverns to
become a tourist attraction,
receiving visitors as early as
the 17th century. However, it
lost prominence when the
nearby Postojna and Škocjan
Caves were discovered. Visits
to Vilenica were revived in
1963, and about 450 m
(1,480 ft) of stalactite-encrusted
passageways can now be
seen as part of a guided tour.
The Dance Hall, the biggest of
Vilenica's chambers, serves as
the venue for readings during
the Vilenica International
Literature Festival, which
brings together Slovenian and
Central European poets.

🏛 **Tabor Military Museum**
Tel (05) 767 0107. 🕗 *Jan–Feb: by
appt; Mar–Dec: 9am–noon & 2–6pm
Wed–Sun.* 📷

🔆 **Vilenica Cave**
Tel (051) 648 711. 📷 🕗 *Apr–Oct:
3 & 5pm Sun.* 📷 *Vilenica
International Literature Festival (Sep).*
www.vilenica.com

Rock formations at the Vilenica
Cave, near Lokev

Verdant archway in the Botanical Gardens, Sežana

Sežana ⓫

Road Map A4. 45 km (28 miles) NE of Koper. 12,600. from Koper, Ljubljana & Nova Gorica. from Nova Gorica. Partizanska 63; (05) 731 0128. www.kras-carso.com

An unassuming market town serving the hill villages of the western karst, Sežana is an important hub for travellers looking at visiting nearby attractions such as the Lipica Stud Farm and the Vilenica Cave. It also holds a variety of minor attractions in its own right, the most popular of which is the restful **Botanical Gardens**.

The gardens were laid out by the Scaramanga family, a Trieste-based trading dynasty who were enthusiastic horti-culturalists, and collected plants from all over the globe. An elegant 19th-century palm house provides the garden's geometrically arranged flower-beds with a focal point. Beyond the palm house lies an extensive arboretum, with a high number of evergreens that help to keep the gardens colourful all year round.

♣ Botanical Gardens
Partizanska cesta 2. **Tel** (05) 731 1200. 7am–3pm Mon–Fri, 9am–noon & 3–6pm Sat & Sun. www.ksp-sezana.si

Lipica ➓

Road Map A4. 48 km (30 miles) NE of Koper. from Sežana. www.lipica.org

Located by the Italian border, the village of Lipica is synony-mous with the Lipizzaner horses bred here since 1580. Established by the Habsburg Archduke Charles of Styria, the **Lipica Stud Farm** crossed Andalusian horses with local steeds, resulting in the grace-ful white Lipizzaner horses. The breed immediately found favour with the prestigious Spanish Riding School in Vienna, and has been con-sidered an aristocrat in the equine world ever since.

Today, Lipica has riding stables, two hotels, a casino, a nine-hole golf course and the Museum Lipikum (Muzej lipicanca). Many of Lipica's 400 horses can be seen grazing in the extensive paddocks that adjoin the stud farm. Tours of the stables allow visitors to see the beasts at close quarters, while presentations by the Classical Riding School show the highly trained horses performing complex routines. Ponies are available for rides, and horse-drawn carriage tours of the farm and pastures are on offer from April to October. Enthusiasts can book one-week courses ranging from horse riding for beginners to advanced dressage training.

Occupying a room in one of the older stable complexes is the **Avgust Černigoj Gallery** (Galerija Avgusta Černigoja), honouring Černigoj (1898– 1985), the Modernist artist

who spent the last years of his life at Lipica. The collection ranges from Constructivist paintings from the artist's youth to the collages he worked on in his later years. The gallery is designed according to the avant-garde aesthetics of Černigoj's early years, with grey metal stair-cases, bright red pillars and a circular viewing platform on the second floor.

Lipica Stud Farm
Tel (05) 739 1708. hourly; Apr–Oct: 10am–5pm Mon–Fri, 10am–6pm Sat & Sun; Oct–Mar: 10am–3pm daily. www.lipica.org

🏛 Avgust Černigoj Gallery
Tel (05) 739 1740. Apr–Oct: 10am–5pm Mon–Fri, 10am–6pm Sat & Sun; Oct–Mar: 10am–3pm daily. www.lipica.org

Typical white Lipizzaner horses grazing at the Lipica Stud Farm

LIPIZZANER HORSES

Inspired by the need to produce a strong cavalry horse, Habsburg Emperor Maximilian II decided to breed white Andalucian horses with local horses. The experiment was continued by his brother Archduke Charles, who founded a stud farm at Lipica. After the break-up of the Habsburg Empire in 1918, the Austrians established a new Lipizzaner stud farm in Piber, Austria, while the Slovenians continued breeding the horses at Lipica. The horses are dark-coloured when young, and develop their distinctive off-white coats only after the age of five.

Škocjan Caves ⑫
Škocjanske jame

Located in rolling countryside just outside the town of Divača, the Škocjan Caves are one of Slovenia's most spectacular karst features. The UNESCO World Heritage site's labyrinthine complex of caverns and passageways is reckoned to be the world's largest network of subterranean chambers, and to this day, remains only partially explored. About 3 km (2 miles) of passageways are open to the public, accessible by a 90-minute guided tour. As well as a spectacular array of stalagmites and stalactites, visitors can marvel at underground waterways and rock bridges. The surrounding landscape, featuring limestone gorges, pastureland, traditional stone-built villages and deciduous forest, is a protected nature area.

Visitors outside the main entrance to the caves

Entrance

Škocjan Village
The restored barns of Škocjan Village contain a number of museum collections, with a model of the cave system and Bronze Age archeological finds among the exhibits.

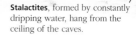

Stalactites, formed by constantly dripping water, hang from the ceiling of the caves.

★ **The Bowls**
This sequence of cup-like formations, arranged in tiers and formed by the sediment left by dripping water, is one of the more unusual sights here.

STAR SIGHTS

★ The Bowls

★ Cerkveník Bridge

★ The Organ

★ **Cerkvenik Bridge**
The most breathtaking moment for many visitors is the walk across this man-made bridge, hovering 45 metres (148 ft) above the twisting underground Reka river.

Velika Dolina
Velika Dolina (literally, Great Valley) is where the Reka river disappears underground, carving out the chambers of the Škocjan Caves before re-emerging near the Adriatic Sea.

Church of St Cantianus is dedicated to the local patron saint. The name, Škocjan, is the local dialect for St Cantianus.

Škocjan Village

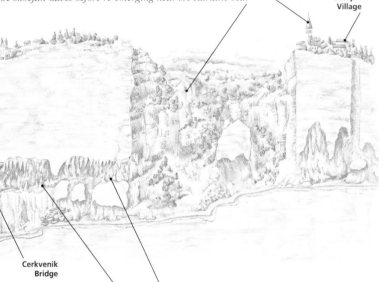

Cerkvenik Bridge

★ **The Organ**
This is one of the most alluring rock formations, so called due to a ribbed curtain of limestone that resembles the pipes of a church organ.

Paradise Cave
Among Škocjan's set-piece caverns, the Paradise Cave is famous for the fluted pillars of glistening rock that connect the floor to the ceiling.

Colourful façade of the Veno Pilon Gallery, Ajdovščina

Vipava ⑬

Road Map A4. 58 km (36 miles) N
of Koper. 🏛 *5,200.* 🚌 *from Nova
Gorica & Ljubljana.* 🛈 *Glavni trg; (05)
368 7041.* **www**.vipavska-dolina.si

Pressed against the sheer
grey flanks of the Nanos
ridge, the small town of
Vipava stands at the centre
of the Vipava valley wine
producing area. Dominating
the main square is the ochre
17th-century mansion built
by the Lanthieri Counts,
who ruled over Vipava
until World War I. A building on the town's main
square houses the tourist
information centre and
the **Vinoteka**, where white
wines made from the indigenous zelen and pinela
grapes are available for
sampling and purchase.

Beyond the square, Vipava's
street plan of narrow twisting
alleyways protects houses
from the *burja*, the bone-
chilling northeasterly wind
that blasts down from the
mountain ridges above.
Alleyways behind the main
square lead to an attractive
waterside area near the
source of the Vipava river,
which emerges from the
limestone slopes of Nanos
mountain. From here, trails
lead up towards the jagged
ruins of Vipava's 13th-century

castle. For those keen to
embark on longer hikes,
several marked paths
lead up towards Nanos's
main ridge, beyond
which lies a rolling
plateau of evergreen
forest and pastures.
Perched on a small hill
2 km (1 mile) west of
Vipava is the 17th-century
Zemono Manor, a
famously beautiful
arcaded building,
which now houses the
Pri Lojzetu restaurant
(see p209).

Vinoteka
Glavni trg 1. **Tel** *(05) 368 7041.*
⬜ *Jun–Sep: 9am–7pm daily;
Oct–May: 10am–5pm Mon–Fri,
9am–2pm Sat.* 🔲

Ajdovščina ⑭

Road Map A4. 65 km (40 miles)
N of Koper. 🏛 *18,100.* 🚌 *from
Ljubljana & Nova Gorica.* 🛈 *Lokarjev
drevored 8; (05) 365 9140.*
www.tic-ajdovscina.si

The main town of the Vipava
valley, the semi-industrial
Ajdovščina began life as a
Roman fortified camp, ruins
of which can still be seen
around town. It became an
important centre of milling
and metalworking in the
Middle Ages, its workshops
powered by the gushing
waters of the Hubelj river.
More recently, Ajdovščina has
become noted as the home
of the Pipistrel aviation company, whose innovative
gliders can frequently be seen
at the airfield west of town.

Relics from Ajdovščina's
ancient origins are most
visible on the eastern side of
the centre, where a surviving
medieval gateway and
adjoining section of Roman
wall preside over a grassy
park facing the river.
Inside the gate lies a
tightly woven web of
narrow streets, where the
Veno Pilon Gallery
(Pilonova galerija)
honours the locally
born painter, Veno Pilon
(1896–1970), with
displays of paintings
and mementos from his
lifetime. The collection starts
with Pilon's subtly dramatic
watercolours of the Russian
town of Lipeck, where he was
interned as a prisoner of war
during World War I. Most

**Wine bottle,
Vipava**

Vista of vineyards from Zemono Manor, Vipava

'iew of an entrance gate to the ancient hilltop town of Štanjel

ıtriking of Pilon's later works ıre the Expressionist portraits, n which the sitters are ɔortrayed with asymmetrical aces, overlarge hands or ·longated torsos.

A 30-minute walk on a vell-signed and easy-going ıature trail on the northern ·ide of town leads to the ource of the Hubelj river, vhich emerges from the rocky ıillside in the form of a ;ushing waterfall.

Veno Pilon Gallery
Prešernova 3. ***Tel*** *(05) 368 9177.*
8am–4pm Tue–Fri.
www.venopilon.com

Vipavski Križ ⓯

Road Map A4. 67 km (42 miles) N ɔf Koper. *180.*

Occupying a low ridge in the niddle of the Vipava valley, Vipavski Križ was an insignificant village until the late 15th century, when the Counts ɔf Gorizia realized that they ıeeded a forward line of defence to protect themselves ıgainst Ottoman attacks. Križ vas quickly transformed into a fortress, with the ensuing nflux of soldiers, builders ınd churchmen transforming t into a major regional centre.

Today, Križ is a sleepy settlement, with long stretches ɔf defensive wall intact, and he stark remains of the fortress looming above the ts eastern end. Dominating he town is the 17th-century Capuchin Monastery Church (cerkev kapucinskega samostana), famous for a monumental Baroque painting of the Holy Trinity which hangs upon the high altar. The monastery's **Library** contains a prized collection of manuscripts and prayer books.

Library
9am–noon & 1–5:30pm Tue–Sat.

Štanjel ⓰

Road Map A4. 59 km (37 miles) NE of Koper. *340.* *from Nova Gorica & Sežana.* *from Nova Gorica & Sežana.* *(05) 769 0056.* www.kras-carso.si

The best-preserved of the ridgetop settlements to the southwest of the Vipava valley is Štanjel, once an important way-station on the trade route between Vipava and the coast. Sacked by Ottoman raiders in 1470, the town was re-fortified in the 16th century by the Kobenzl family.

The main approach to the town leads through the west gate, adorned with the deer and eagle motifs of Štanjel's coat of arms. Beyond lies a knot of narrow, unpaved alleys lined with sturdy cottages. Presiding over this stone warren is the arresting cone-shaped belfry of St Daniel's Church (Cerkev sv Danijela), a late-Gothic structure with Baroque altars.

On Štanjel's hill is the 16th-century Castle (Kaštel), much of which is in ruins; a restored lower section abuts a pleasant courtyard. Occupying one of the castle buildings is the **Lojze Spacal Gallery** (Galerija Lojzeta Spacala), housing a comprehensive collection of works by the Trieste-born artist Lojze Spacal (1907–2000), famous for his depictions of the karst and the coast. Staff at the gallery also show visitors around the nearby Karst House (Kraška hiša), a traditional hill-village home. The ground floor was used as a storage room and barn, while the upper storeys served as living quarters.

Statue at the entrance to Štanjel

Just beyond the Karst House, the town's eastern boundary is marked by the Kobdilj Tower (Kobdiljski stolp), a gateway topped with castellations. Running in an arc below the tower is Ferraris' Garden (Ferrarijev vrt), a landscaped park designed by architect Max Fabiani, featuring a lake with a Venetian-style ornamental bridge. The views from the garden are stunning.

Lojze Spacal Gallery
Grad Štanjel. ***Tel*** *(05) 769 0197.*
daily. www.spacal.net

Boating through an underground lake, Križna Cave ▷

View of Gorizia from the Franciscan Monastery of Kostanjevica, Nova Gorica

Nova Gorica 🄬

Road Map A3. 85 km (53 miles) N of Koper. 🚗 13,900. 🚆 from Ljubljana. 🅘 Bevkov trg 4; (05) 330 4600. **www**.novagorica-turizem.si

The main administrative centre of western Slovenia, Nova Gorica owes its origins to post-World War II peace treaties, which awarded the city of Gorizia to Italy but left the villages immediately to the east in Slovenian hands. The Slovenians decided to build a new town on their side of the border that would serve as an economic and social centre for the local rural population, and Nova Gorica (New Gorizia) was the result. Largely constructed in the 1950s under the guidance of urban planner Edvard Ravnikar, the town centre has a functional, grid-plan appearance. However, there is a surprising wealth of historical sights scattered throughout the suburbs.

Dominating a hill south of the centre, the **Franciscan Monastery of Kostanjevica** (Frančiškanski samostan na Kostanjevici) started out as a Carmelite foundation established in the early 17th century. Re-founded by the Franciscans in 1811,

Coat of arms, Sveta Gora

it holds the burial vault of France's last Bourbon king, Charles X (1757–1836), who reigned for six years until the revolution of 1830 forced him to take refuge in Habsburg-ruled Gorizia. The monastery's library contains many historic volumes, most notably a copy of Adam Bohorič's first-ever Slovenian grammar, published in 1584.

Around 4 km (3 miles) east of central Nova Gorica, Kromberk Castle is a Renaissance château surrounded by ornamental gardens. It provides a fittingly grand home for the **Nova Gorica Museum** (Goriški muzej), whose extensive art collection spans everything from Gothic altar panels to graphic prints by local artist Lojze Spacal (1907–2000). The museum's ethnographic and archeological collections are housed in the **Villa Bartolomei** in Solkan, a leafy suburb made up of the summer villas of Gorizia's middle classes. The ethnography display is particularly engaging, including the kind of copper pots and pans that would have been used in a 19th-century Slovenian kitchen. Spanning the Soča river on Solkan's northern boundary is Nova Gorica's most treasured architectural monument,

the Solkan railway bridge (Solkanski most). Opened in July 1906, the bridge's 85-m (280-ft) high central arch is the biggest of any stone-built bridge in the world. Despite being blown up by the Austrian army to prevent its capture by Italian forces in 1916, it was rebuilt by the Italians in 1927. The bridge is best viewed from the grassy banks of the Soča river.

Looming to the east of the Solkan Bridge is Sveta Gora hill, its 684-m (2,245-ft) high summit crowned by the **Sveta Gora Monastery** (Frančiškanski samostan Sveta Gora) and its Pilgrimage Church of the Assumption. The church contains a 16th-century picture of the Virgin that is popularly believed to answer the prayers of the faithful.

🄰 **Franciscan Monastery of Kostanjevica**
Škrabčeva ulica 1. **Tel** (05) 330 7750. ☐ daily. 🎫 🛈 **www**.samostan-kostanjevica.si

🏛 **Nova Gorica Museum**
Grajska 1. **Tel** (05) 335 9811. ☐ daily. 🎫 🛈 **www**.goriskimuzej.si

🏛 **Vila Bartolomei**
Pod Vinogradi 2. **Tel** (05) 335 9811. ☐ 8am–5pm Mon–Fri. **www**.goriskimuzej.si

🄰 **Sveta Gora Monastery**
Sveta Gora 2. **Tel** (05) 330 4020. 🅘 7am & 5pm Mon–Sat; 8am, 10am, 11:30am & 4pm Sun & holidays. **www**.svetagora.si

A Tour of the Goriška Brda Region ⑱

Stretching northwest of Nova Gorica is the Goriška Brda region, characterized by green slopes and hilltop villages. It is one of Slovenia's foremost wine regions, famous for the light white rebula as well as international varieties such as Merlot and Chardonnay. Wine can be tasted at innumerable local establishments, ranging from big wineries in the main villages to family farmsteads out on country roads.

Bottle of red wine

TIPS FOR DRIVERS

Starting point: Nova Gorica.
Length: 45 km (28 miles).
Duration: Allow a full day.
Driving conditions: There are single-lane roads in the region; road crosses through Italy too.
Stopping-off points: The region is full of wineries. Among the most popular are Vinoteka Brda and Vinska klet Goriška Brda in Dobrovo.
Tourist information: Dobrovo: Grajska cesta 10, (05) 395 9594, www.brda.si

Vipolže ⑦
Home to a ruined castle circled by cypresses, the village of Vipolže is surrounded by vineyards, olive trees and orchards.

Nova Gorica ①
A 20th-century town, this is the administrative centre of the region.

Dobrovo ⑥
Goriška Brda's main settlement is also one of the most convenient places to sample and buy local wine.

Šmartno ⑤
The most attractive of Goriška Brda's villages, Šmartno is known for its local produce.

Solkan Bridge ②
This masterpiece of engineering, with the largest single-span stone arch in the world, opened to railway traffic in 1906.

Vrhovlje pri Kojskem ④
Perched on a verdant ridge, Vrhovlje's pilgrimage church offers a wonderful panorama of the countryside.

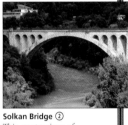

SLOVENIA

Goriška Brda

ITALY

KEY

— Tour route
--- Other road
🛈 Information centre
☆ View point
— Railway
–·– International boundary

0 km 2
0 miles 2

Kojsko ③
This tranquil village is famous for the semi-fortified Holy Cross Church, home to a winged Gothic altarpiece.

Idrija ⓚ

Road Map B3. 102 km (63 miles) N of Koper. 🚹 *12,000.* 🚏 *from Ljubljana .* 🏢 *Vodnikova, (05) 374 3916.* 🎭 *Idrija Lace Festival (late Jun).* **www**.idrija-turizem.si

Accessed via notoriously winding roads, Idrija's location at the base of a valley, amidst green hills, is spectacular. Mining began here in 1490 when, according to local legend, a barrel-maker was soaking his wares in a nearby stream and discovered mercury. Idrija became the second largest mercury-mining centre in Europe, providing 13 per cent of the global output.

Statue in the centre of the town

After mining came to a halt in 2008, the town became a major centre of industrial tourism. This mining heritage is apparent everywhere in Idrija – even the tourist office is housed in a former pit-head building, home to a lovingly polished 19th-century winding machine. The best place to view Idrija's industrial legacy is the **Town Museum** (Mestni muzej), housed in the Gewerkenegg Castle, perched on a hilltop above the centre. Lumps of ruddy ore along with displays of drilling equipment and photographs of helmeted workers illustrate the history of mining in the town. One section of the museum is devoted to the story of the manufacture of Idrija lace, a home industry begun by miners' wives to supplement modest family incomes, and still going strong today. The display includes everything from tablecloths to alluring lacy evening dresses. A first hand experience of mining conditions is provided at **Anthony's Shaft** (Antonijev rov). This atmospheric network of tunnels, initially excavated in 1500, is located to the south of the castle. A tour of the shaft starts at the former administrative building known as the Šelštev House, where a video presentation introduces the growth of mining in the town. Visitors are then led down the shaft itself, where mining techniques of the past are demonstrated.

Several other industrial monuments are strewn around the centre of the town: the pit-head pavilion at Francis's Shaft (Jašek Frančiške) contains an absorbing display of mining machinery, while the nearby steep-roofed Miner's House (Rudarska hiša) reveals the cramped living conditions of 19th-century families. On the western outskirts of town is a large stone building containing the Kamšt, an impressive waterwheel built in 1790 to pump floodwater from the mineshafts below. With a diameter of 14 m (45 ft), it was the biggest waterwheel in Europe and was in use until 1948.

Immediately beyond the Kamšt is the Zgornja Idrijca Landscape Park, where a path runs alongside the Rake – a man-made water course that fed the waterwheel – below wooded hills. Keen walkers can follow forest trails towards the Klavže, 18th-century dams that controlled the flow of water on local mountain torrents, making it possible to float locally cut timber downstream.

Idrija has a major culinary claim to fame in the *žlikrofi*, ravioli-like pockets of pasta stuffed with potato, bits of bacon and onion. Freshly made *žlikrofi* is served in most of the local restaurants.

🏛 **Town Museum**
Prelovčeva 3. **Tel** (05) 372 6600.
⏰ 9am–6pm daily. 🏷 📷 **www**.muzej-idrija-cerkno.si **Note:** check here about access to Francis's Shaft & the Kamšt.

🏛 **Anthony's Shaft**
Kosovelova 3. **Tel** (05) 377 1142.
📷 10am & 3pm Mon–Fri, 10am, 3pm & 4pm Sat & Sun. 🏷 📷
www.rzs-idrija.si

Courtyard of the Gewerkenegg Castle, home to Idrija's Town Museum

For hotels and restaurants in this region see pp192–4 and pp207–9

Cerkno town with the mountains in the background

Cerkno ⑳

Road Map B3. 20 km (13 miles) NW of Idrija. 🚶 5,000. 🚌 from Idrija. 🏠 Močnikova, (05) 373 4645. 🎭 Laufarija processions (Shrovetide), Cerkno International Jazz Festival (May). **www**.cerkno.si/turizem

Stretched out beneath the 1,632-m (5,354-ft) high ridge of Mount Porezen, the village of Cerkno is a popular base for summer hiking and winter skiing. The main attraction in the village itself is **Cerkno Museum**, which contains an arresting collection of wood-carved carnival masks worn by the local pre-Lenten revellers, the *laufarji*.

The Cerkno tourist office can organize visits to the Divje Babe cave, a major archaeological site rich in Neanderthal remains, between April and September. In 1996, archaeologists discovered what is claimed to be the world's oldest musical instrument, a 55,000-year-old flute carved from bear bone. The bone is exhibited in the National Museum of Slovenia, Ljubljana (see p62), although the question of whether it is really a flute or simply a bone with holes in it is the subject of long-running academic debate.

🏛 **Cerkno Museum**
Bevkova 12. **Tel** (05) 372 3180. 🕐 9am–3pm Tue–Fri, 10am–1pm & 2–6pm Sat & Sun. **www**.muzej-idrija-cerkno.si

Franja Partisan Hospital ㉑
Partizanska bolnica Franja

Road Map B3. 25 km (16 miles) N of Idrija. **Tel** (05) 372 3180 🕐 Apr–Sep: 9am–6pm daily; Oct: 9am–4pm daily; Nov–Mar: pre-arranged groups only. 🦽 🎫 **www**.muzej-idrija-cerkno.si

In the densely wooded and picturesque Pasica gorge lies the Franja Partisan Hospital, a timber-built field hospital used by Slovenian resistance fighters during World War II. Active from December 1943 to 1945, the hospital's 13 wooden huts once housed wards that were fully equipped with x-ray machines, operating theatres, and an electricity generator. Over 1,000 partisans and Allied soldiers were treated here during the war. Medical supplies, dropped by Allied aircraft throughout Slovenia, allowed this and other field hospitals to remain operational. Staff and patients were blindfolded on their way to and from the hospital to ensure maximum secrecy.

Converted into a memorial after the war, the site was named after partisan doctor Franja Bojc Bidovec (1913–85), the hospital's administrator from January 1944 until the end of the war.

The site was badly damaged by floods in September 2007. However, renovation is underway and several buildings have already been rebuilt and are open to visitors.

View of the huts at the Franja Partisan Hospital

THE CERKNO LAUFARJI

Some of Slovenia's strangest and most colourful carnival customs take place in Cerkno. The *laufarji* (runners) are local young men who cavort through the village in stylized costumes welcoming the spring. They appear on the first Sunday of the year and increase in number as the weeks go by. Their main task is to accompany the *Pust* – played by a local man clad in fir-tree branches, a symbol of winter that has to be confronted before spring can commence. The *Pust* is put on trial in the village square on the Sunday before Shrove Tuesday. He is then symbolically executed with a *bot*, a forester's hammer, on Shrove Tuesday. The *Pust* is policed by the *terjasti* – *laufar* with skull-like wooden masks featuring grotesque teeth – who also entertain the public by dancing and leaping.

Typical *laufar* mask and costume

Predjama Castle

Predjamski grad

There are few fortresses more dramatically situated than Predjama Castle, which sits half way up a hillside carved into a huge cave. The site was fortified in the 13th century, although most of what can be seen today is the result of 16th-century rebuilding. Most famous of the castle's many owners was the 15th-century knight Erasmus Lueger, a bandit-like figure who was killed during a siege in 1484. In July, a tournament is held in the castle to celebrate the medieval period with jousts and parades.

Erasmus Lueger

Rocky entrance leading to the interior of the castle

Upper Vantage Point

Dining Room
The 16th-century furnishings and costumes, displayed in the restored dining room, provide an insight into the aristocratic lifestyles of the time when castles became residential chateaux.

★ **Torture Room**
The castle has a series of tableaux featuring wax dummies. This room shows a prisoner being tortured prior to interrogation in the inquisitor's room next door.

Karst caves below the castle can be visited by guided tour.

Drawbridge
Accessible via wooden bridges that could be hastily removed, Predjama was considered impregnable. A reconstructed drawbridge leads to the part that is located within the cave.

STAR SIGHTS

★ Torture Room

★ Pietà in the Chapel

★ Upper Vantage Point

Chaplain's Room

This room is one of several interiors redecorated to provide a flavour of castle life during the late 16th century, when Predjama was owned by the noble Kobenzl family.

VISITORS' CHECKLIST

Road Map B4. 13 km (8 miles) NW of Postojna. ℹ *Postojna Caves Visitor Centre, (05) 700 0163.* ⬤ *Jul & Aug: 9am–7pm; May, Jun & Sep: 9am–6pm; Apr & Oct: 10am–5pm; Nov–Mar: 10am–4pm daily.* 🎫 🗝 *Tours of karst caves: May–Sep: 11am, 1, 3 & 5pm.* 🏰 *Erasmus Knights' Tournament (mid Jul).* **www**.predjamski-grad.si

★ Pietà in the Chapel

Located in the castle's Chapel of St Anne, a serene white space decorated with wooden pews and a simple cross, this tender and moving pietà from 1420 is one of the high points of late-Gothic art in Slovenia.

Castle entrance

★ Upper Vantage Point

Staircases ascend to the highest of the castle's five levels, from where the viewing terrace offers an extensive panorama of the valley below.

ERASMUS LUEGER

Born in Trieste, Erasmus Lueger became the owner of Predjama Castle in 1478. He fell foul of the authorities after killing one of the Emperor's kinsmen, and used the castle as a base from which to mount raids on the surrounding territory. In 1484, Baron Ravbar of Trieste laid siege to Predjama Castle for more than a year in an attempt to starve Erasmus into submission. The defenders brought in food through a secret tunnel, taunting Ravbar's men by tossing fresh cherries at them from the castle walls. Erasmus was ultimately killed by a cannonball, which hit the castle privy just when he happened to be squatting inside.

Portrait of Erasmus Lueger in Predjama Castle

Postojna Caves ㉓
Postojnska jama

Slovenia's most popular natural attraction, Postojna Caves constitute the longest subterranean system in the country, with over 20 km (12 miles) of chambers and tunnels. They were formed by the seeping waters of the Pivka river and its tributaries, which carved out several levels of underground galleries over a period of roughly three million years. The caves were first opened to visitors in 1819, with Austrian Emperor Francis I as the guest of honour. The site currently receives just under half a million visitors a year, making it one of the most popular natural attractions in Europe. Inside, magnificent formations of stalactites and stalagmites seem to stretch endlessly in all directions.

Visitors outside the main entrance to Postojna Caves

Subterranean Railway
The 2-km (1-mile) long underground railway offers an exhilarating introduction to the caves, speeding visitors through dramatically illuminated chambers. With the train swerving between dangling stalactites, it is almost like a fairground ride.

Russian Bridge
Built by Russian prisoners during World War I, the Russian Bridge leads to the Macaroni Hall, which is covered with stunning pure-white stalactites.

Stalactites, formed by constantly dripping water, hang from the cave ceiling.

STAR SIGHTS
★ Concert Hall
★ White Passage
★ The Diamond

Guided Tours
Lasting 90 minutes, guided tours begin with a train ride into the heart of the caves, followed by a walk through a series of halls with intricate rock formations.

★ **Concert Hall**
Before returning by train to the cave entrance, visitors emerge into the Concert Hall, a vast space where orchestral performances are occasionally held.

VISITORS' CHECKLIST

Road Map B4. 53 km (33 miles) S of Ljubljana. 🚆 *from Ljubljana.* 🚌 *from Ljubljana.* 🛈 *Jamska Cesta 9, Postojna, (05) 720 1610.* **www**.tdpostojna.si ◯ *Jan–Mar & Nov–Dec: tours at 10am, noon & 3pm; Apr & Oct: tours at 10am, noon, 2pm & 4pm; May, Jun & Sep: tours hourly 9am–5pm; July & Aug: tours hourly 9am–6pm.* 🦽 🚻 🍴 🖻 🛍 **www**.postojnska-jama.si

Big Mountain
This 45-m (147-ft) high rocky mound was created when the ceiling collapsed.

★ **White Passage**
One of the series of chambers known as Beautiful Caves, the White Passage is crammed with impressive stalagmites and stalactites.

★ **The Diamond**
This huge stalagmite, also called "Brilliant", on account of its dazzling white surface and peculiar shape, is one of the highlights of the spectacular Winter Chamber.

Proteus Anguinus
The caves are the natural habitat of this rare amphibian, known as the human fish.

Entrance to the famous Postojna Caves

Exploring Postojna

The history of the town of Postojna, situated midway between Ljubljana and the Adriatic coast, is inextricably linked with that of the Postojna Caves, the famous sequence of caverns that can be entered from the western edge of town. Known since the Middle Ages, the caves were visited by the famous geographer Janez Vajkard Valvasor *(see p91)* in the late 17th century and became a destination for mass tourism in the 19th century.

The arrival of the railway in 1857 made the cave accessible to visitors from all over Central Europe. This also spurred the development of Postojna itself, which was transformed from a provincial market town into a major administrative centre. The town fell under Italian rule after World War I, and it became a heavily garrisoned military base on the frontier with the erstwhile Kingdom of Yugoslavia. Barrack buildings can still be seen on the outskirts of town. The **Postojna Regional Museum**, which occupies the former military garrison headquarters, has on display exhibits relating to the natural history, archaeology as well as the ethnography of the entire karst region.

Today, the cave remains Postojna's main attraction, drawing an average of half-a-million visitors every year. The cave is particularly rich in stalagmites, stalactites and other rock formations, thanks mainly to the region's high rainfall, which helps to produce the constantly dripping water from which stalactites are formed. The temperature in the cave is a constant 10° C (50° F); visitors are advised to wear warm clothing.

A World War II tank

🏛 Postojna Regional Museum
Ljubljanska 10. **Tel** (05) 721 1080. ☐ *9am–3pm Tue–Fri, 10am–1pm & 2–6pm Sat & Sun.* **www**.notranjski-muzej.si

Pivka Cave ㉔
Pivka jama

Road Map B4. 3 km (2 miles) N of Postojna. 📷 *by appointment from the ticket office.*

Just north of the entrance to the Postojna Caves is the lesser known Pivka Cave. A steep descent via a stairway and a walk along the path that runs beside a submerged stretch of the Pivka river takes visitors to the caverns. A man-made passageway leads through to the neighbouring Black Cave (Črna jama), so named due to the smooth, black calcite rock that gives lustre to some of the caverns.

Pivka Park of Military History ㉕
Park vojaške zgodovine

Road Map B4. 16 km (10 miles) S of Postojna. **Tel** (05) 721 2180. ☐ *Jun–Sep: 10am–5pm daily; Oct–May: 10am–3pm Sat & Sun.* 📷 📷 📷

Occupying the former Italian and subsequently Yugoslav barracks at the southern end of Pivka village is this major collection of military artifacts. Much of the exhibition is made up of artillery pieces and tanks used by Italian and German occupiers during World War II. Alongside these is military hardware used by the Yugoslav People's Army in the 10-day conflict of June–July 1991. A circular walking route named the Trail of Military History (Krožna pot vojaške zgodovine) runs up and down the neighbouring hills, passing fortifications dating from the inter-war era, when the area was a highly militarized zone on what was then the Italian-Yugoslav border. The whole trail takes about 4 hours to negotiate, although visitors can choose a shorter 45-minute stretch that runs to Primož hill, site of an inter-war Italian artillery fort.

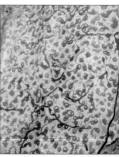

Unusual spotted walls of the Pivka Cave

Entrance to the spectacular Planina Cave

Planina Cave ㉖
Planinska jama

Road Map B4. 12 km (8 miles) NE of Postojna. *Tel (04) 133 8696.*
Jun–Aug: 5pm daily; Apr, May & Sep: 3pm & 5pm Sat, 11am, 3pm & 5pm Sun. Oct–Mar: by appt only. **www**.planina.si

The Planina Cave is one of Slovenia's most spectacular water caves. The cave has passageways carved by the subterranean Pivka river, which flows here from Postojna Cave, and the Rak, which flows from the Rakov Škocjan gorge. The rivers meet inside Planina to form the Unica river, which emerges from the cave's northern end. It is an important habitat for the amphibious *Proteus anguinus (see p19)*, which can be seen swimming in the rivers. Tours of the cave take visitors through the huge arched tunnel carved by the Unica before ascending to the Great Hall, so named because of its 70-m (230-ft) high ceiling. Further inside is the confluence of the Pivka and the Rak, with the Rak tumbling over a small waterfall. Deeper 4-hour explorations of the cave, including dinghy trips on subterranean lakes, are available if booked well in advance.

Rakov Škocjan Regional Park ㉗

Road Map B4. 7 km (5 miles) E of Postojna. **www**.notranjski-park.si

Rakov Škocjan is a rugged limestone canyon formed by the collapse of an underground tunnel carved by the rushing waters of the Rak river. Parts of the tunnel still survive in the form of two rock bridges, with the delicate 40-m (140-ft) high arch of the Small Natural Bridge (Mali naravni most) marking the eastern end of the gorge. The lower, but much longer Great Natural Bridge (Veliki naravni most), lies 3 km (1 mile) further down. A well-marked trail runs between the two bridges. At the far end of the Great Natural Bridge, the Rak disappears into Tkalca Cave, before joining the Pivka river in the Planina Cave.

Lake Cerknica ㉘
Cerkniško jezero

Road Map B4. 22 km (14 miles) E of Postojna. **www**.notranjski-park.si

Just south of the town of Cerknica is the "disappearing" Lake Cerknica, a broad karstic depression that fills with water during wet spells, especially during the spring thaw, but gradually dries as the water seeps away into its porous limestone underlay. The lake is in a constant state of growing and shrinking, and may disappear entirely during dry summers, when it becomes a reedy marsh. At its fullest extent the lake covers an area of 26 sq km (10 sq miles).

Lake Cerknica is a popular venue for boating and fishing in spring. It is surrounded by a network of quiet country roads, which make for ideal cycling terrain. The lake's popularity with ducks, corncrakes and wading birds has made it a major attraction for birdwatchers.

View of the "disappearing" Lake Cerknica during the dry season

Križna Cave ㉙
Križna jama

Road Map B4. 30 km (19 miles)
SE of Postojna. **Tel** (04) 163 2153.
☐ Apr–Sep. ☑ ☒ Apr–Jun: 3pm
Sat & Sun; Jul–Aug: 11am, 1pm, 3pm
& 5pm daily; Sep: 11am, 1pm & 3pm
daily; 3–4 day notice advisable.
www.krizna-jama.si

Famous for its subterranean
lakes, Križna Cave offers
one of Slovenia's unique
speleological experiences.
Fed by underground water
sources from both the Bloke
and Cerknica plateaus, the
8-km (5-mile) long cave
contains a string of 22 lakes,
separated from each other by
smooth rock barriers formed
by mineral deposits.

The cave is not fully fitted
with electric lighting so
visitors are supplied with
portable lamps on entering
the cave, making the tour all
the more atmospheric.

Guided tours last about an
hour and begin with a trip
through Bears' Corridor –
so-called because of the huge
number of skeletons of the
prehistoric cave bear found
here – before culminating
with a boat trip on the first of
the cave's lakes – a shallow
body of water with sloping
stone banks that resemble

Egyptian room in the Snežnik Castle

inviting beaches at first sight.
For visitors who wish to
explore more, there are
longer 4-hour tours, which
use small dinghies to venture
further into the underground
lake and river system. This
journey terminates at the
Calvary Hall, where a
submerged forest of stalagmites glitters beneath the
crystal clear water. This
longer tour is limited to four
people per day so it is best to
reserve well in advance.

The temperature inside the
cave remains a constant 8° C
(47° F) through the year and
it is advisable to wear or carry
some warm clothing.

The Križna Cave is also an
important habitat for bats,
with seven different species
nesting here during winter.

Snežnik Castle ㉚
Grad Snežnik

Road Map B4. 38 km (24 miles) SE
of Postojna. **Tel** (01) 705 7814. ☐
Apr–Sep: 10am–6pm daily; Oct–Mar:
10am–4pm Tue–Sun. ☑ ☒ hourly;
obligatory. ☒

A Renaissance chateau rising
behind picturesquely turreted
walls, Snežnik Castle was
owned by some of Slovenia's
leading landowning families
throughout the centuries.

The guided tours lead
visitors through a series of
historic interiors, each filled
with a rich array of period
furniture. Outside, the castle's
verdant landscaped park is
the perfect place for a
relaxing stroll.

The castle's former dairy
now houses the **Snežnik
Dormouse Museum**, which
informs visitors on traditional
dormouse-hunting techniques,
as well as different ways to
cook the animal once it is
caught. There is also a display
of hats fashioned from
dormouse fur.

🏛 **Snežnik Dormouse
Museum**
Grad Snežnik. **Tel** (01) 705 7516.
☐ mid-May–Oct: 10am–noon &
3–7pm Wed–Fri; 10am–1pm &
2–7pm Sat & Sun. ☑ ☒

Snežnik Plateau ㉛
Snežniška planota

Road Map B4. 40 km (25 miles) SE
of Postojna. ℹ Loz, (08) 160 2853

Snežnik Castle is one of the
main trail heads for mountain-
biking, horse riding and
walking on the Snežnik

Well-lit section of the Križna Cave

Plateau, a typically rugged limestone landscape characterized by rocky outcrops, frequent abysses and dense forests. The plateau enjoys some of the highest precipitation in the whole of Slovenia, which mostly falls in winter as snow – hence the name Snežnik, which roughly translates as snowy.

Snow remains for much of the year on the upper slopes of the 1,796-m (5,892-ft) high Veliki Snežnik, the cone-shaped mountain at the centre of the plateau. Despite a bare, rocky summit Veliki Snežnik is not a difficult climb for seasoned hikers.

Veliki Snežnik is a long day's walk from both Snežnik Castle and the other main starting point, Ilirska Bistrica. Alternately, visitors can drive to Sviščaki, a small settlement just east of Ilirska Bistrica, which has a mountain hut, and pick up the shorter trail to the mountain from there.

The other major holiday centre on the plateau is Mašun, midway between Snežnik Castle and Veliki Snežnik. It has B&B accom-modation in the local farm-houses and a floodlit ski slope during winter.

Ilirska Bistrica ❷

Road Map B4. 33 km (21 miles) S of Postojna. 🚶 5,000. 🚌 from Ljubljana. 🛈 Bazoviška Cesta 12; (05) 710 1384. **www**.ilirska-bistrica.si

A quiet and uneventful town located on the road and rail route linking Ljubljana with the Croatian port of Rijeka, Ilirska Bistrica is best known as a starting point for walkers who wish to explore the nearby Snežnik Plateau.

At the centre of the town is St Peter's Church, which has a Gothic presbytery, a collection of 17th-century Baroque altars and paintings by 20th-century artist, Tone Kralj. Around the church lies an engaging huddle of 19th-century buildings.

The information centre in the town can help organize private accommodation here.

Remains of a castle in the Mašun village

Reka river valley ❸

Road Map B4. 37 km (23 miles) S of Postojna.

Rising on the south side of Snežnik Plateau, the Reka river flows northwest before disappearing into the Škocjan Caves *(see pp138–9)*, only to emerge 33 km (21 miles) later

Reka river flowing through the Škocjan Caves

on the Italian side. To the west of Ilirska Bistrica, the river is particularly scenic.

The swift flowing waters were once used to power sawmills, such as in the **Novak Farmstead** (Novakova domačija) below Smrje village. The restored 19th-century mill has a water wheel and a traditional farmhouse kitchen.

Just north of Smrje, the riverside village of Prem is a fine example of the stone-built settlements that once characterized the area. The well-preserved **Prem Castle** (Grad Prem) offers fine views and contains a display of arti-facts found at Bronze Age hill forts on the Brkini plateau south of the river.

🏛 **Novak Farmstead**
Topolc 75C. **Tel** (05) 714 5987.
⭘ by appt.

⛪ **Prem Castle**
Prem. **Tel** (05) 710 1384. ⭘ May–Sep: noon–7pm Sat & Sun. 🗺

THE ŠKOROMATI OF HRUŠICA

Located on the Brkini plateau to the west of Ilirska Bistrica, Hrušica village is famous for preserving pre-Lenten carnival customs with pagan undertones. Revellers known as the *škoromati* run through the streets on the Saturday preceding Shrove Tuesday, clad in sheepskin jerkins, wooden masks and hats. They are led by the sinister *škopiti*, a black-clad figure wielding a huge pair of tongs. His job is to catch unmarried girls and smear them with ash, ensuring their fertility. On Ash Wednesday, an effigy known as the *Pust* is burnt outside the village, guaranteeing good fortune and healthy crops for the coming year.

Traditional masked *škopiti*

SOUTHERN AND EASTERN SLOVENIA

*B*ordered by Austria, Hungary and Croatia on three sides, and encompassing five of Slovenia's nine administrative districts, Southern and Eastern Slovenia is a melting pot of cultures and histories. The landscape here varies from sub-alpine hills to vast green plains and idyllic vineyards to virgin forests such as Kočevski rog, full of deserted villages, brown bears and lynx.

Southern and Eastern Slovenia, because of its location between larger nations, has long been subject to a tug-of-war between European powers. The region's turbulent history began with the Bronze Age Hallstatt tribes. The Romans arrived in the 1st century AD, creating powerful military and merchant colonies such as Poetovio (Ptuj) and Celeia (Celje).

The Germanic aristocratic dynasties conquered swathes of territory in the early Middle Ages. The beleagured Slovenian aristocrats rallied briefly under the banner of the counts of Celje, but, with the assassination of Ulrich II in Belgrade in 1456, resistance crumbled. By the end of the century, the Habsburgs held sway over all territory except the land to the east of the Mura river, which was claimed by the Hungarian crown.

From the early 15th century, the regions that bordered Croatia were attacked by the Ottomans. These attacks lasted for two centuries, leading to the rapid fortification of feudal castles on the borders. In addition to the Bronze Age archaeology, Roman antiquities, remote monasteries and Baroque fortresses, this region has more than its fair share of scenery. It is also home to Slovenia's most colourful festivals such as Kurent in Ptuj or the folk jamborees in Bela Krajina. The local wine culture established by the Romans continues in the east, and thermal spa resorts such as Dolenjske Toplice and Rogaška Slatina marry historic architecture with luxury wellness facilities. Maribor, Slovenia's second-largest settlement, has a range of shops and restaurants in its historic heart.

Swimming complex under a glass roof, Terme Čatež

◁ Magnificent Knight's Hall in Brežice Castle

Exploring Southern and Eastern Slovenia

Compared to Ljubljana, or the regions of Gorenjska and
Primorska in the west, Southern and Eastern Slovenia is
toured by fewer foreign visitors. This diverse region
divides roughly into three areas. The north is characterized by the sub-alpine Pohorje massif, which extends
from the west of Maribor to the pretty town of Slovenj
Gradec. The area south of the Krka river valley is a
land of small towns and folk customs, with border
fortresses and sun-kissed wine hills along the
eastern border. The region of Prekmurje beyond
the Mura river is distinct due to centuries of
Hungarian rule. Historic towns such as Ptuj, a
cradle of civilization for two millennia, Celje
and Maribor have modern hotels and are
good bases for excursions. Charming country
inns and splendid castle hotels provide an
excellent incentive to explore the area further.

SIGHTS AT A GLANCE

Villages, Towns and Cities
Bogojina ⑩
Celje pp170–71 ⑲
Črnomelj ⑩
Dravograd ㉓
Kočevje ③
Laško ㉗
Lendava ㊷
Ljutomer ㊱
Maribor pp176–7 ㉛
Metlika ⑪
Murska Sobota ㊳
Novo Mesto ⑥
Ormož ㉟
Ptuj pp178–9 ㉜
Ribnica ①
Rogaška Slatina ⑰
Slovenj Gradec ㉑
Slovenske Konjice ㉙
Šentanel ㉔
Velenje ⑳
Velika Polana ㊶
Žužemberk ⑧

Castles and Manors
Podsreda Castle ⑮
Štatenberg Manor ㉞

Monasteries
Olimje Monastery ⑯
Pleterje Monastery ⑫
Žiče Monastery ㉘

Tours
*A Tour of the
Krka Valley p165* ⑬

Museums and Galleries
Gallery of Naive Artists ⑦
Rogatec Open-air
Museum ⑱

Churches
Church of the Virgin
Protectress ㉝
Church of the
Assumption ②

Areas of Natural Beauty
Kolpa valley ⑤

Spa Resorts
Dolenjske Toplice ⑨
Kope ㉒
Moravske Toplice ㊴
Radenci ㊲

Sites of Interest
Bizeljsko-sremiška
Wine Road ⑭
Kočevski Rog ④
Peca Underground
Mine ㉕
Rogla ㉚
Roman
Necropolis ㉖

SEE ALSO
• *Where to Stay pp195–7*
• *Where to Eat pp209–11*

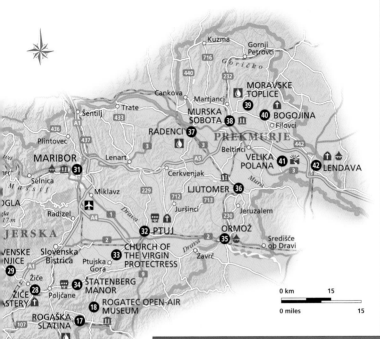

Theatre and concert hall, Lendava

GETTING AROUND

There is an international airport at Maribor. The A1 motorway from Ljubljana provides access to all destinations to the east as far as Lendava, passing through Maribor. Off the highways, travel is often slow due to single-lane roads. There are good international rail connections to Austria and Croatia from this region. Maribor and Celje are the hubs of regional rail and bus transport in the east, while Novo Mesto is the centre of rail and bus transport in the south; links to villages are limited.

KEY

✈ International airport

═══ Motorway

─── Main road

═══ Minor road

⊷ Railway

::::: Road tunnel

▬▬▬ International border

△ Peak

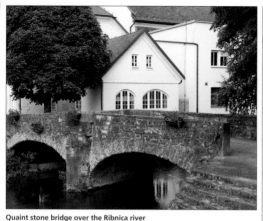

Quaint stone bridge over the Ribnica river

Ribnica ❶

Road Map C4. 43 km (27 miles)
SE of Ljubljana. 🚉 9,200. 🚌 from
Ljubljana. 🛈 Škrabčev trg 21; (01)
836 9355. 🎭 Dry Goods Fair
(1st Sun of Sep). **www**.ribnica.si

The modest market town
of Ribnica has long been
renowned for its woodcraft.
The town's cottage industry
flourished when, in an attempt
to restore prosperity in his
kingdom after Turkish raids,
the Austrian Emperor Frederick
III (r.1452–93) gave Ribnica
free licence to trade in his
territory in 1492. As a result,
peddlers hawked locally made
spoons, butter pats, wicker
sieves, wooden buckets and
even toothpicks throughout
the Habsburg Empire.

A fascinating collection of
woodcraft as well as displays
on the peddlers' lifestyle are
highlights of the Municipal
Museum in **Ribnica Castle**
(Grad Ribnica), a restored
Renaissance stronghold
situated on a river islet.
Visitors can purchase craft
souvenirs at the tourist office.

Located in front of the castle
is the Church of St Stephen
(Cerkev sv Štefana). Its two
bell towers, crowned with
classically inspired obelisks
and pediments, were designed
by the Modernist architect,
Jože Plečnik (see p73).

🏛 **Ribnica Castle**
Škrabčev trg 40. **Tel** (01) 836
9335. ⬜ 10am–1pm & 4–7pm
Tue–Sun. 🎫

Church of the Assumption ❷
Cerkev Marijinega vnebovzetja

Road Map C4. 6 km (4 miles) W
of Ribnica; Nova Štifta 3.
Tel (01) 836 9943. ♿

Perched on a hill and
shaded by ancient linden
trees in the tranquil
farming village of Nova
Štifta is the mid-17th-
century Church of the
Assumption, the most
revered pilgrimage
church of the Dolenjska
region. The church's
octagonal design,
fronted by a curious
arcade and capped by a
lantern, introduced the
Lombardy Mannerist style to
Slovenia and was later copied

Tombstone,
Regional Museum

Frescoed Holy Steps in the Church
of the Assumption

throughout Dolenjska. The
frescoed Holy Steps were
added to the rear of the
church in 1780 to accom-
modate the flood of pilgrims.

The church's plain interior
only heightens the impact
of the spectacular Baroque
furnishings decorated in
shades of ruby, emerald
and gilt. The carved high
altar by the 17th-century
sculptor Jurij Scarnos is
especially rich – a riot of
gilded carvings on which
Mary is lifted heavenwards
by a flock of cherubs.

Kočevje ❸

Road Map C4. 17 km (11 miles) SE
of Ribnica. 🚉 17,000. 🚌 from
Ljubljana & Novo Mesto. 🛈 Trg
zbora odposlancev 72; (01) 893
1460. **www**.obcinakocevje.si

During World War II,
the Kočevski Rog plateau
was a wellspring of
Partisan Resistance.
Kočevje – today, an
administrative centre of
the "Land of Forests"
("Dežela gozdov") on
the Kočevski Rog –
hosted the inaugural
assembly of the
Delegates of the
Slovenian Nation.
This assembly, held
between 1 and 3
October 1943, effec-
tively led to the birth of the
modern Slovenian nation.

The parliament was held
at Šeškov dom, which is
now the **Regional Museum**
(Pokrajinski muzej). The hall
where the delegates convened
bears a banner that reads
Narod si bo pisal sodbo sam
(The nation shall choose its
fate alone). It also displays
superb reportage-style
sketches of the assembly as
well as of the Partisan
Resistance by the 20th-
century Novo Mesto-born
artist, Božidar Jakac. A section
in the museum covers the
lifestyles and the sudden
flight of the Germanic
Gottscheer population from
Kočevski Rog in 1941.

Another memento of partisan
activity is the heroic monument to the Communist

Baza 20, the Partisan Resistance camp in Kočevski Rog

struggle, erected postwar in the central square, Trg zbora odposlancev.

🏛 **Regional Museum**
Prešernova 11. **Tel** (051) 269 972.
⏰ 8am–3pm Mon–Fri. 🅿 ♿
www.pmk-kocevje.si

Kočevski Rog ❹

Road Map C4. 37 km (23 miles) SE of Ribnica. **Tel** (07) 306 6025.
🚌 from Apr–Oct by the Dolenjska Museum in Novo Mesto.
www.dolmuzej.com

The limestone plateau east of Kočevje is cloaked in one of Europe's last virgin forests, its pine and beech woods home to brown bears, wolves and lynx. Habsburg rulers resettled German immigrants, known as Gottscheers, in this remote region from the 14th century. The immigrants made the area one of the most developed in the region by the early 20th century but fled fearing reprisals at the outbreak of World War II.

The Partisan Resistance set up camp here in 1943 and established **Baza 20**, located 7 km (4 miles) west of the town of Dolenjske Toplice (*see p163*). Concealed in limestone depressions, this nerve centre for the anti-Fascist struggle was never discovered despite several attempts by the Nazis, and is preserved as the only serving headquarters of European wartime resistance. At its peak, around 200 people lived and worked in the 26 huts, which contained a

hospital, workshops, a printing press and barracks. All but two with display boards are empty, yet the silent forest makes the visit a haunting experience.

The base is now tainted by the partisans' massacre of thousands of pro-German Slovene Home Guard in the forest at the end of the war. Their mass graves were a secret until the 1970s and the exact number of people executed remains unknown.

Kolpa valley ❺

Road Map C5. 49 km (31 miles) S of Ribnica. ℹ Osilnica 16; (01) 894 1594. 🍴 🅿 ⛺ **www**.osilnica.si

Due to its natural beauty and one of the cleanest – and, in summer, warmest – rivers in

Europe, this tranquil river valley is a favourite holiday destination among Slovenians. Walking and fishing are popular, as is rafting on the gentle rapids of the Kolpa river that snakes along the Croatian border. The hub of all activity is Osilnica, 18 km (11 miles) west of the international border crossing. It has the only bank and supermarket in the area, as well as the Stane Jarm Gallery (Galerija Staneta Jarma), featuring works of local sculptor Stane Jarm (b.1931). Gallery visits can be organized at the tourist office.

East of Osilnica, in Ribjek, the diminutive Church of St Egidius (Cerkev sv Egidija), is a pretty shingle-roofed structure dating from 1681, with naive frescoes and painted glass windows, a traditional Slovenian folk art. It is said that the guard depicted on the right of the high altar is a commandant who fought in one of the many Turkish incursions of the 16th century.

Another folk hero of the valley is Peter Klepec, a shepherd boy who is said to have been given superhuman strength by local fairies. A legend relates that he uprooted the largest tree in the valley to defeat Turkish forces. This is depicted in a roadside sculpture by Stane Jarm a short distance west of Ribjek; the figure weilds a tree and glares eastwards.

RAFTING ON THE KOLPA

The clear Kolpa river provides delightful opportunities for rafting between April and September. While rafting on small whitewater rapids is possible early in the season, tranquil trips on inflatable rafts or canoes are possible in mid-summer; the river is at its swiftest between Stari trg and Vinica. Hotel Kovač in Osilnica and Tine & Co on Stari trg organize rafting trips.

Visitors rafting on the Kolpa river

Impressive façade of the Town Hall, Novo Mesto

Novo Mesto ❻

Road Map D4. 58 km (36 miles)
E of Ribnica. 🏠 22,000. 🚊 *from
Ljubljana.* 🚌 *from Ljubljana &
Dolenjske Toplice.* 🛈 *Glavni trg 6;
(07) 393 9263.* 🚢 *Mon & Fri.*
www.novomesto.si

Located on the banks of the
Krka river, Novo Mesto is
the largest city in southeastern
Slovenia and the capital of
Dolenjska region. Although its
name literally means New
Town, historical evidence
suggests that a settlement has
occupied this spot since prehistory. Today's city was
founded in 1365 by the
Habsburg Archduke Rudolph
IV (1339–65), who had
christened it Rudolphswert.
Novo Mesto blossomed into
an important trading centre in
the Middle Ages, and then
into an industrial centre.
    The modernity of the city's
outskirts has not affected its
historic centre. The oldest site
in Novo Mesto is the Church
of St Nicholas (Cerkev sv
Nikolaja), built at the highest
point on the river promontory.
It features an altarpiece by the
Venetian Renaissance artist
Tintoretto (1518–94), as well
as Slovenia's only Gothic crypt,
built to prop up the presbytery
and now a repository for
bishops' tombstones.
    The grand attraction of
the town, however, is the
Dolenjska Museum (Dolenjski
muzej) beyond the church,
which holds some of the
richest ancient archaeological
exhibits in the country.
Particularly outstanding are the

grave-finds of Celtic Hallstatt
tribes of the late Iron Age,
notably the armour of a high-
ranking warrior, as well as
exceptional stitulae (bronze
cremation urns) forged with
vivacious images of warriors
and hunters. An adjacent
building showcases exhibits
of regional ethnography.
    Glavni trg, the former
merchant centre, is a
picturesque cobbled
throughfare with
several cafés and, at
the centre, the 1903
Town Hall (Rotovž).
The Franciscan
St Leonard's Church
(Fračiškanskan cerkev
sv Lenarta), a block
behind the town hall,
has a Neo-Gothic and
Secessionist façade
and houses illuminated the
manuscripts in the attached
library; the tourist office can
arrange visits.
    At the end of Glavni trg
is **Jakčev House** (Jakčev dom),
a gallery of works by the
artist Božidar Jakac who was
born in this riverside quarter.
Displays rotate, but include
charming images of Novo

Situlae at the
Dolenjska Museum,
Novo Mesto

Mesto and the Dolenjska
countryside as well as lively
sketches made when the artist
travelled to Europe and
America in the 1920s and 30s.

🏛 **Dolenjska Museum**
Muzejska ulica 7. **Tel** *(07) 373 1130.*
🕐 *9am–5pm Tue–Sat, 9am–1pm
Sun.* 🎫 **www**.dolmuzej.com

🏛 **Jakčev House**
Sokolska ulica 1. **Tel** *(07) 373
1131.* 🕐 *9am–5pm Tue–Sat,
9am–1pm Sun.* 🎫

Gallery of
Naive Artists ❼
Galerija likovnih
samorastnikov

Road Map C3. 20 km (13 miles)
NW of Novo Mesto; Goliev trg 1,
Trebnje. **Tel** *(07) 348 2100.* 🚊 *from
Novo Mesto.* 🚌 *from Novo Mesto &
Ljubljana.* 🕐 *10am–noon & 3–6pm
Mon–Fri, 10am–noon Sat.* 🎫 **www.**
ciktrebnje.si

The otherwise anonymous
town of Trebnje war-
rants a visit for its
Gallery of Naive Artists.
Located above a shop-
ping centre, Slovenia's
only naive art museum
displays the works of a
village artists' collec-
tive established in
the 1950s, modelled
after the Hlebine
school in northern Croatia.
Characterized by sharp lines
and bright clear colours,
the art here depicts happy
peasants, fairy tale forests and
bountiful fields. Their unconventional compositions are
influenced by Slovenian folk
arts such as painted beehive
panels and oil-on-glass votive
art. The gallery also displays
works by affiliated international artists.

Paintings and sculptures at the Gallery of Naive Artists, Trebnje

View of Žužemberk Castle from the banks of the Krka river

Žužemberk ❽

Road Map C4. 24 km (15 miles) W of Novo Mesto. 🏃 *1,100*. 🚌 *from Ljubljana & Novo Mesto*. 🎭 *Medieval Days (mid Jul)*. **www**.zuzemberk.si

The geographical and administrative hub of the broad Krka river valley, this market town was built around a defence tower in the Middle Ages. **Žužemberk Castle** (Grad Žužemberk) was built in the 16th century by the Auersperg princes and retained offices, a court and prison cells until it began to collapse in 1893. It was reduced to a shell in 1945, but restoration, ongoing since the 1960s, has returned some of the visual impact of its five circular bastions. The castle now serves as a venue for concerts between June and September.

🏰 **Žužemberk Castle**
Grajski trg 1. **Tel** (07) 388 5180.
🕐 Jul–Aug: 10am–6pm Sat & Sun.

Dolenjske Toplice ❾

Road Map D4. 13 km (8 miles) SW of Novo Mesto. 🏃 *3,300*. 🚌 *from Novo Mesto*. ℹ️ *Sokolski trg 4; (07) 384 5188*. **www**.dolenjske-toplice.si

The oldest medicinal spa resort in Slovenia, Dolenjske Toplice lies at the foot of the Kočevski Rog plateau. Slovenian chronicler Janez

Vajkard Valvasor *(see p91)* recorded tourists coming to bathe in its thermal spring waters in the mid-1600s, when the Auersperg princes promoted its warm and mud baths. The small town prospered at the close of the 19th century as a fashionable health resort of the Austro-Hungarian Empire.

Today, Dolenjske Toplice remains popular with visitors who come for medicinal cures; the 36° C (96.8° F) calcium-rich water is said to work wonders for rheumatism. Recreational visitors come to the Balnea Wellness Centre, which has a complex of pools, saunas, and massage rooms.

Handicrafts at Primožič House

Spire of the Church of St Peter, Črnomelj

Črnomelj ❿

Road Map D4. 33 km (21 miles) S of Novo Mesto. 🏃 *5,800*. 🚉 *from Ljubljana*. 🚌 *from Novo Mesto & Metlika*. ℹ️ *Trg svobode 3; (07) 305 6530*. 🎭 *Jurjevanje Folk Festival (mid-Jun)*. **www**.belakrajina.si

The administrative capital of the Bela Krajina region is celebrated for a wonderful folk festival that attracts dancers and musicians from throughout Slovenia, as well as for its pre-Roman history.

Črnomelj Castle (Črnomaljski grad), modified into offices and barely recognizable as a Romanesque stronghold from its façade, contains a small municipal museum. The **Church of St Peter** (Cerkev sv Petra), located diagonally opposite, is notable for its collection of fragments of Roman tombstones near the choir. Behind it, at the far end of the street, **Primožič House** (Primožičeva hiša) displays and sells regional handicrafts such as painted eggs (*pisanica*) and wickerwork.

🏛 **Črnomelj Castle**
Trg svobode 3. **Tel** (07) 305 6530.
🕐 8am–4pm Mon–Fri, 9am–noon Sat. 🎭

🏛 **Primožič House**
Ulica Mirana Jarca 18. 🕐 8am–4pm Mon–Fri, 9am–noon Sat.

Tri Fare churches in Rosalnice, near Metlika

Metlika ⓫

Road Map D4. 27 km (17 miles) SE of Novo Mesto. 🏠 3,400. 🚌 from Novo Mesto & Črnomelj. 🅸 Metlika Castle, Trg svobode 4; (07) 363 5470. 🎉 Vinska Vigred (3rd weekend of May). **www**.metlika-turizem.si

Set in the lovely countryside, this wine-producing town near the Kolpa river is the most picturesque in the Bela Krajina region. Given the historic architecture in its town centre, it is hard to believe the town was frequently attacked and occupied by Turkish forces in the 15th and 16th centuries, and gutted by fire in 1705.

During the Turkish raids, Metlika Castle (Grad Metlika) was a Renaissance fortress; today's aristocratic manor is a result of renovation in the 18th century. A wing of the castle houses the **Bela Krajina Museum** (Belokranjski muzej), which has displays on the region. An audio-visual slideshow introduces the themes – local history, notably Hallstatt grave finds and Roman remains excavated near Črnomelj; and rural lifestyles and crafts, including wine-making and displays of the white embroidered folk costume after which Bela Krajina (literally, White Carniola), according to one theory, is named. The cellars house a wine bar serving local wines. Another wing of the castle contains the Slovenian Firefighting Museum (Slovenski gasilski muzej), which has displays of old fire engines; the country's first fire brigade was established in Metlika in 1869.

The heart of the old town is Mestni trg, a pretty square with small, pastel-coloured houses. At the square's end, fronted by the Maltese crosses of the Teutonic Knights and with a fresco of the Last Judgment, is the Church of St Nicholas (Cerkev sv Nikolaja).

Environs
Located just over 2 km (1 mile) east of Metlika in Rosalnice are the **Tri Fare** (literally, Three Parishes) – a trio of Gothic pilgrimage churches set side by side and enclosed within a low wall. Historians speculate that the churches may have been built to cater to a mixed denomination of Croats, Slovenians and Greek Orthodox worshippers or to cope with a surge in pilgrims in the early 1500s. The largest and smallest, the Lady of Our Sorrows and Ecce Hommó

respectively, contain fine Baroque frescoes. The churches are usually locked; it is best to consult the tourist office in Metlika for the whereabouts of the keys.

🏛 **Bela Krajina Museum**
Trg svobode 4. **Tel** (07) 306 3370. ◔ 9am–5pm Mon–Sat, 10am–2pm Sun. 🌐 **www**.belokranjski-muzej.si

Pleterje Monastery ⓬
Samostan Pleterje

Road Map D4. 17 km (11 miles) E of Novo Mesto; Drča 1, Šentjernej. **Tel** (07) 308 1225. 🕐 7:30am–5:30pm Mon–Sat. **www**.kartuzija-pleterje.si

The Carthusian Order was permitted by the Count of Celje to found a monastery in this remote location in 1407. Today, white-cloaked monks remain in the monastery despite Turkish raids in the 16th century and the order's dissolution by Emperor Joseph II in 1784; the buildings were reclaimed in 1899. The monastery is screened by a high wall and visitors have access only to the Gothic Church of the Holy Trinity (Cerkev sv Trojice) – bare but for a medieval rood screen – and a shop that sells fruit brandies, wines, honey and beeswax candles made by the monks.

Bottle of pear brandy

In an attempt to deflect attention from the monastery, an **Open-air Museum** (Pleterje Skansen) was built in an adjacent field. Historic buildings from the region were rebuilt here to re-create a traditional farmstead, centred around a snug 19th-century cottage with a "black kitchen" hung with smoke-cured meats and cabin-like bedrooms with corn-sheaf mattresses. A toplar or double hayrack and a small farmyard of animals complete the picture.

Interior of a house, Open-air Museum, Pleterje Monastery

🏠 **Open-air Museum**
Drča 1, Šentjernej. **Tel** (07) 308 1050. ◔ Apr–Nov: 10am–5pm daily; Dec–Mar: 10am–4pm daily. 🌐 **www**.skansen.si

A Tour of the Krka Valley ⑬

East of Novo Mesto, the Krka river snakes through a broad valley and passes a succession of large castles. These are a legacy of the Ottoman Turk expansion during the 16th century, when the Habsburg Emperor Ferdinand II established a military frontier *(vojna krajina)* to fight off raids from across the border. Modified later into palaces by feudal rulers, the strongholds on this route now house museums, galleries, spas and hotels.

TIPS FOR DRIVERS

Starting point: *Otočec, on the 419 from Ratež to Mokrice.*
Length: *42 km (26 miles).*
Duration: *Full day.*
Driving conditions: *Single-lane country roads till Brežice.*
Stopping-off points: *There are restaurants at every stop off en route that serve good traditional cuisine.*

Konstanjevica na Krki ②

This pretty village, located on an island in the river, is home to a former Cistercian monastery, with one of the largest Renaissance court-yards in Europe. Inside the monastery is the outstanding Božidar Jakac Gallery, with paintings and sketches by the 20th-century Slovenian artists such as France and Tone Kralj.

Otočec ①
This 13th-century Renaissance mansion on an island in the Krka river has been restored as a five-star hotel. Famous guests include President Tito and actor Roger Moore, among others.

Leskovec

Cerklje

Šentjernej

Ratež

Gabrje

SLOVENIA

CROATIA

Mokrice Castle ⑤
Legend has it that the crow on the coat of arms of this triangular Renaissance fortress fell into the courtyard with an arrow through its neck, alerting the owners to the Turkish forces amassed nearby. It is now a hotel with an excellent golf course.

0 km   3
0 miles   3

KEY

— Tour route
— Motorway
— Other road
— Railway
-•- International boundary

Terme Čatež ④
Developed in the 1960s as a spa for people suffering from rheumatism, Terme Čatež is today the largest and most popular resort in the country.

Brežice ③
Located at the confluence of the Krka and Sava rivers, this town centres around a Renaissance stronghold housing exquisite frescoes in the Knight's Hall as well as a regional museum.

The 13th-century hilltop Podsreda Castle

Bizeljsko-sremiška Wine Road ⑭

Bizeljsko-sremiški vinorodni okoliš

Road Map E3. 51 km (32 miles) NE of Novo Mesto. 🏠 *Cesta prvih borcev 18, Brežice; (07) 499 0680.* 🍴 🗿 www.visitbrezice.com

The lower Sava valley area, north of Brežice *(see p165)*, is known for excellent sparkling and blended white wines cultivated in sandy, mineral-rich soils. The greatest concentration of winemakers lies 10 km (6 miles) north of Brežice on highway 219, around the villages of Stara vas, Brezovica and Bizeljsko. **Istenič** at Stara vas is one of Slovenia's premier sparkling wine producers and organizes cellar tours and tastings. A local attraction are the repnice cellars, cave-like sandstone cellars used by many winemakers. These were dug as natural refrigerators for farmers' crops, but their constant 6–8°C (43–47°F) temperatures and humidity proved ideal for laying down wines. Most of the repnice vineyards are located in Brezovica. The cellars also give refuge to bee-eating birds, which can be seen nesting between May and July near Bizeljsko.

> 🏠 **Istenič**
> Stara vas 7. **Tel** (07) 495 1559.
> 🕐 1–8pm Mon–Thu, 1–10pm
> Fri, noon–10pm Sat, 10am–8pm
> Sun. 🗿 🍴 www.istenic.si
> **Note:** Book in advance.

Podsreda Castle ⑮

Grad Podsreda

Road Map E3. 57 km (35 miles) NE of Novo Mesto; Podsreda 45. **Tel** (03) 580 6118. 🕐 Apr–Oct: 10am–6pm Tue–Sun. 🗿 🖥 www.kozjanski-park.si

With its sheer slab-sided walls and a perch on a high wooded spur above the valley, Podsreda Castle appears every inch the romantic castle. Originally erected in the 13th century and then owned by a succession of feudal dynasties, including the counts of Celje and Ptuj, this rectangular fortress was a near total ruin after World War II. Its impressive looks today are the result of three decades of renovation; only

Black and golden altar at the church in Olimje Monastery

the medieval kitchen looks as it did when the castle was built. Other rooms, which host an exhibition of glasswork, are bare and sometimes startlingly modern.

The castle's commanding position affords sweeping views of the lower Sava valley all the way to the low mountains in Croatia.

Olimje Monastery ⑯

Minoritski samostan Olimje

Road Map E3. 78 km (49 miles) NE of Novo Mesto; Olimje 82. **Tel** (03) 582 9161. 🚑 **Pharmacy** 🕐 Mar–late Oct: 10am–7pm daily; late Oct–Feb: 10am–5pm daily. 🗿 www.olimje.net

Prettily located at the head of a valley near the Croatian border, Olimje Monastery is a squat Renaissance castle that was given to Pauline monks in the mid-17th century. The monks added a Baroque church to the original structure, in which they installed one of Slovenia's most extravagant religious artworks – an altar (1680), which fills the choir with jet-black and gilt carving.

The church also features Baroque frescoes by the Pauline monk Ivan Ranger (1700–1753), a leading Baroque painter of Central Europe, which rise to a trompe l'oeil lantern. Contemporary frescoes adorn a side chapel dedicated to St Francis.

The former south tower, just off the cloisters, contains what is claimed to be Europe's third oldest pharmacy. This low-vaulted circular room retains a low Baroque cabinet and frescoes that depict physicians from Christianity and antiquity as well as scenes of Christ healing. The **Pharmacy** has a vestibule, where the Pauline monks sell herbal cures. The chocolatier, located on one side of the monastery gardens, is also popular with visitors.

Baroque fresco, Olimje Monastery Pharmacy

many ailments – spout within this hall. The hall also offers massages, aromatherapy and fango mud treatments.

Visitors can also spend time in the **Rogaška Riviera** a complex of thermal mineral water pools.

⚑ Rogaška Riviera
Stritarjeva 1. *Tel* (03) 811 2000.
⊙ *daily.* www.terme-rogaska.si

Rogatec Open-air Museum ⓲
Muzej na prostem Rogatec

Road Map E2. 8 km (5 miles) NE of Rogaška Slatina; Ptujska cesta 23. *Tel* (03) 818 6200. 🚉 *from Rogaška Slatina.* 🚌 *from Rogaška Slatina.* 🛈 *Trg 22; (03) 810 7286;* www.rogatec.net. ⊙ *Apr–Nov: 10am–6pm Tue–Sun.* 🅿 🛈 www.muzej-rogatec.si

The market town of Rogatec is home to the largest open-air museum in Slovenia. A short distance from the town centre, ten agricultural buildings gathered from Štajerska, a region in northern Slovenia, have been rebuilt to simulate a village, providing an insight into rural and religious folk-culture between the 18th and early 20th centuries.

The centrepiece cottage – the boyhood home of Slovenian poet Jože Šmit (1922–2004) – has hollowed

Façade of the Grand Hotel Rogaška, Rogaška Slatina

tree trunks for gutters. The windows of the room in the *hiška* (home), where the older daughters of the house slept, have hinged iron grills to deter amorous suitors. Traditionally, the hinges were left unoiled so that it would be difficult to open the windows. The village also has a toplar double hay-rack unique to Slovenian rustic architecture, a pigsty fronted by a rack on which turnip and carrot leaves were dried for winter feed, and a cluttered 1930s grocer's store selling traditional souvenirs.

Demonstrations of domestic crafts such as baking, smithery and basket-weaving from corn husks are sometimes staged late on Friday or Saturday afternoons during the high season.

Rogaška Slatina ⓱

Road Map E3. 88 km (57 miles) NE of Novo Mesto. 🚶 *5,500.* 🚉 *from Celje.* 🚌 *from Celje & Maribor.* 🛈 *Zdraviliški trg 1; (03) 581 4414.* www.rogaska-slatina.si

No other Slovenian spa town retains the air of its imperial heyday like Rogaška Slatina. Austro-Hungarians acclaimed the therapeutic power of the thermal waters after the Croatian viceroy Petar Zrinski was cured here in 1665. The arrival of Archduke Johann von Habsburg in 1810 propelled Rogaška Slatina into a fashionable resort frequented by Austro-Hungarian royalty and Viennese high society.

Its heart is the central park, Zdraviliški trg, with mani-cured lawns and immaculate flowerbeds. Here, the Habsburg-era health spa, Zdraviliški dom, now the Grand Hotel Rogaška (*see p197*), is one of the grandest Neo-Classical buildings in Slovenia and has an opulent ballroom in which composer Franz Liszt once entertained imperial spa-goers.

The original 19th-century drinking-temple lends its name to Rogaška Slatina's Temple mineral water, on sale throughout Slovenia. The focus of many of today's visitors, however, is the modern drinking hall (*pivnica*) at the far end of the square. Several mineral springs, including Donat – a potent magnesium-rich water, hailed as a cure for

Agricultural buildings at the Rogatec Open-air Museum

Plague Monument in the Main Square, Maribor ▷

Celje ⑯

The sobriquet "City of Counts and Princes" seems inconsistent with the modest appearance of Slovenia's third-largest town. Yet Celje, founded over Celeia, the administrative centre of the Roman province of Noricum during the 1st to 5th centuries, rose to become a regional superpower under the dukes of Celje in the Middle Ages. Until Count Ulrich II was assassinated by a rival in Belgrade in 1456, their feudal dynasty stood alone against the Habsburgs, an act of defiance that put their three-star crest onto the Slovenian flag. Modernization and damage during World War II erased the medieval glory, yet Celje's riverside core harbours appealing museums and a splendid castle. The largely pedestrianized Old Town is located on the bank of Savinja river.

Marian pillar in Glavni trg with St Daniel's church as the backdrop

🏛 Glavni trg

Ringed by cafés and shaded by plane trees, this picturesque cobbled square is a favourite place for locals to relax. It developed as the administrative heart of the Old Town and is surrounded by Baroque townhouses of wealthy citizens. The house at No. 8 still retains its frescoes. A votive Marian pillar (1776) stands at the centre above statues of St Rok, protector against plague; St Florian, Catholic firefighter; and St Joseph, the patron saint of families and workers. The pillar itself was installed two centuries ago and became the place where criminals were publicly shamed.

Mounted into a townhouse behind the pillar is a Roman tombstone from Celeia.

🔒 St Daniel's Church

Slomškov trg.
Celje's principal church (Cerkev sv Danijela) stands on Slomškov trg, a square named to honour the 19th-century bishop, Anton Martin Slomšek, who was born near Celje and beatified in 1999. This large Gothic church was built in the early 14th century to replace a smaller predecessor when Celje's wealth and power had begun to rise.

Within the church's dark, atmospheric interior are several frescoes, including one of an Adoration procession that spans the presbytery arch, and fine tombstones of the Celje dukes in full armour in one aisle. The highlight of the church is the late-Gothic chapel – named

Chapel of Our Lady of Sorrows after its medieval pietà – to the altar's left.

Located behind the church is the Water Tower, the most impressive bastion of medieval defences, so called for its riverside location.

🏛 Celje Regional Museum

Muzejski trg 1. *Tel* (03) 428 0962.
☐ Mar–Oct: Tue–Sun; Nov–Feb: Tue–Sat. 🎫 🎦 obligatory.
www.pokmuz-ce.si
Located in a Renaissance palace, this museum (Pokrajinski muzej Celje), showcases the town's past from prehistory to the early 20th century and its ducal rulers. A ghoulish case contains 18 of their skulls – that of the ill-fated Ulrich II is almost sliced in half. The other star attraction is a

Beautifully painted ceiling of the Celje Regional Museum

For hotels and restaurants in this region see pp195–7 and pp209–11

painted ceiling (1600) that was uncovered during renovation of the ceremonial hall in 1926 and is so fragile that it is kept in dim light. Art historians dispute its attribution to the Dutch master, Almanach. Its trompe l'oeil is a spectacular work with guards and noble-women gazing down at viewers from galleries that seem to fade into the distance, while images of the four seasons and battles frame the edges.

Elsewhere, rooms hold a selection of furnishings and oil paintings in styles ranging from Renaissance to Biedermeier. Other sections of the museum contain prehistoric archaeology, including the world's oldest needle and a lapidarium of votive slabs from Celeia.

🏛 Museum of Recent History

Prešernova 17. **Tel** (03) 428 6410.
⏰ 10am–6pm Tue–Fri, 9am–1pm Sat. 🌐 www.muzej-nz-ce.si

Located in the town hall, this museum (Muzej novejše zgodovine) offers an entertaining narrative of Celje from the late 19th century. Short films introduce local history and the "Street of Craftsmen" upstairs. There is a splendid re-creation of shops and ateliers in the mid-20th century with displays of tools and ephemera.

The museum also contains Herman's Den (Hermanov brlog), the only children's museum in Slovenia. Opposite the museum is a former Minorite monastery, nick-named Old Pot (Stari pisker), that served as a World War II

VISITORS' CHECKLIST

Road Map D3. 100 km (62 miles) N of Novo Mesto. 🏙 50,000. 🚉 from Ljubljana, Maribor & Velenje. 🚌 from Ljubljana, Maribor & Murska Sobota. 🛈 Krekov trg 3, (03) 428 7639; Old Castle, (03) 544 3690. 🌐 www.celeia.info

penitentiary. Nazis shot 374 hostages in six mass executions in its courtyard in 1941 and 1942.

⚓ Old Castle

Cesta na grad 78. **Tel** (03) 544 3690.
⏰ May & Sep: 9am–8pm daily; Jun–Aug: 9am–9pm daily; Oct–Apr: 9am–5pm daily. 🌐 🖥

The scale of one of Slovenia's largest castles, Stari grad, testifies to Celje's power under late-medieval counts. Originally a Romanesque stronghold on a sheer bluff southeast of the centre, the castle acquired its form during the late 14th century. The Celje counts built a palace and the four-storey defensive Friedrich Tower. After centuries of decay, it has been restored to some of its former glory and now doubles as an exhibition space. There are splendid views over Celje from a belvedere near the palace, and from the tower.

Historical performance in progress at the Old Castle

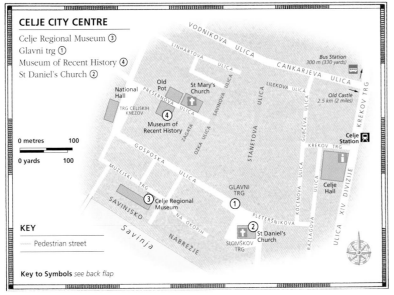

CELJE CITY CENTRE

VODNIKOVA ULICA
LINHARTOVA ULICA
CANKARJEVA ULICA
Bus Station 300 m (330 yards)
National Hall
Old Pot
PREŠERNOVA ULICA
St Mary's Church
LILEKOVA ULICA
SAVINOVA ULICA
ULICA
GUBČEVA ULICA
Old Castle 2.5 km (2 miles)
KREKOV TRG
TRG CELJSKIH KNEZOV
④
Museum of Recent History
ZAGATA
OZKA ULICA
STANETOVA
Celje Station
GOSPOSKA ULICA
KREKOV TRG
ⓘ
MUZEJSKI TRG
KOCENOVA ULICA
Celje Hall
SAVINJSKO
③ Celje Regional Museum
NA OKOPIH
GLAVNI TRG
①
RAZLAGOVA
ULICA XIV DIVIZIJE
Savinja
NABREŽJE
② St Daniel's Church
PLETERŠNIKOVA ULICA
SLOMŠKOV TRG

0 metres 100
0 yards 100

KEY

---- Pedestrian street

Key to Symbols see back flap

Collection of African masks, Velenje Museum

Velenje ⑳

Road Map D2. 24 km (15 miles) NW of Celje. ⧉ *33,800.* ▤ *from Celje.* ▭ *from Celje & Ljubljana.* ⓘ *Stari trg 3; (03) 896 1860.* **www**.velenje-tourism.si

Slovenia's fifth-largest town and one of the newest, Velenje is an interesting architectural piece of Communist Yugoslavia. It grew rapidly in the 1950s as the country's coal mining expanded. The town architect thought that since miners spent days underground, the town should be filled with light and space: achieved via tower blocks and squares. "Tito's Velenje", named in honour of Josip Broz Tito, was completed by 1959.

Velenje Castle (Velenjski grad) crowns a low hill to the south of town. The castle, first documented as a stronghold to control the north-south trade routes in the 13th century, was modified in the 16th century. The **Velenje Museum** (Muzej Velenje) hosts ten different collections, the most absorbing relate to sacral and folk works, African art and ritual objects and modern Slovenian art.

The **Coal Mining Museum of Slovenia** (Muzej premogovništva Slovenije) offers tours to explore the shafts below.

🏛 **Velenje Castle & Museum**
Ljubljanska cesta 54. **Tel** *(03) 898 2630.* ◯ *10am–6pm Tue–Sun.* 🖭 www.muzej.velenje.si

🏛 **Coal Mining Museum of Slovenia**
Stari Jašek, Koroška cesta. **Tel** *(03) 587 0997.* ◯ *8:30am–5pm Tue–Sun.* 🖭 ☒ *last tour 3pm.* ☐ ☐ www.rlv.si/muzej

Slovenj Gradec ㉑

Road Map D2. 51 km (32 miles) NW of Celje. ⧉ *8,000.* ▭ *from Celje & Velenje.* ⓘ *Glavni trg 24, (02) 881 2116.* **www**.slovenjgradec.si

Reputedly the coldest town in Slovenia – four decades ago, schoolchildren would be sent home because the ink froze in their pens – this small town is better known as the birthplace of composer Hugo Wolf (1860–1903) and for its artistic heritage that dates to the 18th century, when a local workshop made sacred sculpture. A

Baroque altar of Church of St Elizabeth, Slovenj Gradec

Modernist arts collective in the 1930s spawned the **Gallery of Fine Arts** (Galerija likovnih umetnosti), a pastel-tinted medieval building with modern sculpture. The gallery hosts works by local 20th-century artists such as Jože Tisnikar and international names such as Ossip Zadkine, a Russian-born, Paris-educated Cubist. The building was originally the town hall and the exhibits of regional archaeology in the incorporated **Koroška Regional Museum** (Koroški pokrajinski muzej) are displayed in old cells. These include glass and jewellery from Colatio, a 3rd-century Roman settlement that preceded Slovenj Gradec.

The **Church of St Elizabeth** (Cerkev sv Elizabete) lies on Trg svobode, off Glavni trg. Its sombre late-Romanesque exterior conceals a late-Gothic interior with Baroque furnishings. Austrian sculptor Johan Jacob Schoy (1686–1732) carved an altar so large it just squeezes into the presbytery while the altarpiece is by Franz Strauss, leading artist of Slovenj Gradec's Baroque workshop.

The adjacent Church of the Holy Spirit (Cerkev sv Duha) contains fragments of Roman tombstone embedded in its walls and Gothic frescoes of Christ's martyrdom. The tourist office can provide access when mass is not in progress.

🏛 **Gallery of Fine Arts**
Glavni trg 24. **Tel** *(02) 884 1283.* ◯ *9am–6pm Tue–Fri, 10am–1pm & 2–6pm Sat & Sun.* 🖭 ☐ www.glu-sg.si

🏛 **Koroška Regional Museum**
Glavni trg 24. **Tel** *(02) 884 2055.* ◯ *9am–6pm Tue–Fri, 10am–1pm & 2–6pm Sat & Sun.* 🖭 ☐ www.kpm.si

---

JOŽE TISNIKAR (1928–98)

Few Slovenian painters are as instantly recognizable as Jože Tisnikar. After an impoverished childhood as one of eight children to an alcoholic father, he took a job performing autopsies and preparing cadavers in the pathology department of Slovenj Gradec hospital. The experience shaped his work. *Autopsy* (1955) established the style of the self-taught artist: haunted and bleak.

The Flute Player, 1971, by Jože Tisnikar

The Romanesque Church of St Vitus, Dravograd

Kope ❷

Road Map D2. 63 km (39 miles) N of Celje. **ℹ** *Glavni trg 41, Slovenj Gradec; (02) 882 2740.* **www**.pohorje.org

A narrow road running east from Slovenj Gradec ascends slowly through villages to this small resort among the highest hills of the Pohorje massif. It is a popular destination for skiing as the snow cover can last from November to late spring, while in summer, hikers and families come for the clean, cool air and easy walking trails.

Hour-long walks from a car park at an altitude of 1,370 m (4,500 ft) ascend to the neighbouring peaks, Velika Kopa and Črni vrh. From the latter, at 1,540 m (5,060 ft), the path continues to hilltops Mali Črni vrh and Ribniški vrh to reach a pretty alpine lake covered with waterlilies.

Dravograd ❷

Road Map D2. 60 km (37 miles) NW of Celje. **🚶** *3,400.* **🚆** *from Maribor.* **🚌** *from Maribor, Celje, Velenje & Slovenj Gradec.* **ℹ** *Trg 4 julija 50, (02) 871 0285.* **www**.dravograd.si

On the Austrian border, this small town wraps around the confluence of the Drava, Meža and Mislinja rivers. The location made it strategic for rafters, who bound felled logs at its quay then transported them as far away as Hungary, Romania and Serbia. Pleasure trips by raft *(flos)* are organized for groups *(see pp220–21).*

Dravograd's name was tarnished in the last century, due to its association with a Gestapo prison in the basement of the town hall at Trg 4 julija. In its five cells, punishment and torture was meted out to Slovenian resistance fighters and troublesome Russian prisoners who were forced to build a hydroelectric dam on the Drava river. The cells can be visited through the tourist office during weekday office hours.

Nearby, in the town centre is the Romanesque Church of St Vitus (Cerkev sv Vida), built in 1170, when Dravograd first found mention in the records.

Šentanel ❷

Road Map C2. 78 km (49 miles) NW of Celje. **🚶** *200.*

This sleepy farming hamlet clusters around its church on a sun-drenched south-facing

hillside. With good views and a lazy pace of life, Šentanel is a lovely destination at which to sample rural tourism, stop overnight in a traditional alpine farmhouse or sample the local cider *(mošt)* in the village centre inns. Opposite the church are two farmsteads with a few small rooms on the ground floor and an attic storage space accessed by ladder. The village is also a popular base for some of the finest mountain biking trails. The Eko Hotel Kmetija Koroš *(see p197)* runs tours.

Bicycle tour of the museum in the Peca Underground Mine

Peca Underground Mine ❷
Podzemlje Pece

Road Map C2. 46 km (29 miles) NW of Celje; Glančnik 8, Mežica. **Tel** *(02) 870 0180.* **🚌** *from Dravograd & Črna na Koroškem.* **ℹ** *Park kralja Matjaža, Center 100; (02) 823 8269.* 📷 📷 *Tue–Sun.* **Museum** ⬜ *9am–3pm Tue–Sun.* **www**.podzemljepece.com

Although the Romans are believed to have sourced lead ore from Mount Peca, it was not until 1665 that a mine was dug at Mežica to extract lead and zinc. Mining intensified in the early 20th century and when the mine ceased production in 1994, about 19 million tonnes (21 million tons) of ore had been extracted. Visitors can tour the mine by a train that descends 3.5 km (2 miles), or on bicycles. A **Museum** on the ground level focuses on miners' lifestyles and geology.

Traditional tourist farm, Šentanel

Mausolea at the Roman Necropolis, Šempeter

Roman Necropolis **26**
Rimska nekropola

Road Map D3. 12 km (8 miles) W of Celje; Ob rimski nekropoli 2, Šempeter. **Tel** (03) 700 2056. 🚌 from Celje. 🚃 from Celje. 🕐 1–15 Apr: 10am–3pm daily; 16 Apr–Sep: 10am–6pm daily; Oct: 10am–4pm Sat & Sun. 🎫 ♿ www.td-sempeter.si

In 1952, villagers digging in an orchard in the town of Šempeter discovered a female statue, thereby unearthing a well-preserved Roman cemetery on the former Ljubljana to Celje road. The cemetery survived the reigns of the Roman Emperor Trajan and the Severi Dynasty (AD 96–235), but was abandoned around AD 270 when the Savinja river flooded. The silt preserved the 100-plus mausolea of Celeia (Celje) families, which have been reconstructed; the park is called Roman Necropolis.

The most impressive epitaph is the marble mausoleum of the Spectatii, a monument over 8 m (26 ft) high, built for a Celje dignitary and his family. There is an image of Medusa at the apex intended to protect their remains from grave-robbers, while on the base are reliefs of Roman civilization – images of hunting and sporting, depictions of the four seasons and one of a satyr flirting with a nymph.

The richest carving adorns the mausoleum of the Ennius family. The style of its reliefs dates it back to the mid-1st century AD. It is fronted by an image of Europa being carried out to sea by Zeus disguised as a bull. Canopied

by a richly carved baldachin are images of Ennius family. Both monuments were created when Celje was at its most wealthy. The oldest tomb, that of Gaius Vindonius Successus, with images of Hercules leading Alcestis to the underworld, and the simple late 3rd-century tomb of Statucius Secundianus, reflect the rise then wane of a rich society. A section of the Roman road itself lies to the east of the cemetery.

Relief on a tombstone

Laško **27**

Road Map D3. 11 km (7 miles) S of Celje. 🏃 4,000. 🚌 from Celje. 🚃 from Celje. 🚏 Trg svobode 8; (03) 733 8950. 🎪 Beer & Flowers Festival (2nd week of Jul). www.stik-lasko.si

The road to the south of Celje follows the Savinja river to this small town famous as

Swimming pool at the spa resort in Laško

the home of the lager, Laško pivo. It was first brewed in 1825 by the owner of a honey and mead shop that grew into one of the largest breweries in Yugoslavia. The town's brewery (pivovarna) lies to the south of the medieval town centre and houses a small museum with displays on brewing techniques.

Laško's second claim to fame is its mineral springs. The Romans, medieval missionaries and the Austro-Hungarian Emperor Franz Josef I (r.1848–1916) himself bathed in the 34° C (93° F) waters that bubble up just north of the Old Town. Today's spa resort is a modern complex named Wellness Park Laško (Zdravilišče Laško) with pools and a massage centre. The town also boasts the fine early Gothic Church of St Martin (Cerkev sv Martina), which has a Romanesque tower.

Žiče Monastery **28**
Žička kartuzija

Road Map E2. 20 km (12 miles) NE of Celje; Stare Slemene 24, Loče. **Tel** (03) 759 3110. 🕐 May–Oct: 9am–7pm daily; Nov & Feb–Apr: 10am–6pm Mon–Fri. 🎫 🎪 📷 🛍 🍴 **Apothecary** 🌙 winters.

Magical for its peace and isolation in the Valley of St John, Žiče Monastery might well be the most evocative ruin in Slovenia. The Carthusian monastery was founded in 1160 – the story goes that St John appeared in a dream to the Styrian ruler Otakar III of Traungau (1124–64), who had recently returned from the Crusades, and instructed him to create a self-sufficient community. The monastery withstood Turkish raids behind high defence walls in the 15th century and prospered until its dissolution by Emperor Joseph II in 1782.

At the heart of the complex is the shell of the Romanesque Church of St John the Baptist (Cerkev

Defensive towers guarding the entrance to Žiče Monastery

sv Janeza Krstnika) and an octagonal Gothic chapel that houses a model of the monastery. Surrounding buildings have been restored and now house a museum with a lapidarium; the cellar of the acclaimed winemaker Zlati Grič; and, in a defence tower, the **Apothecary** that sells medicinal liquors and herbal cures prepared to ancient Carthusian recipies. The Gostišče Gastuž (1467) by the entrance is reputed to be the oldest operating inn in Slovenia.

Bottle of Zlati grič wine

Slovenske Konjice ㉙

Road Map D2. 19 km (12 miles) NE of Celje. ⋔ 13,900. ₪ from Celje, Ljubljana & Maribor. ⓘ Stari trg 29; (03) 759 3110. **www**.slovenskekonjice.si

Persevere through the modern suburbs and the Old Town lives up to the charm suggested by Slovenske Konjice's tag line "City of Flowers and Wine". Historic townhouses, painted in shades of peach, cream and butterscotch with flowerbox-lined windows stretch along the banks of a stream that is spanned by tiny bridges. A local tale explains that these early 18th-century houses survived where their medieval predecessors burned because their builders had

incorporated sacred boulders from the Žiče Monastery in the walls. The village-like medieval core, Stari trg, is enchanting.

At Stari trg 15, the Riemer Gallery (Galerija Riemer) displays a private collection of period furniture and art amassed by a wealthy local businessman. Tours can be organized through the tourist office.

Another attraction is the Church of St George (Cerkev sv Jurija), an unusual two-nave Gothic construction with a frescoed Baroque chapel. Beyond it is the **Trebnik Manor** (Dvorec Trebnik), an erstwhile 17th-century residence, which now serves as a gallery and shop where organic herbal beauty products and foods are sold.

Rogla ㉚

Road Map D2. 36 km (22 miles) N of Celje. ₪ from Zreče. ⓘ Cesta na Roglo 15, Zreče; (03) 757 7100. 🏠🖥📷🍴 **www**.rogla.eu

The rounded highlands north of Slovenske Konjice are the central section of the Pohorje massif extending west of Maribor. Once home only to isolated dairy farmsteads and a cottage timber industry, the lightly forested upland is known today for its ski resort on the summit of Rogla at 1,520 m (4,980 ft), north of the town of Zreče. Once the snow thaws, hiking and mountain biking take over on a variety of trails through Alpine meadows and pine forests.

Shelves lined with produce at the Trebnik Manor shop, Slovenske Konjice

Ptuj ㉜

Sculpture of St George

Scenically located on the banks of the Drava river, Ptuj is furnished with a wealth of monuments that testify to a history spanning two millennia. The town was founded in AD 69 as a self-governing Roman city-state named Colonia Ulpia Traiana Poetovio. At its height, 40,000 people lived in Poetovio, making it the largest Roman settlement in what is now Slovenia. The medieval town later blossomed under the governance of Austrian nobility and the archdiocese of Salzburg. Its influence, however, was weakened by the Ottoman Turkish attacks and then by fires in the 17th century. By the 1700s, Ptuj was just the provincial town it now appears to be at first glance.

View of the Church of St George and its neighbourhood, Ptuj

🏠 Mestni trg

The tidy main square, popular with locals for their morning coffee and evening drinks alike, has been the civic heart of Ptuj since medieval times. The grandest of the historic buildings on the square is the Germanic Neo-Gothic Town Hall built in 1907 to replace the late-Gothic original. Statues on its corner oriel window depict the Roman emperor Trajan, who awarded Ptuj full colonial rights; and St Victorin, the town's first bishop in the early 4th century.

A statue on the votive column in the middle of Mestni trg depicts St Florian, protector against fire, as a Roman soldier. This statue is a replica of the original, which was erected in 1745 after four catastrophic fires hit the city in a span of 60 years. The St Florian Column seems to have worked at protecting the town from fires – the inferno in 1744 was Ptuj's last.

🏠 Minorite Monastery

Minoritski trg. *Tel (02) 748 0310.*
The Minorite Order set up this monastery (Minoritski samostan) when they arrived in Ptuj in 1261. Having survived the purges of autocratic Joseph II in 1784 and persecution by the Nazis, the order still remains in the monastery, which possesses what is said to be the oldest Baroque façade in Slovenia. Its interior has a beautiful summer refectory with rich stucco work and frescoes. In the library is one of only three surviving New Testaments by the 16th-century Lutheran Primož Trubar (*see p35*), who published the first books in the Slovenian language. Visits to the monastery can be arranged through the tourist office.

The adjoining modern church is a replica of the one destroyed by Allied bombs in 1945 – only the Gothic presbytery remains of the original. The gilded votive Marian pillar outside was erected in 1655 to safeguard against plague.

🏠 Church of St George

Slovenski trg. *Tel (02) 748 1970.* 🔲
Built in the 9th century over a Roman basilica, the Church of St George (Cerkev sv Jruija) is an atmospheric hybrid of late-Romanesque and Gothic styles whose walls are decorated with frescoes. The abundance of finely carved altars reveal the wealth of the medieval town – an *Adoration of the Magi* (1515) in the south aisle is a highlight. The church's most acclaimed sculpture is a 15th-century work that portrays its patron as a boyish knight. The sculpture is protected in a glass case in the vestibule.

The baptismal chapel at the rear of the south aisle contains a 15th-century colour-saturated polyptych of the death of the Virgin Mary by Konrad Laib, a Salzburg master influenced by Italian high art. One wing of the polyptych shows St Heronymous wearing a red cape, holding a model of the original church.

🏠 Orpheus Monument

Slovenski trg.
This 5-m (16-ft) high Roman tombstone stands where it was unearthed sometime in the Middle Ages. Carved from white Pohorje marble for a 2nd-century mayor of Poetovio, and later used as a medieval pillory, this monument (Orfejev spomenik) is named after the worn relief of Orpheus, the legendary musician in Greek mythology. Here he is shown surrounded by the animals attracted by his songs of lament for Eurydice,

Frescoes in the summer refectory, Minorite Monastery

his wife. Carvings in the tympanum depict Selene, goddess of the moon.

More modest tombstones from Poetovio are mounted around the base of the City Tower (Mestni stolp) behind, a five storey campanile, which doubled as a watchtower during Turkish raids.

🏛 Dominican Monastery

Muzejski trg 1. **Tel** *(02) 748 0360.* ☐ *15 Apr–Nov: 9am–6pm daily.* 🌐 **www.**pok-muzej-ptuj.si

Thick floral stucco and sgraffiti, sculptures of friars and a candy-pink colour scheme give the Dominican Monastery (Dominikanski samostan) the most joyful façade in Ptuj. The decoration was added to the original Gothic building that housed the order after it arrived in Ptuj around 1230.

Inside, medieval frescoes in the cloister and Gothic vaults provide an atmospheric setting for the superb antique and medieval exhibits of the **Ptuj Regional Museum** (Pokrajinski muzej Ptuj).

🏛 Ptuj Castle

Na gradu 1. **Tel** *(02) 748 0360.* ☐ *9am–6pm daily.* 🌐 ✚ 🔊

Like the Celts and Romans before them, the Salzburg archbishops built Ptuj Castle (Ptujski grad) on the high ground above the Drava river, in the 11th century. It was leased to the lords of Ptuj and was renovated into a palace by the Leslie Dynasty in the 17th century. A tour of the castle's rooms is included in the entry fee to the Ptuj Regional Museum. The lower floors house period furnishings and objets d'art. The floors above display musical instruments, costumes of Ptuj's famous Kurent carnival and devotional art.

Environs

Around 2 km (1 mile) west of Ptuj, a pavilion, signposted off Mariborska cesta, shelters

the remains of the 3rd-century **Mithra Shrine**. Its finest sacrificial relief depicts the Roman sun god Mithras as he sacrifices a bull to create the world. Prize finds are displayed in the Dominican Monastery.

Kurenti costumes, Ptuj Regional Museum

THE KURENT

Somewhere between a fertility ritual and a rite of spring, the Kurent is named for its Kurenti – scary figures who dress in shaggy sheepskins, wear horns or a feather head-dress and have beak-like noses and red tongues that hang to the chest. On Shrove Tuesday, the Kurenti gambol between houses, flailing wooden clubs and clanking cowbells to scare off evil and winter spirits. Spectators smash clay pots for good luck and some women give handkerchiefs to win favour with the male Kurenti.

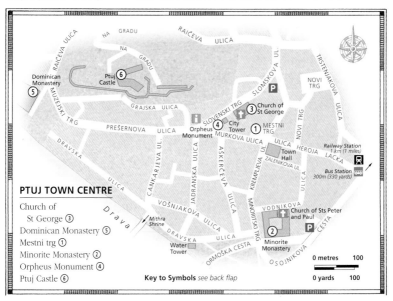

PTUJ TOWN CENTRE

Church of
St George ③
Dominican Monastery ⑤
Mestni trg ①
Minorite Monastery ②
Orpheus Monument ④
Ptuj Castle ⑥

Key to Symbols *see back flap*

0 metres   100
0 yards   100

Church of the Virgin Protectress ⓷⓷
Cerkev Marije Zavetnice

Road Map E2. 11 km (7 miles) SW of Ptuj. **Tel** (02) 794 4231. 🚌 from Ptuj. 🛈 Ptujska Gora 36, (02) 794 0027. **www**.ptujska-gora.si

Dating from the beginning of the 15th century, the Church of the Virgin Protectress is located above Ptujska Gora village. Funded by Ptuj's Lord Bernard III, the church was fortified during Turkish incursions in the middle of the century.

According to a local legend, the Virgin Mary draped her cloak over the hill as a black cloud to conceal the church from raiders – a miracle that elevated it to one of the most revered churches in Slovenia.

The story is probably related to the extraordinary *Virgin as Protector* (1410) high altar, the highlight of a beautifully spacious three-nave Gothic interior. Its centrepiece depicts a host of angels lifting the Madonna's dusty green cloak to reveal a kneeling crowd sheltered beneath. Among the 82 aristocrats, clergy and commoners depicted are portraits of Bernard III with his wife Valburga, presumably the two figures on the Virgin's left staring back at viewers. The south aisle contains a superb high-Gothic baldachin that was created to canopy the tomb of Celje's Count Frederick II; the three-star crest of the Celje

Dynasty – adopted in 1991 on the national flag – is just one feature among the exquisite carving. In the sanctuary, to the right of the main portal, is a finely executed Gothic fresco of St Dorothy and Jesus in the rose garden, with its donor depicted kneeling at the side.

Štatenberg Manor ⓷⓸
Dvorec Štatenberg

Road Map E2. Štatenberg 86, Makole. 18 km (11 miles) SW of Ptuj. **Tel** (02) 803 0216. 🕙 10am–10pm Wed–Sun. 📷 for tours only. 📕 book in advance. 🍴

Set above the valley 9 km (6 miles) west of Ptujska Gora, this two-storey palace was commissioned by Count Ignaz Maria Attems in the early 18th century. Intended to replace a medieval castle in nearby Makole, it was designed by an Italian architect and served as a summer residence for the powerful aristocratic Styrian family.

Štatenberg Manor's emblem

The four-wing palace was created in one go and has not been altered by subsequent owners. While decades of neglect have left the exterior semi-derelict, the courtyard is a delight of restrained Baroque style. There is a restaurant on the palace's ground floor. The rest of the interior, much of which is in poor condition, can only be seen on tours. The highlight is the ceremonial two-storey hall in the central

Štatenberg Manor, with the garden in the forefront

wing, where the Attems held banquets and balls beneath a ceiling whose allegorical frescoes of mythology, arts and sciences, are framed by stucco work. The surrounding English-style parkland, though neglected, is rather pleasant to explore.

Ormož ⓷⓹

Road Map F2. 23 km (14 miles) E of Ptuj. 👥 2,300. 🚉 from Ptu &, Murska Sobota. 🚌 from Ptuj. 🛈 Kolodrorska cesta 9, (02) 741 5556; second office in castle.

A location on a terrace abutting the Slovenian border has put Ormož on the front line throughout modern history. Between the 15th and 17th centuries, the town was attacked by Hungarians and Ottoman Turks, prompting the lords of Ormož to fortify the 13th-century castle. **Ormož Castle** retains the Romanesque tower, but the Baroque courtyard palace is the product of renovation during peacetime in the 18th century. When the castle was being restored, allegorical Classical paintings were put up in its halls. These paintings are now located on the first floor and are the highlight of the small museum within the castle, which also has displays on the town's history. The museum's displays include photographs from the Ten Day War (27 June–6 July, 1991) when Ormož was again back on the barricades of Slovenia as tanks of the Yugoslav Army invaded from Croatia *(see p39)*.

Virgin as Protector relief, Church of the Virgin Protectress, Ptujska Gora

For hotels and restaurants in this region see pp195–7 and pp209–11

The countryside north of Ormož is idyllic to explore at leisure. Isolated houses are scattered atop hills whose sun-drenched slopes nurture the vineyards of one of the country's premier wine regions. Details of the wine cellars *(vinska klet)* are available at the tourist office.

Environs
About 11 km (7 miles) north of Ormož lies the somnolent wine village, Jeruzalem. The story goes that it was christened by German Crusaders who were reminded of the holy city by the local hospitality. They are said to have brought a pieta icon, a replica of which is on the altar of the Church of St Mary (Cerkev sv Marije).

🏛 Ormož Castle and Museum
Kolodvorska 9. *Tel (02) 741 7290.* 🔲 *May–15 Oct: 8am–3pm Mon–Fri, 9am–2pm Sat; 16 Oct–Apr: 9am–4pm Mon–Fri, 9am–2pm Sat.* 📷 🚻

View of the lush green vineyards, north of Ormož

Ljutomer 🟠36

Road Map F2. 44 km (27 miles) NE of Ptuj. 🏘 *3,400.* 🚉 *from Ormož & Murska Sobota.* 🚌 🛈 *Jureša Cirila 4, (02) 581 1105; Glavni trg, (02) 584 8333.* **www**.jeruzalem.si

This region to the south of the Mura river has long been associated with horse breeding. This helps to explain why its administrative and cultural centre, Ljutomer, hosted

Nineteenth-century buildings in the main square, Ljutomer

Slovenia's first horse-racing meet – only the second in the Austro-Hungarian empire – in 1875. Between April and September the racing society stages trotting races on two Sunday afternoons a month on a racecourse about 1 km (0.6 mile) north of the centre. Ljutomer's heart is its spacious main square, Glavni trg, with a votive plague column of the Virgin Mary and saints Rok and Boštjan (1729). The **Ljutomer Museum** in the former town hall at the back of the square focuses on the Tabor Movement in Ljutomer (1868–71), when young Slovenian intellectuals initiated mass open-air forums *(tabors)* to rally support for a united Slovenia. More absorbing, perhaps, is footage from the oldest movies shot in Slovenia, filmed by cameraman Karol Grossmann in 1905.

🏛 Ljutomer Museum
Glavni trg 2. *Tel (02) 581 1295.* 🔲 *8am–3pm Mon–Fri.* 📷 📹 🚻

Radenci 🟠37

Road Map F1. 31 km (19 miles) N of Ptuj. 🏘 *1,800.* 🚌 *from Ljutomer & Murska Sobota.* **www**.zdravilisce-radenci.si

Until the arrival of a young Austrian medical student, Karl Henn, in 1833, local peasantry believed the 30–33° C (86–91° F) waters that bubbled up from the ground at Radenci

were caused by the cooking of subterranean witches. Henn, by now a doctor, returned to the area in 1869 and began to export the naturally carbonated water to the imperial court in Vienna and the papal palace in Rome. Branded with a three-hearts logo, the water is popular throughout Slovenia.

The medicinal spa resort established by Henn in 1882, Zdravilišče Radenci, is located at the eastern fringe of a large wooded park east of modern Radenci. Its waters are believed to treat cardiovascular problems. Renovation has added Terme Radenci, a spacious modern spa hotel with a wellness centre and large thermal swimming pool. Both are open to visitors as well as guests.

Visitors at the thermal pool in the spa resort, Radenci

Murska Sobota ❸❽

Road Map F1. 47 km (29 miles)
NE of Ptuj. 🏚 *12,600.* 🚉 *from
Ljubljana & Ptuj.* 🚌 *from Radenci,
Maribor & Celje.* 🛈 *Zvezna ulica 10;
(02) 534 1130; Slovenska ulica 25;
(02) 534 8822.* **www**.murska-
sobota.si

Until it was absorbed into the
Kingdom of Serbs, Croats and
Slovenes in 1919, Murska
Sobota was a backwater of
Hungary and, therefore, has
few historical monuments.
Today, the town is the capital
of the Prekmurje region. The
Regional Museum (Pokrajinski
muzej) in Murska Sobota
Castle (Murski grad) is worth a
visit. An erstwhile residence of
the counts of Murska Sobota,
and notable for its ceremonial
Baroque portal, this massively
turreted Renaissance palace
sits in an English-style parkland in the centre of the town.

The restored Baroque
festive hall, with splendid
frescoes and stuccowork, is
arguably the highlight among
the museum's archaeology
and ethnology exhibits. One
section has black pottery jugs
crafted by potters in the
northeastern village of Filovci,
and displays on customs of
the region. There is also
footage of ferries that plied
the Mura river until the 1930s
– the region was cut off from
Slovenia by road until a
bridge was built over the
river in 1924. One room
details the liberation of
Murska Sobota by Russia,

Visitors bathing in a thermal pool in Terme 3000, Moravske Toplice

after a second Hungarian
occupation at the end of
World War II. A Soviet-style
victory monument in the town
centre celebrates the Red
Army's arrival in April 1945.

🏛 **Regional Museum**
Trubarjev drevored 4. **Tel** *(02) 527
1706.* ⏰ *9am–5pm Tue–Fri,
9am–1pm Sat & Sun.* 📷 ♿
www.pok-muzej-ms.si

Moravske Toplice ❸❾

Road Map F1. 54 km (34 miles)
NE of Ptuj. 🏚 *700.* 🚌 *from Murska
Sobota.* 🛈 *Kranjčeva 3; (02) 538
1520.* **www**.moravske-toplice.com

Several hot-water springs were
discovered on the Prekmurje
plains during the search for
oil in the 1960s. This is where
the spa town of Moravske
Toplice was established. The
mineral-rich waters here
proved to be extremely popular with those seeking relief
from rheumatism.

Every day in summer,
hundreds of visitors come to
the **Terme 3000** spa to take a
dip in the waters, which
emerge at over 70°C (158°F)
but are cooled to around
36°–38°C (97°–100°F). The
resort's complex of hotels and
pools includes a medical faci-
lity, a wellness centre offering
massages and saunas and a
holiday area that is popular
with young families.

Environs
The small village of **Martjanci**
lies 2 km (1 mile) to the east
of Moravske Toplice. Although

its church appears to be an
anonymous Gothic construction, its presbytery contains the
finest medieval frescoes in the
Prekmurje area. They were
painted in 1392 by the artist
Janez Aquila. The frescoes,
which draw many visitors to
the town, are intended
to represent a heavenly
Jerusalem. Apostles – St Peter
with the key to the pearly
gates, St James with his staff
and scallop shell of pilgrimage
and St George spearing a
dragon – are depicted mingling
with dying Crusaders while
saints look on from the roof.
Aquila chose a unique way
to leave his signature on his
work – he painted himself into
the work as the tonsured
monk kneeling in a corner.

🌡 **Terme 3000**
Kranjčeva ulica 12. **Tel** *(02) 512
2200.* ⏰ *daily.*

Bogojina ❹❶

Road Map F1. 56 km (35 miles)
NE of Ptuj. 🏚 *570.* 🚌 *from
Murska Sobota.*

Bogojina is a village of
Hungarian-style L-shaped
cottages, many of which are
crowned by large nests of
white storks. The village's main
attraction is the **Church of the
Ascension** (Cerkev
Gospodovega vnebohoda),
easily visible on a low slope
on the northern outskirts. This
parish church was remodelled
by Slovenia's Modernist
architect Jože Plečnik *(see p73)*
in his idiosyncratic style; it is
popularly known as Plečnik's

**Baroque room in the Regional
Museum, Murska Sobota**

Church (Plečnikova Cerkev). The church's spire is a cylindrical construction, like an observation tower, crowned by a curious turret. The interior has been transformed from a single-nave Baroque construction into an impressive hall-like space that is broken only by a massive column of charcoal-grey marble in the centre. From this radiate four white-washed arches, all the more impressive for their simplicity. The most curious element of all is the wooden high altar. It has locally-made pottery hanging from it, somewhat like the kitchen dresser of a Roman emperor. The church's oak-beamed ceiling is covered with ceramic plates glazed in the colours of the Prekmurje countryside – pale straw, moss green and terracotta.

Approach to the Church of the Ascension, Bogojina

Velika Polana ⓵

Road Map F2. 63 km (39 miles) NE of Ptuj. 🏠 800. 🛈 Velika Polana 2117; (02) 573 7327. **www**.strk.si

From late spring, this village in southeast Prekmurje hosts more breeding pairs of white storks than anywhere else in Slovenia. Around ten couples, who mate for life, migrate here, travelling 12,000 km (7,450 miles) from sub-Saharan Africa. For five months, until early August, these black-and-white birds stalk frogs and small rodents in the wetlands near the Mura river and then return at dusk to their nests – large baskets

Stork's nest on a telegraph pole, Velika Polana

of twigs perched on roofs, chimneys and even telegraph poles. These nests are repaired and expanded over successive migrations and can grow very heavy. Locals welcome the returning birds, believing they are a sign of good luck and a premonition of a new baby in the family, according to folklore.

Locally-born writer Miško Kranjec (1908–1983) eulogized the grasslands, woods, people and storks' nests in his works.

Lendava ⓶

Road Map F2. 72 km (45 miles) NE of Ptuj. 🏠 3,400. 🚌 from Murska Sobota & Moravske Toplice. 🛈 Glavna ulica 38; (02) 578 8390. **www**.lendava-turizem.si

Equidistant from the Croatian and Hungarian borders, Lendava is the easternmost town in Slovenia. Founded by Romans on the Poetovio-Savaria route (today Ptuj-Szombathely), it developed into a medieval market town under Hungarian feudal rulers. The L-shaped **Lendava Castle** (Lendavski grad) sits on a terrace above the town. It houses a municipal museum whose displays include Bronze Age archaeology and folk art from Hetés, a Hungarian region known for its textiles.

On Glavna ulica are many Secessionist buildings that were built during a trading boom after the town was made the district centre in 1867. **No. 52**, distinct because of its

canary yellow colour, contains a museum on contemporary trade and bourgoise lifestyle.

Much of the town's prosperity was driven by its large Jewish population. Although the Jewish community was deported by Hungarian forces during World War II, the town's **Synagogue** has been restored and is one of only two in Slovenia. Its square-shaped, galleried hall has a small display on the Jewish community and plays host to temporary art exhibitions. The building opposite the synagogue is a cultural centre designed by 20th-century Hungarian architect Imre Makovecz. Perched among vineyards above the town is the **Church of the Holy Trinity** (Cerkev sv Trojice). It has a mummified corpse on display, which, according to legend, is that of Captain Mihael Hadik, who died defending his home town from Turkish forces in 1603 – a deed so noble that his corpse was preserved by its own sanctity. Although Hadik died in battle, his body was not found until 1733, preserved by the lime-rich soil.

🏛 **Lendava Castle**
Banffyjev trg 1. **Tel** (02) 578 9260.
🕙 8am–4pm Mon–Fri, 9am–2pm Sat. 🚹

⭐ **Synagogue**
Trg Györgya Zale 1. **Tel** (0) 577 6020.
🕙 10am–noon Tue–Sun. 🚹

⛪ **Church of the Holy Trinity**
Lendavske gorice. **Tel** (02) 578 8330.
🕙 11–11:30am & 3:30–4pm Tue–Sun. 🌨 during snowfall. 🚹 👶 🚻

Lendava Castle, perched above the town, Lendava

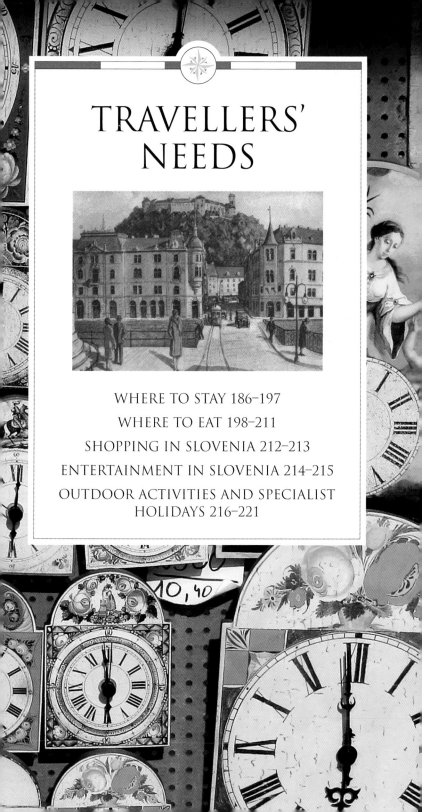

TRAVELLERS' NEEDS

WHERE TO STAY

Slovenia is a relatively new holiday destination as compared to Croatia, Italy or Austria. It is in the last two decades that its holiday accommodation facilities have increased in number to rival those of its neighbouring countries. Over the years, hotels have been renovated to provide modern facilities and bland business hotels have been refurbished with relaxed styles that also appeal to holiday makers. Boutique-style accommodation in the form of small luxury

Door handle
at a hotel

hotels, mostly in historic buildings, have become popular too. Yet much of the charm is in the country's smaller establishments and pensions. Family-run hotels make up in character what they lack in facilities. Slovenia has also seen a rise in the number of tourist farms that offer a few simple rooms or apartments – a chance to experience the hospitality and home cooking for which the country is renowned. As ever, the national tourist board website is a mine of information.

HOTELS

Tourism blossomed at resorts such as Bled, Bohinj, Portorož and at thermal spas from the 1970s. Most resort hotels from that era have been renovated to offer facilities such as flat-screen televisions, minibars, Internet access and room service. Large hotels often have a small gym, a spa and sauna and perhaps a plunge pool. There are few international chain hotels in Slovenia.

Grander establishments from the late 19th century can be found in Ljubljana, Bled and in contemporary spa resorts such as Rogaška Slatina and Dolenjske Toplice. The best have been luxuriously updated and even those that retain their late-1970s decor have a certain faded grandeur, though en suite facilities can be disappointing.

The most interesting hotels in Slovenia are the boutique residences in historic buildings. Three of the best include Vila

Tourist farm with horses near Stična

Bled at Bled, Kendov dvorec near Idrija and Otočec Castle. The independent family-run hotels in destinations such as the Bled area, the Soča Valley, Piran and Ptuj offer modest luxury, character and personal service. Most rooms in hotels are en suite, but air conditioning is most prevalent in modern hotels and on the coast. Many hotels in coastal resorts such as Portorož close from November to March.

BUDGET ACCOMMODATION

Geared for young visitors, hostels in Slovenia are affiliated to **Hostelling International**. There are smart private hostels in Ljubljana, Piran and Novo Mesto. Dormitory accommodation of up to ten beds is standard, but most also have two- or three-bed rooms, which should be reserved in advance. Facilities – generally shared – typically include a kitchen, a laundry, a common room and Internet access.

For around the same price, visitors can source *sobe* (rooms) and *apartmaji* (apartments) in a *gostilna* (inn) or in houses through private tourist agencies; the tourist board brochure *Rates for Accommodation in Private Rooms and Apartments* also lists options. In large numbers on the coast and in the Julian Alps, these are categorized from one to three stars: a one-star offers shared facilities

Façade of the Palace Hotel in Portorož

◁ **Hand-painted clocks at a flea market in Ljubljana**

Facilities for children at a hotel in Radenci

but provides a basin; two-star and the plusher three-star rooms have en suite facilities.

The most appealing budget accommodation option is the tourist farm. Around 200 *turistične kmetije* (private farms) affiliated to the **Association of Slovenian Tourist Farms** now offer homestays in everything from traditional alpine farms to modern houses with orchards. Accommodation is homely rather than luxurious and graded by "apples" – from one (basic rooms with shared facilities) to four (en suite rooms). The *Friendly Countryside* brochure lists options.

RATES AND RESERVATIONS

Accommodation in Slovenia represents good value compared with much of Europe. Prices are highest in Ljubljana and Maribor and major resorts such as Bled. Rates peak from mid-June to August except in the capital, where rates are consistently high. However, hotels in ski resorts such as Kranjska Gora or Mariborsko Pohorje have a second season from December to February, when rates are higher. A nominal tourist tax is charged per person per night in all hotels, and a 30 per cent surcharge is levied for stays of under three days in many resorts and farmstays.

It is advisable to make a reservation year-round in Ljubljana and Maribor, both of which are consistently busy, and in summer at Bled and the Triglav National Park, on the coast or in Ptuj.

CHILDREN

Most of the hotels accept children, so travel in Slovenia will present few difficulties. Tourist farms are a particular delight. Most types of accommodation can provide a cot or extra bed and have high chairs. Generally, only larger resort hotels offer baby-sitting services. Hotels offer a discount of 30 to 50 per cent for children up to the age of 14 to 17 staying in their parents' room. Toddlers – usually up to three or four years old – can stay free of charge.

DISABLED TRAVELLERS

Care for the disabled is good in city business hotels and large hotels in resorts, which usually have lifts and ramps. Elsewhere, accommodation options for disabled visitors are limited. Few older hotels and tourist farms are suitable for those with restricted mobility. The **Paraplegics**

Tents set up at a camp site in the Alps, Trenta

DIRECTORY

BUDGET ACCOMMODATION

Hostelling International
Gospostvetska cesta 84, Maribor.
Tel (02) 234 2137.
www.youth-hostel.si

Association of Slovenian Tourist Farms
Trnoveljska cesta 1, Celje.
Tel (03) 491 6481.
www.turisticnekmetije.si

DISABLED TRAVELLERS

Paraplegics Association of Slovenia
www.zveza-paraplegikov.si

Association of Slovenia provides further information on accommodation options for those with special needs.

MOUNTAIN HUTS

Planinski domovi (mountain huts) are located in the northwest, and nearly a third of the 170 available are in the Triglav National Park. Intended as overnight refuges for hikers, they vary from basic shelters with bunkbeds to cottages with rooms for guests. Most huts in the high Alps open from June to September only, while those at lower altitudes operate from April to October. All take reservations but it is essential to secure a bed near the summit of Mount Triglav in July and August.

CAMPING

Standards at Slovenian *kampi* (camp sites) are universally high. The larger sites on the coast, or around Bled and Bohinj and in the spa resorts of eastern Slovenia have a supermarket and restaurant. Clusters of sites are in the Bled area, in the Soča Valley around Bovec, and on the coast; all are busy in the high season. It is best to source a copy of the national tourist board's *Camping in Slovenia* brochure for full details. Most camp sites open from late-April to October. Camping in the wild is strictly forbidden.

Choosing a Hotel

Most of the hotels and resorts in this guide have been selected across a wide price range for their good value, facilities and location. Hotels are listed by area and arranged alphabetically within the same price category. For map references, see pages 96–9 for Ljubljana and the inside back cover for the rest of Slovenia.

PRICE CATEGORIES
Price categories are for a standard double room per night in high season, including tax and service charges. Breakfast is not included, unless specified.
€ under €50
€€ €50–€70
€€€ €70–€100
€€€€ €100–€150
€€€€€ over €150

LJUBLJANA

AROUND THE CENTRE Hostel Print €
Rožna dolina IV/34, 1000 **Tel** *(051) 387 111* **Rooms** *22*

A swanky hostel with a bed-and-breakfast approach to comforts, Print offers two- and three-bed rooms, many with en suite facilities, rather than multi-bed dorms. A variety of social areas, including outdoor terraces, are on offer for guests. A range of dishes is available for breakfast. **www.hostelprint.com**

AROUND THE CENTRE Hostel Celica €€
Metelkova 8, 1000 **Tel** *(01) 230 9700* **Rooms** *29*

An interior design classic among Europe's hostels, Celica makes full creative use of the former Yugoslav military police station it is housed in. Each room was decorated by a different team of international artists. Double rooms and dorms are available, and a basic breakfast is included. Book well in advance. **www.hostelcelica.com**

AROUND THE CENTRE MartaStudio €€
Tržaška cesta 24, 1000 **Tel** *(05) 902 0452* **Rooms** *4*

Comprising well-kept apartments in a suburban courtyard southwest of the centre, MartaStudio is a brisk walk or short bus ride from Slovenska cesta. Accommodation includes three two-person studios with a kitchenette and TV, and a family-sized two-bedroom apartment with lounge, dining table and kitchen. **www.martastudio.eu**

AROUND THE CENTRE Hotel Park €€€
Tabor 9, 1000 **Tel** *(01) 300 2500* **Rooms** *201*

A bland-looking grey high-rise conceals a good mid-price choice with small but well-appointed rooms and good views from the upper storeys. Several floors offer hostel-style two- and four-bed rooms (44 rooms), which are sparsely furnished and come without TVs. Some rooms have shared facilities down the hallway. **www.hotelpark.si**

AROUND THE CENTRE A Hotel €€€€
Cesta dveh cesarjev 34D, 1000 **Tel** *(01) 429 1892* **Rooms** *26*

Housed in a pleasant three-storey suburban building on the southern fringes of Trnovo, this amenable three-star hotel offers contemporary rooms decorated in creamy-brown colours. Bicycles are available on rent to get around the city and the hotel's terrace-garden café-bar is a good place to relax. **www.ahotel.si**

AROUND THE CENTRE Ljubljana Resort €€€€
Dunajska 270, 1000 **Tel** *(01) 568 3913* **Rooms** *60*

Located in the suburb of Ježica, 6 km (4 miles) north of town, this is a grassy open park with two- and three-room bungalows and a camp site. Its proximity to Laguna Beach Aquapark and its range of sporting facilities from table tennis to volleyball make the resort popular. **www.ljubljanaresort.si**

AROUND THE CENTRE Austria Trend €€€€€
Dunajska 154, 1000 **Tel** *(01) 588 2500* **Rooms** *214*

Located 3 km (2 miles) north of the centre, Austria Trend is well placed for those interested in the sporting and cultural events at the nearby Stožice Arena. The four-star rated rooms are sizeable and stylish, and those on the upper storeys come with fine views. The hotel also has spa facilities. **www.austria-trend.at**

AROUND THE CENTRE Hotel Mons €€€€€
Pot za Brdom 55 **Tel** *(01) 470 2700* **Rooms** *114*

Situated 5 km (3 miles) west of the city centre, this secluded four-star hotel and conference centre offers chic fully-equipped rooms in a modern building. The buffet breakfast is a veritable feast. A free minibus service runs to the centre of town at set times throughout the day. **www.hotel.mons.si**

NEW TOWN Alibi M14 Hostel € **City Map** D3
Miklošičeva 14, 1000 **Tel** *(01) 232 2770* **Rooms** *12*

A sister operation to a hostel in Old Town, M14 is housed in a 19th-century apartment block and offers both bunk-bed dorms and neat en suite double rooms, all decked out in warm colours and with parquet floors. There is a small kitchen where guests can make their own breakfast. The laundry service costs a few euros extra. **www.alibi.si**

Key to Symbols *see back cover flap*

NEW TOWN Hotel Center

📋 €€

Slovenska cesta 51, 1000 **Tel** *(01) 520 0640* **Rooms** *8* ***City Map** C1*

A friendly and intimate establishment on the main shopping street, Hotel Center's rooms are small but have high ceilings and are decorated in soothing shades of chocolate. Rooms on the courtyard-facing side are quieter than those looking out on to Slovenska cesta. Breakfast from the café-bar downstairs costs extra. **www.hotelcenter.si**

NEW TOWN Vila Veselova

🔄 €€

Veselova 14, 1000 **Tel** *(05) 992 6721* **Rooms** *8* ***City Map** B3*

This rather grand looking 19th-century villa on the edge of Tivoli Park conceals a simple but friendly hostel-cum-pension. Guests can choose between self-contained double rooms, or six- to eight-bed dorms, some of which have en suite facilities, while others have shared facilities. Free Internet access is available for guests. **www.v-v.si**

NEW TOWN City Hotel

🔄 P 🍴 📋 €€€

Dalmatinova 15, 1000 **Tel** *(01) 239 0000* **Rooms** *204* ***City Map** D2*

A popular mid-range choice, City Hotel is conveniently located midway between the Old Town and the train and bus stations. The spacious rooms are decked out in warm reds and creams and come with contemporary touches such as flat-screen TVs. Free Internet access is available for guests. **www.cityhotel.si**

NEW TOWN Emonec

P 📋 €€€

Wolfova 12, 1000 **Tel** *(01) 200 1520* **Rooms** *41* ***City Map** D3*

Small, simply furnished but pleasant en suite rooms are available at the Emonec, one of the few low cost options in the heart of the city. Basic breakfast, bike hire and Internet access are among the facilities provided. Prešernov trg *(see p48)* and the Old Town are a stone's throw away. **www.hotel.emonec.com**

NEW TOWN Prenočišče Slamič

🔄 €€€

Kersnikova 1, 1000 **Tel** *(01) 433 8233* **Rooms** *11* ***City Map** C1*

This homely pension-style hotel is located midway between the main shopping area and Tivoli Park. Decked out in soothing cream and brown, the rooms come with a minibar and free Internet access. The hotel has suites as well as double rooms. Breakfast is served in the next-door café. **www.slamic.si**

NEW TOWN Pri Mraku

🍴 €€€

Rimska 4, 1000 **Tel** *(01) 421 9600* **Rooms** *345* ***City Map** C4*

Located just around the corner from Trg francoske revolucije, this medium-sized pension offers adequate rooms with TVs and en suite showers. Not all the rooms have air conditioning, and some of the fabrics used are old-fashioned. Top-floor rooms have attic ceilings. **www.daj-dam.si**

NEW TOWN Central Hotel

🔄 📋 €€€€

Miklošičeva 9, 1000 **Tel** *(01) 308 4301* **Rooms** *74* ***City Map** D2*

The name of this smart and efficient hotel is an accurate indication of its location; it is a 3-minute walk from Prešernov trg. Rooms are well furnished and there is a varied breakfast. Guests can use the swimming pool and sauna facilities of the Union hotel just down the street. **www.centralhotel.si**

NEW TOWN Grand Hotel Union

🔄 P 🍴 🏊 📺 📋 €€€€€

Miklošičeva 1, 1000 **Tel** *(01) 308 1989* **Rooms** *327* ***City Map** D2*

This is a handsome Art Nouveau building near the Triple Bridge *(see pp48–9)*. Executive rooms in the main building are spacious and stylish, while business rooms in the annexe are more contemporary in style. The eighth-floor pool and spa is a great place to relax. A breakfast buffet is on offer for guests. **www.gh-union.si**

NEW TOWN Hotel Lev

🔄 P 🍴 📺 📋 €€€€€

Vošnjakova 1, 1000 **Tel** *(01) 433 2155* **Rooms** *173* ***City Map** C1*

This ten-storey tower in the centre of the city is a 1960s Modernist landmark that has hosted everyone from President Tito to Luciano Pavarotti. The rooms come in a variety of sizes but offer all facilities. Breakfast is lavish. There is a casino in the basement. **wwww.hotel-lev.si**

NEW TOWN Slon

🔄 🍴 📋 €€€€€

Slovenska cesta 34, 1000 **Tel** *(01) 470 1100* **Rooms** *168* ***City Map** C2*

Habsburg Emperor Maximilian II once stayed at this spot, before the hotel was built, with an elephant *(slon* in Slovenian; hence the name). Located on the main shopping street and near the Old Town, it offers rooms decorated in muted colours. Parquet floors and flat-screen TVs constitute a nice mix of old and new. **www.hotelslon.com**

OLD TOWN Alibi Hostel

📋 €

Cankarjevo nabrežje 27, 1000 **Tel** *(01) 251 1244* **Rooms** *26* ***City Map** D3*

A venerable Old Town building with a grand wooden staircase and high ceilings, this hostel comprises a mix of dorms and three-bed or four-bed rooms. The sparsely furnished rooms are brightened up by graffiti-style murals; several come with sunny riverside views. The common room has a drinks machine. **www.alibi.si**

OLD TOWN Antiq Hotel

🔄 📋 €€€

Gornji trg 3, 1000 **Tel** *(01) 421 3560* **Rooms** *16* ***City Map** D4*

Located in the heart of the Old Town, this boutique hotel has rooms ranging from snug economy doubles with shared facilities to regular rooms with en suite bathrooms. The hotel's split-level four-person apartment will suit those travelling as a group. Warm colours and antiques create a homely atmosphere. **www.antiqhotel.si**

OLD TOWN Maček　　　　　　　　　　　　　　　　€€€
Krojaška 5, 1000 **Tel** *(01) 425 3791* **Rooms** *5*　　　　　　　　**City Map** D4

This is a friendly and informal bed-and-breakfast accommodation on the banks of the Ljubljanica, with rooms above their popular café-bar. The en suite rooms have laminated wooden floors and are decorated in cheerful colours. There are two apartments available for those travelling as a group. **www.sobe-macek.si**

OLD TOWN Allegro　　　　　　　　　　　　　　　▤　€€€€
Gornji trg 6, 1000 **Tel** *059 119 620* **Rooms** *17*　　　　　　　**City Map** D4

The intimate and cosy Allegro is located in a historic house in the Old Town. With reproduction furniture, loud fabrics and modern bathrooms, this will suit travellers who like their comforts to be a bit flamboyant. The top-floor rooms have attic ceilings, while others come with tiny courtyard-facing balconies. **www.allegrohotel.si**

THE ALPS

BLED Mulej Tourist Farm　　　　　　　　　　　 P 🏃　€€
Selo pri Bledu 20, 4260 **Tel** *(04) 574 4617* **Fax** *(04) 574 4617* **Rooms** *8*　　　**Road Map** B2

Simple en suite rooms and an apartment are available in this family farm in Selo village, 1 km (half a mile) south of Bled. Children can feed farm animals and go horse riding. Breakfasts feature organic foods such as breads, jams, cheese and sausages produced on the farm. Dinner is also served. **www.mulej-bled.com**

BLED Penzion Mayer　　　　　　　　　　　　 P 🍽 🏃　€€€
Želeška cesta 7, 4260 **Tel** *(04) 574 1058* **Fax** *(04) 576 5741* **Rooms** *12*　　　**Road Map** B2

This is a family-run pension above Lake Bled that provides a more peaceful stay than the large hotels in the centre. Occupying a 19th-century house, it has small but good-value rooms with parquet flooring and excellent bathrooms plus a two-bed garden chalet. The hotel also has a fine Slovenian restaurant *(see p205)*. **www.mayer-sp.si**

BLED Vila Prešeren　　　　　　　　　　　　 📶 P 🍽　€€€€
Veslaška promenada 14, 4260 **Tel** *(04) 575 2510* **Rooms** *8*　　　　**Road Map** B2

Renovated in 2008, this 19th-century lakeside villa beneath Bled Castle offers stylish accommodation. Though rather compact, rooms feature wrought-iron beds and statement wallpaper. Those on the first floor enjoy excellent views of the lake; the suites have balconies and the terrace is perfect for breakfast. **www.vilapreseren.si**

BLED Grand Hotel Toplice　　　　　　 📶 P 🍽 🏊 🏃 ▤　€€€€€
Cesta svobode 12, 4260 **Tel** *(04) 579 1000* **Fax** *(04) 574 1841* **Rooms** *87*　　**Road Map** B2

A luxury five-star hotel on Lake Bled's shore, the grande dame of Bled's hotels has hosted international statesmen and celebrities since it was built in the 1850s. The antiques and opulent decor are from the 1930s, yet the modern facilities are first class and service is flawless. The hotel also has a good spa. **www.hotel-toplice.com**

BLED Vila Bled　　　　　　　　　　　　 📶 P 🍽 ▤　€€€€€
Cesta svobode 26, 4260 **Tel** *(04) 575 3710* **Fax** *(04) 575 3711* **Rooms** *31*　　**Road Map** B2

Now an exclusive hotel, Vila Bled, located at the southwest end of the lake, was the private summer holiday home of President Tito. It remains a splendid period piece from the 1950s, with contemporary decor in rooms and suites. There is a sauna and steam bath and the garden affords superb views of the lake. **www.vila-bled.com**

BOHINJ Hotel Jezero　　　　　　　　 📶 P 🍽 🏊 🏃 📺　€€€€
Ribčev Laz 51, 4265 **Tel** *(04) 572 9100* **Fax** *(04) 572 9039* **Rooms** *76*　　**Road Map** A2

Although rather expensive, this well-managed medium-sized hotel is unrivalled for its location beside the lake. Following renovation in 2008, rooms are comfortable, modern and have balconies; the best rooms have views over the lake. Facilities include a pool, saunas and a gym. **www.bohinj.si/alpinum/jezero**

BOHINJ Hotel Kristal　　　　　　　　　　 P 🍽 🏃　€€€€
Ribčev Laz 4a, 4265 **Tel** *(04) 577 8200* **Fax** *(04) 577 8250* **Rooms** *30*　　**Road Map** A2

What began as a small pizzeria at the entrance to the village has grown into a medium-sized hotel whose smart rooms offer good value for money. Facilities such as a minibar, TV and Internet are available, and most rooms have a balcony with great views. Family rooms with three or four beds are available. **www.hotel-kristal-slovenia.com**

BOHINJ Vila Park　　　　　　　　　　　　　 P 🍽　€€€€
Ukanc 129, 4265 **Tel** *(04) 572 3300* **Fax** *(04) 572 3312* **Rooms** *8*　　　**Road Map** A2

This smart villa at the western end of the lake is an excellent choice for an expensive escape for adults – children are not allowed. Set in tranquil gardens beside the Savica, the alpine-styled house has modern rooms furnished in understated luxury. Service is good and there is a pleasant shared lounge with a fireplace. **www.vila-park.si**

BOVEC Hotel Alp　　　　　　　　　　　　 P 🍽 🏊 🏃　€€
Trg golobarskih žrtev 48, 5230 **Tel** *(05) 388 4000* **Fax** *(05) 388 4002* **Rooms** *103*　　**Road Map** A2

Located in the heart of Bovec, Hotel Alp makes an economical base for adventure-sport enthusiasts. Rooms are small with 1980s furnishings, but have en suite facilities and TVs. Some rooms have a balcony. Guests have free use of a Finnish sauna and steam bath to rejuvenate after a day's activities. **www.alp-hotel.si**

Key to Price Guide *see p188* **Key to Symbols** *see back cover flap*

KAMNIK Malograjski dvor
🏠🍴🏃 €€€

Maistrova 13, 1240 **Tel** *(01) 830 3100* **Fax** *(01) 830 3123* **Rooms** *22* **Road Map** *C3*

A stone's throw from the cafés on the main square, this restored 18th-century townhouse contains elegant en suite rooms furnished to reflect its historic character. Superior rooms are spacious and have mountain views. There is also a pretty terrace for breakfast in summer. **www.hotelkamnik.si**

KOBARID Hiša Franko
🅿🍴 €€€€

Staro selo 1, 5222 **Tel** *(05) 389 4120* **Fax** *(05) 389 4129* **Rooms** *13* **Road Map** *A2*

Run by the charming hosts Valter and Ana, Hiša Franko is a highly personal retreat with a taste for unfussy romantic design – wooden floors, streamlined modern furniture and muslin drapes. An adjacent house provides three cheaper basic rooms. The restaurant *(see p206)* is very good. **www.hisafranko.com**

KOBARID Nebesa
🅿🚻🍴 €€€€€

Livek 39, 5222 **Tel** *(05) 384 4620* **Rooms** *4* **Road Map** *A2*

Nebesa, meaning heaven, refers both to a location high on the slopes of Mount Kuk and the interior design of the four chalets that enjoy astonishing views over the valley. The hotel also has a beautifully furnished shared dining room with a kitchen. **www.nebesa.si**

KRANJ Hotel Creina
🏠🅿🍴🗒 €€€

Koroška cesta 5, 4000 **Tel** *(04) 281 7504* **Fax** *(04) 281 7499* **Rooms** *87* **Road Map** *B3*

This is a central business hotel that is more comfortable inside than suggested by its unprepossessing exterior, thanks to renovations in 2005. Five rooms have been modified for disabled visitors and there are dedicated smoking rooms; the quietest rooms are located at the rear. **www.hotelcreina.si**

KRANJ Hotel Kokra
🅿🍴🗒 €€€€€

Predoslje 39, 4000 **Tel** *(04) 260 1501* **Rooms** *66* **Road Map** *B3*

The smartest hotel in the Kranj area is a plush four-star set in the grounds of Brdo Castle, a restored aristocratic residence 3 km (1 mile) east of Kranj. The hotel also has 11 apartments, a spa and golf course; guests can go fishing for trout and horse riding in the parkland. Ljubljana and Bled are a 20-minute drive away. **www.brdo.si**

KRANJSKA GORA Hotel Kotnik
🗒🅿🍴 €€€

Borovška cesta 75, 4280 **Tel** *(04) 588 1564* **Fax** *(04) 588 1859* **Rooms** *15* **Road Map** *A2*

This classy family-run hotel in the heart of the village is a good alternative to the larger resort hotels. Its tastefully decorated rooms have all facilities, Internet access and minibar. A couple of three- or four-bed rooms are available for families. The popular Pino pizzeria and a good restaurant are part of the hotel. **www.hotel-kotnik.si**

KRANJSKA GORA Hotel Miklič
🅿🍴🏃🚻 €€€

Vitranška 13, 4280 **Tel** *(04) 588 1635* **Fax** *(04) 588 1634* **Rooms** *17* **Road Map** *A2*

This hotel is close to the lower terminal of the ski lifts. It has spacious rooms with pale wood furniture and pastel wall colours. There are interconnected rooms and holiday apartments for families. Facilities include Wi-Fi, sauna, a children's playroom and storage for bikes and skis. The restaurant *(see p206)* is excellent. **www.hotelmiklic.com**

KRANJSKA GORA Vitranc
🅿🍴 €€€

Podkoren 94, 4280 **Tel** *(04) 580 9520* **Rooms** *15* **Road Map** *A2*

Located in a village 2 km (1 mile) west of Kranjska Gora, this shuttered inn is a great alternative to large resorts. Hand-painted furniture and bright curtains are typical of the modern alpine style in the individually decorated en suite rooms, some with four beds for families. The restaurant serves hearty Slovenian fare. **www.vitranc.si**

LOGARSKA DOLINA Hotel Plesnik
🗒🅿🍴🚻🏃 €€€€

Logarska dolina 10, 3335 **Tel** *(03) 839 2300* **Fax** *(03) 839 2312* **Rooms** *30* **Road Map** *C2*

Scenically located in the valley, Hotel Plesnik has country-style rooms in the main building and a wing where smaller rooms retain a traditional charm; most rooms have a balcony. The hotel also has a pool and sauna, and manages a century-old tourist farm nearby. **www.plesnik.si**

RADOVLJICA Gostilna Lectar
🍴🗒 €€

Linhartov trg 2, 4240 **Tel** *(04) 537 4800* **Fax** *(04) 537 4804* **Rooms** *5* **Road Map** *B2*

This 500-year-old inn in the Old Town offers enchanting bed-and-breakfast accommodation. Cosy and individual en suite rooms live up to charm of their gingerbread signs – a traditional craft practised here for centuries. Each room has painted furniture and a modern bathroom, a minibar, cable TV and Wi-Fi. **www.lectar.com**

ROBANOV KOT Govc-Vršnik Tourist Farm
🅿🍴🏃 €€

Robanov kot 34, 3335 **Tel** *(03) 839 5016* **Fax** *(03) 839 5017* **Rooms** *10* **Road Map** *C2*

Tranquility reigns on this large tourist farm. Rooms are clean, pleasant and simply decorated with modern pine furniture. Its location in a beautiful alpine valley attracts nature lovers and walkers. The sauna and Jacuzzi are welcome after a hike, and breakfast on the terrace in summer is a delight. **www.govc-vrsnik.com**

TRENTA Kekčeva domačija
🅿🍴 €

Trenta 76, 5232 **Tel** *(04) 141 3087* **Rooms** *13* **Road Map** *A2*

Reached via a track halfway down Vršič Pass, this traditional farmstead amid astonishing scenery has a fairy tale-like quality. Featured in the 1963 film *Good luck, Kekec*, it is arguably the most idyllic mountain retreat in Slovenia. It has nine rooms and four apartments; plans are afoot to build a pool and sauna. **www.kekceva-domacija.si**

COASTAL SLOVENIA AND THE KARST

ANKARAN Hotel Convent   €€€€
Jadranska 25, 6280 **Tel** *(05) 663 7300* **Rooms** *24*   **Road Map** *A4*

Housed in a former Benedictine convent with a lovely arcaded courtyard, the Adria shares sporting facilities, including an indoor pool, with the camp site next door; the seafront is a mere 5-minute walk away. The en suite rooms are old-fashioned but comfortable. **www.adria-ankaran.si**

CERKNO Hotel Cerkno   P 🍴 ☰ 📺   €€€
Sedejev trg 8, 5282 **Tel** *(05) 374 3400* **Rooms** *75*   **Road Map** *B3*

Located in the heart of Cerkno, this establishment provides comfortable rooms in a tranquil setting, with easy access to local walks. It is a good base for exploring the northern karst, and is only 10 km (6 miles) away from the Cerkno Ski Centre. There is a sauna and a swimming pool fed by thermal springs. **www.hotel-cerkno.si**

DIVAČA Domačija Pr’ Vncki   €
Matavun 10, 6215 **Tel** *(05) 763 3073* **Rooms** *5*   **Road Map** *A4*

A delightfully rustic bed-and-breakfast in a historic farmhouse, this hotel is located in the village of Matavun, a short distance from the Škocjan Caves *(see pp138–9)*. Rooms are traditionally furnished with wooden furniture and the house features a "black kitchen". The en suite two- and three-bed rooms have Internet access.

DUTOVLJE Youth Hostel Pliskovica   €
Pliskovica 11, 6221 **Tel** *(05) 764 0250* **Rooms** *6*   **Road Map** *A4*

A wonderfully well-maintained farmhouse in a typical wine-producing Kras village is the idyllic site of this welcoming hostel. The choice is between bunk-bed dorm accommodation and private double rooms. Breakfast is included. The hostel rents out bicycles and offers advice on where to ride them. **www.hostelkras.com**

GORIŠKA BRDA Breg   P 🍴 ☰   €€
Breg pri Golem Brdu 3, 5212 **Tel** *(05) 304 2555* **Rooms** *6*   **Road Map** *A3*

Housed in a pair of beautifuly restored village houses on the western edge of the Brda wine-growing region, Breg offers cosy rooms with rustic but smart furnishings, exposed stonework and wood-burning stoves. Regional recipes and local wines are served in the restaurant, and bikes are available for rent. **www.turizembreg.com**

GORIŠKA BRDA Belica   P 🍴 ☰ ☰   €€€
Medana 32, 5212 **Tel** *(05) 304 2104* **Rooms** *10*   **Road Map** *A3*

Surrounded by green fields and vineyards, this modern farmstead and wine cellar in the heart of the Goriška Brda wine producing region offers en suite double rooms decked in a mix of rustic and contemporary furnishings. Many rooms have additional beds for children; family-sized apartments are also available. **www.belica.net**

IDRIJA Kendov dvorec   P 🍴 ☰   €€€€€
Na griču 2, Spodnja Idrija, 5281 **Tel** *(05) 372 5100* **Rooms** *11*   **Road Map** *B3*

The spacious rooms in this five-star hotel are furnished in late 19th- to early 20th-century style, complete with lush fabrics and a fair sprinkling of antiques. Lush gardens and rural landscape add to the sense of tranquility. The restaurant is a well-known local gastronomic destination. **www.kendov-dvorec.si**

IZOLA Hotel Marina   🍴 ☰   €€€€
Veliki trg 11, 6310 **Tel** *(05) 660 4300* **Rooms** *52*   **Road Map** *A5*

The Hotel Marina may not be the most attractive building in Izola but its harbour-front location makes it the perfect base from which to enjoy this medieval town. Rooms are functional but those on the western side have great views. There is a spa and an excellent seafood restaurant *(see p207)*. **www.hotelmarina.si**

KOPER BIO   P 🍴 📺 ☰   €€€
Vanganelska cesta 2, 6000 **Tel** *(05) 625 8884* **Rooms** *30*   **Road Map** *A4*

Located in the south of town, some 3 km (2 miles) from the centre, this low-rise hotel has a pleasant suburban feel. The en suite rooms are simply furnished but bright and airy, and there is a Jacuzzi and sauna on site. As well as regular double rooms, there are several triple-bed rooms. **www.hotel-bio.si**

KOPER Hotel Pristan   P ☰   €€€
Ferrarska 30, 6000 **Tel** *(05) 614 4000* **Rooms** *16*   **Road Map** *A4*

The Pristan is located in a port-side area, within easy walking distance of the Old Town. From the outside, the hotel building looks somewhat like a ship. Inside, the functional-but-smart en suite rooms come with a TV and minibar. Some triple-bed rooms and suites are also available. **www.pristan-koper.si**

KOPER Hotel Vodišek   ☰   €€€
Kolodvorska 2, 6000 **Tel** *(05) 639 2468* **Rooms** *35*   **Road Map** *A4*

Rooms at the Vodišek are simply furnished but neat en suites in a rather staid-looking block that also houses apartments and offices. The location, midway between the train and bus stations and the Old Town, is a major plus point. Koper's biggest shopping centres are right at the hotel's doorstep. **www.hotel-vodisek.com**

Key to Price Guide *see p188* **Key to Symbols** *see back cover flap*

KOPER Hotel Koper 🔢📋 €€€€
Pristaniška 3, 6000 **Tel** *(05) 610 0500* **Rooms** 60 *Road Map A4*

With prim en suite rooms, Hotel Koper is ideally located – a short walk from the main square and just across the road from the marina and the market. Noise from the nearby cafés can be a problem in summer. The price includes free access to the aquapark at its sister hotel, Žusterna. **www.terme-catez.si**

KOPER Hotel Žusterna 🔢🏊🏋️📺📋 €€€€€
Istrska cesta 67, 6000 **Tel** *(05) 610 0300* **Rooms** 113 *Road Map A4*

This hotel has simple no-frills en suite rooms in a large modern building just west of Koper on the coastal road to Izola. The main attraction is the on-site aquapark, with both indoor and outdor pools, water slides, spa and a children's section complete with a pirate ship. North-facing rooms have views of the sea. **www.terme-catez.si**

LIPICA Maestoso €€€€
Lipica 5, 6210 **Tel** *(05) 739 1580* **Rooms** 66 *Road Map A4*

Built in the 1970s and boasting a loud 70s decor, the three-star Maestoso is a comfortable base from which to explore the soutwestern karst. Rooms have views of Lipica's grazing white horses, it has a good café-restaurant *(see p207)* and the nearby spa centre has a range of massages and beauty treatments. **www.lipica.org**

NOVA GORICA Hotel Sabotin 🔢📇🔢📋 €€€
Cesta IX. korpusa 35, 5250 **Tel** *(05) 336 5000* **Rooms** 76 *Road Map A3*

Occupying a Renaissance villa that has been expanded with modern annexes, Hotel Sabotin contains a sizeable warren of en suite rooms with TVs, most of which are small but comfortable. The hotel is located in the low-rise suburb of Solkan, a good 20-minute walk from the centre of Nova Gorica. **www.hotelsabotin.com**

NOVA GORICA Perla 🔢📇🔢🏊📋 €€€€
Kidričeva 7, 5000 **Tel** *(05) 336 3000* **Rooms** 249 *Road Map A3*

The pearl in gaming-company HIT Gorica's crown, the Perla rises above an extensive entertainment complex, comprising a casino, swimming pool and spa. Rooms are decked in warm colours and a generous breakfast is on offer. A number of luxury suites cater to guests who want to be pampered. **www.hit.si**

PIRAN Alibi Hostel 📋 €
Bonifacijeva 11, 6330 **Tel** *(03) 136 3666* **Rooms** 20 *Road Map A5*

Alibi offers a varied collection of rooms and dorms spread over three sites in the atmospheric Old Town of one of the Adriatic's most evocative old ports; the reception is at Bonifacijeva 11. The en suite double rooms with terraces are well worth the stay. Breakfast is not included but there are bakeries nearby. **www.alibi.si**

PIRAN Val €
Gregorčičeva 38a, 6330 **Tel** *(05) 673 2555* **Rooms** 22 *Road Map A5*

Hidden in the alleys of the Old Town, the family-run Val offers simply furnished two-, three- and four-bed rooms, with shared showers and toilet off the hallway. A buffet breakfast is included in the price and there is a small kitchen with a cooker and fridge. **www.hostel-val.com**

PIRAN Max 📇 €€
Ulica IX. korpusa 26, 6330 **Tel** *(05) 673 3436* **Rooms** 6 *Road Map A5*

Located near Piran's cathedral, Max offers a handful of cosy en suite rooms, squeezed into a tall thin house with a steep narrow staircase. Rooms are decorated in warm-coloured fabrics and have TVs. The upper storeys offer attractive views. Breakfast is served in a room with exposed stonework and quirky paintings. **www.maxpiran.com**

PIRAN Miracolo di Mare €€€
Tomšičeva 23, 6330 **Tel** *(05) 921 7660* **Rooms** 12 *Road Map A5*

Enjoying a peaceful alley-side location near Piran's small-boat harbour, this bed-and-breakfast offers small but pleasant rooms kitted out in citrus-coloured fabrics with shower cubicles and TVs. In summer, breakfast is served in the backyard patio, which features a fragrant herb garden. **www.miracolodimare.si**

PIRAN Hotel Piran 🔢📇🔢📋 €€€€
Stjenkova 1, 6330 **Tel** *(05) 690 7000* **Rooms** 89 *Road Map A5*

Located in the town centre, the three-star Piran offers a mixed bag of rooms, with those in the smarter modern annexe marginally more comfortable than those in the older wing. The sea-facing rooms with balconies are well worth booking. The fourth-floor breakfast room with a terrace deserve a visit. **www.hoteli-piran.si**

PIRAN Hotel Tartini 📇🔢📋 €€€€
Tartinijev trg 15, 6330 **Tel** *(05) 671 1000* **Rooms** 46 *Road Map A5*

A medium sized hotel on Piran's Italianate main square, Hotel Tartini offers comfortable en suite rooms decorated with contemporary furniture and bold colours. The balconied rooms on the hotel's west side have sea views and the penthouse suite comes with its own roof terrace. **www.hotel-tartini-piran.com**

PIVKA Pri Andrejevih 📇🔢 €
Narin 107, 6257 **Tel** *(05) 753 2070* **Rooms** 6 *Road Map B4*

A renovated farmstead in the village of Narin, 4 km (3 miles) south of Pivka, Pri Andrejevih has comortable two-, three- and four-bed rooms overlooking a farmyard. It is a good base from which to explore the Reka valley. Delicious home-cooked food is on offer. **www.andrejevi.si**

PORTOROŽ Grand Hotel Bernardin

🅿 🅿 ⅋ ≋ ⚡ ⅋ 🗏   €€€€€

Obala 2, 6320 **Tel** *(05) 695 1000* **Rooms** *241*   **Road Map** *A5*

Built into the cliffside midway between Portorož and Piran, Bernardin is a 1970s-era hotel renovated to modern five-star standards. Rooms are on the bland side but facilities are second to none, with a beach, spa centre, shops, numerous bars and cafés, and a covered pool fed by sea water. **www.h-bernardin.si**

PORTOROŽ Grand Hotel Portorož

🅿 🅿 ⅋ ≋ ⅋ 🗏   €€€€€

Obala 33, 6320 **Tel** *(05) 692 9001* **Rooms** *194*   **Road Map** *A5*

This five-star seafront establishment makes the perfect place for a bit of pampering, with crisply decorated rooms, faultless service, swimming pool and an extensive range of spa, massage and beauty treatments. All rooms have balconies, with prices rising according to how good a view of the Adriatic the room gives. **www.lifeclass.net**

PORTOROŽ Hotel Riviera

🅿 🅿 ⅋ ≋ ⅋ 🗏   €€€€€

Obala 33, 6320 **Tel** *(05) 692 6020* **Rooms** *183*   **Road Map** *A5*

The Riviera is among the best-equipped of the many four-star hotels grouped along Portorož's seafront, with spa facilities lending the place the air of a self-contained health resort. Spacious bedrooms come with decent-sized bathrooms, most with a full-size tub. Sea-facing rooms are slightly more expensive. **www.lifeclass.net**

PORTOROŽ Kempinski Palace

🅿 🅿 ⅋ ≋ ⅋ 🗏   €€€€€

Obala 45, 6320 **Tel** *(05) 5692 7000* **Rooms** *181*   **Road Map** *A5*

Once home to the likes of Archduke Franz Ferdinand and Sophia Loren, this 19th-century seafront palace and its modern annexe are now a five-star hotel with smartly-furnished rooms. Indoor and outdoor pools, spa and beauty treatments and a lavish breakfast ensure that guests are well pampered. **www.kempinski.com**

POSTOJNA Hotel Garni Kras

🅿 🅿 🗏   €€€

Tržaška cesta 1, 6230 **Tel** *(05) 700 2300* **Rooms** *27*   **Road Map** *B4*

Housed in a modern building in the centre of Postojna and within walking distance of the caves, the Garni Kras offers smart rooms decorated in warm colours. The top-floor suites have excellent views of the town centre and the surrounding countryside. The ground-floor café serves mouthwatering cakes and pastries. **www.hotel-kras.si**

POSTOJNA Hotel Sport

🅿 ⅋   €€€

Kolodvorska 1, 6230 **Tel** *(05) 720 2244* **Rooms** *40*   **Road Map** *B4*

Near the centre of Postojna, the Sport is a three-storey 19th-century building with simply furnished but bright rooms. Apart from the standard double rooms, the three-bed and four-bed rooms will suit families or groups of friends. Hostel-type dorms are also available. Bike hire and a beauty parlour are on site. **www.sport-hotel.si**

RAKEK Hotel Rakov Škocjan

🅿 ⅋   €€€

Rakov Škocjan 1, 1381 **Tel** *(01) 709 7470* **Rooms** *13*   **Road Map** *B4*

A welcoming country hotel offering cosy en suite rooms with TVs, this hotel is located on the southern side of the Rakov Škocjan gorge. Situated within easy walking distance of the gorge's sights, it is also an ideal base from which to visit Postojna, Cerknica and the Planina Cave. **www.h-rakovskocjan.com**

SEČA Forma Viva

🅿 ⅋   €€

Seča 159, 6320 **Tel** *(04) 036 9003* **Rooms** *27*   **Road Map** *A5*

With simple but warmly decorated rooms in a two-storey villa, Forma Viva is located right at the summit of the Seča peninsula and commands terrific views. The shaded terrace, bordered by a palm-filled garden, is a great place to relax. Half- and full-board arrangements are available. Open Apr–Oct. **www.formaviva-portoroz.com**

ŠKOCJAN Jankovi

🅿 🗏   €€

Vremski Britof 11, 6217 **Tel** *(03) 133 5166* **Rooms** *5*   **Road Map** *B4*

A large farmstead in the village of Vremski Britof, 3 km (2 miles) from the entrance to the Škocjan Caves, Jankovi offers a handful of two-, four- and six-person apartments, each equipped with modern fittings. Local grocery shops are nearby, and the farmstead is ideally situated for local walks and bike rides. **www.kmetija-jankovi.com**

SPODNJA IDRIJA Na Kluk'

🅿   €

Govejk 14C, 5281 **Tel** *(05) 377 9007* **Rooms** *7*   **Road Map** *B3*

This is a rural bed-and-breakfast in a large country house set amidst verdant hills northeast of Idrija. Rooms feature parquet floors and bright colours. A range of hiking and biking possibilities are accessible. Most rooms are doubles although a multi-bed family room is also available. **www.nakluk.si**

TOMAJ Škerlj

🅿 ⅋ ≋   €€

Tomaj 53a, 6221 **Tel** *(05) 764 0673* **Rooms** *7*   **Road Map** *A4*

This rural bed-and-breakfast in the village of Tomaj, Škerlj offers a range of two-, three-and four-bed rooms grouped around a traditional farmhouse courtyard. There is a small outdoor pool and bicycles can be hired. Arrangements for half-board with home-cooked food can be made. **www.skerlj.eu**

VIPAVA Na Hribu

🅿 ⅋   €

Slap 93, 5271 **Tel** *(05) 364 5708* **Rooms** *10*   **Road Map** *A4*

Located in the village of Slap just across the valley from Vipava, this large farmstead contains a clutch of small, simply furnished but homely en suite rooms. There are a number of three-bed rooms, and a four-person apartment. The restaurant serves local cuisine and home-produced wine. **www.nahribu-zorz.veha.net**

Key to Price Guide *see p188* **Key to Symbols** *see back cover flap*

SOUTHERN AND EASTERN SLOVENIA

CELJE Hotel Štorman
🔲 P 🍴 €€
Mariborska cesta 3, 3000 **Tel** *(03) 426 0426* **Rooms** *52*   **Road Map** D3

A business hotel in a towerblock on the south-bound dual-carriageway into Celje, Hotel Štorman has small and dated though acceptable en suite rooms. The Old Town is a five-minute walk away. A bar-restaurant incorporated into the hotel provides decent meals. **www.storman.si**

CELJE Hotel Evropa
🔲 🍴 📋 €€€
Krekov trg 4, 3000 **Tel** *(03) 426 9000* **Rooms** *61*   **Road Map** D3

Behind its 19th-century façade, Hotel Evropa is a fine modern business hotel with a slick modern style that will appeal to visitors. Superior rooms are worth the extra cost for twice the space. Wi-Fi is accessible throughout. The restaurant and café are the best in town. **www.hotel-evropa.si**

DOLENJSKE TOPLICE Hotel Balnea
🔲 P 🍴 ♨ €€€€
Zdraviliški trg 7, 8350 **Tel** *(07) 391 9400* **Rooms** *62*   **Road Map** D4

This hotel is a little more expensive than its older neighbours but is in another league in terms of comfort. From a lofty glass atrium to retro-modern styled bedrooms and romantic suites with four-poster beds, the Balnea offers a comfortable stay. The resort's spa offers good deals for guests. **www.terme-krka.si**

KOLPA VALLEY Kovač
P 🍴 🏃 €€
Sela 5, 1337 **Tel** *(01) 894 1508* **Fax** *(01) 894 1655* **Rooms** *35*   **Road Map** C5

During summer holidays this hotel-cum-activities centre in Osilnica is often taken over by school groups. At other times, its pleasant bedrooms with terracotta tiles and crisp white sheets provide a quiet base from which to explore the Kolpa valley. Its owners organize river trips and offer advise on fishing. **www.kovac-kolpa.com**

KOPE Hotel Luka
🔲 P 🍴 🏃 📋 €€
Kope, 2383 **Tel** *(02) 883 9850* **Rooms** *180*   **Road Map** D2

Only 100 m (328 ft) from the summit of Kope, this hotel is popular with skiing families in winter and training athletes in summer. The best rooms are those with balconies on the first and second floors. Family suites and chalets are also available. Facilities include ski storage, bike hire, a spa and a children's disco. **www.vabo.si**

LAŠKO Hotel Savinja
🔲 P 🍴 €€
Valvasorjev trg 1, 3270 **Tel** *(05) 922 1076* **Rooms** *10*   **Road Map** D3

First a Renaissance courtyard townhouse, then the site of the town's first brewery, this refurbished building in the heart of medieval Laško now houses a small hotel with accommodation in high ceilinged rooms whose maple furnishings are from the 1930s. It also has a good restaurant and a riverside terrace bar. **www.savinja-lasko.si**

LAŠKO Vila Monet
P 📋 €€
Savinjsko nabrežje 4, 3270 **Tel** *(08) 205 0751* **Fax** *(08) 205 0758* **Rooms** *6*   **Road Map** D3

This is a centrally located pension in a restored riverside 19th-century villa that feels secluded despite being just off the main square. It has quietly sophisticated rooms with modern conveniences such as a minibar, satellite TV and Wi-Fi. It offers good value for money, especially for two-night deals. **www.vilamonet.si**

LAŠKO Wellness Park Laško
🔲 P 🍴 ♨ 🏃 📺 📋 €€€€
Zdraviliška cesta 6, 3270 **Tel** *(03) 423 2100* **Rooms** *180*   **Road Map** D3

Far from cheap, this resort hotel to the north of the centre is one for the whole family. Under one roof is an astonishing range of pools, waterslides and wave machines as well as spas with a world of massages and beauty treatments. It offers more modern style than the average large hotel. **www.thermana.si**

MARIBOR Hotel Bolfenk
🔲 P 🍴 ♨ 🏃 📋 €€€
Hočko Pohorje 131, 2208 **Tel** *(02) 220 8841* **Fax** *(02) 220 8849* **Rooms** *20*   **Road Map** E2

This family-friendly apartment hotel complex sits right at the base of the ski piste on the Mariborsko Pohorje. It is great in winter, while in summer there are all sorts of activities for kids nearby, as well as a spa. Bright apartments have balconies that give them a rural feel. Some have fireplaces. **www.pohorje.org**

MARIBOR Hotel Orel
🔲 P 🏃 📋 €€€€
Volkmerjev prehod 7, 2000 **Tel** *(02) 250 6700* **Fax** *(02) 251 8497* **Rooms** *71*   **Road Map** E2

The Orel is a decent three-star with modest, comfortable rooms, half of which are air conditioned. All rooms have en suite facilities and Internet access, with Wi-Fi in some areas. The real draw is the hotel's location in the heart of the Old Town. **www.termemb.si**

MARIBOR Grand Hotel Ocean
🔲 P 🍴 🏃 📋 €€€€
Partizanska cesta 39, 2000 **Tel** *(05) 907 7120* **Fax** *(05) 907 7130* **Rooms** *23*   **Road Map** E2

A small, boutique four-star hotel opposite the train station, the Grand Hotel Ocean is named after the first train to stop in Maribor in 1846. The rooms are tasteful and quietly elegant with thick carpets, neutral colours, orthopaedic mattresses and all modern conveniences, including massage showers. **www.hotelocean.si**

METLIKA Hotel Bela Krajina
⚂ **P** ⑪ 🗏 €€€

Cesta bratstva in enotnosti 28, 8330 **Tel** *(07) 305 8123* **Fax** *(07) 363 5281* **Rooms** *26* **Road Map** *D4*

Unmissable because of its bright orange façade, this small hotel provides a comfortable base from which to explore the Bela Krajina region. Its simple en suite rooms are comfortable, with modern bathrooms that are a bit small. The wine bars in the Old Town of Metlika are within walking distance. **www.hotel-belakrajina.si**

MOKRICE Grad Mokrice
P ⑪ €€€€€

Rajec 4, 8261 **Tel** *(07) 457 4240* **Fax** *(07) 495 7007* **Rooms** *28* **Road Map** *E4*

Not as glamorous as the nearby Otočec Castle, this restored Renaissance castle has a certain bygone grandeur – chateâu-style furniture and parquet floors. The round suites in corner turrets are vast. Guests have access to the pools at Čatež. One of Slovenia's best golf courses is in the castle grounds. **www.terme-catez.si**

MORAVSKE TOPLICE Prekmurska vas
P 🏊 🏃 €€€€

Kranjčeva 12, 9226 **Tel** *(02) 512 2200* **Fax** *(02) 548 1607* **Rooms** *12* **Road Map** *F1*

These self-catering apartments that accommodate up to six people in pretty Prekmurje-style cottages are the best option for the most appealing stay at Terme 3000. Free entry to the resort's pools, plus a location in central Prekmurje make this a family-friendly base from which to enjoy the resort. **www.terme3000.si**

MURSKA SOBOTA Hotel Štrk
P ⑪ 🏊 🏃 📺 🗏 €€

Polana 40, 9000 **Tel** *(02) 525 2158* **Fax** *(02) 525 2157* **Rooms** *24* **Road Map** *F1*

Named after the storks that nest annually on its chimney, Štrk is located 4 km (3 miles) northwest of Murska Sobota. It has everything from traditional touches to comforts such as air conditioning, high-tech showers and thick carpets. There is a small spa, bikes for hire and a fishing pond. **www.lovenjakov-dvor.si**

MURSKA SOBOTA Sončna hiša
P 🏃 🗏 €€€€€

Banovci 3c, 9241 **Tel** *(02) 588 8238* **Fax** *(02) 588 8239* **Rooms** *5* **Road Map** *F1*

A newcomer to Slovenia's roster of aspirational residences, Sončna hiša, literally Sun House, 12 km (8 miles) south of Murska Sobota, feels less a boutique hotel and more a chic homestay. It offers accommodation for up to 18 guests with five individually designed suites; the Stork room has baby facilities. **www.soncna-hisa.si**

NOVO MESTO Hostel Situla
⑪ €

Dilančeva ulica 1, 8000 **Tel** *(07) 394 2000* **Fax** *(07) 394 2001* **Rooms** *20* **Road Map** *D4*

Funky and friendly, the Situla is an excellent choice. Its murals and printed linen are designed after the Iron Age situla urns displayed in the Dolenjska Museum. There are three- or four-bed dorms and larger eight-bed rooms, all but one share a bathroom. Facilities include a laundry and an Internet café. **www.situla.si**

NOVO MESTO Hotel Krka
⚂ **P** ⑪ 🗏 €€€

Novi trg 1, 8000 **Tel** *(07) 394 2100* **Rooms** *53* **Road Map** *D4*

Fairly dated in decor, this business hotel is the only one of its kind in central Novo Mesto. Facilities include cable TV, minibar, air conditioning, Internet and Wi-Fi access and a massage salon. One room has facilities for disabled visitors. Guests also have free use of pools in nearby spa resorts. **www.terme-krka.si**

OLIMJE Penzion Amon
P ⑪ €€

Olimje 24, 3254 **Tel** *(03) 818 2480* **Fax** *(03) 582 9026* **Rooms** *13* **Road Map** *E3*

A fine golf course and winery, Amon is also a good choice for an overnight stay. Total refurbishment in 2010 has created accommodation that is crisp and modern, with colourful walls to enliven natural fibre carpets and pale wood furniture. Front rooms have a balcony and ample sunlight and are worth the extra euros. **www.amon.si**

ORMOŽ Penzion Merkež
🛏 **P** ⑪ €€

Brezovica 16, 8259 **Tel** *(07) 495 1311* **Rooms** *5* **Road Map** *F2*

The Merkež family opened this traditional-style pension in 2009 and named its bedrooms and suite after the grape varieties they once cultivated behind the house; guests can ask to see the family's wine cellar. The en suite rooms blend cosy country style with modern facilties such as Wi-Fi. **www.merkez.si**

ORMOŽ Dvorec Jeruzalem
P ⑪ 🗏 €€€€

Jeruzalem 8, 2259 **Tel** *(02) 719 4805* **Fax** *(02) 719 4807* **Rooms** *10* **Road Map** *F2*

Buried deep in the idyllic wine hills north of Ormož, this is a classy small hotel in a restored 17th-century manor. There are views of vineyards on all sides, while the hamlet itself is soporific. Bedrooms come with flat-screen TVs and Wi-Fi as well as rich wood floors, mahogany furniture and brass fittings. **www.dvorec-jeruzalem.si**

OTOČEC Grad Otočec
⚂ **P** ⑪ 📺 🗏 €€€€€

Grajska cesta 2, 8222 **Tel** *(07) 384 8900* **Rooms** *30* **Road Map** *D4*

A classic among Slovenian hotels for its history and architecture, this island castle is now a Relais & Chateâux address. Sensitive refurbishment has introduced modern boutique glamour that is in harmony with the historic structure. Guest have free use of nearby tennis courts and pools. **www.terme-krka.si**

OTOČEC Šeruga
🛏 **P** €€

Sela pri Ratežu 15, 8222 **Tel** *(07) 334 6900* **Fax** *(07) 334 6901* **Rooms** *12* **Road Map** *D4*

There are few Slovenian tourist farms as idyllic as this one 3 km (2 miles) southwest of Otočec. The Šeruga family has converted a barn into pretty en suite rooms full of understated charm, offering top value for money. They also offer meals. Activities for children include feeding the livestock. **www.seruga.si**

Key to Price Guide *see p188* **Key to Symbols** *see back cover flap*

PTUJ Grand Hotel Primus

Pot v toplice 9, 2251 **Tel** *(02) 749 4500* **Fax** *(02) 749 4523* **Rooms** *122*   **Road Map** *E2*

This is a large glossy hotel 2 km (1 mile) west of the Old Town. Slickly managed, with four-star comforts and spa treatments and balconies in all rooms, it is adjacent to an outdoor pools complex and the town's golf course. There is free bus and train travel into the Old Town every few hours. **www.terme-ptuj.si**

PTUJ Hotel Mitra

Prešernova ulica 6, 2250 **Tel** *(02) 787 7455* **Fax** *(02) 787 7459* **Rooms** *29*   **Road Map** *E2*

A budget boutique hotel, the Mitra is housed in a 16th-century house in the Old Town. The rooms are themed after a Ptuj narrative, though more noticable is the impeccable blend of designer and historic decor. The attic rooms are smaller but still lovely. There is also a spa, fine wine cellar and garden. **www.hotel-mitra.si**

PTUJ Park Hotel

Prešernova 38, 2250 **Tel** *(02) 749 3300* **Fax** *(02) 749 3301* **Rooms** *15*   **Road Map** *E2*

The Park has loads of character to go with that provided by its restored 16th-century building – rooms are individually furnished with an eclectic blend of late-1800s antiques. Art, old and new, adorns the walls in public areas. There is an appealing café-bar too. **www.parkhotel-ptuj.si**

RIBNICA Penzion Makšar

Breže 18, 1310 **Tel** *(01) 837 3160* **Fax** *(01) 836 3433* **Rooms** *6*   **Road Map** *C4*

Hidden in a village between Ribnica and Nova Štifta, this restaurant and pension is the area's most pleasant stay. Although it opened in 2009, modernity is softened by rustic details such as wooden furniture, apple-green walls in rooms and terracotta floors in the bathroom. Flat-screen TVs in every room. **www.penzion-maksar.si**

ROGAŠKA SLATINA Hotel Slatina

Celjska cesta 6, 3250 **Tel** *(03) 818 4100* **Fax** *(03) 818 4102* **Rooms** *61*   **Road Map** *E3*

This is a good-value option away from the central square that is popular with visitors on health and spa treatment programmes, both in the town and in the on-site mineral water swimming pool. A slick glass wing attached to the original 19th-century hotel contains more modern superior rooms with minibars. **www.hotelslatina.com**

ROGAŠKA SLATINA Grand Hotel Donat

Zdraviliški trg 10, 3250 **Tel** *(03) 811 3000* **Fax** *(03) 811 3732* **Rooms** *167*   **Road Map** *E3*

This large resort hotel is attached to the drinking hall and contains a sophisticated spa with wellness and medical treatments. Bedrooms are comfortable and modern throughout whether facing the park or forest. All en suite rooms are spacious and have a balcony. Deluxe rooms are individually styled. **www.ghdonat.com**

ROGAŠKA SLATINA Grand Hotel Rogaška

Zdraviliški trg 14, 3250 **Tel** *(03) 811 2000* **Fax** *(03) 811 2012* **Rooms** *83*   **Road Map** *E3*

Occupying the palatial Neo-Classical building where Austro-Hungarian emperors stayed and composer Franz Liszt played waltzes in the ballroom, is the Grand Hotel Rogaška. The bedrooms, although showing their age, are comfortable enough with dated decor and grand proportions. **www.terme-rogaska.si**

ŠENTANEL Koroš

Jamnica 10, 2391 **Tel** *(02) 870 3060* **Fax** *(02) 870 3061* **Rooms** *8*   **Road Map** *C2*

While this tranquil eco tourist farm is a base for mountain bike holidays, its relaxed atmosphere, typified by an honour-system bar, and the beautiful panorama from a spur north of Šentanel will delight anyone who stays here. The charming en suite rooms are simply decorated; breakfasts feature local produce. **www.mtbpark.com**

SLOVENJ GRADEC Rotovnik-Plesnik Tourist Farm

Legen 134, 2383 **Tel** *(02) 885 3666* **Fax** *(02) 885 3059* **Rooms** *6*   **Road Map** *D2*

This charming tourist farm is a hugely relaxing place to stay. Located 2 km (1 mile) from Slovenj Gradec on the road to Kope, the farmhouse has six pretty en suite rooms. Two rooms are for families and there is a children's playground. Tasty home-cooked food is served and half-board is recommended. **www.rotovnik-plesnik.si**

TREBNJE Gostilna Rakar

Gorenje Ponikve 8, 8210 **Tel** *(07) 346 6190* **Fax** *(07) 346 6191* **Rooms** *24*   **Road Map** *C3*

This celebrated restaurant *(see p211)* 1 km (half a mile) east of Trebnje offers accommodation in an adjacent wing. The decor is minimalistic, with only a large modern oil painting adding colour to the pale woods and cream fabrics in rooms, each with a whirlpool bath. A good base from which to tour the region. **www.rakar.si**

VELENJE Hotel Razgoršek

Stari trg 1, 3320 **Tel** *(03) 898 3630* **Fax** *(03) 898 3672* **Rooms** *30*   **Road Map** *D2*

With its ornate gold-trimmed furniture and reproduced Old Masters, the Razgoršek has a theatrical faux Baroque decor. This small hotel beneath the castle at the edge of modern Velenje has six standard business-style rooms. Air conditioning is only available on the first floor; satellite TV is in all rooms. **www.hotelrazgorsek.com**

ŽUŽEMBERK Koren

Dolga vas 5, 8360 **Tel** *(07) 308 7260* **Rooms** *6*   **Road Map** *C4*

Located on the bank of the river opposite the town, this tourist farm enjoys good views of the castle. The rooms in the wing are simple, with pine furnishings and flooring, but the riverside setting is relaxing and guests have free use of bikes and canoes. Half- or full-board deals are recommended. **www.turizem-koren.com**

WHERE TO EAT

Slovenian cuisine is something of an unknown entity to a majority of foreigners. Nevertheless, you can eat very well here, whether at an international eatery in the city, a new type of country restaurant where master chefs elevate seasonal and local produce to gourmet heights, or just at a village inn. A bad meal is rare in a country that takes fresh produce for granted, although it helps if

Menu outside a restaurant, Piran

visitors like hearty dishes. Apart from the national cuisine *(see pp200–201)*, Slovenians have a taste for the ethnic dishes of the Balkans – both Serbian grilled meats and Croatian Adriatic fish – as well as Austrian and Italian cuisine, whose pizzas are ubiquitous. However, other European food is poorly represented, while Asian cooking tends to be limited to cities and large towns.

RESTAURANTS

The term *restavracija* (restaurant) is used to define any formal establishment that offers fine local as well as international cuisine. As a rule of thumb, most are located in cities, large towns or, to a lesser extent, resorts. More widespread – and almost always more appealing in terms of their rustic atmosphere – is the *gostilna*. This roughly approximates to a British country inn and is just as varied in quality. Like celebrated British gastro-pubs, the finest Slovenian *gostilna* can provide the most memorable dining experiences in the country thanks to the efforts of master chefs who produce creative country cooking from seasonal and local ingredients. Others offer nothing more fancy than soups and schnitzels.

Whether it is gourmet country cuisine or the no-nonsense pub or bar food, the menus are usually traditional and at weekends many urban Slovenians head out of town for a long lunch in a country *gostilna* – which is highly recommended. A *gostišče* is similar but also offers accommodation.

For a quick informal meal, there is the pizzeria as well as the *okrepčevalnica,* or snack bar, which typically prepares Serbian meat snacks such as *čevapčiči* (meat rissoles with spicy sauce) or the filled filo pastry snack *burek.* A café (sometimes known as a *kavarna*) will offer pastries, fresh gateaux and ice cream. No matter where you eat, smoking has been banned indoors since 2007. Even the few restaurants that have smoking rooms cannot serve food and drink within them.

MENUS

Except in cafés and simple village inns, all restaurants and the majority of *gostilna* will provide an English translation of the menu. However, many places prepare extra dishes in addition to the standard menu. Such daily specials will be chalked up in Slovenian on a blackboard or handwritten and presented with the menu at upmarket addresses. Since by definition these are the freshest dishes, generally prepared from whatever is in season and usually to local recipes, such offers are always worth investigating. The staff, especially the younger ones, will be able to help translate the more obscure words on the menu *(see pp254–6)*. More upmarket dining establishments usually display a menu with prices outside.

Outdoor seating at a restaurant near Vršič Pass

Cafés with outdoor seating in Tartini Square, Piran

PRICES, TIPS AND PAYMENT

Like most other countries, the cost of a meal in Slovenia varies according to the location. Eating out in Ljubljana, Maribor, Bled and the coast area is far more expensive than in the south and east. Many restaurants provide good-value set menus, which permit a choice from two or three dishes in each course. Similarly, the tasting menus of gourmet restaurants, usually with five to eight smaller dishes, can work out as good value and a chance to sample many dishes. The price of alcohol varies, but beer is the cheapest drink.

Prices include tax but not always service. In a smart restaurant and upmarket *gostilna*, it is usual to add a tip of 10 per cent for good service. In an inn, the standard practice is to round up the final sum, while loose change is perfectly acceptable in cafés.

Payment by credit card, normal enough in most of Europe regardless of the size of the establishment, is also the practice in Slovenia. Generally, MasterCard is accepted in almost all major establishments. However, American Express cards may well pose a bit of a problem in some places, so do carry enough cash with you. Restaurants and inns that accept credit cards display the logos of acceptable cards near the entrance. Do check if a minimum charge is applied to customers paying by card.

OPENING HOURS

Cafés generally open from 8am and *gostilna* from 11am, although many of those that serve as a hub for the local community may open around 9am. Restaurants usually open from noon, with a break from around 3 to 6pm; some city establishments open for dinner only. Dinner is eaten earlier in Slovenia than in neighbouring areas such as Dalmatian Croatia and Italy, usually around 7pm or even 6pm in remote country inns, some of which stop serving food by 9pm. Many inns and restaurants close on Mondays or Tuesdays.

RESERVATIONS AND DRESS CODES

A prior reservation is essential only in the best restaurants. However, Friday and Saturday nights and Sunday lunchtimes are busy in highly regarded local *gostilna*, so a reservation is worthwhile if visitors want

to eat at a particular place at a certain time or if they prefer a specific restaurant. Dress codes are informal and comfortable, with smart attire only required in the very best city restaurants, and even then nothing more formal than a jacket for men. However, visiting an upmarket *gostilna* mud-spattered after a walk may well be frowned on.

CHILDREN

Slovenians are fond of children and welcome them to all but the very choicest city restaurants. Most *gostilna* and restaurants can provide a high chair for toddlers and there will be light dishes for children particularly during the lunch period. Pizza and pasta or hamburger-like snacks such as *pljeskavica* and *čevapčiči* are readily available and make for a good choice for children.

VEGETARIANS

Slovenia likes its meat dishes and there are few dedicated vegetarian restaurants outside a handful in the capital. Nevertheless, there is a growing awareness of vegetarian needs and most *gostilna* offer three or four vegetarian dishes. In addition, fresh salads are popular and vegetarian soups, typically of beans or mushrooms, are standard fixtures on menus nationwide. Fish-eaters will find life easier due to the wide variety of Adriatic and freshwater fish on menus.

Cosy interior of the popular Petit Café, Ljubljana

The Flavours of Slovenia

If Slovenia has surprisingly wide-ranging tastes for such a small nation, it is because its regional cuisines are shaped by neighbouring Italy, Austria, Hungary and the Balkans. Most of its best-loved dishes are rooted in the country's peasant past – the tenets of Slovenian cooking are simple, sturdy and meaty, and seasonal local produce is rightly celebrated. Small wonder, then, that the best Slovenian chefs retain a place for traditional recipes on their menus and, rather than striving to impress with high-concept cookery, let good ingredients do the talking.

Walnut potica

Freshly harvested wild mushrooms for sale in autumn

COUNTRY CUISINE

The frugal roots of much Slovenian cookery can be seen in the ingredients that make up many of its classic dishes. Vegetables such as potatoes, cabbage, squashes, turnips and pumpkins, which keep well through the winter months, appear in many forms. A national favourite is wild mushrooms, which are gathered and served fresh in autumn, then dried for use throughout the year.

Sweet dishes often feature orchard fruits, such as apples, cherries, pears and plums. Nuts, especially walnuts, and poppy, pumpkin and sunflower seeds, appear in many cakes and stuffed dumplings, often sweetened with local honey. Soured cream and soft curd cheese are widely used as well.

The focus of most Slovenian meals, however, is meat, usually pork *(svinjina)*. Pork lard is often used to flavour side dishes, and sausage-making is a great tradition.

Perhaps the most distinctive Slovenian culinary feature is the use of buckwheat; *žganci*, a buckwheat mash often served with mushrooms or pork crackling as a side dish, was dubbed "the pillar of Slovenia" in the 1800s.

Walnuts

Cottage cheese

Pumpkin

Poppy seeds

Carr saus

Pea

Buckwh

Selection of produce featured in many traditional Slovenian dishes

SLOVENIAN DISHES AND SPECIALITIES

Dine at a farmstay *(see p187)* or a restaurant that specializes in regional food and you will taste Slovenian cuisine at its most authentic and appealing. A typical starter is soup *(juha)* – often a hearty bowlful such as *jota* or mushroom soup *(gobova juha)*, sometimes served in a hollowed-out loaf as a bowl. The main course is generally of the meat-and-two-vegetables variety; pork is ubiquitous, often served as escalopes or schnitzel, but veal *(teletina)* and beef *(govedina)* are also popular, as is game in season, particularly venison *(srna)*, pheasant *(fazan)* and rabbit *(zajec)*. Freshwater trout *(postrv)* is delicious fried in corn flour or lightly smoked. Aside from fruit-filled *štruklji* and *prekmurska gibanica*, the classic Slovenian dessert is *potica*, a filling, ring-shaped cake made with nuts and honey.

Honey

Jota *is a hearty soup made with sauerkraut, root vegetables, cured pork and red kidney beans.*

Traditional, lavishly decorated cookies in a Radovljica bakery

nowhere is this more evident than in its use of paprika. This is the region of rich, spicy *golaž* (goulash) and steaming pots of *bograč* stew, a dish so highly revered that Lendava stages the Bogračfest cooking competition every August. Prekmurje's traditional autumn slaughter supports its reputation for fine hams (*šunka*) and pork sausages (*klobase*), hot with paprika, aromatic with garlic, thickened with buckwheat or millet porridge, and served fresh or cured.

ITALIAN INFLUENCES

Flavours and cooking styles begin to change the further one travels west in Slovenia. In the Italian border region of Primorska, the food is noticeably lighter, and menus might feature home-made *njoki* (gnocchi) and *rižota* (risotto), often with wild mushrooms and herbs. Idrija is known for its ravioli-like *žlikrofi*, traditionally filled with potato, bacon, onion and chives. Arguably the most famous ingredient from this part of the country is *pršut*, a delicious air-dried ham, like Italian prosciutto, that originates in the karst and Istrian Slovenia. In these southwesterly areas and along the Adriatic coast, fish and seafood, fine wines, lashings of olive oil and excellent restaurants come as standard.

A TOUCH OF SPICE

Hungarian influences take over at the opposite end of Slovenia. Prekmurje, in the far east of the country, has a regional cuisine that is as distinctive as the Italianate food of west Slovenia, and

Fresh fruits and vegetables on a stall in Ljubljana market

WHAT TO DRINK

Water (*voda*) Sparkling water (*mineralna*) is standard unless still (*negazirana*) is specified.

Coffee (*kava*) As in Italy and the Balkans, this is served strong and black unless milk (*mleko*) is requested.

Tea (*čaj*) This is less common than coffee and always served black. Herbal tea is *zeliščni čaj*.

Beer (*pivo*) Slovenian beer – Union brewery's *Zlatorog* or *Laško* – is a thirst-quenching Pilsner-style brew.

Wine (*vino*) Whether white (*belo*) or red (*rdeče*), Slovenian wines are of a high standard. Look especially for wines from the Goriška Brda region.

Pear brandy (*viljamovka*) This is a popular, often home-made fruit schnapps. Some of the best is distilled and sold at Pleterje Monastery (*see p164*).

Bograč, *a spicy, meaty stew from Prekmurje, is named after its traditional earthenware cooking pot.*

Štruklji *are dumplings, stuffed with ground walnuts and spices. They are served as a side dish or a dessert.*

Prekmurska gibanica *is a pie with layers of filo pastry, cottage cheese, poppy seeds, walnuts and spiced apple.*

Choosing a Restaurant

The restaurants in this guide have been selected across a range of price categories for their location, atmosphere, good food and value. All the entries are arranged alphabetically within price categories and by region. For map references, see pages 98–9 for Ljubljana and the back inside cover for the rest of Slovenia.

PRICE CATEGORIES
Price ranges are based on the price per person for a three-course meal with half a bottle of wine, including cover charge, service and tax.

€ under €20
€€ €20–€30
€€€ €30–€50
€€€€ €50–€80
€€€€€ over €80

LJUBLJANA

AROUND THE CENTRE Celica café   V   €
Metelkova 8, 1000 **Tel** *(01) 230 9700*

Even if you are not staying at Celica's hostel you can eat in its funkily designed café. The menu concentrates on inexpensive but filling fare, with a choice of vegetarian options. The daily menu of soup, main course and cake is a real bargain. Popular with local students, it is also a convenient stop-off for vistors looking around the area.

AROUND THE CENTRE Gostilna Rožnik   €
Cankarjev vrh 1, 1000 **Tel** *(01) 251 3429*

For a taste of traditional mountain food head for this lovely 19th-century building below the summit of Rožnik Hill, just a short hike from the city centre. Sausages, chops and thick soups such as *ričet* (barley and beans) form the backbone of the menu. A slice of *pehtranova potica* (tarragon cake) is recommended.

AROUND THE CENTRE Kavarna SEM   €€
Metelkova 2, 1000 **Tel** *(01) 300 8700*

The Slovene Ethnographic Museum's stylish ground-floor café is the perfect place to recharge one's batteries. Its menu of moderately priced salads, soups, sandwiches and cakes provides the ideal material for a light lunch or afternoon tea. The garden terrace includes a merry-go-round and a see-saw for children.

AROUND THE CENTRE Gostilna pod Rožnikom   €€€
Cesta na Rožnik 18, 1000 **Tel** *(01) 251 3446*

Known to the locals as Čad, this 19th-century house below Rožnik Hill is one of the best addresses in town for Balkan-style grilled meats. *Ražnjiči* (skewer grilled strips of pork) and *čulbastija* (tender pork chops) are among the favourites, while *prebranac* (baked beans) is the garnish of choice.

AROUND THE CENTRE Pri Škofu   €€€€
Rečna 8, 1000 **Tel** *(01) 426 4508*

Pri Škofu has a long-standing reputation for good food at a good price and is a delightful place for a traditional meal. Its quiet location and simple wooden tables lend to its magic. There is a refreshing air of informality and the menu is not always written; ask the waiters for what is available.

AROUND THE CENTRE Yildiz Han   €€€
Karlovška cesta, 1000 **Tel** *(01) 426 5717*

Occupying a quiet canal-side location on the east of Ljubljana's castle hill, Yildiz Han serves traditional Turkish grilled meats and kebabs. The colourful carpet-swathed interior plays host to belly dancers on weekends and hookahs can be enjoyed on the summer terrace.

NEW TOWN Ajdovo zrno   V   €
Trubarjeva cesta 7, 1000 **Tel** *(04) 169 0468*   **City Map** *D2*

A clean and bright self-service canteen, Ajdovo zrno offers a choice of vegetarian-only hot dishes and a well-stocked salad bar. Located in a courtyard only a few steps away from the central Prešernov trg, it is the perfect venue for a quick healthy meal between bouts of sightseeing. Closed Sat and Sun.

NEW TOWN Le Petit Café   €€
Trg Francoske revolucije, 1000 **Tel** *(01) 251 2575*   **City Map** *C4*

A popular French-style café, Le Petit has a large – and frequently crowded – terrace looking out towards Jože Plečnik's Illyrian Monument. People flock here for the fresh pastries and croissants, but there is plenty in the way of more substantial meals, with soups, salads and pastas predominating on the menu.

NEW TOWN Figovec   €€€
Gosposvetska 1, 1000 **Tel** *(01) 426 4410*   **City Map** *C1*

Located on one of central Ljubljana's most prominent street corners, Figovec has always been renowned for its horsemeat – as a starter in the form of horse carpaccio, and also in main courses such as foal steak. There are plenty of mainstream meat dishes such as wiener schnitzel and some spicy goulashes too.

Key to Symbols *see back cover flap*

NEW TOWN Joe Peña's
🍴 🍷 €€€
Cankarjeva 6, 1000 **Tel** *(01) 421 5800*
City Map *C2*

A Mexican-themed restaurant with bare floorboards and low-key lighting, this is a reliable option for those seeking big portions and moderate prices. Half of the menu is made up of chimichangas, fajitas and other spicy fare, although there are plenty of mainstream pork and steak choices too. It is also a good place for cocktails.

NEW TOWN Šestica
€€€
Slovenska cesta 40, 1000 **Tel** *(01) 242 0855*
City Map *C2*

A popular main street restaurant with an attractive garden courtyard, Šestica's menu covers most regions of Slovenia, with goulash from the plains of eastern Slovenia and squid and grilled fish from the coast. The *prekmurska gibanica* (poppy-seed-and-cottage cheese cake) makes an outstanding dessert. Closed Sun.

NEW TOWN Gostilna As
🍴 🍷 €€€€
Čopova 5a, 1000 **Tel** *(01) 425 8822*
City Map *C2*

This smart but not over-formal venue has long been a favourite among local gourmets. The blend of Mediterranean and Central European cuisine makes full use of local ingredients. The adjoining As lounge serves inexpensive pastas and salads alongside an impressive range of cocktails.

NEW TOWN Shambala
€€€€
Križevniška 12, 1000 **Tel** *(03) 184 3833*
City Map *C4*

Occupying an arcaded courtyard that has been covered to create a dining room, Shambala offers an exquisite selection of Asian dishes, with Thai curries, spicy grilled fish and Chinese stir-fries. The fixed-price lunches are excellent value and there is a respectable list of cocktails, Slovenian wines and fiery fruit brandies.

NEW TOWN JB Restavracija
🍷 €€€€€
Miklošičeva 17, 1000 **Tel** *(01) 433 1358*
City Map *D2*

The culinary baby of Slovenian super-chef Janez Bratovž, JB Restavracija is arguably the leading destination in town for Mediterranean and Central European fusion. A small, seasonally changing menu sources the best local ingredients and the wine cellar is one of the best-stocked in the capital. Closed Sun and Mon.

NEW TOWN Pri vitezu
🍴 🍷 €€€€€
Breg 18–20, 1000 **Tel** *(01) 426 6058*
City Map *D4*

A 300-year-old inn on the banks of the Ljubljanica, "At the Knight's Place" offers upscale dining in a soothing barrel-vaulted space. Adriatic seafood and Central European meat dishes form the backbone of the menu. Most dishes come with an innovative modern European twist. Lunchtime menus represent great value for the quality.

OLD TOWN Café Romeo
€€
Stari trg 6, 1000 **Tel** *(01) 426 9011*
City Map *D4*

Romeo is a firm favourite with those seeking a reasonably priced lunch in a fun café environment. It serves pastas, tortillas, sandwiches and salads in a pop-art interior dominated by bold blacks and reds. Outdoor seating stretches down towards the riverbank and the choice of cocktails may tempt you to linger.

OLD TOWN Abecedarium
€€€
Ribji trg 2, 1000 **Tel** *(01) 426 9514*
City Map *D3*

Abecedarium admirably fits the bill for good food and a riverside setting. The menu is Slovenian-Mediterranean, offering a selection of roast meats, freshwater fish, seafood and pasta dishes. The Slovenian 16th-century language reformer Primož Trubar lived in this building, hence the alphabet-themed decor that fills the barrel-vaulted interior.

OLD TOWN Čajna hiša Cha
€€€
Stari trg 3, 1000 **Tel** *(01) 252 7010*
City Map *D4*

This attractive barrel-vaulted tea-house in the heart of the Old Town is the ideal place to relax over a pot of fresh tea, with a variety of speciality brews on offer. There is also a good choice of sandwiches and salads. A shop here sells loose tea and crockery. Closed Sun.

OLD TOWN Gostilna na Gradu
V €€€
Grajska planota 1, 1000 **Tel** *(08) 205 1930*
City Map *D3*

Occupying a barrel-vaulted building in the Ljubljana Castle courtyard, Gostilna na Gradu uses contemporary furnishings to create a winning combination of tradition and modernity. The menu focuses on traditional Slovenian country cuisine, stylishly presented, with deer goulash, oxtail and pan-fried trout featuring among the mains.

OLD TOWN Sokol
€€€
Ciril-Metodov trg 18, 1000 **Tel** *(01) 439 6855*
City Map *D3*

A popular national restaurant, Sokol occupies a warren of rooms in the Old Town. Hearty pork and steak dishes predominate, although the menu also includes game, freshwater fish and eastern Slovenian specialities such as *telečja obara* (paprika-rich veal stew). Try their own beer, which comes in both light and dark versions.

OLD TOWN Vodnikov hram
€€€
Vodnikov trg 2, 1000 **Tel** *(01) 234 5260*
City Map *E3*

Housed in a roomy traditional inn with plenty of exposed stonework and arched brick ceilings, this inn is located right beside Ljubljana's Market. It is an excellent place to tuck into meaty Slovenian favourites such as stuffed veal schnitzels, lean steaks and black blood-and-groats sausages. The window seats are usually snapped up quickly.

OLD TOWN Julija ♟ €€€€
*Stari trg 9, 1000 **Tel** (01) 425 6463* **City Map** D4

An elegant and relaxing place on the Old Town's main street, Julija strikes a good balance between Slovenian and international cuisine, with risotto and pasta choices alongside substantial steak and seafood dishes. For those eager to learn more about Slovenian wines, Julija's wine list is a good place to start.

OLD TOWN Lunch Café Marley & Me 🖼 V €€€€
*Stari trg 9, 1000 **Tel** (08) 380 6610* **City Map** D4

By no means only a café and certainly not just for lunch, this intimate restaurant is a nice mix of Minimalist decor and rustic furnishings. The fare is mostly Mediterranean, with fresh pasta, fish and substantial portions of salads predominating. There are only nine tables, so book in advance.

OLD TOWN Most 🖼 V ♟ €€€€
*Petkovškovo nabrežje 21, 1000 **Tel** (01) 232 8183* **City Map** D2

Right beside the Butchers' Bridge and with a pavement terrace facing the colonnaded fish market, Most, literally meaning bridge, embraces both Adriatic and inland Slovenian cuisine, with fish and steaks on the menu. The risottos and pastas make superb lighter meals. The wine list features organic white wines from Goriška Brda.

OLD TOWN River House 🖼 ❚❚ V V €€€€
*Gallusovo nabrežje 31, 1000 **Tel** (01) 425 4090* **City Map** D4

This combined restaurant and lounge-bar enjoys an ideal location, with an outdoor terrace overlooking the Ljubljanica river. Pasta dishes and Mediterranean salads share space on the menu with traditional Slovenian meat and fish main courses. It is also a popular nightlife venue, with DJs performing on weekend evenings.

OLD TOWN Špajza 🖼 ♟ €€€€
*Gornji trg 28, 1000 **Tel** (01) 425 3094* **City Map** D4

This relaxed diner's interior is composed of a cluster of small rooms decorated with folksy bric-a-brac. The menu includes fresh fish from the Adriatic, as well as inland Slovenian classics such as breast of duck, horsemeat steaks and game. Seasonal specials are chalked up on a board outside and the set lunches are well worth trying.

OLD TOWN Valvas'or 🖼 ♟ €€€€
*Stari trg 7, 1000 **Tel** (01) 425 0455* **City Map** D4

With a tasteful designer interior, Valvas'or delivers a delicate blend of Slovenian and international cuisine, impeccably prepared and served. The gourmet menus are recommended, and there is always a handful of affordable dishes of the day chalked up outside.

OLD TOWN Zlata ribica €€€€
*Cankarjevo nabrežje 5–7, 1000 **Tel** (01) 241 2680* **City Map** D3

Occupying a historic riverside building, the "Little Goldfish" is a pleasant spot in which to sample a traditional Slovenian menu of grilled fish, Adriatic *brodet* (fish soup) and treats from inland Slovenia such as baked *štruklji* (stuffed flour and cheese dumplings) and hearty pork and game dishes. They have reasonable lunch menus too.

FURTHER AFIELD Ledinek 🖼 €€
*Šmarna gora 4, 1000 **Tel** (01) 511 655*

Located at the top of Šmarna Gora hill and with benches pushed against the walls of the pilgrimage church, this traditional inn is famous for its own recipe of *planinski čaj* (herbal tea) and *na žlico* – literally "by spoon" – hearty soups thick with chunky vegetables. Expect freshly baked cakes and pastries at weekends.

FURTHER AFIELD Gorjanc €€€
*Tržaška 330, 1000 **Tel** (01) 423 1111*

With a trio of wood-panelled rooms just off the main road to Vrhnika, this traditional inn is a good place to visit after exploring the Ljubljana Marshes or Bistra castle. The menu revolves around filling, meat-heavy country dishes such as roast pork, horse steaks and succulent *pečenice* (roasted) sausages. Closed Fri and Sat.

FURTHER AFIELD Kašča €€€
*Spodnji trg 1, Škofja Loka, 4220 **Tel** (04) 512 4300*

Located in the basement of a 15th-century granary and with an interior seperated by wooden partitions, Kašča is a comfortable place to enjoy moderately priced Slovenian staples. Hearty mains of veal, pork or freshwater fish are augmented by cheaper lunchtime options such as *pot kašča* (sausage and cabbage stew). Closed Sun.

FURTHER AFIELD Maček 🖼 ❚❚ ♟ €€€
*Spodnje Gameljine 28, 1211 **Tel** (01) 563 2348*

This traditional village inn located in a village east of Šmarna Gora has a bar where locals gather for a glass of wine. It has a large wooden-beamed dining room, where pictures of mushrooms provide a clue to the establishment's seasonal specialities. Also on offer are rural treats such as game goulash, trout and venison.

FURTHER AFIELD Pri Kopač 🖼 €€€
*Tržaška 418, Brezovica, 1000 **Tel** (01) 365 3066*

Midway between Ljubljana and Vrhnika, "The Digger" has been drawing in customers for more than 100 years. Its trademark rustic dishes include roast veal, pork knuckle and the house favourite – *Ljubljanski zrezek* (veal or pork-stuffed schnitzel covered in mushroom sauce). Closed Sun and Mon.

Key to Price Guide *see p202* **Key to Symbols** *see back cover flap*

THE ALPS

BLED Belvedere Paviljon

€

Cesta svobode 26, 4260 **Tel** *(04) 575 3710* **Road Map** *B2*

This café and patisserie is in housed in a lofty, wood-panelled room decorated with photos of President Tito with various world leaders, taken in Vila Bled. Belvedere Paviljon has superb views of the lake and island and guests can sit outdoors on the belvedere, which curves around the shore.

BLED Gostilna Pri Planincu

€

Grajska cesta 8, 4260 **Tel** *(04) 574 1613* **Road Map** *B2*

A cheerful, unpretentious alpine-styled inn that has hosted mountaineers since 1903. Today, it is divided between a front bar where workmen down beer at lunchtime and the rear dining rooms with wooden panelling and beams. The menu includes steaks, pizzas and Balkan grilled meat snacks such as *čevapčiči* (rissoles). The portions are large.

BLED Penzion Mayer

€€€

Želeška cesta 7, 4260 **Tel** *(04) 574 1058* **Road Map** *B2*

This pension-cum-restaurant prepares excellent, well-priced country cuisine. Dishes change with the seasons but expect the likes of mushroom soups thickened with buckwheat, fresh grilled trout, turkey with walnuts and home-made *koline* (pork) sausages. Closed Mon.

BLED Okarina

€€€

Ljubljanska cesta 8, 4260 **Tel** *(04) 574 1458* **Road Map** *B2*

A rather smart fusion restaurant Okarina's off-beat interior has Indian paintings and textiles. It is no surprise, then, that Indian dishes feature on the menu, some baked in a traditional tandoor clay oven, alongside Adriatic fish and seafood and a few meat dishes and pastas. Open for dinner, Mon–Fri.

BLED Vila Prešeren

€€€

Veslaška promenada 14, 4260 **Tel** *(04) 575 3710* **Road Map** *B2*

Attached to a small boutique hotel, this slick café and restaurant has one of the finest lakeside terraces in Bled. Rattan loungers and parasols on a timber deck lend a Mediterranean style to match the light cuisine; expect risottos, pastas, salads, Adriatic fish and grilled meats. The dining room is restrained and modern.

BLED Topolino

€€€€

Ljubljanska cesta 26, 4260 **Tel** *(04) 574 1781* **Road Map** *B2*

Though modest in appearance, this antique-furnished address is the gourmet destination of the area. Its food is fresh, seasonal and creative. Sample dishes include superb spinach gnocchi covered with smoked goat cheese or steamed baby shrimp over puréed carrots with a sauce of caramel and balsamic vinegar. Closed Tue.

BOHINJ Gostišče Mihovc

€

Stara Fužina 118, 4267 **Tel** *(04) 572 3390* **Road Map** *A2*

This traditional inn lies at the heart of a lovely village 3 km (2 miles) northwest of Ribčev Laz. With modest decor and a vintage mechanical music box, it is frequented largely by locals and caters to local tastes – chunky home-style dishes such as bean soup with local sausage or goulash. There is a small terrace at the back.

BOHINJ Gostilna Rupa

€€€

Srednja vas 87, 4267 **Tel** *(04) 572 3401* **Road Map** *A2*

Located 4 km (2 miles) northwest of the lake, this eatery has alpine styling with embroidered cushions and checked curtains in the dining room, waitresses in traditional attire and a folk band once a week in summer. The fresh Bohinj trout is faultless. Great views from the terrace. There is a children's playground as well. Closed Mon.

BOVEC Martinov hram

€€

Trg golobarskih žrtev 27, 5230 **Tel** *(05) 388 6214* **Road Map** *A2*

A reliable inn in the heart of the village, Martinov hram has a popular vine-covered terrace. The interior is airy and modern, decorated with local paintings. Specialities include Soča river trout, local fare such as sheep's cheese with potatoes, game, pastas, risottos and Balkan snacks. Ask about daily specials. Closed Mon.

KAMNIK Kavarna Veronika

€

Glavni trg 6, 1240 **Tel** *(05) 997 0949* **Road Map** *C3*

This is where locals go to gossip over coffee and perhaps an ice cream or slice of cream gateau. The café occupies a prime location beneath Mali grad on the corner of its main largely traffic-free high street. A wicker chair on its terrace is the ideal position from which to watch the town's comings and goings.

KAMNIK Gostilna Čubr

€€€€

Križ 53, 1218 **Tel** *(01) 834 1115* **Road Map** *C3*

Semiformal and family-run, the Čubr has a reputation for upmarket Slovenian cuisine cooked with precision and presented with flair. À la carte favourites include soups of wild garlic or tarragon with home-made breads, colt steak with red peppers, roast kid or fresh fish. Ask about daily specials. Closed Sun and Mon.

KOBARID Gostilna Breza
🔼 ♿ 🚗   €€€
Mučeniška ulica 17, 5222 **Tel** *(05) 389 0040*   **Road Map** *A2*

Overlooked by most visitors as it is located behind the main square, this family restaurant serves upmarket home-made dishes from the Dolenjska and Bela Krajina regions. Expect sausages, venison with blueberries or turkey in a tarragon sauce. Tables are laid in the garden in summer. Closed Wed and Thu.

KOBARID Hiša Franko
🔼 ♿ 🚗 🍷   €€€€
Staro selo 1, 5222 **Tel** *(05) 389 4120*   **Road Map** *A2*

This is a cult culinary destination thanks to the master chef's creations – beautifully presented seasonal dishes such as pigeon breast with chicory, coffee sauce and wild cherries or venison tartare with green apple sauce. Tasting menus are recommended. Closed Mon and Tue (open for dinner on Tuesdays in summer).

KOBARID Kotlar
🔼 ♿ 🚗 🍷   €€€€
Trg svobode 11, 5222 **Tel** *(05) 390 1110*   **Road Map** *A2*

Sails strung across the roof and a boat-shaped bar add to the family-run Kotlar's reputation for style and outstanding cuisine. Fresh Adriatic seafood and fish is the main attraction and include squid and lobster dishes. The wine list is also sensational. Closed Tue and Wed.

KRANJ Gostilna Kot
🍴 🔼 🚗 🍴 🍷   €
Maistrov trg 4, 4000 **Tel** *(04) 202 6105*   **Road Map** *B3*

This inn at the entrance of the Old Town, where the locals go for simple food at low prices, spills on to the pedestrianized square in summer, while it has cosy wood-panelled rooms for winter. The food is mostly solid fare such as sautéed veal or sausages with horseradish, but there are light options such as trout with garlic and parsley.

KRANJ Pr' Matičku
🔼 🚗 🍴 🍷   €
Jezerska cesta 41, 4000 **Tel** *(04) 234 3360*   **Road Map** *B3*

This respected country-style restaurant in a residential suburb in Kranj. The rustic terrace appeals in summer and the interior, full of hunting trophies and old photographs, is a delight. Food is similarly traditional, with a good choice of game dishes and a decent wine list.

KRANJSKA GORA Gostilna Cvitar
🔼 🚗 🍴 🍷   €€
Borovška cesta 83, 4280 **Tel** *(04) 588 3600*   **Road Map** *A2*

Located beside the church, this restaurant in a historic inn has a terrace overlooking the pedestrianized central square. There is a good menu of Slovenian dishes such as game goulash with potato dumplings or veal stew with buckwheat polenta and Soča trout. The wine list is reasonable.

KRANJSKA GORA Gostilna Pri Martinu
🔼 🍴 V 🍷   €€
Borovška cesta 61, 4280 **Tel** *(04) 582 0300*   **Road Map** *A2*

Buckwheat grains with mushrooms or turkey with walnuts and tagliatelle are local touches on a menu that has a large choice of meat and fish dishes. The restaurant is frequented by both locals and tourists. It has a small vegetarian menu. The inn is divided into alpine-styled rooms, some with traditional furniture.

KRANJSKA GORA Hotel Miklič
🔼 ♿ V 🍷   €€€
Vitranška 13, 4280 **Tel** *(04) 588 1635*   **Road Map** *A2*

This is the fine-dining restaurant of the resort *(see p191)*, providing an international menu in a smart dining room with a bright conservatory. Game dishes are well represented alongside local fish and spit-roast specials. A good menu caters to vegetarians too. Some of the finest Slovenian wines are represented on the wine list.

LOGARSKA DOLINA Gostilna Raduha
🔼 🍷   €€€€
Luče 67, 3334 **Tel** *(03) 838 4000*   **Road Map** *C2*

Raduha is one of Slovenia's finest restaurants thanks to owner-chef Martina Breznik. Fifth in her family to own the inn, she lifts Slovenian cooking to gourmet heights. Expect nettle soup or home-smoked brook trout on seasonal menus showcasing local produce. Tasting menus are recommended. Closed for lunch, Mon and Tue.

RADOVLJICA Gostilna Avsenik
🔼 ♿ 🎵 🚗 🍴 🍷   €€
Begunje 21, 4275 **Tel** *(04) 533 3402*   **Road Map** *B2*

Slovenia's most successful musical group, the Avsenik Brothers, have transformed the original family restaurant into a destination for fans. It now has several large dining rooms and a dance floor. The waitresses in traditional attire and lively performances several times a week are all good fun. Closed Mon.

RADOVLJICA Izletniška kmetija Globočnik
🍴 🔼   €€
Globoko 9, 4240 **Tel** *(04) 073 6930*   **Road Map** *B2*

The creation of an artist-chef, this village eaterie is as much an ethnological experience as it is culinary. The restored 17th-century cottage has a "black kitchen" and a ceramic stove in the simple dining room. The food is a buffet of traditional farm fare created from whatever is fresh. Reservation essential. Open Mon–Thu.

RADOVLJICA Gostilna Lectar
🔼 🚗 🍴 🍷   €€€
Linhartov trg 2, 4240 **Tel** *(04) 537 4800*   **Road Map** *B2*

This 600-year-old inn in the Old Town has an old-world atmosphere along with good traditional cooking. Upmarket country dishes such as pork and sour turnip haggis or buckwheat fritters with cottage cheese are served in the lovely individually-styled rooms. The rear terrace has views of the mountains. Closed Tue.

Key to Price Guide *see p202* **Key to Symbols** *see back cover flap*

COASTAL SLOVENIA AND THE KARST

GORIŠKA BRDA Klinec   €€€
Medana 20, 5212 **Tel** *(05) 304 5092*   **Road Map** *A3*

A family-run establishment in Medana village, Klinec excels in western Sovenia's traditional cuisine, with home-cured *pršut* (ham) the inevitable starter and hearty mains of grilled or roast meat with fresh vegetables from the garden. Home-baked bread and wines from the family vineyard complete the picture.

HRASTOVLJE Švab   €€
Hrastovlje 53, 6275 **Tel** *(05) 659 0510*   **Road Map** *A5*

A traditional-style village restaurant serving Istrian staples such as home-made sausages, *fuži* (pasta twirls) with a variety of sauces, roast veal and *ombolo* (lightly-smoked pork chop). As so often in the karst, a platter of home-cured meats such as *pršut* and pancetta is the best way to kick off a meal.

IDRIJA Kos   €€
Tomšičeva 4, 5280 **Tel** *(05) 372 2030*   **Road Map** *B3*

This family-owned, homely pub-restaurant serves Slovenian staples such as grilled sausage, veal cutlets and freshwater fish. The speciality of the house is *idrijski žlikrofi*, a unique local form of ravioli stuffed with either potato or mushrooms. They are usually served with roast pork or goulash. Closed Sun.

IZOLA Marina   €€€€
Veliki trg 11, 6310 **Tel** *(05) 660 4100*   **Road Map** *B3*

This hotel restaurant serves top-quality seafood on a wonderful terrace facing Izola's *mandrač* (small-boat harbour). The fresh grilled fish (sold by weight) is excellent, although be sure to look out for great-value daily specials and set lunches. The wine cellar is one of the best-stocked on the coast.

KOPER Istrska klet Slavček   €
Župančičeva 39, 6000 **Tel** *(05) 627 6729*   **Road Map** *A4*

A dark woody interior and checked tablecloths set the tone for this unpretentious tavern, serving local wines direct from the barrel and a filling range of cheap local dishes. Thick soups such as *jota* (bean-and-sauerkraut soup) or *fažol* (beans and smoked pork) come highly recommended. Closed Sat.

KOPER Kroštola   €
Kopališko nabrežje 1, 6000 **Tel** *(05) 627 8178*   **Road Map** *A4*

A relaxing timber-ceilinged pavilion with outdoor seating facing the sea shore, this café is the place to come for a lovingly-baked lemon meringue pie, tiramisu, or local favourite *koprska rožica* (biscuit with a swirl of jam). Look out for the persimmon pie during autumn. Other light-bite fare includes toasted sandwiches and *pršut* platters.

KOPER Skipper   €€€
Kopališko nabrežje 3, 6101 **Tel** *(05) 626 1810*   **Road Map** *A4*

A plain façade conceals a cosy dining room with an outdoor terrace overlooking Koper's yachting marina. The excellent seafood ranges from the best scampi and grilled white fish to simple and filling gnocchi and shrimp dishes. White wines from Vipava and Goriška Brda will help to wash the meal down.

KOPER Za gradom   €€€€
Kraljeva 10, 6000 **Tel** *(05) 628 5505*   **Road Map** *A4*

Some distance from Koper's Old Town in the western suburb of Semedela, Za gradom is well worth the trip on account of its superbly prepared and presented Adriatic seafood, fresh from the Koper market. Leave some room for the glorious desserts. Closed Sun and Mon. Reservations are essential.

LIPICA Bistro Favory   €€€
Lipica 5, 6210 **Tel** *(05) 739 1580*   **Road Map** *A4*

The café-restaurant of the Maestoso hotel, with a selection of cakes, pastries and traditional Slovenian meals, is the best place to seek refreshment after a visit to the Lipica stables. Soups of the day represent great value and the fixed-price lunches are well worth a try. Vipava whites and teran reds comprise the respectable wine list.

LOKEV Muha   €€€
Lokev 138, 6219 **Tel** *(05) 767 0055*   **Road Map** *A4*

Located in the village of Lokev, close to the Vilenica Cave and Lipica stud farm, Muha serves up traditional food in large portions. Start with local *pršut* before tucking into sausages, steaks or roast ham washed down with teran or refošk wines. Closed on Thu and Fri.

NOVA GORICA Pri Hrastu   €€€
Kromberška cesta 2, 5000 **Tel** *(05) 302 7210*   **Road Map** *A3*

Housed in a wood-beamed house, "Under the Oak" lives up to its name with a secluded tree-shaded courtyard. Adriatic fish and local game feature heavily on the menu. The outdoor stove comes into its own during summers when veal and octopus are baked under a charcoal-covered lid known as a *peka*.

NOVA GORICA Dam
🍴 🍷 ♿   €€€€€
Vinka Vodopivca 24, 5000 **Tel** *(05) 333 1147*   **Road Map** *A3*

This elegant restaurant in the suburb of Kromberk specializes in seafood, with oven-baked fish and fresh Adriatic scampi among its stand-out dishes. Consider the fixed-price gourmet menus, which offer a little bit of everything. The superb wine list provides an excellent introduction to west Slovenian viticulture.

NOVA GORICA Pikol
🍴 🍷 ♿   €€€€€
Vipavska 94, Rožna Dolina, 5000 **Tel** *(05) 302 2562*   **Road Map** *A3*

Located in a secluded wooden pavilion just off the old road to Ajdovščina, this highly regarded seafood restaurant is the place for exquisite fish dishes, Adriatic scampi and shellfish. The multi-course gourmet menus offer good value. Begin with Pikol's trademark starter, seabass carpaccio with herbs. Closed Tue and Wed.

PIRAN Čakola
♿   €€
Partizanska 2, 6330   **Road Map** *A5*

A cosy café-bar on a characterful Mediterranean square, Čakola's interior looks like a cross between a modern lounge bar and a 19th-century living room. Apart from being a popular night-time drinking venue, Čakola offers speciality teas, fresh sandwiches and platters of sliced cold meats including home-cured *pršut*.

PIRAN Neptun
€€€
Županičeva 7, 6330 **Tel** *(05) 673 4111*   **Road Map** *A5*

An excellent seafood restaurant that is frequently overlooked by the tourists, Neptun occupies a quiet street close to the main square. There are few better places to sample fresh Adriatic fish, expertly grilled. There is a good choice of squid, scampi and lobster if you want to push the boat out. Closed Tue.

PIRAN Pri Mari
🍷   €€€
Dantejeva 17, 6330 **Tel** *(05) 673 4735*   **Road Map** *A5*

With folksy furnishings and maritime prints establishing an appropriately warm and homely tone, Pri Mari is one of the best places on the coast to try out traditional grilled and baked fish dishes. Tasty western Slovenian staples such as *jota* and *bobiči* (bean soup with sweetcorn) are also on the menu.

PIRAN Verdi
♿   €€€
Verdijeva 18, 6330 **Tel** *(05) 673 2737*   **Road Map** *A5*

This snug Old Town restaurant occupies an L-shaped space decorated with an enviable collection of prints by local artist Lojze Spacal. It is an outstanding place to sample succulent scampi and calamari dishes, as well as more expensive grilled white fish and lobster.

PIVKA Pri Cunarju
♿   €€
Jurišče 1, 6257 **Tel** *(05) 757 8082*   **Road Map** *B4*

This village inn, 10 km (6 miles) east of Pivka, is the place to come for traditional country cooking, featuring home-cured meats, roast lamb and sausages made from lamb and game as well as thick filling stews. The home-made fruit and herb brandies are well worth trying.

PORTOROŽ Santalucia
♿   €€€€
Obala 26, 6320 **Tel** *(05) 677 9104*   **Road Map** *A5*

One of a handful of bar-restaurants clustered around Portorož's tennis club, Santalucia offers the best in Adriatic seafood, with some excellent oven-baked fish dishes alongside shellfish and squid. Look out for inexpensive daily specials and set lunches chalked up on a board outside.

POSTOJNA Špajza
🅅 ♿   €€€
Ulica 1, maja 1, 6230 **Tel** *(05) 726 4506*   **Road Map** *B4*

Checked tablecloths, knick-knacks and wicker-bottomed chairs create a relaxing environment in which to feast upon a well-chosen menu of Mediterranean-Slovenian fare, with superb risottos, seafood pastas, fresh white fish and substantial steaks. The set lunches are good value and there is a good choice of wines.

PREDJAMA Gostilna Požar
♿   €€€
Predjama 2, 6230 **Tel** *(05) 751 5252*   **Road Map** *XX*

Located on the access road to Predjama Castle and with an outdoor terrace that offers superb views, Požar features a broad-based Slovenian menu with plenty in the way of schnitzels, sausages and thick soups. Game, freshwater fish and summer barbecues are among the house specialities.

ŠTANJEL Grad
♿   €€€
Štanjel 1a, 6222 **Tel** *(05) 769 0118*   **Road Map** *A4*

Occupying the courtyard of Štanjel's 16th-century castle, Grad is the ideal place to sample Slovenian karst cuisine. Home-cured *pršut*, wild mushrooms and home-made pasta feature heavily on the menu, alongside lamb, game and Adriatic seafood. Local Teran wines are the ideal accompaniment. Closed Mon and Tue.

VIPAVA Gostišče Podskala
♿   €€
Glavni trg 9b, 5271 **Tel** *(05) 366 5357*   **Road Map** *A4*

With a tree-shaded terrace overlooking the bubbling Vipava river this is an idyllic place in which to enjoy west Slovenian cuisine, with freshwater trout, Adriatic seafood and local game jostling for attention on a wide-ranging menu. Local favourite *vipavska jota* (bean-and-sauerkraut soup) makes an ideal good-value lunch.

Key to Price Guide *see p202* **Key to Symbols** *see back cover flap*

VIPAVA Majerija

⚑ €€€€

Slap 18, 5271 **Tel** *(05) 368 5010* **Road Map** *A4*

Located just outside the village of Slap across the valley from Vipava, Majerija is a stone-built farmstead serving up hearty local meat dishes accompanied by vegetables from their own garden. There is a good list of Vipava and Goriška Brda wines, with some hard-to-resist home-brewed spirits. Open Fri–Sun.

VIPAVA Pri Lojzetu

⚑ €€€€€

Dvorec Zemono, 5271 **Tel** *(05) 368 7007* **Road Map** *A4*

Housed in a Renaissance manor house just outside Vipava, Pri Lojzetu is famous throughout Slovenia for its creative cuisine, blending Adriatic seafood with ingredients from the Vipava valley and the karst. Lamb, bear and Adriatic scampi feature among the mains and there's a great wine list. Closed Mon and Tue.

SOUTHERN AND EASTERN SLOVENIA

BIZELJSKO-SREMIŠKA WINE ROAD Pri Peču

🎄 🛏 🍴 🍷 €€

Stara vas 58, 8259 **Tel** *(07) 452 0103* **Road Map** *E3*

A snug cocoon of old stone and wood on a country lane, this is a fine place for a lunch while gazing across the fields to the vineyards of Croatia. It is not fancy but it is appealing to get off the beaten track and sample a menu of local wines while tucking into hearty smoked meats; there is also a small fish menu. Closed Tue.

BREŽICE Ošterija Debeluh

🎄 🛏 🅥 🍷 €€€

Trg Izgnancev 7, 8250 **Tel** *(07) 496 1070* **Road Map** *E3*

The restaurant's chef updates traditional recipes using the freshest produce to create dishes such as beef with a pesto of dandelion and dried tomato. Good-value tasting menus of three to six courses allow you to explore a range of seasonal dishes. The wine list features over 200 national wines. Closed Sun.

CELJE Gostilna Amerika

🎄 🎵 €€€

Mariborska cesta 79, 3000 **Tel** *(03) 541 9320* **Road Map** *D3*

This lively restaurant has long been the best place in Celje for Serbian food, despite its anonymous location on a dual carriageway; it is directly opposite the City Centre shopping complex. It is a vegetarian no-go zone, where all manner of meats are grilled over charcoal and served in large portions. There is live music during weekends.

CELJE Gostilna Francl

🎄 🛏 🅥 €€€

Zagrad 77, 3300 **Tel** *(03) 492 6460* **Road Map** *D3*

The best restaurant in the region according to locals, this traditional village establishment is located just south of Celje and is a popular destination at weekends. It is known for home-made *štruklji* and *koline*. There are also good venison and fish dishes. Leave room for the tasty apple strudel. Closed Tue.

ČRNOMELJ Gostilna Müller

🎏 🎄 🛏 🍴 🍷 €€

Ločka cesta 6, 8343 **Tel** *(07) 356 7200* **Road Map** *D4*

Located beside the Lahinja river this inn is popular among locals for a drink as much as a weekend meal. It has a passable selection of Bela Krajina dishes including roast leg of veal with horseradish and desserts including *potica* and Balkan snacks such as *čevapčiči*. Closed Mon.

GOSTIŠČE LOVEC Dolenjske Toplice

🎄 🛏 €€

Pionirska cesta 2, 8350 **Tel** *(07) 306 5639* **Road Map** *D4*

Pub food served in large portions is the stock in trade of this central inn. Starters such as game sausage in tart cviček wine preceed a wide selection of main courses such as turkey with cheese and *pršut*, venison with cranberries or Balkan grilled meats. It is more popular with youngsters for its menu of cheap pizzas.

KOLPA VALLEY Kovač

🎄 ♿ 🛏 €€

Sela 5, 1337 **Tel** *(01) 894 1508* **Road Map** *C5*

The dining room of the modern hotel just beyond Osilnica is hall-like, but warmed by its pleasant rustic decor which includes murals of folk hero Peter Klepec and craggy carvings in the style of local sculptor Stane Jarm. There is a terrace that looks across river meadows. The menu is strong on game and Kolpa trout.

KOSTANJEVICA NA KRKI Gostilna Kmečki hram

🎄 🛏 €€€

Oražnova ulica 11, 8311 **Tel** *(07) 498 7078* **Road Map** *D4*

Renovation has added style to the outside seating of this central inn, yet at its core it remains a low-ceilinged "Peasant's House", every inch of which exudes bucolic charm. Baked Krka carp, fillet of wild boar with mushrooms or venison in plum sauce are a cut above peasant fare. In summer, tables extend through the garden to the river.

LENDAVA Lovski dom

🎄 🛏 €€

Lendavske gorice 238a, 9220 **Tel** *(02) 575 1450* **Road Map** *A2*

Tables in a thatched open barn make up for a dated dining room in this restaurant. Ask the waitress to explain the Slovenian-only menu of classic regional fare such as *ciganska pečenka* (gypsy roast pork), *koline*, *bograč* (spicy thick goulash) and *dödoli* (potato dumplings). Closes at 8pm Mon and Sun.

MARIBOR Čajek Café
Slovenska ulica 4, 2000 **Tel** *(02) 250 2986*   **Road Map** *E2*

Popular with students, this is a wonderfully eccentric café among the chain stores of the Old Town, whose mismatched decor and old china lend it a rather artistic air. Come for an astounding array of fresh teas, which are served in pots with a timer to guarantee the perfect brew, coffee and a slice of home-made cake.

MARIBOR Gril Ranca
Dravska ulica 10, 2000 **Tel** *(02) 252 5550*   **Road Map** *E2*

Gril Ranca's Balkan-style grilled meats are hugely popular with Maribor diners for a quick bite. Favourites include *čevapčiči*, *pleskavice* (hamburger-style patties) and *vešalice* (grilled pork kebabs). Its location on the side of Lent river is an added attraction. The food is simple but delicious.

MARIBOR Novi svet pri Stolnici
Slomškov trg 5, 2000 **Tel** *(02) 250 0486*   **Road Map** *E2*

Located on a corner of the cathedral square, this fish restaurant is Maribor's finest address. It is charmingly styled as a Dalmatian *konoba* (traditional inn), with old lanterns and fishing nets. The Adriatic fish and seafood is excellent, though dishes priced by weight can be expensive. Closed Sun evenings.

MARIBOR Pri treh ribnikih
Ribniška ulica 9, 2000 **Tel** *(02) 234 4170*   **Road Map** *E2*

Named after the "three fishponds" nearby, this is a smarter-than-average traditional restaurant at the northern end of the city park, so is a popular destination after a weekend stroll. There are fish dishes such as fried trout with pumpkin and sunflower seeds and rather expensive meats, especially game. A limited menu caters to vegetarians.

METLIKA Grajska klet
Trg svobode 4, 8330 **Tel** *(07) 305 8998*   **Road Map** *D4*

The classy wine bar in the Renaissance courtyard and cellars of Metlika Castle is an excellent opportunity to sample the produce of Bela Krajina's winemakers. White wines feature, especially those of local producer Šturm, although wines from as far away as Primorska are also kept in stock.

MURSKA SOBOTA Gostilna Lovenjak
Polana 40, 9000 **Tel** *(02) 525 2158*   **Road Map** *F1*

This pleasant restaurant is attached to a village hotel. Dining is on a vine-covered terrace or indoors. The food is a modern take on traditional Prekmurje dishes such as frog's leg soup, buckwheat porridge with roast porcini mushrooms and Hungarian *bograč*. A folk band plays on summer weekends. Closed Sun.

MURSKA SOBOTA Gostilna Rajh
Soboška ulica 32, Bakovci, 9000 **Tel** *(02) 543 9098*   **Road Map** *F1*

The food in this restaurant gives Prekmurje flavours a gourmet twist. Regional favourites *bograč* and *gibanica* (cake with cottage cheese, walnuts, poppy seeds and apples) are served alongside excellent home-cured meats; try the Prekmurje charcuterie with turnip sauerkraut. Closed Mon and Sun eve.

NOVO MESTO Čajarna Krojač
Grajski trg 17, 8000 **Tel** *(07) 337 0160*   **Road Map** *D4*

Not just the *čaj* (tea) from all over the world but also a short menu of sandwiches such as baguettes with mozzarella and *pršut*, plus snacks such as olives are served at this laid-back café beside the bridge at the end of Glavni trg. Apart from terrace tables, there is a tiny balcony high above the river that is just big enough for two.

NOVO MESTO Gostišče Loka
Župančičevo sprehajališče 2, 8000 **Tel** *(07) 332 1108*   **Road Map** *D4*

Located near a footbridge on the banks of the Krka river, Loka is a good choice for a lazy meal on warm days. The menu covers everything from fish dishes to pizzas, while an attached café is a popular weekend destination for coffee, ice creams and creamy gateaux. Closed Sun.

OLIMJE Amon
Olimje 24, 3524 **Tel** *(03) 818 2480*   **Road Map** *E3*

One of the first independent small winemakers in Slovenia, Amon's restaurant remains a delight. Rough plastered walls, wooden furniture, lace and fine crystal create a classy rustic atmosphere. It serves upmarket country cooking with home-made soups and *štruklji* and main courses of rich beef and venison goulash *Kozje*.

ORMOŽ Taverna Kupljen
Svetinje 21, Jeruzalem, 2259 **Tel** *(02) 719 4128*   **Road Map** *F2*

Kupljen, one of the finest winemakers of the Jeruzalem region, serves its mostly dry or semi-dry white wines in a taverna. The food is good enough to make this the choice for lunch by locals. The barn-like dining hall is appealing but where the taverna really scores is its hilltop location above sun-drenched vineyards.

OTOČEC Gostilna Vovko
Ratež 48, 8321 **Tel** *(07) 308 5603*   **Road Map** *D4*

A good choice for a relaxed meal, this understated address has a pleasant dining room with chunky wood furniture and an old wine press. The inn is renowned for its charcoal-grilled meat dishes, and also offers game and lighter vegetarian meals of *štruklji* or pumpkin gnocchi. Closed Mon and Tue.

OTOČEC Grad Otočec
🖼️ 🍴 €€€€

Grajska cesta 2, 8222 **Tel** *(07) 384 8900* **Road Map** *D4*

The restaurant of this boutique hotel in a restored castle is elegant – brown leather, white linen, dark woods and stone walls. The menu includes classy Slovenian food such as steak with truffles, venison in cranberry sauce or local fish. The *gibanica* is one of the best. Reservations are essential.

PTUJ Bo Café
🍴 🚶 🏠 €

Slovenski trg 7, 2250 **Tel** *(02) 784 1384* **Road Map** *E2*

The Bo presumably refers to bohemian, which is a good description for the wicker chairs and mismatched old furnishings arranged beneath the Gothic vaults of this small café. It is a lovely place for tea and coffee. In summer, tables spill out around the Orpheus Monument, a 2nd-century Roman relic.

PTUJ Amadeus
🚶 🍴 🍷 €€€

Prešernova ulica 36, 2250 **Tel** *(02) 771 7051* **Road Map** *E2*

This centrally located bar and restaurant specializes in *štruklji*, a staple of Slovenian cuisine. The menu also includes plenty of mainstream meat dishes – the house special is steak with dried plums and buckwheat *štruklji* – and there are also cheap Balkan snacks such as *čevapčiči* to go with a glass of beer. Closed Sun eve.

PTUJ Gostilna Ribič
🚶 🏠 €€€

Dravska ulica 9, 2250 **Tel** *(02) 749 0635* **Road Map** *E2*

Friendly and quietly stylish, this fish restaurant is a fine choice for a memorable meal. All sorts of Adriatic seafood and freshwater fish are served. There is a short vegetarian menu and good salads. The vaulted dining rooms are pleasant, but it is the terrace, with tables set near the river under a pergola, that is inviting. Closed Mon.

ROGAŠKA SLATINA Gostišče Jurg
🚶 🏠 🍴 🍷 €€€

Brestovec 4a, 3250 **Tel** *(03) 581 4788* **Road Map** *E3*

Turn off the Zagreb road towards Brestovec and follow the signs to find this relaxed garden inn tucked away in the hills. It is a local favourite, held in high esteem because of the friendly welcome and home-made food prepared from fresh ingredients, from salami to bread or truffles; ask about daily specials. Closed Mon.

ROGAŠKA SLATINA Kaiser
🚶 ♿ 🏠 🍷 €€€€

Zdraviliški trg 14, 3250 **Tel** *(03) 811 4000* **Road Map** *E3*

By far the smartest option in town, this hotel-restaurant serves a wide range of international and upmarket Slovenian dishes. The conservatory, looking on to a 19th-century drinking temple, is modern and stylish. The cherry-wood furnishings of the vaulted dining room allude to the belle époque grace of Rogaška Slatina's heyday.

ŠENTANEL Gostilna Marin
🚶 🏠 €€

Šentanel 8, 2391 **Tel** *(02) 824 0550* **Road Map** *C2*

This farm's restaurant is a good place for a rural retreat. Its emphasis is on the sort of home cooking typified by country platter *kmečka pojedina*, a feast of sausages, buckwheat mash, larded beans and potatoes. There are some vegetarian dishes also. Try local *mošt* (cider) and *borovničevo žganje* (blueberry brandy).

SLOVENJ GRADEC Gostilna Murko
🚶 🏠 €€€

Francetova cesta 24, 2380 **Tel** *(02) 883 8103* **Road Map** *D2*

Located north of the centre, this family-owned restaurant prides itself on home-made produce; dishes such as *mežerli* (a mix of offal, spices, bread and eggs) or *pečenice* (sausages cooked in wine) are made from their great-grandparents' recipes. There are small vegetarian and fish menus. Local *mošt* is served. Closed Sun eve.

SLOVENSKE KONJICE Gostilna Grič
🚶 🏠 🍴 €€€

Škalce 86, 3210 **Tel** *(03) 758 0361* **Road Map** *D2*

This restaurant, affiliated to celebrated winemaker Zlati Grič, sits above vineyards on a low hill, a 10-minute drive north of Slovenske Konjice. Meals on the terrace shaded by birch trees are idyllic. With its pastel peach walls and old wood, the interior has a relaxing country air. The menu is strong on meat dishes and keenly priced.

TREBNJE Gostilna Javornik
🚶 🍴 🍷 €€€

Rakovnik 6, 8232 **Tel** *(07) 343 4534* **Road Map** *C3*

It is worth travelling off the beaten track to reach this *gostilna* that is especially popular on weekends. The dining rooms are pretty and the cooking tasty. The chef is famous for his chicken liver pâté, steak with mushrooms or ribs in a wine sauce – much of it cooked in a wood oven. The tasting menus offer good value. Closed Mon and Tue.

TREBNJE Gostilna Rakar
🚶 ♿ 🏠 🍴 €€€€

Gorenje Poikve 8, 8210 **Tel** *(07) 346 6190* **Road Map** *C3*

Favoured for fine dining, this is the most sophisticated restaurant in the area *(see p197)*. Fish is the speciality, with Adriatic dorade, langoustines and *škampi bouzzara* (scampi gently simmered in wine, tomatoes, garlic and herbs) on the menu alongside local trout. The selection of Slovenian wines is excellent. Closed Tue.

ŽUŽEMBERK Gostilna Pri Gradu
🚶 🏠 🍴 🍷 €

Grajski trg 4, 8360 **Tel** *(07) 308 7290* **Road Map** *C4*

This is a popular meeting place among locals for coffee and a bite, not least because of its location on the main square opposite the castle. The menu includes pizza and pasta as well as basic mains such as schnitzel. The tables beneath the shade of a spreading lime tree are appealing.

SHOPPING IN SLOVENIA

Slovenia tempts visitors to spend at every turn. The chain stores are mainstays of shopping in towns, but you will find the abundant smaller workshops in the capital and tourist destinations more interesting. Here you will discover goods that make excellent souvenirs: laceware and folk craft such as *pisanice* (painted eggs), crystal glassware from Rogaška Slatina and paintings or jewellery crafted by artisans who draw on traditional styles. While you may find crafts at markets, their mainstay is seasonal foodstuffs, much of it organic. Homemade fruit brandies, honey and seed oils are worth a try. Notwithstanding the growth of malls, most shopping is in pedestrian precincts which feature a department store or two, high fashion brands, an ice cream parlour and cafés.

Hand-painted wine bottle

Paintings for sale in a street, Kranj

OPENING HOURS

As a rule of thumb, shops open from 8am to 7pm on weekdays and until 1pm on Saturdays. However, this will vary depending on the size of the town and location. Major chain stores in city shopping centres may open on Sunday morning, while many shops on the coast keep more Mediterranean hours in summer, with about one or two hours' break for lunch and late evening opening. Similarly, shops in smaller towns often close from 12:30pm until 2pm. Apart from the large chains in shopping centres, the only shops that are open on Sundays are some of the bakeries, and even then only for a few hours in the morning. Everything is shut on public holidays. Outside of these hours, the only places to purchase supplies are large petrol stations on major routes, most of which have basic supermarkets; and kiosks at major train stations.

PRICES AND PAYMENT

Prices in shops are fixed and it is not accepted practice to haggle in major stores. Owners of craft studios may be open to negotiation, although remember that the owner may well be the artist, too. Though prices are usually displayed in markets and street stalls, it is permissible to attempt to negotiate a lower price for goods if done with goodwill – gentle humour is more persuasive than tough talk in Slovenia.

In department stores, shopping centres and independent shops in large towns, it is possible to pay in cash or by using an internationally recognized credit card. In the smaller shops and in places such as markets, payments are always in cash.

VAT REFUNDS

Visitors from non-European Union countries can obtain a refund on the value-added tax (DDV), levied on purchases by requesting a form at the point of sale. This is filled out by the seller, then certified by customs authorities upon presentation of the original receipt as you exit the country. Note that to qualify for a refund, goods must be unopened and taken out of the country within three months of purchase. The tax – 20 per cent of the purchase price – is refunded by the institutions indicated on the tax-free purchase form. Refunds cannot be requested for mineral oils, alcohol and alcoholic beverages or for tobacco products.

MARKETS

The street markets of Slovenia are wonderfully colourful and lively places to browse. In large towns these are generally held on weekdays, and occasionally on Saturday morning, and display a fine array of seasonal

Façade of the Citypark mall, Ljubljana

produce from local farmers, plus a small quota of imported foods. No visit to Ljubljana is complete without a stroll around the excellent open-air Market *(see p50)* located near St Nicholas's Cathedral. Alongside fruit and vegetables, you can expect to find honey and beeswax, excellent charcuterie stalls and often patterned *medeni kruhek* (honey bread) fashioned into rings or hearts. Ljubljana and Maribor *(see p176)* have enjoyable flea markets on Sundays and the last Saturday of the month respectively. These are great places to unearth unusual Slovenian items from a bygone era.

SHOPPING CENTRES

High streets aside, the hubs of modern shopping in cities and large towns are the large shopping centres located in the more modern outskirts beyond the old centres. Here you will find a variety of fashion chain stores, perhaps a department store, and usually a branch of the national supermarket giant, Mercator.

HANDICRAFTS AND MODERN GOODS

With a tradition of trade guilds it can trace to medieval times, Slovenia boasts a wide array of regional crafts that make novel souvenirs. Local tourist information centres often sell a selection of goods

Small wine shop in a family-owned cellar in Medana, Goriška Brda

or can point you to a studio. Common novelty items in the alpine northwest include tall brimmed hats or pipes from the Bohinj area. Radovljica, with its apiary museum, is a good source of painted beehive panels *(see p111)* decorated with witty folk designs, while nearby Kropa is celebrated for decorative wrought-iron pieces. Idrija *(see p146)* is renowned for lace handicrafts made with great skill and patience. Ribnica is the home of *suha roba,* (traditional household wares crafted from wood and wicker) while the Bela Krajina region specializes in traditional rustic crafts such as *pisanice* (painted Easter eggs) and wicker baskets; try a store in Črnomelj *(see p163).*

Modern Slovenian brands stocked countrywide include lead crystal glass, manufactured in Rogaška Slatina, and stylish Lisca lingerie. Though not unique to Slovenia, the traditional alpine Sunday-best clothes such as collarless jackets and dirndl-bodiced skirts, sold in upmarket traditional stores, also make unusual gifts.

FOOD AND WINE

Slovenian herbal teas, sea-salt skimmed from pans near Portorož *(see p132), bučno olje* (nutty pumpkin-seed oil) and apiarian products such as honey, beeswax and propolis are sold throughout Slovenia.

Necklace made of felt

Mass-produced examples are sold in supermarkets, but higher quality produce is available from specialist shops or from markets, where it is sold by producers. In the Alps, look out for cheeses produced by alpine farmers in the Triglav National Park. Shops at the monasteries of Pleterje *(see p164)* and Stična *(see p89),* whose monks maintain a centuries-old tradition of self-sufficiency, sell herbal and apiary produce as well as herbal remedies. However, Pleterje monastery is most celebrated for fruit brandies produced from the monastic orchards and said to be beneficial to health; bottles of *viljamovka* (pear spirit), with a whole fruit inside, make excellent gifts. Mass-produced fruit and berry liquers are sold in wine shops and supermarkets. The finest Slovenian wines are rarely exported and are a good souvenir: Simčič and Movia wines are highly rated by sommeliers.

Traditional beehive paintings on sale in a souvenir shop

Visitors at one of the local pastry shops, Piran

ENTERTAINMENT IN SLOVENIA

From professional opera to punk, metal and jazz ensembles to alpine polka groups, Slovenia has a small but diverse entertainment scene. Inevitably, the wellspring of culture is the capital, Ljubljana – whether for music, theatre, opera, or nightclubs. For such small cities, Ljubljana and Maribor boast an impressive cultural scene throughout the year, though the main institutions reduce their output in July and August.

Street performer, Koper

Maribor's scene is supported by its large student population. Many of the small towns and villages boast their own folk heritage ensembles which stage regular performances. Particularly memorable are the outdoor cultural festivals staged throughout the country – from Ljubljana's Jazz Festival, and the folk extravaganza at Črnomelj to the reggae and rock festivals at Tolmin, there is some form of entertainment for everyone.

Entrance to the Kolosej theatre, Koper

INFORMATION AND TICKETS

Local tourist information centres are the most reliable sources of information on entertainment in Slovenia. Their offices stock flyers and posters for upcoming events and their websites generally publish dates of festivals and major concerts. The website of the Slovenian Tourist Board *(see p221)* is also useful for planning. In Ljubljana the "Kažipot" section of the daily newspaper *Delo* offers up-to-date listings. Tickets are available at the door or in advance at the box office of venues such as Križanke *(see p69)* Major venues also allow online booking and collection from the box office.

THEATRE AND FILM

Plays are almost universally staged in the Slovenian language, which will marginalize the theatre as a source of entertainment for all but the

most ardent theatre-goer. On the plus side, Slovenian theatre has a penchant for visual flair, so performances are often enjoyable nonetheless. The Slovene National Theatre *(see p95)*, a splendid Art Nouveau edifice that hosts the national theatre company in Ljubljana, is the nation's premier stage. Its secondary

Performance by the Maribor Puppet Theatre

arm, the **Slovene National Theatre Maribor** has an excellent reputation nationwide, while the **Prešernovo gledališče Kranj** supports its own city theatre. Other theatres include the **Mladinsko Theatre** (Slovensko mladinsko gledališče) and Gledališče Glej *(see p95)*. Puppet theatre (Lutkovno gledališče) is a charming tradition that excels in fantastical visuals. Dedicated venues are the **Ljubljana Puppet Theatre** and the **Maribor Puppet Theatre**.

All large towns have multiplex cinemas (kino) such as **Kolosej**. Foreign films are shown in their original language with Slovenian subtitles. Of special interest is the Ljubljana International Film Festival (LIFFe), which hosts a fortnight of international cinema in November.

CLASSICAL MUSIC, OPERA AND DANCE

Five professional orchestras operate in Slovenia. It may come as a surprise to many visitors to learn that the nation's elite orchestra, the Slovenian Philharmonia *(see p68)*, is one of the oldest in Europe, having been formed in 1701. The **Cankarjev dom**, an arts and conference centre in Ljubljana, also hosts classical concerts, including international artistes.

The Slovene National Opera and Ballet *(see p95)* are the leading companies in their fields and share a splendid historic **Opera House** in the

Poster of the annual Mladi Levi festival

capital. Again, a secondary offshoot of the company performs in Maribor, sharing a venue with the national theatre. Slovenian mezzo-sopranos Bernarda Fink, born to Slovenian parents in Buenos Aires, and Marjana Lipovšek, are great cultural ambassadors for Slovenian opera, and both regularly perform in Slovenia. The Exodos and the Mladi Levi international festivals have a reputation for daring contemporary pieces.

ROCK, JAZZ AND FOLK

Slovenian rock music came roaring into the public consciousness with the birth of a Ljubljana punk scene in the late 1970s. Bands Laibach and Pankrti were deemed a civil threat and suppressed by the authorities. Re-formed and as confrontational as ever, the former still tours. Other heavyweights of the Slovenian

rock and pop scenes include evergreen stadium rock group Siddharta; Vlado Kreslin, who create tuneful folk pop, and ethno-pop singer Magnifico. Student population in the two main cities continue to support a thriving alternative live scene; Ljubljana's Metelkova Mesto *(see p77)* is a counter-culture legend with associations such as **Menza pri koritu** promoting culture and the arts. The capital's Orto Bar *(see p95)* hosts national rock bands and DJs in its nightclub. In Maribor, **Klub MC** is the bastion of student rock bands and local DJs. Tolmin-based music festivals **Metalcamp** and **Reggae Riversplash** draw thousands of music fans to the Soča Valley in July.

Both Ljubljana and Maribor have jazz venues that host Slovenian groups plus touring foreign artists; Ljubljana's Cankarjev dom is the main stage for major international names. The Jazz Club Gajo *(see p95)* organizes music events during the summer. Events such as the Ljubljana Jazz Festival are also a must for any visiting jazz fan.

Lovers of traditional music are spoilt for choice in Slovenia. The country retains a strong folk tradition that can be heard in the music of groups such as Terra Folk (actually a quartet of class-ically trained musicians) or Katalena, who blend folk and jazz. No country festival is complete without a folk group, especially in the Bela Krajina and Prekmurje regions – the Jurjevanje festival at Črnomelj is the

high point of the folk calendar. In the alpine area, visitors can hear chirpy accordion music. No group is more famous than the gold-disc selling Avsenik Brothers, whose polkas are copied throughout Germanic Europe. Regular concerts are held at their restaurant in Begunje near Bled *(see p206)*.

DIRECTORY

THEATRE AND FILM

Kolosej
Šmartinska 152, Ljubljana.
Tel (01) 520 5500.
www.kolosej.si

Mladinsko Theatre
Vilharjeva 11, Ljubljana.
Tel (01) 425 3312.
www.mladinsko.com

Ljubljana Puppet Theatre
Krekov trg 2, Ljubljana.
City Map E3. *Tel* (01) 300 0970.
www.lgl.si

Puppet Theatre Maribor
Vojasniski trg 2, Maribor.
Tel (02) 228 1978. www.lg-mb.si

Slovene National Theatre Maribor
Slovenska ulica 27, Maribor.
Tel (02) 250 6100.
www.sng-mb.si

Prešernovo gledališče Kranj
Glavni trg 6, Kranj.
Tel (04) 201 0200. www.pgk.si

CLASSICAL MUSIC, OPERA AND DANCE

Cankarjev dom
Trg republike, Ljubljana.
City Map C3. *Tel* (01) 241 7100.
www.cd-cc.si

Opera House
Župančičeva 1, Ljubljana.
City Map C2. *Tel* (01) 241 1764.
www.cd-cc.si

ROCK, JAZZ AND FOLK

Menza pri koritu
www.menzaprikoritu.org

Klub MC
www.klub-mc.si

Metalcamp
www.metalcamp.com

Reggae Riversplash
www.riversplash.si

Façade of the Cankarjev dom with the monument of Ivan Cankar in front

OUTDOOR ACTIVITIES AND SPECIALIST HOLIDAYS

Visitors who revel in scenery and the great outdoors are spoilt for choice in Slovenia. The country's diverse landscape ranges from snow-capped mountains and lush wine slopes towards the coast and virgin woods. The Triglav National Park and Kamniško-Savinjske Alps offer ample opportunities for walking, hiking, cycling and paragliding during summer and for skiing and snowboarding in winter. The country's numerous rivers are popular with fishing enthusiasts as well as with those interested in adventure sports such as hydroboarding and canyoning; sailing, windsurfing and diving are popular in coastal Slovenia. The numerous spas in the country also attract a large number of visitors every year and offer patrons a wide variety of thermal cures as well as therapeutic massages.

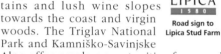

Road sign to Lipica Stud Farm

WALKING AND HIKING

No one should contemplate a visit to Slovenia without good walking shoes. There are walking trails everywhere and one can take anything from a stroll along the boardwalk at Vintgar gorge *(see p110)* to a month-long hike along Slovenia's alpine spine. All routes, except themed trails, are indicated by a white dot within a red circle. Themed trails currently have their own symbols, although a programme to replace these with a new symbol – a white dot within a yellow circle – began in 2010. Nevertheless, maps are advisable for all but the shortest tourist trail. Produced by the **Alpine Association of Slovenia** (Planinska zveza Slovenije), these maps are available in Ljubljana and at visitor centres or agencies. The decision about where to go is limited only by the traveller's imagination and stamina. Mountain routes are clear of snow and the weather is usually stable from mid-June to September, although conditions in the Alps change rapidly year-round.

The most popular destination for walking in Slovenia is the Triglav National Park *(see pp112–5)*. The most famous hike is the two-day ascent of Mount Triglav. Lake Bohinj *(see pp114–5)* offers an excellent base for all walks in the National Park; local agencies organize hikes during the season. Logarska dolina *(see p122)* is a good base for excursions into the Kamniško-Savinjske Alps. The **Slovenian Mountain Guide Association** provides detailed information on guides and hiking. Other popular walking areas include the sub-alpine Pohorje massif, accessible from Kope *(see p172)*; Rogla *(see p175)*; Maribor *(see pp176–7)*; the karst; the high meadows of Velika Planina *(see p121)* and Robanov kot *(see p122)*. The **Slovenian Tourist Board** publishes *Hiking in Slovenia*, a brochure providing a good overview of options. The trekking guide publisher Cicerone produces two guides to walking in Slovenia – *Trekking in Slovenia* and *The Julian Alps of Slovenia*

Slovenia has also developed the 500-km (310-mile) long Slovene Alpine Trail, from Maribor via the Slovenian Alps to Ankaran on the Adriatic coast. The walk takes around 30 days to complete.

Breathtaking views while hiking in the Alps

Skiers at a slalom race at a popular skiing destination

ROCK CLIMBING

Bled *(see pp108–9)* and Lake Bohinj are the focus for rock climbing, known as *športno plezanje* (sports climbing), in Slovenia. All the 340-plus routes in this spectacular limestone area are bolted and offer a good range of climbing grades, the majority in the 5a to 7b range according to the French Free Climbing Grading System. The ideal time to visit Bled for rock climbing is from May to October. Beginners are advised to book a trip with an activities provider in Bled or Bohinj.

Other destinations for climbing include Osp, east of Koper *(see pp134–5)*, and around Celje *(see pp170–71)*. Sidarta publishes details of 3,600 routes in 84 areas in its guidebook the *Slovenia Sports Climbing Guidebook*.

SKIING AND SNOWBOARDING

Skiing is a very popular sport in Slovenia; one in five Slovenians ski and the most popular pistes are those in the alpine areas of Gorenjska and on the Pohorje massif. Of the 48 ski centres in the country – which combined, provide upto 50,000 skiers with over 272 km (169 miles) of pistes – 15 qualify as resorts. Only a few are as developed or offer skiing as challenging as that in Austria, Italy or the French Alps. However, this means fewer skiers, lower prices and a large variety of slopes *(see pp26–7)* in a small area.

Depending on the weather, the skiing season generally runs from late November to March or April, and sometimes even early May on the high slopes of Kanin in the Soča Valley. The peak season is from late December to mid-February. Cable cars or ski pulls, ski hire and ski coaching are available at all resorts.

The most popular resort for foreign visitors is Kranjska Gora *(see p116)*, which has 30 km (19 miles) of pistes ranging from easy to moderate. In the northwest, Krvavec, northeast of Kranj *(see p120)*, is well equipped and popular with skiers from Ljubljana at weekends; visitors should be prepared for long queues. Vogel, beside Lake Bohinj, has off-piste routes and superb views, as does Kanin near Bovec *(see p118)*, offering the only pistes over 2,000 m (6,562 ft) high. Slovenian skiers also enthuse about Cerkno *(see p147)*; none of its 18 km (11 miles) of trails are higher than 1,300 m (4,265 ft) but the downhill skiing is famously challenging.

The most popular slopes to the east are at Rogla and Mariborsko Pohorje *(see p177)*. The latter has the largest ski area in the country with 220 ha (544 acres) laid with 80 km (50 miles) of pistes, of which 10 km (6 miles) make up Europe's longest night run. Snowboarding is popular at

Krvavec, Vogel – which has a dedicated snowboard park – and Rogla, all of which have half-pipes and jumps. Popular off-piste ski areas include those around Komna, above Lake Bohinj, and the foothills of Mala Mojstrovka, above Vršič Pass *(see pp116–7)*; a local guide is recommended for both areas.

Cross-country skiing is a delight. Trails are laid out through picturesque glades or fairy-tale snowy forests and are usually free. The best-known trails are on Pokljuka plateau, although the unspoilt valley of Logarska dolina is peerless for scenery.

Further details of resorts are available in *Skiing in Slovenia*, a brochure brought out by the Slovenian Tourist Board. Each resort also has its own individual website, which generally offers maps of pistes, contacts, links to local schools, information on hire companies and often a web-cam showing snow conditions. Links to all resorts are available on the **Active Slovenia** website.

GOLF

The first golf course was laid for the King of Yugoslavia at Bled in 1937, but was neglected by subsequent rulers. Redesigned in 1972 by golf architect Donald Harradine, the **Bled Golf & Country Club** is the nation's premier course, with its 5,900 m (6,000 yard), par 73, 18-hole course set against the backdrop of the Alps. There is also a par 36 nine-hole course on offer.

Guests are also welcome to courses at Lipica *(see p137)* – open year round – Volčji Potok near Kamnik, Mokrice, Ptuj, Slovenske Konjice and Podčertek, among others. Clubs can be hired at all courses except in Slovenske Konjice. The Slovenian Tourist Board website provides information on courses; details of major courses, contacts and addresses, hole breakdowns as well as maps.

Teeing off in Lipica

CYCLING

Mountain biking and cycling are very popular in Slovenia. Quiet country roads through diverse landscapes present opportunities for superb scenic touring. This variety also means there are opportunities for cyclists of all abilities and ages. All children under 14 must wear a helmet while cycling on Slovenian roads.

There are lovely country routes to explore around Bled and Bohinj and the gravel tracks that circuit these lakes also offer great opportunities for cycling. Other destinations include the wine hills of Goriška Brda (*see p141*) or around Jeruzalem (*see p181*), the little visited roads of Idrija (*see p146*) and the karst, as well as Prekmurje, the flattest region of Slovenia. Twisting mountain roads such as those around Vršič Pass or ascents to the ski resorts at Kope or Rogla pose a challenge even for experienced cyclists.

With abundant uplands crisscrossed by old cart tracks, options for mountain biking abound in Slovenia. Bike Park Pohorje in Mariborsko Pohorje is the venue for the downhill Mountain Bike World Cup. Challenging free-ride routes in bike parks in Bovec and

Elderly visitors cycling in Slovenia

Kranjska Gora satisfy those seeking adventure in the Alps. Less challenging dirt tracks lie in the Koroška hills around Jamnica, west of Dravograd (*see p173*) – visitors can even cycle underground through the disused Peca Underground Mine (*see p173*), near Mežica, and on the sub-alpine meadows at Velika Planina, which is accessible by cable car.

The Slovenian Tourist Board has information on 14 cycling regions in its brochure *Cycling in Slovenia*. Its website is also a mine of information for cyclists. Bikes can be hired via tourist agencies throughout the country. Most agencies stock

maps of biking routes and the staff can advise on cyclist-friendly hotels and camp sites, which receive one-to five-wheel accreditation instead of star ratings. Agencies in premier cycling regions such as Bled and Bovec organize guided trips. One of the agencies that provides information on guided tours, trails and accommodation is **Mountain Bike Nomad**.

The best weather for cycling is between May and late September. July and August can be hot, especially in central and eastern Slovenia; the Alps, however, are cooler.

Children taking horse riding lessons in Roznik Hill, Ljubljana

HORSE RIDING

Slovenia's most famous equestrian export are the Lipizzaner horses bred at Lipica *(see p137)* since the 17th century. The **Lipica Stud Farm** offers riding classes as well as tours – a must-do for any horse enthusiast.

Smaller, local riding schools and tourist farms that provide riding for guests are located throughout Slovenia and managed by the Ljubljana-based **Slovenian Equestrian Association**. The tourist board website provides information on accredited schools. Its *Friendly Countryside* brochure of tourist farms uses icons to indicate those that offer riding for guests.

PARAGLIDING

With numerous hills and mountains to use as launch pads, Slovenia has taken to paragliding with enthusiasm. The finest venues for a flight are Krvavec; Mount Vogel, where a 1,200-m (3,937-ft) height difference between the take-off and landing points ensures flights of around 20 minutes; and the Mangart or Kanin mountains near Bovec. The last two enjoy superlative views of Mount Triglav and the Triglav National Park.

For visitors, paragliding is only possible in tandem with an experienced instructor. The activities agencies **Pac Sports** and **Avantura** in Bohinj and Bovec respectively are of good repute.

FISHING

Slovenia's unpolluted rivers and lakes offer great sport for fishing enthusiasts. The fishing season runs from April to October. Visitors are required to possess a licence issued by the **Fisheries Research Institute** of Slovenia (Zavod za ribistro Slovenije). Available at the local tourist boards and select hotels, these cost between 30 and 100 euros a day depending on the area, although catch-and-release permits are cheaper. Rods can only be hired by visitors who opt for

Fishing in the Pivka river, near Postojna Caves

guided trips. Indigenous fish species vary according to whether rivers drain into the Danube basin or the Adriatic Sea. Those in the former, which accounts for three-quarters of the rivers in Slovenia, include brown trout, the grayling and the huchen – a relative of the taimen and salmon. Rivers that drain into the Danube include the Krka around Žužemberk *(see p163)* and the Kolpa.

The prize catch of rivers draining into the Adriatic is Europe's largest trout species, the marble trout.The premier Adriatic fishing ground is the Soča river, renowned as a fly-fishing venue from June onwards; other forms of fishing are banned in some sections. The Sava Bohinjka river and Lake Bohinj offer

Visitor paragliding in the Slovenian Alps, Tolmin

good sport for char, mostly from boats, while Lake Bled is famous among anglers for its trophy carp, which weigh over 20 kg (44 lb).

Information about each area including links to local clubs, which manage 94 per cent of Slovenian fishing waters, can be found on the Slovenian Tourist Board website.

SAILING AND WINDSURFING

Though overshadowed by the islands of neighbouring Croatia, Slovenia's 47-km (29-mile) long coastline permits it to promote itself as a Mediterranean yachting destination. The majority of yacht charter companies are based at Izola *(see p131)*, home to one of three Slovenian marinas; the others are at Koper and Portorož *(see p130)*. Visitors who want to hire a yacht need to present proof of their sailing qualifications. It is also possible to charter a yacht along with an experienced captain – some companies offer sailing lessons with the hire – or take a day trip along the coast. Again, Izola is the principal base for day trips along the coast.

If the coastline is limiting for yachtsmen, it is ideal for those visitors who are new to windsurfing. Winds rarely rise above a gentle breeze in summer and the sea temperatures are warm. Outlets hiring out windsurfing equipment line the beachfront at Portorož.

Adventure-sports enthusiasts kayaking on the Soča river

RAFTING, KAYAKING AND CANOEING

The Soča river is the premier adventure destination for Slovenians, ranking among the top five whitewater rafting and kayaking destinations in Europe. Sections of the river have rapids ranging from easy to difficult, with the added appeal of a turquoise river and impressive alpine scenery. Bovec and Kobarid *(see p118)* are the hubs of activity and several watersports agencies in the towns organize 1.5–2 hour trips. The season runs from April to October; April and early May, when the river is swollen with snow thaw, are best for experienced rafters. In August and early September, the river is safe for families.

Among Slovenians, rafting is popular on the Kolpa river, where the mid-sections pro-vide gentle, unchallenging rapids. There are agencies such as **Soča Rafting** and **Bovec Rafting Team** that hire out rafts to paddle at leisure.

Canoeing is a relatively new activity in Slovenia. You can hire canoes from agencies that serve the Kolpa, and from the shores of Lake Bled and Lake Bohinj. Canoeing along the Ljubljanica river, through Ljubljana to the Ljubljana Marshes *(see p88)*, is a marvellous trip.

HYDROBOARDING AND CANYONING

These are new additions to the roster of adventure sports in Slovenia. Many aficionados consider hydroboarding – racing through rapids with a large float – the most extreme watersport in the country. A wetsuit and protective helmet are obligatory.

Canyoning treats the river gorge as a giant adventure playground. Snug in a wetsuit and wearing a helmet, visitors can swim through rock pools, sluice down waterfalls, and abseil over low cliffs to negotiate a river canyon.

The Soča river and its tributaries are the focus for both activities. Due to their inherent dangers, a guide is compulsory; agencies such as Soča Rafting and Bovec Rafting Team organize trips between April and October.

DIVING

The sea between Piran *(see pp132–3)* and Strunjan is the first choice for Slovenian scuba divers due to the variety of its marine flora and fauna. Other sights include wrecks of cargo vessels and warships sunk during World War II. The Piran-based company **Sub-net** rents equipment, leads guided trips to dive sites and runs

Professional Association of Diving Instructors (PADI) scuba courses from April to October. Diving is also pos-sible in Slovenia's rivers and lakes. Lake Bled is the focus of scuba diving for novices, with local agencies such as **3glav Adventures** organizing trips. The **Slovenian Diving Federation** publishes lists of accredited instructors on its website.

For expert divers, Slovenia's many karst springs offer the opportunity for cave-diving adventures. Scuba divers are still exploring the karst sump of the Wild lake (Divje jezero) near Idrija; in 1997 divers descended to 170 m (558 ft), yet did not reach the bottom.

Deep-sea diving in the Adriatic Sea off the coast at Piran

SPA TOURISM

Slovenia has a tradition of spa tourism that can be traced back to Roman days. Today, alongside private spa facilities in upmarket hotels throughout the country, there are around 15 dedicated health and spa resorts where wellness is the priority. There are two resorts on the coast at Portorož and Strunjan. The others are at natural thermal springs in Dolenjska and Prekmurje.

Over the last decade, "taking the waters" has shifted from simply meaning a health cure to pampering. Consequently, most resorts now provide a hedonistic range of exotic massages and beauty treatments as well as medicinal facilities, which are typically for rheumatism or cardiovascular complaints. This shift is reflected in the move by spas to use the Italian word *terme* or wellness rather than *toplice*, the Slovenian word for spa.

The slick Balnea Wellness Centre at Dolenjske Toplice *(see p163)* typifies the move. Others, such as Moravske Toplice *(see p182)* and Terme Čatež on the outskirts of Brežice *(see p165)*, with their numerous warm swimming pools, promote themselves as family holiday destinations.

The best-known spa resort is Rogaška Slatina *(see p167)*, which retains the architecture and grandeur of its time as a fashionable Austro-Hungarian spa resort in the late 1800s.

Visitors at the spa in Dolenjske Toplice

DIRECTORY

WALKING AND HIKING

Alpine Association of Slovenia
Dvoržakova 9, Ljubljana.
Tel (01) 434 5680.
www.pzs.si

Slovenian Mountain Guide Association
Dvoržakova 9, Ljubljana.
www.zgvs.si

Slovenian Tourist Board
Dunajska cesta 156, Ljubljana. *Tel (01) 589 1840.* www.slovenia.info

SKIING AND SNOWBOARDING

Active Slovenia
www.activeslo.com
(in Slovenian only)

GOLF

Bled Golf & Country Club
Kidričeva cesta 10, Bled.
Tel (04) 537 7711.
www.golfbled.com

CYCLING

Mountain Bike Nomad
Jamnica 10, Prevalje.
Tel (02) 870 3060.
www.bikenomad.com

HORSE RIDING

Lipica Stud Farm
Lipica 5, Sežana.
Tel (05) 739 1580.
www.lipica.org

Slovenian Equestrian Association
Celovška cesta 25, Ljubljana. *Tel (01) 434 7265.* www.konj-zveza.si
(in Slovenian only)

PARAGLIDING

Avantura
Trg golobarskih žrtev 19, Bovec. *Tel (04) 171 8317.*
www.avantura.org

Pac Sports
Ribčev laz 50, Lake Bohinj.
Tel (04) 086 4202.
www.pac-sports.com

FISHING

Fisheries Research Institute
Sp. Gameljne 61, Ljubljana-Šmartno.
Tel (01) 244 3400.
www.zzrs.si

RAFTING, KAYAKING AND CANOEING

Bovec Rafting Team
Mala vas 106, Bovec.
Tel (05) 388 6128. www.
bovec-rafting-team.com

Soča Rafting
Trg golobarskih žrtev 14, Bovec.
Tel (05) 389 6200.
www.socarafting.si

DIVING

3glav Adventures
Ljubljanska 1, Bled.
Tel (04) 163 8184.
www.3glavadventures. com

Slovenian Diving Federation
Celovška cesta 25, Ljubljana.
Tel (01) 433 9308.
www.spz.si
(in Slovene only)

Sub-net
Prešernovo nabrežje 24, Piran. *Tel (05) 673 2218.*
www.sub-net.si

SURVIVAL
GUIDE

PRACTICAL INFORMATION

Slovenia was always the most progressive of the Yugoslav nations. Its acceptance into the European Union in 2004 and integration into the European Monetary Union in 2007, coupled with the growth of tourism, has left it well prepared to welcome visitors. Economic integration has simplified border formalities and monetary issues for tourists. Major investment in infrastructure – motorways, roads and a reliable rail service – has made transport quick and easy. Most of the Slovenians themselves are eager to promote their newly independent nation. Every town, large and small, has an enthusiastic tourist information centre that helps to source accommodation and provides information about local attractions as well as activities.In addition, most Slovenians speak a second language – English is popular among the younger population and German among the older generation.

Information centre sign

WHEN TO VISIT

Slovenia's location, where the Alps, the Adriatic Sea and the Pannonian plain converge, results in a diverse climate. The southwest is characterized by a Mediterranean climate of hot summers and mild winters. The northwest is typically alpine, with warm summers, cold winters and heavy snowfall. The north and east have the dry, airless hot summers and bitter winters typical of a continental climate. Mean national temperatures over 24 hours are 20°C (68°F) in summer and 0°C (32°F) in winter.

The busiest tourist season is between June and August, when popular destinations such as Ljubljana, the Adriatic coast and Lake Bled are crowded. Resorts are at their busiest from late July to mid-August. That said, Ljubljana's café society is also at its most effervescent and the high Alps at their most accessible for hiking at this time too; the alpine plateaux provide relief from the often suffocating heat in the centre and east. Summer is also the busiest time for festivals and most towns stage some form of summer event.

November is the wettest month of the year, especially in the Alps, and many coastal hotels close for winter. However, mountain resorts prepare for the start of the ski season that is in full swing throughout the country by December and January. Winters are at their mildest on the coast but are extreme in the continental north and east, compensated for by the lowest precipitation in the country.

Crowds thin and prices fall in spring (April to early June) and autumn (mid-September to early November), both of which are lovely times to visit. The countryside begins to bloom during the former while the latter sees it luxurious and fruitful.

WHAT TO PACK

What you pack depends on when and where you visit. A waterproof jacket is recommended at all times (albeit lightweight in summer). Walking boots are essential and alpine hikers should come prepared for adverse conditions even in summer.

Visitors enjoying the sun on the promenade at Portorož

◁ **Cable cars to help skiiers reach higher alpine slopes**

Tourist information counter at Ljubljana airport

PASSPORTS AND VISAS

Slovenia became a member of the European Union on 1 May 2004. Consequently, holders of full, valid EU, US, Canadian, Australian and New Zealand passports do not need a visa to enter Slovenia for up to 90 days.

There are no border controls in the EU, although the police may conduct checks at major border crossings with Austria, Italy and Hungary. A passport or photo ID is sufficient from Croatia.

European Union passports

EMBASSIES AND CONSULATES

The embassies or consulates of most countries including **Australia**, the **UK**, **Canada** and the **US** are located in Ljubljana.

CUSTOMS INFORMATION

Customs regulations have been harmonized with EU standards: EU nationals over 17 years can import a limitless amount of goods, but only for personal use. Reasonable limits for entrants within the EU are 800 cigarettes/400 cigarillos/200 cigars/1 kg (35 oz) of tobacco; plus 10 litres (21 pints) of spirits, 90 litres (190 pints) of wine and 110 litres (233 pints) of beer.

Non-EU arrivals have to pass through customs inspections at Brnik airport.

These are generally cursory but are subject to the following cap on imports: 200 cigarettes/100 cigarillos/50 cigars/250g (9 oz) of tobacco; 1 litre (2 pints) of spirits, 4 litres (9 pints) of wine; perfumes and electronic goods up to €430 value. A maximum of €10,000 can be imported in cash; larger sums must be declared on arrival. On leaving, non-EU travellers can apply for a refund on Slovenian VAT (DDV) if they can prove a one-day, single-retailer spend of over €70 *(see p212)*.

VISITOR INFORMATION

A well-developed network of tourist information centres caters to visitors' needs. Denoted by "TIC" (Turistično-informacijski center), these are generally run by city, town or the regional authorities and manned by friendly staff who speak excellent English. Apart from information on local accommodation, attractions, tour and activity providers, most of the centres provide maps of their region free or for a nominal fee. Most also stock excellent brochures from the national tourism co-ordinator, the **Slovenia National Tourist Office**. Its main office beside the Triple Bridge *(see pp48–9)* in Ljubljana's Old Town bursts with information about the country.

Private tourist agencies fill in the gaps in towns where there is no official bureau, often located around rail or bus transport hubs.

Most destinations in Slovenia maintain a website and provide pages in English and often a searchable database of entertainment and festivities, accommodation listings and details of tourist sights. The national tourist office's website is also a wealth of information.

OPENING HOURS

Public and private offices operate from 9am to 4 or 5pm on weekdays. Banking hours *(see pp230–31)* generally include an hour's break from 12:30pm. Post offices *(see p233)* and pharmacies tend to operate slightly longer hours. Standard shop opening times are from 8am–7pm on weekdays and until 1pm on Saturdays, although these vary with the size of the town; those in large city shopping centres may open on Sunday morning, for example. Bear in mind that 24-hour petrol stations on major routes have basic supermarkets and that country petrol stations generally operate shop hours, so may close on Sunday. Museums and galleries typically open from 9 or 10am until 5 or 6pm on Tuesdays to Sundays; details are provided with each entry. *Odprto* means open, *zaprto* means closed.

Supermarket at a petrol station in Bled

Ticket booth at Tolmin gorge

ADMISSION CHARGES

A small charge is levied for entry to most museums and galleries in Slovenia. Expect to pay a couple of euros at small town museums and up to four euros for showpiece galleries in towns and cities. Entry to churches and to the Triglav National Park is free.

LANGUAGE

The south Slavic tongue of Slovenia is not the easiest language, even to anyone with a smattering of other European languages. This is apart from the fact that there are about 40 or so dialects.

Fortunately, most people in Slovenia speak at least one other language, so visitors should be able to make themselves understood easily. The standard of English is excellent among the younger generation – seek out a student or young person if you need to ask for help – and German is common among older citizens and around the Austrian border. Italian is widely understood in the border areas. Nevertheless, attempting a few local words *(see pp254–6)* is appreciated.

RELIGION

Although 40 religious denominations are registered, Slovenia is overwhelmingly Roman Catholic. The 60 per cent of Slovenians who define themselves as Catholic dwarfs the second-largest religious group, the 2.3 per cent Muslim population. The church is treated with respect even among the less religious younger generation and religious services are broadcast regularly on national radio. It is highly insensitive to enter a church when a service is in progress and negative comments about religion may offend deeply, especially the elderly.

Sign at the Slovenia airport

DISABLED TRAVELLERS

Although awareness is improving, Slovenia still has some way to go until it becomes disabled-friendly. Public transport, except international and modern intercity trains such as the service between Ljubljana and Maribor, usually has steps. Larger train stations can provide boarding ramps on request. Similarly, steps rather than ramps are standard in museums and only larger hotels have wheelchair-friendly rooms and lifts.

Change is slowly being made as buildings are modernized. For example, Slovenia created the world's first footpath for the disabled; a 15 km (9 miles) wheelchair accessible trail from Vodranci near Ormož. The most comprehensive source of information is the **Paraplegics Association of Slovenia** (Zveza paraplegikov Republike Slovenija), whose website has an English translation.

GAY AND LESBIAN TRAVELLERS

Recent educational campaigns have softened attitudes – the registration of same-sex

Ornate altars of the church at Olimje Monastery

Fresh farm produce for sale at a farm near Šmartno

partnerships was legalized in 2006 – and physical attacks are rare. Nevertheless, Slovenia remains deeply conservative in regard to the gay and lesbian communities. It is rare to see same-sex couples walking hand-in-hand. Similarly, sourcing gay-friendly accommodation can prove problematic – discretion is the best policy.

The focus of the nation's gay and lesbian community is in Ljubljana, which hosts the Pride Parade in June and the Festival of Gay and Lesbian Films in December. The capital also has a traditional Sunday get-together at a city-centre club. Internet resources include the Slovenian-language only **Slovenian Queer Resources Directory** and **Out in Slovenia**, a sports and activities organizer.

ELECTRICITY

Mains voltage is 220V, 50Hz. British, Australian and Irish appliances require a standard two-prong, round-pin adaptor. North American appliances require a transformer.

TIME

Slovenia operates Central European Time, so it is one hour ahead of Greenwich Mean Time (GMT), six hours ahead of US Eastern Standard Time, and 10 hours behind Australian Eastern Standard Time.

RESPONSIBLE TOURISM

Two-thirds of Slovenia is covered in natural forest, making it the second most forested country in Europe. Over a third is protected as by the European Union's Natura 2000 network of important habitats. There is a growing awareness of environmental issues, promoted by the government-aided Council for the Environmental Protection of the Republic of Slovenia and the sustainable development pressure group, Umanotera. The national tourist board has also declared its commit-ment to promote green and sustainable ethics.

Recycling is commonplace in urban centres, where there are separate bins for waste. Ecotourism is growing at around 20 per cent per anum. Under the Association of Slovenian Tourist Farms *(see p187)*, there are 200 or so farmstays, concentrated in the north and west. They are small

Clock on a public building in Stara Loka

DIRECTORY

EMBASSIES AND CONSULATES

Australia
Železna cesta 14, Ljubljana.
Tel *(01) 234 8675,
(01) 234 8676.*

UK
4th Floor, Trg republike 3, Ljubljana. **City Map** C3.
Tel *(01) 200 3910, (01) 425 0174.* **www**.british-embassy.si.

Canada
Trg republike 3, Ljubljana.
City Map C3. **Tel** *(01) 252 4444, (01) 252 3333.*

USA
Prešernova cesta 31, Ljubljana.
City Map B3. **Tel** *(01) 200 5500, (01) 200 5555.*
www.usembassy.si.

DISABLED TRAVELLERS

Paraplegics Association of Slovenia
Štihova 14, Ljubljana.
Tel *(01) 432 7138.*
www.zveza-paraplegikov.si

GAY AND LESBIAN TRAVELLERS

Out in Slovenia
www.outinslovenija.com

Slovenian Queer Resources Directory
www.ljudmila.org/siqrd

VISITOR INFORMATION

Slovenian National Tourist Office
Krekov trg 10, Ljubljana.
City Map E3. **Tel** *(01) 306 4575, (01) 200 5555.*
www.slovenia.info

holdings practising low-impact agriculture and some are accredited "Eko" to signify their healthy environment and organic food. Organic farming has enjoyed a surge and the fresh fruit and vegetables at daily markets is generally produced without chemical sprays. Packaged organic produce is labelled "Bio".

Personal Security and Health

Emblem of the police

Slovenia is one of the safest European countries to visit. The capital, Ljubljana, is largely crime free – pickpockets are rare and violent crime almost unheard of. Slovenian public health services are also excellent and visitors to the country face no health risks. There are no endemic diseases and water is potable throughout the country. Instead, the most common ailments for visitors relate to the climate. Summers can be suffocatingly hot and sunburn can be an issue. Mountainous regions present the added danger of adverse weather, especially at high altitudes.

POLICE

Slovenian police, known as *policija*, have the task of providing public safety. Dressed in blue uniforms, they are generally courteous and able to communicate in basic English, especially the younger officers. All policemen have the right to request proof of identity from any citizen or visitor: it could be a driving licence, passport, a personal identity card or any other valid official document with a photograph issued by a government authority. While this power is rarely invoked – in practice, only by international border patrols and even then only in unusual circumstances – it is advisable to carry appropriate documents or a photocopy of your passport at all times.

PERSONAL SAFETY AND THEFT

Slovenia enjoys one of the lowest crime rates in Europe, so public places are very safe. Mugging and violent crimes are extremely rare. Visitors might be approached by people begging for money in Ljubljana and Maribor, but they are not dangerous. Petty theft is uncommon, even in these cities. Nevertheless, it accounts for 90 per cent of all crime reported, so take the usual basic precautions to protect valuables. It is advisable to lock cars and close the windows. It is best not to leave cameras, wallets, bags, mobile phones or any other valuables in open view inside cars. Similarly, although street pickpockets are exceedingly rare, it is best to be alert at train and bus stations.

Theft from hotel rooms is rare, but in the highly unlikely event, if anything is stolen, report the loss to the police to receive an insurance number.

By international agreement, any tourist detained for questioning or for any reason has the right to contact a diplomatic representative from their national consulate. The official will be able to advise on and source legal representation, hire a translator and contact family members if required. In the event of a lost passport, inform your consulate or embassy immediately. It will issue a temporary replacement, usually for a small fee – a photocopy of your key information is helpful. Note that replacements must be collected in person at your embassy.

Security guard at the marathon in Ljubljana

INSURANCE

Citizens of the European Union with a European Health Insurance Card (EHIC) are permitted subsidized emergency medical treatment in Slovenia. The form is available in post offices.

Obtain a receipt to ensure reimbursement upon your return home in case you have to pay for any treatment. However, be aware that the reciprocal agreement does not cover medical repatriation, private treatment or dental treatment. Therefore, private medical insurance is a wise precaution for non-EU residents too, as it covers the cost of treatment and return home if required.

Check the small print on these policies to determine which sporting activities are covered, if any. Most insurers exempt "dangerous sports" such as skiing, rafting, climbing, paragliding, mountaineering and sometimes even hiking, from standard policies. Supplements or dedicated policies to cover these activities are more expensive but will refund the cost of services

Blue and white police car

in case of any assistance by agencies or rescue services such as the **Mountain Rescue Association of Slovenia** (Gorska reš'evalna zveza Slovenije), or an airlift to the hospital.

MEDICAL TREATMENT

Trained staff at the *lekarna* (local pharmacy) offer over-the-counter advice, usually in fluent English, and can provide basic medicines for upset stomachs or bad colds as well as prescribe antibiotics. To buy your usual prescription medicines, it is advisable to bring a signed letter from your GP stating the medicine's generic name. Pharmacy hours are between 7am and 7pm from Monday to Friday and from 7am to 1pm on Saturdays. All large towns have a duty pharmacy that is open 24 hours as well as on Sundays. This is organized by rota and a notice with the name of the current incumbent is posted on all pharmacy windows.

Tourist offices and hotel concierges are the best sources for information on the nearest pharmacy as well as the local doctor. Again, the standard of English is excellent. Consulates and embassies have a list of English-speaking doctors for more complex medical

Appropriately dressed visitors at Vršič Pass, northern Slovenia

requirements. These should be your first ports of call in case of sickness. A *bolnica* (hospital) is only for medical emergencies or in the case of a referral.

HEALTH PRECAUTIONS

Slovenian health standards are high and, accidents aside, the only precautions for visitors are likely to be concerned with the climate. Those caught in inclement weather on high alpine peaks are susceptible to hypothermia at any time of the year; heat-stroke and sunburn are possible in summer. It is imperative to wear appropriate clothing for the terrain. To avoid sunburn, always use sunscreen and cover exposed

Slovenian ambulance

skin; it is important to hydrate regularly, especially if taking part in strenuous activity.

British and American embassies warn of the dangers of tick-borne encephalitis in forested areas in summer. This potentially fatal brain infection is contracted from ticks that attach themselves to passing animals. Vaccination is advisable for hikers and campers who intend to stay in heavily wooded areas between May and September. Long socks are a good idea if walks and hikes are part of the agenda.

Less dangerous are the mosquitoes, which drift in clouds near lakes, ponds and slow rivers in summer. None carry diseases, however, a mosquito repellant is handy to avoid uncomfortable bites.

PUBLIC CONVENIENCES

In large cities, *javno stranišče* (public toilets) can be found without much difficulty. Often in the form of automatic cubicles with instructions in several languages on the door, these charge around €1 for use. Toilets can also be found at museums and in bars and cafés, although in the latter, it is courteous to at least buy a drink rather than expect to use the facilities for free. Men should enter *moški*, women *ženske*, occasionally written as M and Ž; there is usually a picture on the door.

Pharmacy on Ljubljana's Prešernov trg

Banking and Currency

Euro symbol

On 1 January 2007, Slovenia woke up to a new year and a new currency when the euro replaced the tolar as the country's official currency. Although many locals complain that this also resulted in prices being surreptitiously hiked, the switch brought Slovenia in line with the bulk of the European Union nations. Consequently, visitors have the option of sourcing currency before they arrive in the country, something that was almost impossible before the switch. Once in the country, access to money is easy thanks to the abundance of exchange offices and ATMs.

An ATM, commonly known as bankomat, in Slovenia

For those who prefer cheques, it is advantageous to buy them in Euro denominations.

BANKS AND CHANGING MONEY

Money can be changed in a *banka* (bank) and at authorized *bureaux de change*. Banks operate between 9am and 5pm on weekdays, although some close for an hour at 12:30pm. *Menjalnice* (exchange offices) keep more flexible opening hours; in heavily touristed areas, such as on the coast, they may open until late in the evening in high summer. They are also located in larger post offices. More flexible still are the numerous other outlets at which to change money – travel agents and hotels in tourist areas, petrol stations on motorways near borders and even large shopping centres.

While banks will change cash for free or levy only a nominal fee on exchanges, other operators will charge a commission on all transactions. Typically this is between 1 and 1.5 per cent for *bureaux de change* and around 3 per cent for other operators, though some may charge up to 5 per cent. Hotels and camp sites tend to provide the poorest value for money.

CREDIT CARDS AND TRAVELLERS' CHEQUES

Major credit cards such as **Visa**, **MasterCard**, **American Express** and **Diners Club** are widely accepted in large towns, popular tourist centres and in large hotels. Outside of these, *gostišče* (inns), pensions and *gostilna* (restaurants) may demand cash – double check if you are in doubt. All petrol stations accept cards. In the event of the loss of your card, it is essential to contact your card provider without delay, so that it can be blocked to prevent illegal use. The rise in ATM withdrawals has made travellers' cheques largely redundant as they restrict access to cash to the working hours of banks and exchange bureaux. Large international hotels may accept them as an alternative to cash.

Credit cards used in Slovenia

ATMS

More convenient for a short visit is to withdraw cash directly from a *bankomat* (ATM). Ubiquitous throughout Slovenian towns and resorts, as well as in motorway petrol stations, these accept international credit cards – usually Visa and MasterCard, and also, to a lesser extent, EuroCard, American Express and Diners Club. To withdraw money, a personal identification number (PIN) is required. However, remember that interest accrues as soon as a transaction is made.

A moderately cheaper option is to use debit cards affiliated to recognized credit systems such as Maestro, Cirrus and Visa Electron Plus. Most card providers will charge a one-off fee at a set rate and or one calculated as a percentage of the sum withdrawn; consult your bank before travelling. Every ATM will

DIRECTORY

CREDIT CARDS AND TRAVELLERS' CHEQUES

American Express
Tel (00) 44 1273 696 933.

Diners Club
Tel (01) 589 6133.

MasterCard
Tel (00) 1 636 722 7111.

Visa
Tel (00) 1 410 581 9994.

Façade of Banka Slovenije in Ljubljana

display the cards it accepts and all have an English-language option.

ATM crime such as illegal "readers" mounted on to a card slot, that scan the cards' magnetic strip, or theft at dispensers are unheard of in Slovenia.

LOCAL CURRENCY

The unit of currency in Slovenia is the euro, which is divided into 100 cents. The designs on the notes are generic architectural details and a European map common to all notes

in the Euro-zone. The coins feature a standard European design on one side and images of Slovenian cultural heroes or icons on the reverse. The uniform currency is a blessing to those travelling across Euro-zone countries.

Bank Notes
Euro bank notes have seven denominations. The 5-euro note (grey in colour) is the smallest, followed by the 10-euro note (pink), 20-euro note (blue), 50-euro note (orange), 100-euro note (green), 200-euro note (yellow) and 500-euro note (purple). All notes show the stars of the European Union.

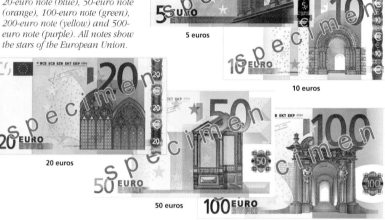

5 euros

10 euros

20 euros

50 euros

100 euros

200 euros

500 euros

2 euros 1 euro 50 cents 20 cents 10 cents

Coins
The euro has eight coin denominations: 1 euro and 2 euros; 50 cents, 20 cents, 10 cents, 5 cents, 2 cents and 1 cent. The 2- and 1-euro coins are both silver and golden in colour. The 50-, 20- and 10-cent coins are golden. The 5-, 2- and 1-cent coins are bronze.

5 cents 2 cents 1 cent

Communications and Media

Communications systems in Slovenia are of a high standard. There is a wide network of public services such as post and telecommunications, both of which function well. The news media is also well organized, although the near-absence of English-language publications presents a barrier for many visitors. Similarly, access to international print media is restricted to large cities and major resorts. However, a large quantity of English-language television and film is screened to compensate for the limited Slovenian output, and nearly all hotels and modern pensions subscribe to satellite channels.

Public telephone at the railway station, Ljubljana

TELEPHONES

Hotels charge a premium for telephone calls made from rooms, so it is cheaper to use public telephones, managed by Telekom Slovenije. Generally in good order, these are operated using *telekartice* (phonecards) – public phones do not accept coins. These cards are sold at post offices and newsagent kiosks; prices range from 3 to 14 euros.

Dedicated international phone booths in post offices provide cheaper rates for longer international calls.

MOBILE PHONES

Slovenia employs a GSM (Global System for Mobile Communications) frequency that is standard for mobile phone networks, compatible with Europe and US tri-band phones, but not with the North American GSM. It is, therefore, advisable to contact your service provider to enable your "roaming" access before travelling to the country. However, providers charge inflated prices for using foreign networks, both to make and receive calls.

Phones set to roaming will automatically switch to the strongest local signal from Slovenia's mobile providers. **Mobitel**, **Debitel**, **Simobil** and **Vodafone** are the largest national operators, supplemented by Austrian and Italian operators near

their respective borders. Network coverage extends across 98 per cent of the country.

If your phone is not tied to a specific network, it is best to invest in a local SIM card – the electronic chip that links your phone to a network. Offered by service providers such as Mobitel and priced at around 10 euros, these SIMs give you a local telephone number and a sum of credit that can be topped-up by prepaid cards sold in mobile phone shops, newsagents, post offices and often motorway service stations. Another option is to source a travel SIM card before travelling. This is a similar concept but it retains a telephone number from your home nation, so standard charges apply for incoming calls.

As elsewhere in Europe, it is against the law to use a mobile phone while driving.

Placard indicating Internet access at a tourist office

INTERNET AND EMAIL

The Internet is slowly gaining popularity in Slovenia. Internet cafés in cities and large towns provide access for around 2 or 3 euros per hour. However, many hotels have a free terminal, as do tourist information centres in popular destinations, generally with a time limit of 15 minutes. Public libraries also permit free access, although these are shut on weekends.

Once the sole preserve of top-end hotels, Wi-Fi networks are on the increase. The **Slovenian Government** website lists *točke* (access points) throughout the country, and the **Wi-Fi Točke** website pinpoints Wi-Fi *točke* on Google maps for the specified location. Both are in Slovenian only and have the

---

DIALLING CODES

- In Slovenia, telephone numbers have two-digit regional codes and seven-digit local numbers.
- To call Slovenia from abroad, dial the international code, then the country code (386) followed by the area code with the first zero omitted, and finally the number of the subscriber.
- Mobile phone numbers have a prefix of 031, 041, 051 or 040, followed by nine digits. Dial first the code then the number when calling a cell phone from a public or private local number; drop the zero if calling from abroad.
- To make a long-distance call, dial the two-digit regional code and then the local number.
- To make an international call from Slovenia, dial the international code (00), followed by the country code then dial the number, again omitting the first zero.
- For directory enquiries, dial 1188.

Post office with the distinct bugle logo, Škofja Loka

inherent problem that you need to be online to use them. Most towns, museums, hotels and tourism agencies and many restaurants now have their own websites.

POSTAL SERVICES

Carved out of the Yugoslav-era communications provider PTT and state-owned since 2002, **Pošta Slovenije** is recognized by its canary-yellow signs with a curled post bugle. There are post offices in any settlement larger than a village, which sell *znamke* (stamps) and *telekartice*, and have fax and photocopying facilities. Larger offices often offer money-changing facilities. Stamps are also available at newsagents.

The price of postage is determined by item and weight. International charges are €0.40 for a *pismo* (standard letter) up to 20 g (0.7 ounces); €0.36 for *razglednica* (postcard); 13.67 for a *paket* (parcel) within the EU and under 2 kg (4 lb); and €38.27 for *pakets* under 2 kg (4 lb) to the US and Canada. Letters can be deposited at the office or in yellow post boxes located at roadsides; parcels must be dropped off at the post office.

Post offices are open from 8am to 6pm, Monday to Friday and from 8am to noon on Saturdays; the main branches in larger towns and cities open a few hours later. Larger hotels may accept post for visitors by prior arrangement. However, if staying for up to

a month, it is more practical to use the poste restante services provided by post offices in the cities and larger towns. Correspondence is held for 30 days; carry proof of identity to collect your post. Please ensure that all mail is marked poste restante and has the recipient's name clearly written.

ADDRESSES

Slovenian street names make more sense when one understands the local names: *ulica* is street, *cesta* is road, *trg* is square. House numbers are written after street names. Numbers in smaller destinations often do not follow a logical order. To add to the confusion, villages generally dispense with street names and give each house a number, such as Ptujska Gora 36 in Ptujska Gora village.

TELEVISION AND RADIO

Slovenia has five domestic public service broadcast channels. Of the largest three, SLO 1 is a general broadcaster, SLO 2 is the main sports provider and SLO 3 covers politics. Unlike print media, large commercial broadcasters are owned by foreign companies, so the two American-owned Pop-TV and Kanal A frequently screen English-language content with Slovenian subtitles. Most hotels also subscribe to international satellite news stations such as BBC World and CNN. When radio frequencies were liberalized after independence, it resulted in a fragmented Slovenian

radio service. Of interest to foreign visitors are the two channels of the national provider, Radio Slovenija.

NEWSPAPERS

Being a small market, Slovenia supports just five daily newspapers, which range from the serious *Delo* to sensationalist tabloid *Slovenske novice*. Foreign media is in limited supply outside Ljubljana, Maribor and premier resorts such as Lake Bled; imported publications are usually a couple of days out of date. Local English-language magazines include the fortnightly news-based *Slovenian Times* and *Hotel*, a bilingual tourism magazine published quarterly. Both are distributed free in upmarket hotels and tourist information centres.

Newspaper kiosk on a street, Ljubljana

TRAVEL INFORMATION

Most visitors to Slovenia from Europe, the US and Australia arrive by air. Jože Pučnik Airport puts the premier tourist destinations of Ljubljana, Lake Bled and the Triglav National Park within an hour's travel of the arrivals lounge, and those travelling further afield will discover that the well-maintained and expanding transport network permits rapid transit across the nation.

Sign to the ticket office, Ljubljana

However, overland crossings from Austria, Italy, Croatia and Hungary are not uncommon. Visitors may choose to arrive in Slovenia by rail, sea or car. Rail travel takes longer and is more expensive than flying. Travelling by car is convenient and is cheaper in the long run. Catamarans, hydrofoils and cruise ships connect Piran to Venice and Trieste in Italy as well as to Poreč and Rovinj in Croatia.

Adria Airways flight at Jože Pučnik Airport

ARRIVING BY AIR

Slovenia has three international airports – **Jože Pučnik Airport** at Brnik, 23 km (14 miles) north of Ljubljana; **Edvard Rusjan Airport** in Maribor; and **Portorož Airport**.

National airline carrier **Adria Airways** operates direct routes from London, Birmingham and Dublin as well as from continental European hubs including Frankfurt, Munich, Vienna, Zurich, Brussels, Paris, Barcelona, Amsterdam, Oslo and Copenhagen. Budget operator **easyJet** also has a scheduled service from London, Milan and Paris.

Other European airlines that offer scheduled services to Slovenia include Austrian Airlines, Air France, Finnair, Czech Airlines, Turkish Airlines and Vueling.

No airline currently operates direct routes to Slovenia from the US, Canada or Australia. Instead, travellers must fly to European travel hubs such as London, Paris, Frankfurt, Vienna or Budapest, and then take connecting flights by other European carriers.

Facilities at the Jože Pučnik Airport, which is open daily from 6am to 10pm, include restaurants, ATMs and *bureaux de change*, a post office, a duty-free shop, free wireless Internet, tourist information offices and car rental agencies.

AIR FARES

Fares on scheduled flights vary from airline to airline and season to season. Fares tend to be the highest during the tourist season in summer, but Slovenia's burgeoning reputation as a ski destination results in a second tourist season in winter. Booking tickets early saves money. However, budget airlines are no longer always the cheapest because major airlines have reduced their fares. It is wise to make a comparative analysis of prices on the airline websites before booking tickets.

SHUTTLE SERVICES

Connecting buses operate from Jože Pučnik Airport to Kamnik and Kranj. Ljubljana presents the greatest number of options for onward travel within Slovenia, although Kranj serves as a convenient starting point to explore the Triglav National Park. Tickets, which can be bought on boarding the bus, cost €2 to €4. Private minibus shuttles operate the same routes at regular intervals as well as one to Bled and Bohinj.

The **Ljubljana Airport Taxi Association** also has a stand here and drivers will chauffeur passengers to any destination in the country. Visitors can expect to pay around €41 to Ljubljana and €55 to Bled. Advance reservations can be made via its website, which also has a list of prices.

Shuttle bus from Jože Pučnik Airport to Ljubljana

Visitors outside the ticket office at the train station in Ljubljana

RAIL TRAVEL

Visitors can get to Slovenia by rail from the UK but the journey is about 20 hours and is expensive – around three times the price of a flight. The route involves changes in Paris and Munich to hook up with the Eurocity 'Mimara' via Salzburg to Ljubljana. From Germany, daily Eurocity (EC) trains via Munich also connect Frankfurt and Stuttgart to Ljubljana. Austria has a regular Salzburg service, daily InterCitySlovenija (ICS) trains from Vienna to Ljubljana and frequent services between Graz and Maribor. From Switzerland, a daily EuroNight (EN) service links Zurich and Ljubljana. Croatia has several routes to the Slovenian capital: eight daily trains from Zagreb, two daily from Rijeka and a daily service from Pula. Italy has an overnight EuroNight connection from Venice to Ljubljana. Other trains to Ljubljana are from Prague, Budapest and Belgrade.

ARRIVING BY SEA

The cruise companies **Kompas**, **Venezia Lines** and Dora operate up to three fast catamarans a week between Venice and Piran from April to late-October. The journey takes around 2½ hours.

In addition, from late April to late September, the fast hydrofoil service of **Trieste Lines** skips along the north Adriatic coast, plying a daily return trip from Trieste in Italy, to Piran, then onwards to Poreč and Rovinj in Croatia.

ARRIVING BY CAR

Travelling to Slovenia by car (or motorbike) is popular with neighbouring countries. Routes are well marked and easy to follow – pan-European road routes have an "E" prefix and are highlighted in green on signs. As part of the European Union, Slovenia abides by the Schengen Agreement that permits free-movement within partner neighbours Austria, Italy and Hungary. Major Slovenian frontier crossings such as those near Villach and Gorizia (Austria), Trieste (Italy) or Nagykanizsa (Hungary) are open 24 hours, year round without border formalities. The police of the transit country may check departing motorists to ensure they comply with local road laws; Austria and Slovenia *(see pp238–9)*, for example, require visitors to buy a vignette to travel on its

Cycles for hire at the tourist office, Ljubljana

(see pp238–9)

---

motorways. Fast motorways also link Zagreb (Croatia) to Maribor and Ljubljana. All international drivers are required to carry a valid driving licence, the car's log book and a green card.

GREEN TRAVEL

Travelling to Slovenia by train reduces the high ecological impact of flying. Within Slovenia, there are hardly any long car drives, as it is a small country. In addition, an excellent public transport network offers rapid links between major tourist destinations and cities. Bikes can be carried on all trains and provide a pleasant way to explore the country. Cycle hire is also available at cheap rates from tourist offices in popular destinations such as Lake Bled and cities such as Ljubljana and Kranj.

If you do not hike or cycle, exploring the remoter countryside without your own vehicle will be difficult as buses are generally slow and infrequent, especially at weekends.

Getting Around Slovenia

Free buggy, Ljubljana

The public transport system in Slovenia is sufficiently widespread to make most destinations accessible. Relatively inexpensive by European standards, the rail network connects the regional centres; Slovenia's small size means travel times are generally short. But, touring beyond the network can prove problematic. While local bus companies operate routes in the countryside, some require careful planning or plenty of time due to a limited service at weekends. Most towns are small enough to be walkable. However, public transport comes into its own in the capital, Ljubljana.

Taxis standing in a queue outside Jože Pučnik Airport, Brnik

TRAVEL IN LJUBLJANA

Those travelling by bus need to buy an Urbana card, which costs €2, and you can then top it up with units. It is best to buy as many units as you think you will need in advance. Each unit, costing €0.80, covers 90 minutes of continuous travel time, including any changes of bus you might make during the journey. Swipe the Urbana card across an electronic card reader situated near the driver's seat, when you enter the bus. These cards can be purchased and topped up at the tourist office and newspaper kiosks. Vending machines located next to principal stops accept both cash and credit cards.

Taxis cost €1–2 initial charge followed by €1.50–2 per km (0.6 miles). Always phone for a taxi if possible. Taxis picked up on the street, especially those parked outside the train station or central hotels, can be more expensive. The recommended taxi services include **Taxi Društvo Ljubljana** and **Taxi Metro**.

TRAINS

The national railway operator, **Slovenian Railways** (Slovenske železnice), is a model of efficiency compared to those of other former Yugoslav nations. Its 1,230 km (764 miles) of track snakes out from the transport hub of Ljubljana to most regions of the country. Carriages are invariably clean and tickets are generally cheaper than those of bus

Train arriving on a platform at Ljubljana's main train station

services. The network is also connected to pan-European routes to permit travel to neighbouring countries.

Prices vary according to the type of train. Top of the range are the express Inter-City Slovenia (ICS) trains. These operate to Maribor and Koper on international lines and reach the highest speeds; the shortest travel time between Ljubljana and Maribor is 1hr 50mins. First-class passengers receive a snack and non-alcoholic drink, which is included in the ticket price. Those in second class have access to a restaurant carriage. Irrespective of the class, all carriages are air-conditioned and comfortable. Naturally, ICS trains are the most expensive; a second-class ticket from Ljubljana to Maribor costs around €14.

Second to this are the InterCity (IC) or EuroCity (EC) trains, which pause at fewer stations than *regionalni vlaki* (regional trains) – these stop at every station on a line. The IC and EC are often faster to return to Ljubljana.

Prices are calculated on the basis of distance covered, and a *povratna vozovnica* (return ticket) costs double that of a *enosmerna vozovnica* (single ticket). First-class tickets cost around 50 per cent more than second-class tickets. Bicycles can be carried free of charge on all trains, except on ICS trains.

SPECIAL TRAIN SERVICES

Two alpine rail services deserve a special mention. A car train operates between Bohinjska Bistrica, near Lake Bohinj, and Most na Soči in the Soča Valley via a tunnel, thereby saving a long ascent over the Soriška planina pass. A heritage steam locomotive known as the Muzejski vlak (Museum Train) operates between April and November up to three times a month. Co-ordinated by the tourism agency **ABC Tourism**, its vintage service travels through the spectacular scenery between Jesenice and Nova Gorica, via Lake

Tourist Office in the main square of Koper

Bled and Bohinjska Bistrica. Timetables are published on the agency's website, through which advance bookings can be made. Tickets can also be booked at local tourist information centres.

TICKETS AND RAIL PASSES

Tickets can be bought from the *železniška postaja* (train station), where yellow timetables list *odhodi* (departures) and white timetables list *prihodi* (arrivals). Slovenia's system of timetable symbols to represent days is difficult to understand for visitors – it is easier to source information directly from an official; information in English is available on Slovenian Railways' website. Credit cards are accepted in all stations. Tickets bought on the train incur a supplementary payment of €2.50. Timetables also list the correct *peron* (platform) for your train.

European Union residents are eligible to purchase an InterRail One Country Slovenia Pass. It enables unrestricted rail travel in Slovenia for three to eight days in a month and costs €50–119, or a third cheaper for travellers under 26. These are valid on all trains, including ICS trains. Non-EU residents qualify for the expensive Eurail Pass, which permits unlimited travel in 20 European countries, so is uneconomical for travel within Slovenia alone. The Turist vikend (Tourist Weekend)

ticket offers 30 per cent discounts to passengers who make return journeys over the weekend.

BUS

Regional private companies operate the bus network in Slovenia. Buses are clean and rarely crowded outside of commuter hours. Departures are regular during the week but reduce dramatically at weekends – Saturday schedules are generally half of those of weekdays, and services on Sunday are almost non-existent. Services to rural areas can be limited too. Conversely, popular routes from Ljubljana to mountain and coastal destinations can sell out on Fridays and public holidays in summer, so purchase in advance from computerized terminals is recommended.

On making a reservation, tickets should be collected two hours prior to departure for local bus lines, and six hours before departure for international lines. Otherwise, tickets can be bought directly before travelling from the *avtobusna postaja* (bus station) or from the driver on boarding. Fares are calculated on the basis of distance travelled, on a sliding scale, regardless of the bus company; €4 for 50 km (31 miles), €9 for 100 km (62 miles) and €17 for 200 km (124 miles). Luggage can be stored in the hold for a few extra euros, depending on size. Timetables are colour-coded to present an organized system of departures and arrivals.

DIRECTORY

TRAVEL IN LJUBLJANA

Taxi Društvo Ljubljana

Tel (01) 234 9000/1/2/3.

www.taxi-ljubljana.si

Taxi Metro

Tel (01) 544 1190.

TRAINS

Slovenian Railways

Kolodvorska 11, Ljubljana.

Tel (01) 291 3332.

www.slo-zeleznice.si

SPECIAL TRAIN SERVICES

ABC Tourism

Celovška cesta 268, Ljubljana.

Tel (05) 907 0500.

www.abctourism.si

CYCLING

Cycling is a popular pastime in Slovenia. The country's small size and the ability to transport bikes by train makes touring by bike feasible. As a rule of thumb, the terrain gets flatter the further east you go. Drivers are generally tolerant of cyclists but it is preferable nevertheless to seek the quietest country lanes. Cycling is not permitted on motorways. Helmets are obligatory for children aged 14 and under. Dedicated cycle lanes exist in most cities where cycling is prohibited in pedestrian areas.

Family cycling on a clear road in Žužemberk

Travelling by Road

Vinjeta sticker, a must for all cars

Touring by car remains, by far, the most enjoyable and rewarding way to see Slovenia. Distances are short, the country roads are largely traffic free and a well-maintained and expanding motorway network permits rapid travel across the nation – it takes just three hours to traverse the 280 km (174 miles) from the Adriatic coast to the Hungarian border, for example. More than anything, your own car puts you right in the heart of Slovenia's stupendous scenery – indeed, a route like the Vršič Pass in the Triglav National Park is a destination in its own right. However, visitors need to be aware that snowfall can close high roads during winters.

RULES OF THE ROAD

Drivers are expected to have with them a full national driving licence and those driving their own car, will be required to present on demand a vehicle registration document and a valid certificate of third-party insurance. Driving is on the right, overtaking on the left and seatbelts are compulsory for all passengers. Drivers are forbidden from using mobile phones at the wheel and dipped headlights are required even during the day. Carrying a reflective, breakdown-warning triangle is mandatory; it should be set up 100 m (328 ft) behind the vehicle if you pull over for anything other than the briefest halt. Other obligatory equipment includes a reflective vest, a spare set of bulbs and a first-aid kit.

Between 15 November and 15 March cars must either be fitted with winter tyres or snow chains must be carried. Speed limits are 130 kph (81 mph) on motorways, 100 kph (62 mph) on secondary or tertiary roads and 50 kph (31 mph) in towns and villages. Fair but determined, traffic police frequently mount radar patrols to snare speeding motorists, often on the outskirts of towns. Offenders are issued on-the-spot, fixed penalty fines for all driving infringements. These start at €40 and rise to €950 – standard fines are €120 for not wearing a seatbelt or using a mobile phone while driving. The maximum blood alcohol limit is currently 0.05 per cent.

Signboard for Vršič Pass

ROADS AND MOTORWAYS

Slovenia has invested huge sums of money in its roads over the last decade. Most of this has gone into extending the *avtocesta* (arterial motorways) the east-west A1 and northeast to southwest A2. The two motorways cross at Ljubljana and are indicated by blue signs (green with an E number for international route numbers). The final sections of the motorway are nearing completion. Having dispensed with tollbooths in 2008, *vinjeta* (vignette) window stickers are obligatory for all vehicles that use motorways. Purchased at large border crossings, motorway petrol stations and post offices, they cost €15 for a week, €30 for a month or €95 for a year. A one-year *vinjeta* (vignette) for motorcycles costs €47.50; a six-month one is €25 and a weekly *vinjeta* is €7.50. Failure to display a valid *vinjeta* can result in fines between €300 and €800.

Signage on all motorways and tertiary roads is excellent. Short cuts on uncategorized back roads – the white routes on a standard road map – often turn into long delays as you enter a maze of unsigned routes. On the plus side, you will experience a

Beautiful mountain scenery viewed from a motorway

Parking outside the National Library, Ljubljana

side of deep rural Slovenia that most visitors never see. *Bencinska črpalka* (petrol stations) dispense *neosvinčen bencin* (unleaded fuel) and diesel between 7am and 8pm on minor roads, have longer opening hours outside cities, and are open 24 hours a day on motorways. Some stations also offer liquified petrolium gas (LPG). All accept standard credit cards.

ROAD SAFETY

Emergency roadside assistance is provided by national auto association the **AMZS** (Avto-moto zveza Slovenije). In the event of an accident, you must call the police. It is illegal to move a vehicle before the police officers arrive.

Be aware that mountains and winters in Slovenia demand caution. Gradients in the Julian Alps can be up to 18 per cent and hairpin bends generally prevent towing of any sort. In addition, snowfall occurs throughout Slovenia during winters, with the possible exception of the coastal strip. While arterial routes are snow-ploughed, roads such as the Vršič Pass can be closed at any time between November and March. Winter equipment, such as snow chains, is required by law during this period.

PARKING

Parking is the greatest problem in cities, especially in Ljubljana. Although the capital has dedicated car parks – follow the blue P to locate them – most parking in Slovenia's towns is on the streets, generally on roads on the periphery of pedestrianized areas and defined by a white line. Payment is on a "Pay and Display" basis, with costs being higher nearer to the centre. Parking in small towns and villages is free and generally easy.

CAR HIRE

Drivers must be over 21 years old (although some hire firms insist they are over 25) and must have held an EU or international driving licence

Car rental offices at the airport in Ljubljana

for at least two years. The major car rental companies operating in Slovenia include **Avis**, **Dollar & Thrifty**, **Hertz** and **Sixt**. Quotes from international rental companies fluctuate between firms and according to the season, but you can expect to pay from €50 per day for a modest two-door vehicle, in summer. Long-term hiring generally brings more favourable day rates, but do check the unlimited mileage clauses. Prices include tax, personal accident insurance, and collision damage waiver (CDW); be warned though, the latter does not usually extend to tyres, wheels, the underside or the interior of the vehicle.

Shopping around with international firms (all of which operate bureaux at Ljubljana airport) before you travel will turn up special deals; local outlets are usually cheaper still if you are not too concerned with appearances. All hire companies require drivers to present a passport, driving licence and credit card (sometimes two) as a deposit upon collection of the car. Double-check whether restrictions apply when crossing international borders, especially if this was part of your travel plans.

General Index

Acknowledgments

Dorling Kindersley would like to thank the many people whose help and assistance contributed to the preparation of this book.

Main Contributors

Jonathan Bousfield was born in the UK and has been travelling in Central & Eastern Europe for as long as he can remember. A student of East European history and languages, he has lived at various times in Belgrade, Sofia, Zagreb, Riga, Vilnius and Cracow. His first travel-writing job involved researching a guide to the former Yugoslavia in 1989. Since then he has authored the *DK Eyewitness Travel Guide to Bulgaria*, the *DK Top Ten Guide to Talinn*, and co-authored the *DK Eyewitness Travel Guide to Eastern and Central Europe*. He is also the author of the *Rough Guide to Croatia*, the *Rough Guide to the Baltic States* and a co-author of the Rough Guides to Austria, Poland and Bulgaria. He has also been a magazine editor, feature writer and rock critic.

James Stewart has been a travel journalist and guidebook author for over 10 years. He writes for several international publications including *The Times*, *Guardian*, *Telegraph*, *Independent*, *Sydney Morning Herald* and *Wanderlust*. He is the author of the *Rough Guide to Tasmania*, the Cadogan guides to *Slovenia* and *Croatia and the Adriatic*, the co-author of *DK Eyewitness Back Roads Germany* and the *Rough Guide to Germany*. He has contributed to Rough Guide's *Make the Most of Your Time on Earth* and *Clean Breaks*.

Fact Checker Ales Fevzer

Proofreader Sandhya Iyer

Indexer Hilary Bird

Editorial Consultant Scarlett O'Hara

Design and Editorial

Publishing Director Clare Currie
Publisher Vivien Antwi
List Manager Christine Stroyan
Project Editors Michelle Crane, Sadie Smith
Project Art Editor Shahid Mahmood
Senior Cartographic Editor Casper Morris
Senior DTP Designer Jason Little
Senior Picture Researcher Ellen Root
Production Controller Louise Minihane

Cartography Credits

Regional mapping supplied by JP Map Graphics, www.jpmapgraphics.co.uk

Additional Photography

M. Balan, Jens Erikesen, Britta Jaschinski, Hanne and Dave King, Shikha Kulkarni, Andrew de Lory, Ian O'Leary, Shruti Singhi, Jonathan Smith, Antony Souter.

Photography Permissions

Dorling Kindersley would like to thank the following for their assistance and kind permission to photograph at their establishment.

Bogenšperk Castle, Brewery Museum, Celje Regional Museum, Cerkno Museum, City Museum of Ljubljana, Kobarid Museum, The Museum of Underwater Activities, Nace's House, National Gallery of Slovenia, The National Museum of Contemporary History of Slovenia, National Museum of Slovenia, Olimje Monastery, Open-Air Museum at the Pleterje Carthusian Monastery, Orthodox Church of Sts Cyril and Methodius, The Pilon Gallery Ajdovščina, Plečnik House, Predjama Castle, The Preseren House, Ptuj Regional Museum, Rogatec Open-Air Museum, Seminary, Slovene Ethnographic Museum, Snežnik Castle, St. Florian Church, St Nicholas Cathedral, Technical Museum of Slovenia, Trebnik Manor, Trebnje Gallery of Naive Artists, Tržič Museum, Turjak Castle, Velenje Museum.

Picture Credits

Key: a-above; b-below/bottom; c-centre; f-far; l-left; r-right; t-top

The publisher would like to thank the following for their kind permission to reproduce their photographs:

4Corners: Guido Cozzi 105b, SIME/Guido Baviera 43tl,/Johanna Huber 100-101,/Arcangelo Piai 102clb.

akg-images: 33br.

Alamy Images: Pat Behnke 103tr, Ladi Kirn 66clb, LatitudeStock 102cla, Lonely Planet Images/ Jonathan Smith 200cl, Cro Magnon 22c, Ian Middleton 19cr, 22bl, Mitja Mladkovic 22br, North Wind Picture Archives 36br, PjrTravel 39tc, David Robertson 17br, Stoz 27br.

Bunker Productions/Festival Mladi Levi: Urška Boljkovac 215tl.

Corbis: Bob Krist 104, Design Pics/Lizzie Shepherd 201cb; Jacques Langevin 39crb, William Manning 47br.

Petra Draskovic: 142-143, 154bl.

European Central Bank: 231 (all images).

Festival Ljubljana: Miha Fras 29c.

FESTIVAL SEVIQC BREŽICE: 29br.

ALEŠ FEVZER: 26cl, 26bl, 27tl, 217tl, 222-223.

GETTY IMAGES: Bongarts 39br, Hulton Archive/ Handout 34t, Photographer's Choice RF/Connie Coleman 201tl.

GOLDEN FOX: 28cl.

HOTEL KOVAČ: 103bl.

JAVNI ZAVOD KINODVOR: Nada Zgank 95tl.

JAZZ CERKNO: Marko Čadež 94bc.

KOROŠKA GALERIJA LIKOVNIH UMETNOSTI SLOVENJ GRADEC, Slovenia, http://www.glu-sg.si/: Jože Tisnikar, *The Flute Player*, Oil and tempera on canvas, 1971, 45 x 35 cm 172br.

LJUBLJANA TANGO FESTIVAL: Branko Čeak 28br.
LUTKOVNO GLEDALIŠČE MARIBOR: Boštjan Lah 214bc.
MARY EVANS PICTURE LIBRARY: 9c, 37tl, 41c, 101c, 185c.

MODERNA GALERIJA, LJUBLJANA: Matija Pavlovec/ Gabrijel Stupica, *The Large Self-Portrait in Light Hues*, 1959 © Marlenka Stupica 25bl.

MUZEJ IN GALERIJE MESTA LJUBLJANA (MGML): Janez Pukšič 73crb.

NATIONAL GALLERY OF SLOVENIA: Bojan Salaj 24cr.
PHOTOLIBRARY: 35tr, 103tl, 103crb, Age footstock/ Tibor Bognár 168-169,/Wojtek Buss 11br,/JD. Dallet 17tc,/Morales Morales 19cla, Art Media 37crb, Barbara Boensch 67crb, Alberto Campanile 23crb, William Cleary 70t, Guy Edwardes 40-41, 124-125, Borut Furlan 220br, Christian Handl 8-9, John Warburton-Lee Photography/Christian Kober 16bl, JTB Photo 10ca, Lonely Planet Images/Grant Dixon 113cra, /Martin Moos 30b, 31cr, Rainer Mirau 112br, National Geographic Society 23tr, Steve Ogle 26tr, Planet Observer 12bl, Peter Schickert 184-185, Science Photo Library/Philippe Psaila 19bc, 151br, Lizzie Shepherd 64-65, Martin Siepmann 113bc.

ŠKOCJAN CAVES PARK: Borut Lozej 138tr, 138cla, 138br, 139tl, 139br.

TURISTIČNO DRUŠTVO SOLČAVA: 2-3, 16t, 216b.

TURIZEM BLED: 109cr.

WIKIPEDIA: 34bc, 35bl, 36tc, 37bl.

ZDRAVILIŠČE RADENCI: 218tr.

Jacket images: Front: 4CORNERS: SIME/Johanna Huber: Back: 4CORNERS: SIME/Johanna Huber tl; CORBIS: Bob Krist cla; DORLING KINDERSLEY: Shruti Singhi bl, Linda Whitwam cl; Spine: 4CORNERS: SIME/Johanna Huber; Front Endpapers: CORBIS: Bob Krist t; PHOTOLIBRARY: William Cleary bc.

All other images © Dorling Kindersley. For further information see: www.dkimages.com

Phrase Book

Pronunciation

c – "ts" as in rats
č – "chi" as in church
g – "g" is a hard g as in get
j – "y" as in yes
š – sh
ž – shown here as "zh", sounds like the "J" in the
French name, Jacques

Emergencies

Help!	Pomóč!	pomoch
Stop!	Stóp!	stop
Call a doctor!	Pokličíite zdravníka!	poklichiite zdrawnika
Call an ambulance	Pokličíte rešilca!	poklichiite resilsa
Call the police!	Pokličíte policijo!	poklichiite policiyo
Call the fire brigade!	Pokličíte gasilce!	poklichiite gasilce
Where is the nearest telephone?	Kjé je najblížji telefón?	kye ye nayblizhyi telefon
Where is the nearest hospital?	Kjé je najblížja bólnica?	kye ye nayblizhya bolnitsa

Communication Essentials

Yes	Dà	da
No	Nè	ne
Please	Prósim	prosim
Thank you	Hvála	hvala
Excuse me	Oprostíte	oprostite
Hello	Živío	zhivyo
Goodbye	Nasvídenje	nasvidenye
Good night	Láhko nóč	lahko nochi
Morning	Jútro	Yutro
Afternoon	Popóldan	popoldan
Evening	Večér	vechier
Yesterday	Včéraj	vchieray
Today	Dánes	danes
Tomorrow	Jútri	yutri
Here	Túkaj	tukay
There	Tàm	tam
What?	Káj?	kay
When?	Kdáj?	kday
Why?	Zakáj?	zakay
Where?	Kjé?	kye

Useful Phrases

How are you?	Kakó ste?	kako ste
Very well, thank you	Zeló dôbró, hvála	zelo dobro, hvala
Pleased to meet you	Me veselí	me veseli
See you soon	Kmálu se vídimo	kmalu se vidimo
That's fine	Odlíčno	odlichino
Where is/are...?	Kjé je/so...?	kye ye/so
How far is it to...?	Kakó dáleč je do...?	kako dalechi je do
How can I get to...?	Kakó láhko pridem do...?	kako lahko pridem do

Useful Words

big	vêlik	velik
small	májhen	mayhen
	vròč	vroch
	hláden	hladen
good	dóber	dober
bad	slab	slab
enough	dovòlj	dovolj
open	odpŕt	odprt
closed	zapŕt	zaprt
left	lévo	levo
right	désno	desno
straight on	narávnost	naravnost
near	blízu	blizu
far	dáleč	dalechi
up	gôr	gor
down	dól	dol
early	zgódaj	zgoday
late	pôzno	pozno
entrance	vhòd	vhod
exit	izhòd	izhod
toilet	stranišče	stranishchie
restaurant	restavrácija	restavratsiya

Shopping

How much does this cost?	Kóliko stáne to?	koliko stane to
I would like...	Želím...	zhelim
Do you have...?	Ali imáte...?	ali imate
I'm just looking	Samó glédam	samo gledam
Do you take credit cards?	Jémljete kreditne kártice?	yemlyete kreditne kartitse
What time do you open?	Kdáj odpréte?	kday odprete
What time do you close?	Kdáj zapréte?	kday zaprete
This one	To	to
That one	Tísto	tisto
expensive	drágo	drago
cheap	pocéni	potseni
size (clothes)	velikóst (oblačila)	velikost (oblachiila)
size (shoes)	velikóst (čévlji)	velikost (chievlyi)
white	béla	bela
black	čŕna	chirna
red	rdéča	rdechia
yellow	ruména	rumena
green	zeléna	zelena
blue	ódra	modra
bakery	pekárna	pekarna
bank	bánka	banka
book shop	knjigárna	knyigarna
butcher's	pri mesárju	pri mesaryu
chemist's	v lekárni	v lekarni

Do you speak English?

Do you speak English?	Govoríte anglêško?	govorite angleshko
I don't understand	Nè razúmem	ne razumem
Could you speak more slowly please?	Láhko govoríte počásneje?	lahko govorite pochiasneye
I'm sorry	Se opravíčujem	se opravichiuyem

market	tržnica	trzhnitsa
hairdresser's	pri frizêrju	pri frizeryu
newsagent's/	raznášalec časopísa/	raznashalec
tobacconist	trafikánt	chiasopisa/
	(trafikántka)	trafikant
		(trafikantka)
post office	pôšta	poshta
shoe shop	trgovína za čévlje	trgovina za
		chievlye
supermarket	súpermárket	supermarket
travel agent	potoválni posrédnik	potovalni
		posrednik

Sightseeing

art gallery	galerija z	galeriya z
	umetnínami	umetninami
castle	grad	grad
cathedral	katedrála	katedrala
church	cérkev	cerkev
forest	gôzd	gozd
garden	vŕt	vrt
island	ôtok	otok
lake	jézero	yezero
mountain	gôra	gora
museum	muzêj	muzey
tourist	cénter za turístične	center za
information	informácije	turistichne
centre		informatsiye
closed for	zapŕto za práznike	zaprto za
holiday		praznike
bus station	ávtobusna postája	avtobusna
		postaya
railway station	žélezniška postája	zheleznishka
		postaya
waterfall	slap	slap

Staying in a Hotel

Do you have a vacant room?	Imáte prosto sôbo?	imate prosto sobo
double room	Dvópósteljna sôba	dvopostelyna soba
single room	Enópósteljna sôba	enopostelyna soba
Is breakfast included?	Je zájtrk vključén?	Je zaytrk vkljuchien
Porter	Portir	portir
Key	Kljúč	klyuchi
I have a reservation	Imám rezervácijo	imam rezervatsiyo

Eating Out

Have you got a table for…?	Imáte mízo za …?	Imate mizo za
I want to reserve a table	Želim rezervírati mízo	zhelim rezervirati mizo
The bill please	Račún, prósim	rachiun prosim
I am a vegetarian	Sèm vegeterijánec/ vegetarijánka	sem vegetariyanets/ vegetariyanka
waiter/ waitress	natákar/natákarica	natakar/ natakaritsa
menu	meni	meni
wine list	vínska kárta	vinska karta
glass	kozárec	kozarets
bottle	stekleníca	steklenitsa

knife	nòž	nozb
fork	vílica	vilitsa
spoon	žlíca	zblitsa
breakfast	zájtrk	zaytrk
lunch	kosílo	kosilo
dinner	večérja	vechierya
main course	glávna jéd	glavna yed
starters	prèdjédi	predyedi
dessert	sladíca	sladitsa

Menu Decoder

krùh	kruh	bread
sól	sol	salt
pôper	poper	pepper
pásta	pasta	pasta
soláta	solata	salad
krompír	krompir	potatoes
krúhovi cmòki	kruhovi tsmoki	potato dumplings
zélje	zelye	cabbage
rèpa	repa	turnip
góbe	gobe	mushrooms
jábolka	yabolka	apples
hrúške	hrushke	pears
slíve	slive	plums
svinjína	svinyina	pork
klobáse	klobase	sausages
šúnka	shunka	ham
ájdova káša	aydova kasha	buckwheat porridge
njoki	nyoki	gnocchi
rižôta	rizhota	risotto
gólaž	golazh	goulash
Telétina	teletina	veal
govédina	govedina	beef
divjáčina	divjachiina	venison
fazán	fazan	pheasant
zájec	zajets	rabbit
postŕv	postrv	trout
máslo	maslo	butter
piščánec	pishchianets	chicken
ríž	rizh	rice
ravióli (slovenske vrste)	ravioli	ravioli (the Slovene type)
mesné króglice	mesne kroglitse	meatballs
dúnajski zrézek	dunajski zrezek	wiener schnitzel
čévápčiči	chievapchiichii	čevapčiči
dágnje	dagnje	mussels
môrski rákci	morski raktsi	shrimp
kalamári	kalamari	squid
štrúklji	struklyi	štruklji
potíca	potitsa	potica
gibánica	gibanitsa	gibanica
zavítek	zavitek	zavitek
sladoléd	sladoled	ice cream
popárjeno	poparyeno	steamed
zavréto	zavreto	boiled
ocvrto	otsvrto	fried
zapéčeno	zapechieno	roasted

Drinks

bélo víno	belo vino	white wine
Čáj	tsay	tea

rdèče víno	**rdeshie vino**	*red wine*
gazírana	**gazirana mineralna**	*sparkling*
minerálna vôda	**voda**	*mineral water*
negazírana minerálna vôda	**negazirana mineralna voda**	*still mineral water*
Kava	**káva**	*coffee*
Žgana pijača	**zhgana peeyatsa**	*spirit*
Voda	**vôda**	*water*

Numbers

0	**nič**	*nichi*
1	**êna**	*ena*
2	**dve**	*dve*
3	**tri**	*tri*
4	**štíri**	*shtiri*
5	**pét**	*pet*
6	**šést**	*shest*
7	**sédem**	*sedem*
8	**ósem**	*osem*
9	**devét**	*devet*
10	**desét**	*deset*
11	**enájst**	*enayst*
12	**dvánajst**	*dvanayst*
13	**trínajst**	*trinayst*
14	**štírinajst**	*shtirinayst*
15	**pétnajst**	*lpetnayst*
16	**šéstnajst**	*shestnayst*
17	**sédemnajst**	*sedemnayst*
18	**ósemnajst**	*osemnayst*
19	**devétnajst**	*devetnayst*
20	**dvájset**	*dvayset*
21	**ênaindvájset**	*enaindvayset*
22	**dvaindvájset**	*dvaindvayset*

30	**trídeset**	*trideset*
31	**ênaintrídeset**	*enaintrideset*
40	**štírideset**	*shtirideset*
50	**pétdeset**	*petdeset*
60	**šéstdeset**	*shestdeset*
70	**sédemdeset**	*sedemdeset*
80	**ósemdeset**	*osemdeset*
90	**devétdese**	*devetdeset*
100	**stó**	*sto*
101	**stoena**	*stoena*
102	**stodve**	*stodve*
200	**dvesto**	*dvesto*
500	**petsto**	*petsto*
700	**sedemsto**	*sedemsto*
900	**devetsto**	*devetsto*
1,000	**tisoč**	*tisochi*
1,001	**tisočena**	*tisochiena*

Time

One minute	**Ena minuta**	*êna minúta*
One hour	**Ena ura**	*êna úra*
Half an hour	**Pol ure**	*pól úre*
Monday	**Ponedeljek**	*ponedéljek*
Tuesday	**Torek**	*tôrek*
Wednesday	**Sreda**	*sréda*
Thursday	**Četrtek**	*chietrtek*
Friday	**Pétek**	*petek*
Saturday	**Sobóta**	*sobota*
Sunday	**Nedélja**	*nedelya*

Road Map of Slovenia